# REFUGEE MENTAL HEALTH

# REFUGEE MENTAL HEALTH

EDITED BY JAMIE D. ATEN AND JENNY HWANG

 AMERICAN PSYCHOLOGICAL ASSOCIATION

Published by
American Psychological Association
750 First Street, NE
Washington, DC 20002
https://www.apa.org

Order Department
https://www.apa.org/pubs/books
order@apa.org

In the U.K., Europe, Africa, and the Middle East, copies may be ordered from Eurospan
https://www.eurospanbookstore.com/apa
info@eurospangroup.com

Typeset in Charter and Interstate by Circle Graphics, Inc., Reisterstown, MD

Printer: Gasch Printing, Odenton, MD
Cover Designer: Nicci Falcone, Potomac, MD

**Library of Congress Cataloging-in-Publication Data**

Names: Aten, Jamie D., editor. | Hwang, Jenny, editor.
Title: Refugee mental health / edited by Jamie D. Aten and Jenny Hwang.
Description: Washington, DC : American Psychological Association, [2021] |
    Includes bibliographical references and index.
Identifiers: LCCN 2020033296 (print) | LCCN 2020033297 (ebook) |
    ISBN 9781433833724 (paperback) | ISBN 9781433835254 (ebook)
Subjects: LCSH: Refugees—Mental health. | Refugees—Mental health services.
Classification: LCC RC451.4.R43 R437 2021 (print) | LCC RC451.4.R43 (ebook) |
    DDC 616.890086/914—dc23
LC record available at https://lccn.loc.gov/2020033296
LC ebook record available at https://lccn.loc.gov/2020033297

https://doi.org/10.1037/0000226-000

*Printed in the United States of America*

10 9 8 7 6 5 4 3 2 1

*To John Makosky, who helped me see and understand
a world beyond the cornfields of my youth.*

—JAMIE D. ATEN

*To my parents, Dave and Jin Hwang, who have helped me
to see the interwoven connection of beauty, brokenness,
and resiliency of the immigrant journey.*

—JENNY HWANG

# Contents

# Contributors

**Samantha Allweiss, MSW,** RefugeeOne, Chicago, IL, United States

**Kent Annan, MDiv,** Humanitarian Disaster Institute, Wheaton College, Wheaton, IL, United States

**Jamie D. Aten, PhD,** Humanitarian Disaster Institute, Wheaton College, Wheaton, IL, United States

**Eugene F. Augusterfer, LCSW,** Harvard Program of Refugee Trauma and Massachusetts General Hospital, Cambridge, MA, United States

**Fred Bemak, EdD,** Professor Emeritus, George Mason University, Fairfax, VA, United States, and Counselors Without Borders

**Nina Campanile, MA,** Harvard Program in Refugee Trauma, Cambridge, MA, United States

**Laura E. Captari, PhD,** The Danielsen Institute at Boston University, Boston, MA, United States

**Ann Chu, PhD,** University of California, San Francisco, CA, United States

**Rita Chi-Ying Chung, PhD,** Professor Emerita, George Mason University, Fairfax, VA, United States

**Monica Connelly, LSW, CADC,** Positive Sobriety Institute, Chicago, IL, United States

**Don E. Davis, PhD,** Georgia State University, Atlanta, GA, United States

**Renee DeBoard-Lucas, PhD,** Treehouse Child Advocacy Center of Montgomery County Maryland, Rockville, MD, United States

**Mina Fazel, PhD,** University of Oxford, Oxford, England

**Monica Gerber, PhD,** The Asian Pacific Development Center, Aurora, CO, United States

**Aimee Hilado, PhD,** Northeastern Illinois University and RefugeeOne, Chicago, IL, United States

**Joshua N. Hook, PhD,** University of North Texas, Denton, TX, United States

**Jenny Hwang, MA,** University of Maryland, Baltimore County, Baltimore, MD, United States

**Allegra Magrisso, LCSW,** RefugeeOne, Chicago, IL, United States

**E. Anne Marshall, PhD,** University of Victoria, Victoria, British Columbia, Canada

**Richard F. Mollica, MD, MAR,** Harvard Medical School, Cambridge, MA, United States

**Hadidja Nyiransekuye, PhD,** University of North Texas, Denton, TX, United States

**Jesse Owen, PhD,** University of Denver, Denver, CO, United States

**Sombo Pujeh, DrPH,** Strengthening Our Ancestors Roots, Washington, DC, United States

**Emily Reznicek, MSW,** RefugeeOne, Chicago, IL, United States

**Derrick Silove, MD, AM,** University of New South Wales, Sydney, Australia

**Rachel Singer, PhD,** Center for Anxiety and Behavioral Change, Rockville, MD, United States

**Alvin Kuowei Tay, PhD,** University of New South Wales, Sydney, Australia, and Centre for Global Health and Social Change, Perdana University, Serdang, Malaysia

**Daryl R. Van Tongeren, PhD,** Hope College, Grand Rapids, MI, United States

**Jolie Shelton Zaremba, MS,** Texas Woman's University, Denton, TX, United States

# REFUGEE MENTAL HEALTH

# 1 INTRODUCTION TO REFUGEE MENTAL HEALTH

JAMIE D. ATEN AND JENNY HWANG

*No one leaves home unless home is the mouth of a shark.*

—Warsan Shire

Kasim, an Iraqi refugee in his late 30s, has been hospitalized after an attempted suicide. You are assigned his case and instructed to follow up with a contingency plan of assessing for further risks and enhancing stability. After Kasim's release from the hospital, his resettlement case manager asks specifically if you can do home visits. The case manager tells you that Kasim has lost a leg from a bomb that destroyed his town. After several years, he fled to Turkey with his family. His injury qualified as a disability, which expedited his resettlement case. However, because he was an adult at the time, only he was given permission for resettlement, meaning he had to leave his family behind. Although it has been more than 8 years since his resettlement, the case manager explains that his case is still open due to his disability and repeated suicide attempts.

When you arrive to Kasim's house, you notice that he has a grave countenance. You look around his apartment and see books, DVDs, and posters in Arabic. He tells you in broken English that "they" stopped giving him Social Security income, his only financial support. He tried to call the Social Security office but struggled to communicate. Without any money, he tells you he does not know how he will survive. He tells you of his recurring nightmares that keep him awake at night. When you ask him if he is part of the local Iraqi community or if he has any social support, he says Iraqis can't be trusted.

https://doi.org/10.1037/0000226-001
*Refugee Mental Health*, J. D. Aten and J. Hwang (Editors)

## PURPOSE OF THIS BOOK

Are you a current practitioner or researcher already working with resettled refugees and looking for more resources? Are you a current student interested in working with refugee communities? Or are you simply interested in learning more about the mental health issues of refugee communities? Whatever your reason may be for picking up this book, we hope it can shed some wisdom, add some skill sets, and encourage you to become part of a community that cares for the millions of people who were forced out of their homes and are rebuilding their lives in a foreign land. Overall, advocating and supporting quality mental health care for resettled refugees is an interdisciplinary and collaborative effort. It relies on concerned practitioners and researchers who are willing to truly listen, engage, and be humbled throughout the process.

Over the past couple decades, the rhetoric supporting refugee mental health resources and services have fallen at two ends of the spectrum: the Westernized medical model and the broad ecological framework of understanding refugee communities. We believe both perspectives bring unique strengths and weaknesses to the overall refugee mental health field. Although the Westernized medical model often provides tangible and easily applicable solutions, it often fails to capture the comprehensiveness of the unique cultural and social experiences of refugees and often places the clients out of context from the factors that influence their mental health. On the other hand, the ecological framework addresses the layers of complexities of the refugee experience, emphasizing the importance of individual, community, and societal intersections. However, this perspective tends to fall heavy in theory and is challenging to translate into tangible actions. This book intends to bridge these seemingly polarized perspectives, introducing both practice-oriented and applicable interventions alongside ecological frameworks of understanding refugee communities.

Although we strongly support the need for quality mental health care for all refugees worldwide, this book focuses specifically on the mental health care intervention and literature for resettled refugees in countries with established mental health care infrastructure. By doing so, we are able to home in on the unique needs of resettled refugee communities and address their specific mental health care gaps. Furthermore, this book focuses on resettled refugee communities in efforts to introduce interventions with history of clinical efficacy. Our aim is to encourage and strengthen existing mental health care services to be genuine healing spaces where breaches of trust and security can be restored holistically with the support of evidence-based interventions.

As the paradigm of mental health rapidly shifts toward alleviating the suffering for the socially vulnerable, we see limitations of traditional mental health care interventions (Miller & Rasco, 2004; Mollica, 2006; Murray et al., 2010). To understand the way in which social vulnerability intersects with mental health, we must thoroughly examine the factors that create and perpetuate social vulnerability. Without doing so, we find ourselves in danger of overgeneralizing, pathologizing, and neglecting the importance of situational context. Refugees resettle into their new country economically disadvantaged, burdened with exposure to highly traumatic and stressful events, and most often with linguistic and cultural barriers. Life after resettlement may exacerbate existing conditions, subsequently increasing social vulnerabilities. Silove et al. (2017) recommended "Creative solutions are thus necessary, including networking of all agencies to ensure the sharing of responsibility of care for refugees with mental disorder" (p. 132).

This book aims to provide a creative and comprehensive compilation of frameworks and interventions that have been adapted and fine-tuned for various refugee communities. It brings together a diverse group of esteemed practitioners and researchers with extensive background in refugee mental health. In each chapter, readers are introduced to new and familiar intervention strategies and challenged to further contextualize them for their own use. Furthermore, readers will repeatedly examine the infrastructural injustices and systematic social vulnerabilities that impact refugee mental health today.

## HISTORY OF THIRD COUNTRY RESETTLEMENT

Before diving into the current status and issues of refugee mental health care, we take our readers back to a pivotal point in history leading to the institutionalization of refugee resettlement.

Involving more than 30 countries, World War II, to this day, remains the deadliest of wars in human history (United Nations High Commissioner for Refugees [UNHCR], 2019a). It took nearly 50 million lives and displaced an estimated total of 40 to 60 million, including extirpated Germans (Zampano et al., 2015). When the United Nations formed in 1945, replacing the League of Nations, it established a new body, the International Refugee Organization (IRO) with the mandate of protecting existing refugee groups in Europe. By 1947, the United Nations Relief and Rehabilitation Administration (UNRRA) was running nearly 800 resettlement camps throughout Europe (Bundy, 2016). Despite the insurmountable devastation, with the efforts of the IRO, UNRRA, and the Allied power, millions of displaced people returned home or emigrated and begin the process of rebuilding their lives. But for tens of thousands (known as "nonrepatriable refugees"), repatriation was not an option due to the possibility of persecution or ongoing political instability in their country of origin. Several of the Allied countries took in quotas of refugees, mainly as designated labor workers. With the passing of the Displaced Persons Act in 1948, the United States authorized entry for more than 200,000 displaced people (Refugee Council USA, 2019). From 1947 to 1951, the IRO resettled well over a million people (UNHCR, 2011).

The atrocities of World War II brought on a collective political will and an awakened sense of humanitarian responsibilities (Bundy, 2016). In 1948, the United Nations proclaimed the Universal Declaration of Human Rights, an agreement on 30 basic rights and fundamental freedoms to which all individuals are entitled with their personhood. Unofficially, it supported demarcating standards for forthcoming political dissensions and warfare. Influenced by the horrors witnessed from previous wars, the declaration outlines freedoms and rights that are most often violated in times of war, intentionally stripping individuals of their sense of security, dignity, and worth. And within these rights specifically addressed was *the right to asylum in other countries from persecution* (Article 14; Amnesty International, 2019).

By the 1950s, all displacement camps closed, along with the dissolution of the UNRRA. In 1951, a multilateral treaty, also known as the 1951 Refugee Convention, led to the formation of the UNHCR replacing the IRO. Much like its predecessor, the purpose of the UNHCR was to provide international protection to refugees and assist governments to find durable solutions for them (UNHCR, 2011). Along with its establishment came the institutionalized definition of a *refugee*: "someone who is unable or unwilling to return to their country of origin owing to a well-founded fear of being persecuted for reasons of race, religion, nationality, membership of a particular social group, or political opinion" (UNHCR, 2020). Any country signing to be a petitionary state of the convention agreed on the parameters of *who* is a refugee and a set of rights that comes with claiming refugee status. Embedded in the convention is a refugee's right to security, work, education, housing, public relief, freedom of religion, issued identity and travel documents, and access to the legal system (UNHCR, 2019b). At the time of establishment, the institutionalized term and rights for refugees only extended to Europeans displaced by World War II. It was not until 1967 that an amendment was made to the 1951 convention upheaving geographic constriction as a criterion for refugee status. The amendment allowed for any person who has (a) a presence outside their home country, (b) a well-founded fear of persecution (being at risk of harm is insufficient reason in the absence of discriminatory persecution), and (c) an incapacity to enjoy the protection of one's own state from the feared persecution to be considered a refugee (UNHCR, 2020). This definition remains unchanged and continues to be the universally accepted criterion for claiming refugee status.

Since its establishment, the UNHCR uses the following three options for permanent solution: voluntary repatriation, local integration, and resettlement. As noted earlier, resettlement was used extensively as a means of resolving the refugee crisis from World War II for those who definitively could not return home or stay in their temporary residence. Since its origin, however, resettlement has been the least preferred of the options because it is the costliest and most cumbersome of solutions. In the decades to follow, however, political agendas and urgent humanitarian needs repeatedly ceased in massive resettlement.[1] Nongovernmental organizations (NGOs) and international organizations played a prominent role in assisting the resettlement process. In efforts to collaborate with other key resettlement organizations, the UNHCR formed the Working Group on Resettlement (WGR), which consisted of resettlement States, UNHCR, and international organizations. WGR meetings became a platform to discuss resettlement policies and efforts to enhance the use of resettlement as a tool of international protection (UNHCR, 2011).

To this day, among the international community, resettlement is still considered the least preferred option, and priority is given to those who are in immediate danger or have serious disabilities. In 2018, there were 70.8 million forcibly displaced people worldwide, of whom 25 million were refugees. Of the 25 million, only 55,680 were resettled (UNHCR, 2019b). Repatriation being the favored solution, refugees wait on average 15 years before they are resettled. Over the years, the process of resettlement has developed into a lengthy and tedious process (Chapters 2 and 5 discuss this more extensively). Once refugees enter their resettlement country, they leave the jurisdiction of international law and protection and become dependent on their resettlement country's infrastructure. Receiving countries, as petitionary states to the refugee protocol, have a responsibility to promote the well-being and dignity of refugees. As historically indicated, refugees needing resettlement are most often the ones in the direst of circumstances, which understandably elicits more complex psychological and emotional concerns.

---

[1] In the 1960s, thousands of Cubans sought refuge to flee the administration of Fidel Castro. In the 1970s, after the Vietnam War, hundreds of thousands of Vietnamese refugees were resettled. The United States also resettled hundreds of thousands of former Soviet Union citizens from the 1970s to the 1990s. In the 1990s, hundreds of thousands of Iraqi refugees fleeing the Gulf War were resettled.

## LIFE AFTER RESETTLEMENT

Many resettlement countries use the 1951 convention and the 1967 amendment as principles for their refugee resettlement policies. Along with the further establishment of human rights advocacy groups and the expansion of WGR, quality of care and services for resettled refugees has improved tremendously. Resettlement countries, whether through government established programs or collaborative NGO networks, aid resettled refugees to access their right to security, work, education, housing, public relief, freedom of religion, identity and travel documents, and to the legal system. In receiving access to these rights, resettled refugees are expected to rebuild their lives and integrate into their new country. But establishing normalcy after years of exposure to violence and uncertainty can be challenging, especially across language and cultural barriers and post-resettlement difficulties (further discussed throughout this book). Rebuilding a life that has been tumultuously upheaved by factors outside one's control is inevitably an idiosyncratic process.

For some resettled refugees, mere access to basic rights may suffice to seamlessly acculturate into their new lives. But for many others, years of research and thousands of recorded narratives indicate a need for deeper interventions and more diverse healing opportunities.


## MENTAL HEALTH THEMES FOR RESETTLED REFUGEE COMMUNITIES

Early studies conducted among Southeast Asian refugees found that addressing mental health issues of refugees is an important aspect of their assimilation to resettled countries (Ying & Akutsu, 1997). In the following 2 decades, there was a burgeoning of epidemiological studies in the refugee mental health field (Silove et al., 2017). Hundreds of studies have examined patterns of psychiatric symptomatology and the effects of ongoing stressors related to displacement (Miller & Rasco, 2004); these studies collectively indicate post-traumatic stress disorders (PTSD) and depression as the two most prevalent disorders in refugee populations (Steel et al., 2002). Meanwhile, systematic reviews suggest that refugees who have resettled in Western countries (such as the United States or Canada) are as much as 10 times more likely to have developed PTSD compared with the general population (Fazel et al., 2005).

It is important to note, however, that the studies do not suggest that all refugees have or will develop PTSD or depression. In a population-based study in 2002 of Vietnamese refugees residing in Australia, researchers found that the majority were free from overt mental illness and existing trauma-related mental illness seemed to reduce over time. Nevertheless, the study also noted that a subgroup of people with a high degree of exposure to trauma had long-term psychiatric morbidity such as depression, anxiety, and PTSD (Steel et al., 2002). These findings resonate with the majority of the existing research that link the degree of the traumatic experiences to the severity of trauma symptoms (Mollica et al., 1993; Norris, 1992). By referencing these studies, it is important to acknowledge their limitations even ones claiming positive cross-validity and reliability tests. According to ecological frameworks on refugee mental health, individual PTSD symptomatology is only one layer to which traumatic experiences can manifest in refugee communities. In their book *The Mental Health of Refugees: Ecological Approaches to Healing and Adaptation*, Miller and Rasco (2004) stated that

> acknowledging the presence of trauma within individuals in no ways contradicts the idea that trauma may also occur as a psychosocial phenomenon that affects entire communities and their underlying fabric of social relationships. (p. 8)

In particular, traumatic exposure to political violence, which many refugees experience, can elicit the development of complex trauma (Herman, 1997). As more research elucidates the impact of post-resettlement issues on the mental health of resettled refugees, we see a shift in the research agenda toward understanding post-resettlement social and economic conditions (Chapter 6 discusses this in more detail). Kim (2016) noted that a lack of reserved resources and community support at the beginning of the resettlement period reflects economic challenges for refugees even decades after they have resettled.

At this point, we reiterate why bridging the medical model perspective and the ecological frameworks can provide both a comprehensive and applicable understanding of refugee mental health needs. By taking an ecological framework to initially grasp the context to which mental health needs exist and cultivate in diverse refugee communities, existing mental health resources and treatment modalities can be appropriately adapted and implemented. In this process, practitioners and service providers can also recognize limitations in services and strategically advocate for better suited treatments. In efforts to leverage both the medical model and the ecological perspective to refugee mental health, this book examines the following:

- research and case studies on the efficacy of Western therapeutic interventions,
- best practices in providing culturally appropriate services,
- examples of ways to culturally adapt existing mental health care services, and
- ecological frameworks for providing holistic care.

## CHALLENGES FOR REFUGEE MENTAL HEALTH INTERVENTIONS

We acknowledge that practice-based evidence in the area of refugee-related interventions is still in its emerging stages despite the availability of a small number of meta-analytic studies examining prevalence of mental health disorders (Fazel et al., 2005; Porter & Haslam, 2005). The demographics of resettled refugees fluctuate each year, making interventions and research catered for a particular ethnic group potentially inapplicable or ineffective (Birman et al., 2008). Birman et al. (2008) stated that "with the unpredictable and under resourced circumstances that confront service providers daily, make it extremely difficult to develop manualized procedures, define a homogeneous sample, and conduct controlled trials" (p. 122). Despite these challenges, we believe practitioners and researchers share a responsibility to continue efforts to enhance services and foster thriving conditions for resettled refugee communities.

## RECOMMENDATIONS FOR USE OF INTERVENTIONS

The guidelines in providing mental health services for refugees have also been a challenge. The diversity and the idiosyncrasy of the refugee experience along with the fluctuating circumstances that force people into refugee status concocts difficulty for standardization of best practice guidelines. Existing resources on refugee mental health recommends a need to take a holistic approach on refugee mental health, bringing the persons in context and fostering the innate wisdom and strengths existing with refugee communities (Murray et al., 2010). So how do mental health professionals bring culturally diverse clients in context? How can we foster innate wisdom and strengths existing within the refugee communities? And how do we take our Western interventions and put them in appropriate context? Birman et al. (2008) stated that because of the challenges of catering to broad and dynamic populations, refugee mental health programs are recommended in the development of generalized principles of "multicultural competence," or an approach that attends to specific cultural perspectives, needs, and circumstances but can be used across diverse cultural groups. Thus, we recommend to readers the following principles outlined by the 2017 American Psychological Association (APA) Multicultural Guidelines to maximize the efficacy of this book:

• Seek to recognize and understand that identity and self-definition are fluid and complex and that the interaction between the two is dynamic.

- Psychologists [mental health professionals] aspire to recognize and under-stand that as cultural beings, they hold attitudes and beliefs that can influence their perceptions of and interactions with others as well as their clinical and empirical conceptualizations. As such, psychologists strive to move beyond conceptualizations rooted in categorical assumptions, biases, or formulations based on limited knowledge about individuals and communities.

- Psychologists [mental health professionals] strive to recognize and under-stand the role of language and communication through engagement that is sensitive to the lived experience of the individual, couple, family, group, community, or organizations with whom they interact. Psychologists also seek to understand how they bring their own language and communica-tion to these interactions.

- Psychologists [mental health professionals] endeavor to be aware of the role of the social and physical environment in the lives of clients, students, research participants, and/or consultees.

- Psychologists [mental health professionals] aspire to recognize and under-stand historical and contemporary experiences with power, privilege, and oppression; as such, they seek to address institutional barriers and related inequities, disproportionalities, and disparities of law enforcement, admin-istration of criminal justice, educational, mental health, and other systems as they seek to promote justice, human rights, and access to quality and equitable mental and behavioral health services.

- Psychologists [mental health professionals] seek to promote culturally adaptive interventions and advocacy within and across systems, including prevention, early intervention, and recovery.

- Psychologists [mental health professionals] endeavor to examine the profession's assumptions and practices within an international context, whether domestically or internationally based, and consider how this globalization has an impact on psychologist's [mental health profes-sionals] self-definition, purpose, role, and function. For example, Western-educated mental health professionals learn to understand positive and maladaptive human behavior and psychological processes in the con-text of Western society. In countries like the United States, self-reliance, self-efficacy, self-actualization, and self-care are emphasized as positive deterrents for functioning. In many cultures, however, the concept of self-psychology is interpreted differently. So as society becomes increasingly more globalized, it is imperative that mental health professionals are aware that their understanding of human behavior is simply part of a bigger narrative.

- Psychologists [mental health professionals] seek awareness and understanding of how developmental stages and life transitions intersect with the larger biosociocultural context, how identity evolves as a function of such intersections, and how these different socialization and maturation experiences influence worldview and identity.

- Psychologists [mental health professionals] strive to conduct culturally appropriate and informed research, teaching supervision, consultation, assessment, interpretation, diagnosis, dissemination, and evaluation of efficacy.

- Psychologists [mental health professionals] actively strive to take a strength-based approach when working with individuals, families, groups, communities, and organizations that seeks to build resilience and decrease trauma within the sociocultural context. (American Psychological Association, 2017)

## OVERVIEW OF THE CHAPTERS

Like any therapeutic work, the process is not linear but involves many detours, impediments, and adaptations. As you read through the chapters of this volume, you will hear from an array of practitioners and researchers who have dedicated their profession to the cause of refugee mental health. Each chapter is based on the authors' clinical experience and supported by existing research and literature. Each chapter is meant to be comprehensive with the acknowledgment that supporting mental health of refugees means work within the walls of the clinic and in the community, whether that means working alongside cultural navigators, conducting home visits, or even doing advocacy work. The chapters are intentionally curated to bridge the medical and ecological approach to refugee mental health by addressing important topics within both disciplines. Each chapter begins with a brief introduction on the scope of the refugee crisis as it relates to the contents of the chapter.

In Chapter 2, Hilado, Reznicek, and Allweiss provide a broad context for understanding the current refugee crisis. The authors examine the current political climate and the global trend in displacement and its impact on refugee resettlement. Furthermore, the authors highlight the political instability of three specific countries—the Democratic Republic of Congo, Myanmar, and Syria—to explain the staggering number of refugees fleeing from these countries. The chapter chronicles the tedious third country resettlement process, which begins from the protracted time in refugee camps and ends with the final resettlement in a new country. As clinicians and researchers based in the United States, the authors focus specifically on the U.S. resettlement procedure. The authors outline several common mental health challenges resettled refugees face during the resettlement process. The chapter ends with a case vignette based on the authors' clinical experience.

In Chapter 3, the authors introduce the vital role humility plays when working with refugee clients and communities. Humility—more specifically cultural humility—has been shown to be critical in working with diverse clients. The authors explore the ways in which mental health professionals can become more self-aware by examining power differences, privilege, and the influence of Western notions of helping. Captari et al. discuss why humility is important to work with cultural differences while providing concrete recommendations for cultivating mental health professional humility. The chapter discusses navigating possible cultural differences, challenges (e.g., mental health stigma), and even mistakes in therapy. A case vignette and a self-awareness exercise are provided. Readers will be challenged to see themselves, refugee clients, mental health issues, and treatment from the perspective of refugees.

In Chapter 4, Singer, DeBoard-Lucas, and Pujeh discuss common ethical issues and dilemmas faced in providing mental health services to refugees. The authors introduce the inevitable gray areas when working with refugee populations and offer ethical guidelines that can help navigate these specific waters. Singer et al. present the applicability of the American Psychological Association Ethical Principles of Psychologists and Code of Conduct when working with refugees and also provide a translation of the World Health Action Plan Guidelines into the domestic context. The authors also discuss culturally sensitive ways to respond ethically to presenting problems that the average mental health professional likely has not encountered. Lastly, they help readers to be mindful of therapist's role and presence and how those in itself may raise ethical dilemmas.

In Chapter 5, Bemak and Chung expand on Chapter 2 to discuss the broad trends in displacement. The authors delve specifically into the modern-day challenges refugees face and how those unique challenges impact their overall mental health and life after resettlement. Bemak and Chung discuss the factors influencing refugee mental health interventions such as cultural beliefs on mental health and employing translators and interpreters. The authors also cover the challenges of facilitating Westernized mental health interventions to individuals and communities who are rooted in more collectivist and holistic cultures. Lastly, they present a comprehensive framework called the multiphase model (MPM) of psychotherapy, social justice, and human rights that encapsulates the complexities of the refugee experience into treatment. The chapter ends with case study examples of using the MPM model.

In Chapter 6, Mollica, Augusterfer, and Campanile begin with a review on the magnitude of the mental health problem for traumatized refugee populations. The authors then introduce examples of emerging evidence-based and culturally adapted therapeutic interventions such as cognitive behavioral therapy, eye movement desensitization and reprocessing, and narrative exposure therapy. This chapter explores the concept of healing and the ways in which alleviating human suffering, especially suffering experienced by refugee communities, involves employing a vast range of psychology, social, cultural, and economic practices. This chapter discusses a new healing model called healing environment and restorative therapy (HEART) where readers build on a universally used basic model of humanitarian relief.

In Chapter 7, Tay and Silove begin with an overview of the modern refugee mental health research. They proceed to discuss the way in which research on refugee mental health shapes and guides the current methods of screening and assessing refugee mental health. The authors introduce the strengths and limitations of various assessment tools and models. Furthermore, Tay and Silove provide evidence-based research on complex refugee mental health needs such as complicated bereavement and explosive anger. They present common refugee mental health needs that service providers should be mindful of when facilitating assessments. Last, Tay and Silove outline how mental health professionals can move toward an evidence-based multilevel approach to refugee mental assessment.

In Chapter 8, Fazel draws from her years of clinical and research experience in working with refugee children. She discusses the ways in which schools can play an integral part in administering mental health care services for refugee children. The author provides both clinical and research support for school-based interventions as well as their limitations. With growing evidence in favor of expressive therapies for trauma-exposed children, Fazel discuss the ways in which different types of expressive therapies (e.g., theatre, music, art, sandplay, narrative exposure) can benefit refugee children, citing empirical evaluations for these interventions. The chapter concludes with the recommendation and need for more empirical evidence to support more expressive therapy programs and school-based interventions for refugee children.

In Chapter 9, Hilado, Chu, and Magrisso encourage readers to diversify treatment settings by working with family units and fostering healthy familial bonds. They discuss how the refugee experience and post-resettlement issues can shift family dynamics and cohesion and consequently cause psychological distress and tension. With research supporting the moderating factors early childhood interventions can have in mental illness prevention, the authors emphasize treatments specifically for families with young children. Readers are introduced to a brief historical background on the treatment models then to their applicability for refugee families. To help readers with contextualization, Hilado et al. draw from their clinical experiences to provide case vignettes for each treatment model. The authors conclude with the benefits and limitations of working with refugee families.

In Chapter 10, Allweiss and Connelly discuss the value of community-based and peer group interventions in fostering sustainable and empowering mental health wellness among refugee populations. Barriers to services are discussed, along with the suggestion of facilitating group psychoeducation classes to lessen those barriers. The authors draw from their direct clinical experience working with RefugeeOne, a refugee resettlement agency in Illinois, to provide examples, benefits, and challenges of administering peer, group, and community-based interventions. They describe successful interventions and their applicability throughout the chapter.

In Chapter 11, Marshall explores the way in which indigenous methods of healing can be integrated into Western therapeutic interventions. The author examines how availability and accessibility of mental health services are not the only impasse for refugee populations in receiving mental health care and how critical the role of cultural understanding of healing plays in working cross-cultural settings. Ecological studies indicate that integrating indigenous methods of healing, such as cultural and religious rituals and cultural practices and beliefs, into existing services could enhance receptivity and provides more effective outcomes (Herman et al., 2005). Marshall provides a variety of ways therapists can blend indigenous or traditional ways and knowledge into existing mental health therapy, demonstrating a multifaceted, hybrid approach. Throughout the chapter, the author provides case studies exemplifying an integrated approach in promoting well-being in refugee populations.

In Chapter 12, Aten, Hwang, and Annan conclude the book by reflecting on the themes and trends from the previous chapters. We discuss the current gaps in refugee mental health services and the research that supports evidence-based interventions specifically for refugee populations. Limitations in the clinical and research settings are discussed, along with suggestions for improving clinical skills and training needed to enhance practice competencies. We offer recommendations for existing refugee mental health programs and provide resources for practicing mental health professionals as well as those in training. Lastly, we highlight the importance of advocacy and its challenges in promoting refugee mental health wellness.

Throughout this volume, all case studies discussed are either fictional or composites, or the client identities and names have been altered to preserve their confidentiality.

## CONCLUSION

In compiling *Refugee Mental Health*, our hope is for readers to become aware of the complex intersection that defines the well-being of millions of refugees. As in the case of Kasim at the beginning of this chapter, understanding the refugee experience means exploring the indiscernibly connected past, present, and future. Our aim is to present readers with mental health interventions and strategies that have been adapted and derived to encompass the multiplicity that underlines refugee well-being. This book is not intended to be a definitive methodology for refugee mental health but rather a collection of best practices to help guide practitioners to provide quality and appropriate services.

## REFERENCES

American Psychological Association. (2017). *Multicultural guidelines: An ecological approach to context, identity, and intersectionality.* http://www.apa.org/about/policy/multicultural-guidelines.pdf

Amnesty International. (2019). *Universal declaration of human rights.* https://www.amnesty.org/en/what-we-do/universal-declaration-of-human-rights/

Birman, D., Beehler, S., Harris, E. M., Everson, M. L., Batia, K., Liautaud, J., Frazier, S., Atkins, M., Blanton, S., Buwalda, J., Fogg, L., & Cappella, E. (2008). International Family, Adult, and Child Enhancement Services (FACES): A community-based comprehensive services model for refugee children in resettlement. *American Journal of Orthopsychiatry, 78*(1), 121–132. https://doi.org/10.1037/0002-9432.78.1.121

Bundy, C. (2016, January 4). Migrants, refugees, history and precedents. *Forced Migration Review, 51*, 5–6. https://www.fmreview.org/destination-europe/bundy

Fazel, M., Wheeler, J., & Danesh, J. (2005). Prevalence of serious mental disorder in 7000 refugees resettled in western countries: A systematic review. *The Lancet, 365*(9467), 1309–1314. https://doi.org/10.1016/S0140-6736(05)61027-6

Herman, H., Saxena, S., & Moodie, R. (Eds.). (2005). *Promoting mental health: Concepts, emerging evidence, practice.* World Health Organization. https://www.who.int/mental_health/evidence/MH_Promotion_Book.pdf?ua=1

Herman, J. (1997). *Trauma and recovery: The aftermath of violence—from domestic abuse to political terror.* Basic Books.

Kim, I. (2016). Beyond trauma: Post-resettlement factors and mental health outcomes among Latino and Asian Refugees in the United States. *Journal of Immigrant and Minority Health, 18*(4), 740–748. https://doi.org/10.1007/s10903-015-0251-8

Miller, K. E., & Rasco, L. M. (2004). An ecological approach for addressing the mental health of refugee communities. In K. E. Miller & L. M. Rasco (Eds.), *The mental health of refugees: Ecological approaches to healing and adaptation* (pp. 1–64). Lawrence Erlbaum Associates. https://doi.org/10.4324/9781410610263

Mollica, R. (2006). *Healing invisible wounds: Paths to hope and recovery in a violent world.* Harcourt.

Mollica, R. F., Donelan, K., Tor, S., Lavelle, J., Elias, C., Frankel, M., & Blendon, R. J. (1993). The effect of trauma and confinement on functional health and mental health status of Cambodians living in Thailand–Cambodia border camps. *JAMA*, *270*(5), 581–586.

Murray, K. E., Davidson, G. R., & Schweitzer, R. D. (2010). Review of refugee mental health interventions following resettlement: Best practices and recommendations. *American Journal of Orthopsychiatry*, *80*(4), 576–585. https://doi.org/10.1111/j.1939-0025.2010.01062.x

Norris, F. H. (1992). Epidemiology of trauma: Frequency and impact of different potentially traumatic events on different demographic groups. *Journal of Consulting and Clinical Psychology*, *60*(3), 409–418. https://doi.org/10.1037//0022-006x.60.3.409

Porter, M., & Haslam, N. (2005). Predisplacement and postdisplacement factors associated with mental health of refugees and internally displaced persons: A meta-analysis. *JAMA*, *294*(5), 602–612.

Refugee Council USA. (2019). *U.S. refugee resettlement.* http://www.rcusa.org/history

Silove, D., Ventevogel, P., & Rees, S. (2017). The contemporary refugee crisis: An overview of mental health challenges. *World Psychiatry*, *16*(2), 130–139. https://doi.org/10.1002/wps.20438

Steel, Z., Silove, D., Phan, T., & Bauman, A. (2002). Long-term effect of psychological trauma on the mental health of Vietnamese refugees resettled in Australia: A population-based study. *Lancet*, *360*(9339), 1056–1062. https://doi.org/10.1016/S0140-6736(02)11142-1

United Nations High Commissioner for Refugees. (2011). *UNHCR Resettlement Handbook.*

United Nations High Commissioner for Refugees. (2019a). *History of UNHCR.* https://www.unhcr.org/en-us/history-of-unhcr.html

United Nations High Commissioner for Refugees. (2019b). *Resettlement data.* https://www.unhcr.org/en-us/resettlement-data.html

United Nations High Commissioner for Refugees. (2020). *What is a refugee?* https://www.unrefugees.org/refugee-facts/what-is-a-refugee/

Ying, Y.-W., & Akutsu, P. D. (1997). Psychological adjustment of Southeast Asian refugees: The contribution of sense of coherence. *Journal of Community Psychology*, *25*(2), 125–139. https://doi.org/10.1002/(SICI)1520-6629(199703)25:2<125::AID-JCOP2>3.0.CO;2-X

Zampano, G., Moloney, L., & Juan, J. (2015, September 22). Migrant crisis: A history of displacement. *Wall Street Journal.* http://graphics.wsj.com/migrant-crisis-a-history-of-displacement

# 2 PRIMER ON UNDERSTANDING THE REFUGEE EXPERIENCE

AIMEE HILADO, EMILY REZNICEK, AND SAMANTHA ALLWEISS

This chapter provides an initial foundation to understanding current global trends in migration and displacement that undergirds the experience of millions of refugees. The refugee experience is further explored by examining the resettlement process specifically in the United States. Last, the chapter discusses how the resettlement process contributes to the overall challenges of providing mental health services to refugees.

According to the 1951 Refugee Convention, a *refugee* is defined as "someone who is unable or unwilling to return to their country of origin owing to a well-founded fear of being persecuted for reasons of race, religion, nationality, membership of a particular social group, or political opinion" (United Nations High Commissioner for Refugees [UNHCR], 2017, p. 3). With few exceptions, to claim refugee status, individuals must cross international borders to register with the UNHCR as a refugee who is seeking asylum in a neighboring country while their claim is processed. Refugees often face perilous journeys while fleeing their country of origin. Moreover, a refugee is typically "someone who has been forced to flee his or her country because of persecution, war or violence. . . . Most likely, they cannot return home or are afraid to do so.

https://doi.org/10.1037/0000226-002
*Refugee Mental Health*, J. D. Aten and J. Hwang (Editors)

War and ethnic, tribal and religious violence are leading causes of refugees fleeing their countries" (USA for UNHCR, 2018b). Thus, all refugees are considered "forcibly displaced," a notably rising category in the bigger picture of international migration.

The International Office for Migration (IOM; 2020) estimates a total of 272 million international migrants. *Migrant* is an umbrella term that defines any person who moves away from his or her place of usual residence, whether within a country or across an international border, temporarily or permanently, and for variety of reasons (IOM, 2020). Some move across country borders to seek economic opportunities (economic migration), some move to escape political regimes and civil unrest (sociopolitical migration), and some move to be closer to family, friends, and other social networks (social migration). For others, migration is a response to adverse effects of climate change, natural disasters, or other environmental factors (environmental migration; USA for UNHCR, 2018b). Migration is therefore often referenced using terms such as "push" and "pull" factors—what pushes a person to leave one's home country and what pulls that person to a new destination. Migration can be broadly categorized into *voluntary migration* and *forced migration*.

In stretches of time marked with massive wars, violence, natural disasters, and/or tumultuous political regimes, forced migration often steers the narrative of international migration patterns. However, for people who are forced into migration for means of survival or security, the demarcation of push and pull factors are ambiguous—what pushes people to leave their homes is what pulls people to their new destination. Furthermore, unlike voluntary migrants or even immigrants,[1] those who are forced into migration often do not have a clear plan of their final destination, diluting the idea that there is a clear pull factor other than the need to seek opportunities to rebuild their lives with safety, dignity, and access to basic resources.

## CURRENT TRENDS IN GLOBAL FORCED DISPLACEMENT

According to the 2018 UNHCR *Global Trends* report, there were 70.8 million forcibly displaced people worldwide, noting a daily average of 37,000 new displacements. Of the 70.8 million forcibly displaced people, 25.9 million

---

[1]From the perspective of the country of arrival, an immigrant is a person who moves into a country other than that of his or her nationality or usual residence, so that the country of destination effectively becomes his or her new country of usual residence (International Migration Law, 2019).

were considered refugees,[2] 41.3 million were internally displaced people, and 3.5 million were asylum seekers (UNHCR, 2018). Figure 1 in *Global Trends: Forced Displacement in 2017* (UNHCR, 2018, p. 6; see https://www.unhcr.org/ 5b27be547.pdf) depicts the increasing trend in global displacements and the countries reporting the largest forcibly displaced populations

In the larger picture of international migration, refugees are a minority but a significant aspect of forced migration. The international standards and requirements, by default, make it difficult to claim refugee status. Crossing international borders, seeking asylum, and proving to have a reason for fear and persecution is a challenging undertaking; it is an experience that requires careful and intentional concern.

## THE REFUGEE EXPERIENCE

Many individuals who have sought refugee status have been abruptly forced into migration, often by targeted threats or mass violence. In the abrupt decision to flee, many individuals may leave without the opportunity to pack essential or precious items. Families may also be separated or make a calculated decision to separate during migration, knowing little of their relatives' safety for extended periods of time. Some refugees are never able to get information about the fates of family members, as they are disappeared in prisons or lost to the ocean in transit. As highlighted by the war in Syria, refugees may face limited or dangerous options of escape, with bordering countries often becoming inhospitable to the onslaught of foreigners attempting to enter during a crisis. Hostile governments may also deter those trying to flee and target their own citizens at the border with force, making the journey even more dangerous.

Because of increased border security around the globe, refugees often turn to smugglers or traffickers to facilitate illegal entry into a border country, but in doing so, many refugees exhaust financial resources and find themselves vulnerable to extortion and physical, sexual, or labor abuse (UNHCR, 2018). Refugees have spoken about the high fees they pay smugglers, and some have described the severe beatings endured when they were unable to pay their smugglers for additional charges while on route. Most refugees discuss their

---

[2]Of the 25.9 million refugees, 20.4 million were under UNHCR mandate, and 5.5 million were under the United Nations Relief and Works Agency mandate for Palestine refugees.

time in a transit as a period of extreme uncertainty focused on a singular goal of escaping the certain danger back home.[3]

Those who make it across borders to a neighboring country often face a new set of challenges. They are placed either in camps or apartments in urban settings; conditions vary depending on the country, but they may be substandard, and access to adequate medical care, education for children, and employment may be limited (Porter & Haslam, 2005). Refugees speak of the discrimination and prejudice they face from native-born citizens, which can be as subtle as indirect social exclusion or as extreme as direct violence, harassment, or hate speech. Although UNHCR protocol states livelihood as a fundamental right for refugees, work authorization is limited, and many refugees find themselves dependent on governmental and nongovernmental aid (American Immigration Council, 2020; Office of Refugee Resettlement, 2020). Compounding unsafe environmental factors may force refugees to stay isolated within their home or limit their mobility, which can increase interpersonal stress among family members.

After conducting a worldwide meta-analysis on mental health outcomes for refugees, Porter and Haslam (2005) asserted: "Worse outcomes were observed for refugees living in institutional accommodation, experiencing restricted economic opportunity, displaced internally within their own country, repatriated to a country they had previously fled, or whose initiating conflict was unresolved" (p. 40). The USA for UNHCR (2018b) reported that two of every three registered refugees are subjected to a protracted refugee situation, which is defined as a stay of 5 or more years in exile from their country of origin. This means that most refugees must remain in a state of flux for prolonged periods of time, facing an uncertain future. Many children experience disruptions in their education while fleeing; others are unable to return to school for the entirety of their displacement. Refugees have often spoken about feeling like they are languishing, with little to no opportunities to improve their situation. This sense of helplessness in itself can feel traumatic, as they are stripped of control over their life and forced to be dependent on others for survival. This reality was outlined in Russell et al.'s (1996) research on the perceptions of leisure time for refugees in Kenya's Kakuma refugee camp, as these authors found that the refugees desired to have opportunities to better their lives and perceived the abundance of free time as a burden, stripping their life of purpose and a sense of meaning.

---

[3] Authors Hilado and Allweiss are mental health professionals in a refugee mental health program. These remarks reflect interview responses from refugees receiving clinical services.

As of 2018, more than two thirds of all refugees worldwide (67%) came from just five countries: Syrian Arab Republic (6.7 million), Afghanistan (2.7 million), South Sudan (2.3 million), Myanmar (1.1 million), and Somalia (0.9 million). Additionally, the majority of these refugees were hosted in just eight countries: Turkey (3.7 million), Pakistan (1.4 million), Uganda (1.2 million), Germany (1.06 million), Sudan (1 million), the Islamic Republic of Iran (979,400), and Bangladesh (906,600; UNHCR, 2018). Figures 2.1, 2.2, and 2.3 provide a visual of these high displacement numbers and the countries supporting them by the end of 2017 (see also UNHCR, 2018, pp. 10 and 15; http://www.unhcr.org/5b27be547.pdf). Refugee numbers have only increased since then, with neighboring countries further strained by the arrivals.

Critical to this conversation are concerns about stability and resources within host countries providing refuge to displaced populations. Many of the countries hosting refugees are also experiencing political instability and economic sustainability concerns for their own citizens, and the majority of these countries do not have the infrastructure to absorb so many displaced refugees without support from NGOs and foreign aid. Most alarming of these statistics is that 52% of all refugees were children under 18 years of age (UNHCR, 2017), a vulnerable population that has unique developmental needs and who are susceptible to illness, trafficking, and recruitment to extremist groups when unable to access adequate food, shelter, opportunities for an education, employment, and vital health resources.

## CURRENT CRISIS REGIONS FOR REFUGEES

In reflecting beyond these staggering numbers, our focus must be on the experiences of individuals, families, and entire communities coming from the various crisis regions. Three countries in particular—the Democratic Republic of Congo, Myanmar (Burma), and the Syrian Arab Republic, in order of numbers displaced represent the largest displacement situations at present—reflect numbers of at-risk populations higher than those recorded over the past decade (UNHCR, 2018). These countries reflect active civil wars, unstable political institutions, and protracted periods of exposure to trauma among those fleeing these respective countries. The refugees from these countries also reflect populations currently being resettled in the United States in large numbers. To help us understand the context of the refugee experience with greater acuity, the following sections provide an overview of the various crisis regions and the specific needs within these respective communities.

**FIGURE 2.1. Populations of Concern to the United Nations High Commissioner for Refugees by Category (End of 2017)**

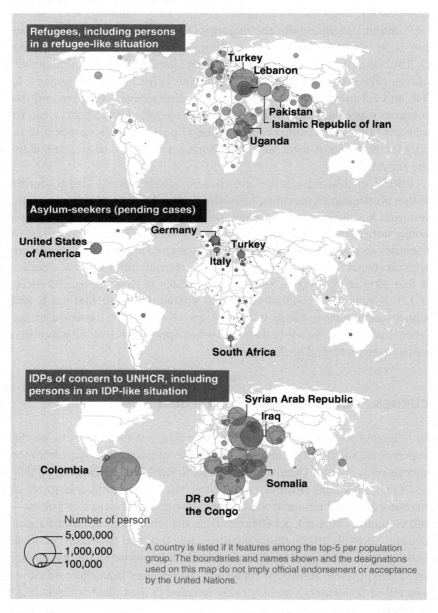

*Note.* DR = Democratic Republic; IDP = internally displaced people; UNHCR = United Nations High Commissioner for Refugees. From *Global Trends: Forced Displacement in 2017* (p. 10), by the United Nations High Commissioner for Refugees, 2018 (http://www.unhcr.org/5b27be547.pdf). Reprinted with permission.

**FIGURE 2.2. Major Source Countries of Refugees**

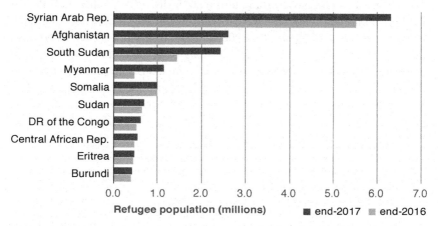

*Note.* DR = Democratic Republic; Rep. = Republic. From *Global Trends: Forced Displacement in 2017* (p. 15), by the United Nations High Commissioner for Refugees, 2018 (http://www.unhcr.org/5b27be547.pdf). Reprinted with permission.

**FIGURE 2.3. Major Host Countries of Refugees**

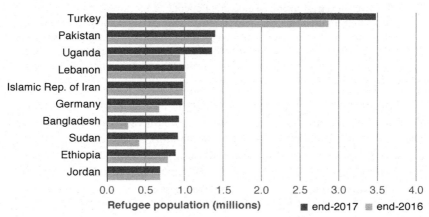

*Note.* Rep. = Republic. From *Global Trends: Forced Displacement in 2017* (p. 17), by the United Nations High Commissioner for Refugees, 2018 (http://www.unhcr.org/5b27be547.pdf). Reprinted with permission.

### Democratic Republic of Congo: The Congolese Refugee Crisis

The crisis in the Democratic Republic of Congo represents the third largest displacement situation. According to the 2018 UNHCR Global Trends Report (2018), 5.4 million Congolese were forcibly displaced, comprising 4.5 million internally displaced persons, 854,000 refugees or asylum-seekers. The crisis in the Democratic Republic of Congo stems from generations of conflict to control a politically unstable country for its precious minerals. For decades, the nation has been fraught with violence by neighboring countries and tribal groups competing for access to the resources. According to Friends of the Congo (2018),

> Congo is arguably the richest country on the planet in terms of natural resources. It is the storehouse of strategic and precious minerals that are vital to the functioning of modern society. Its minerals are key to the consumer electronics industry, the technology industry, automotive, aerospace and military industries. Its diamonds, gold, copper, cobalt, uranium, timber, iron, tin, tungsten, and coltan (mineral that is central to the functioning of our cell phones, laptops and other technology and electronic devices) are coveted from China to America. (sect. 3)

As such, there has been a long history of bloody conflicts involving clans from Rwanda, Burundi, and Uganda invading borders for access to resources with little remarks or action from the international community.

More recently,

> fresh waves of unrest in the Democratic Republic of the Congo have displaced an estimated 5 million people between 2017 and 2019—namely in the Kasai, Tanganyika, and Kivu regions. Hundreds of thousands more have fled to Angola, Zambia and other neighbouring countries. People are fleeing their homes at a worrying pace, as worsening violence destroys lives and livelihoods across the country. (USA for UNHCR, 2018a)

With this mass dispersion of entire communities, exposure to trauma is threaded into the migration experiences. "Human rights violations are still widespread, including physical mutilation, killings, sexual violence, arbitrary arrest and detention in inhumane conditions." (USA for UNHCR, 2018a).

Given the mass displacement, camps in Uganda and Kenya are inundated, as many were already at capacity before the surge of Congolese arrivals. Reports on the ground have indicated shortages in food, lack of adequate medical and mental health care to treat those impacted by the regional conflicts, and overcrowded living quarters that exacerbate disease outbreaks and risk of starvation. Given the nature of the Congolese refugee crisis and the tenuous stability of the refugee camps that have temporarily housed this group, the United States had begun processing and resettling many from this region with arrival numbers of Congolese increasing since 2015. Although there is no immediate end to the regional conflicts in DRC in sight, the United States has remained open to supporting this community through the U.S. Refugee Program.

## Myanmar: The Rohingya Refugee Crisis

The Rohingya people are stateless persons who remain unrecognized by the Myanmar government despite residing in the country for generations. They live in the Rakhine state in Myanmar, making up less than 1% of the ethnic population; they are also a religious minority who practice Islam in a predominantly Buddhist and Christian country. Ethnic tensions between the Rohingya and other religious groups in Myanmar began as early as 2012 with the first recorded incident involving a group of Rohingya men who were accused of the rape and murder of a Buddhist woman. In retaliation, Buddhist nationalists killed and burned Rohingya homes (BBC News, 2017).

Since then, the violence against Rohingya communities has only escalated despite global recognition of human rights violations, instances of documented genocide, and indifference on the part of Myanmar's leadership to recognize the growing civil unrest. Many Rohingya have fled and applied for refugee status through UNHCR resettlement support centers in Malaysia over the past 2 decades. Some wait on average 14 to 17 years before resettlement to countries like the United States, but majority remain displaced in Malaysia indefinitely.

The region hit a tipping point when Rohingya refugees were displaced to Bangladesh in 2017 as a result of intensified violence by the national military involving systematic assault of women and girls, extrajudicial killings, and the burning of entire villages (UNHCR, 2018). Noteworthy of this crisis is the speed of displacement.

> The flight of refugees from Myanmar to Bangladesh occurred at a particularly rapid rate. Over 2017, 655,500 arrived in Bangladesh, mainly concentrated in 100 days from the end of August 9, making the humanitarian response very challenging. In addition, there was a large proportion of infants, children, and pregnant women among refugees and internally-displaced persons from . . . Myanmar, adding a further layer of complexity for interventions. (UNHCR, 2018, p. 6)

Repatriation has been discussed between leaders of Myanmar and Bangladesh, but displaced Rohingya communities are reluctant. As the protracted status of the Rohingya communities in Bangladesh prolongs, hundreds of thousands of people continue to live in makeshift, poorly organized refugee camps with inadequate access to food, shelter, and hygiene facilities, contributing to major public health crises.

## Syria: The Syrian Refugee Crisis

According to a recent report, Syrians were the second largest newly displaced population in 2018, comprising 889,400 people (UNHCR, 2018). As of October 2018, there were 13.1 million forcibly displaced Syrians, comprising approximately 6.3 million registered refugees, 146,700 asylum seekers, and 6.6 million internally displaced persons and 2.98 million in besieged areas that are difficult to reach (USA for UNHCR, 2018b)—all a result of the Syrian civil war that officially began March 15, 2011, when peaceful protests in southern cities were met with violent crackdowns by Syrian security forces (Gilsinan, 2015). According to Huber et al. (2018), the Arab Spring reforms were met with repression from the government while diverse opposition groups failed to unite under one goal. The international community was outspoken and outraged by the violence against peaceful protesters and implemented international sanctions, but the government simply met such action with continued defiance and increased conflict that led to hundreds of thousands of civilian casualties and a destruction of both cities and the institutions that supported the citizens.

Over time, continued protests were met with Syrian military opposition fighting against multiple militant groups that were attempting to take control of different territories. As a result of the civil war, more than 11 million people have been displaced within and beyond Syria's borders (Zong & Batalova, 2017). Moreover, the social infrastructure of Syria has collapsed with "95 percent of people lack adequate healthcare and 70 percent lack regular access to clean water. Half the children are out of school. The economy is shattered, and 80 percent of the population lives in poverty" (Huber et al., 2018). The reports for Syrian children are particularly devastating with data suggesting the war reversed 2 decades of educational progress as more than one third of the schools have not been in use because they were "damaged, destroyed, or occupied" during the civil war (Huber et al., 2018).

Three and a half million Syrian refugees have fled into Turkey, living outside of camps and without access to resources to meet their basic needs. Another estimated one million refugees are in Lebanon, making up almost one fifth of Lebanon's population, while Jordan is housing more than 600,000 refugees across two refugee camps within its city limits. Thousands have fled to other countries including Iraq and Egypt, and millions remain internally displaced within Syria's borders.

Despite the incredible need, the United States has not had a response proportionate to the scale of displacement. Only 18,000 Syrian refugees were resettled since the civil war began, with resettlement coming to a complete halt when the Trump Administration issued executive orders in 2017 suspending the U.S. Refugee Program for 120 days specifically to refugees from Iraq, Syria, Iran, Sudan, Libya, Somalia, and Yemen. This was particularly damaging to Syrian refugee arrivals because Syria was completely blocked from entry. Despite lawsuits, injunctions, and revisions to the executive orders, Syrian refugees continued to be processed in very limited numbers and were subject to extra screening procedures despite Syria being the largest refugee crisis in recent history. In 2018, the United States took in only 11 Syrian refugees—a 98.2% decrease from the first 3 months of 2016 (Gelardi, 2018).

## REFUGEE PROCESSING IN THE UNITED STATES

When refugee designation is assigned, there are only three resettlement options for refugees: repatriation, host country integration, or third country resettlement. *Repatriation* refers to when refugees returns to their home country after a period of time when it is safe to return. *Host country integration* is when permanent residence or citizenship is provided to a refugee candidate by the country providing temporary shelter. Finally, *third country resettlement* is when the refugee (and any family members in the same application) is approved for resettlement to any one of the 37 countries that have agreed to receive refugees under the United Nations Convention Protocol (USA for UNHCR, 2018b).

The UNHCR reports that less than 1% of the world's displaced citizens are resettled to a third country, which indicates that migration stops for millions of people after they reach a neighboring country. Resolution for these individuals is to be absorbed by the country in which they sought asylum or return to their country of origin once the situation in the home country has stabilized and deemed "safe" for repatriation. Unfortunately, recent trends of forced repatriation, as in the case of Syrian refugees, indicates the returning citizens do not always find economic or political stability upon reentry and could be susceptible to the same governmental abuses from which they fled (Radcliffe, 2018; Relief Web, 2018). The problem highlights the politicized nature of the term "refugee," which effectively excludes millions of individuals whose lives are still in grave danger because of the situation within their native country.

The reality is that third-country resettlement is often the only viable option for rebuilding a refugee's life because it affords permanent immigration status and access to resources and opportunities often missing in a refugee's home country. In 2018, 27 countries resettled refugees in collaboration with the UNHCR (see Exhibit 2.1). These countries have been committed to supporting

**EXHIBIT 2.1. Countries Operating Refugee Resettlement Programs in Collaboration With the United Nations High Commissioner for Refugees**

| | | |
|---|---|---|
| Argentina | Finland | Luxembourg |
| Australia | France | Netherlands |
| Austria | Germany | New Zealand |
| Belarus | Hungary | Norway |
| Belgium | Iceland | Portugal |
| Brazil | Ireland | Romania |
| Bulgaria | Italy | Spain |
| Canada | Japan | Sweden |
| Chile | Republic of Korea | Switzerland |
| Croatia | Latvia | United Kingdom |
| Czech Republic | Liechtenstein | United States |
| Denmark | Lithuania | Uruguay |
| Estonia | | |

displaced populations worldwide including those from the three major crisis regions. Despite the increase in available resettlement locations, again less than 1% of refugees are resettled in one of these 27 countries. Third country resettlement is also the most desired option, with many refugee candidates waiting on average 17 years before a resettlement option becomes available. Some wait even longer (25 years and more) without a viable opportunity to move within their lifetime.

The United States for many decades had served as a leader in supporting refugee resettlement, encouraging other countries to be equally accountable and responsive to the needs of vulnerable and displaced populations worldwide. For refugees approved for resettlement in the United States, it is the Department of State that oversees the U.S. Refugee Resettlement Program, a program that was designed to support vulnerable populations fleeing war and persecution since its inception in 1975. As of fiscal year 2016, the U.S. Department of State (2018) reported 3.2 million refugees resettled since 1975, when efforts to diligently track refugee arrivals across the country began.

## Screening and Processing

The process of being resettled as a refugee in the United States is a long multi-step process with no guarantee of admission. It begins with a refugee being referred by UNHCR to a Department of State–funded Resettlement Support Center (RSC). The RSC then conducts an in-depth interview to substantiate the applicant's claim to refugee status. The applicant's information is entered into the Department of State's Worldwide Refugee Admission Processing System (WRAPS) so that all data can be cross-referenced for background checks with other U.S. agencies (American Immigration Council, 2020).

Once the initial information is inputted, security checks begin. This includes all U.S. national security agencies—National Counterterrorism Center, FBI, Department of Homeland Security (DHS), the Department of Defense, and the Department of State, as well as the intelligence community—reviewing the applicant's information that was entered through the RSC. As the screening results from each agency are transmitted back to the Department of Homeland Security and the Department of State, a DHS officer will conduct interviews in the host country, biometric data (i.e., fingerprints) are collected, and the information is entered back into the WRAPS database. Any new information results in another interview and more verifications, biometric data and applicant data are again cross-reference against a number of agencies making this an even lengthier process. If the applicant is cleared of any concerns, the process is allowed to continue to the next phase, which involves cultural orientation and medical screenings.

An applicant that is deemed ready to travel is then assigned to a domestic resettlement agency through an allocation process with nine national Resettlement Agencies that represent all domestic resettlement organizations. Authorization paperwork to travel including the I-94 U.S. Immigrant Visa and travel documents from the IOM are provided, and those with no security concerns are allowed to travel to the U.S. where representatives of their assigned agency meet them to support the adjustment process. The White House provides a clear illustration of the various steps involved in the U.S. refugee screening process (Pope, 2015; see https://obamawhitehouse.archives.gov/blog/2015/11/20/infographic-screening-process-refugee-entry-united-states). As such, it is also important to impress that many refugees wait years to decades for this process to be completed; a prolonged period of waiting that also involves uncertainty and fear for the future, experiences of trauma during the displacement period, and a longing for safety and opportunity that comes when an application is approved.

## Postresettlement Experiences

Once a refugee's case has been selected for resettlement in a specific country after extensive screening, individuals begin the last phase of their journey by traveling to their final destination to start the period of postmigration adjustment. Refugee arrival trends in the United States have continued to decrease due to the strictly limiting arrival quotas set by the newly instated immigration policies under the current U.S. Administration (American Immigration Council, 2020). There has been a dramatic decrease in refugee arrivals nationwide and reductions across major metro areas across the country (see https://www.wrapsnet.org/documents/Graph%20Refugee%20 Admissions%20as%20of%2012-31-19.pdf). As of December 31, 2019, only 3,219 refugees were resettled for the fiscal year despite the fiscal year's (FY2020) quota of 18,000 refugees approved for resettlement; note that the FY2017 ceiling set at 110,000 by the Obama administration was dramatically reduced to 50,000 and then to 18,000 for FY2020 (Refugee Processing Center, 2020). This has been disheartening for many refugees abroad who are awaiting approval for resettlement in the United States as well as family members who hoped to be reunited with their loved ones after long periods of separation. For the latter group, this reality further shapes their post-resettlement experiences.

Although individuals often experience a period of relief at being granted permanent status in a country that has greater political and economic stability, there is also a period of cultural shock (Lysgaard, 1995). This is a time period when circumstances are more challenging or difficult than anticipated, and navigating everyday life feels foreign and possibly frightening. Refugees who arrive to the United States often speak about the misinformation spread through refugee camps that every person in America is wealthy, and their life will be easy once they make it to the United States. Inevitably, the reality of American life is quite different from expectations construed during pre-resettlement, and many refugees adopt a new set of expectations as they transition into the realities of third country resettlement and process the loss of the life they had expected. Each person experiences culture shock during their adjustment period, but the intensity and longevity varies by individual and are rooted in internal and external factors (such as existing coping skills or social supports), which breed or hinder resilience.

To support the initial process, a domestic resettlement agency aids the process of adjustment to a new country. Domestic resettlement agencies are contracted through the Department of State to aid in nearly every aspect of adjustment for new refugee arrivals, which includes securing housing, facilitating initial medical screenings and accessing public benefits, enrollment in English classes for adults, securing survival jobs for heads of the household, and helping young children enroll in school when applicable. Beyond meeting these basic needs, staff within these resettlement agencies also provide the emotional support and connect arrivals with a cultural community—both ethnic communities and faith-based communities when appropriate—to help with the adjustment process. Remarkably, many refugees are able to become self-sufficient within 8 to 10 months (RefugeeOne, 2017); self-sufficiency is defined as securing a job and having sufficient English language skills to pay one's rent, navigate different service systems (medical, education, social service agencies, etc.), and live without overreliance on resettlement agency support for financial and emotional support. These findings indicate that many refugee arrivals who are able to find a community, integrate, and thrive in their own settings despite the trauma history they experience before resettlement (RefugeeOne, 2017). However, some refugee families struggle significantly to meet the high expectations for financial self-sufficiency, which the U.S. State Department sees as the primary marker for success. Critics of this measurement argue that the expectations are unrealistic and do not account for the varied postmigration experiences of refugee clients.

Adjustment can look very different depending on the tangible and social supports available in a refugee's new country. Irrespective of refugee resettlement agency, newly arrived refugees, lacking credit and work history, are typically forced into substandard housing and constrained into low-wage, manual-labor jobs. New arrivals have to adjust to the language and cultural and societal norms of the new country. Cultural differences may include expectations for appropriate dress, conceptualizations of time, acceptable workplace behaviors, and the accessibility of the health care system. Common postresettlement stressors for refugees include housing and food insecurity, underemployment, and limited social supports, all of which potentials as traumatic experiences in itself (APA Presidential Task Force on Immigration, 2013; Beehler et al., 2011). Refugees may be resettled in violent neighborhoods (Beehler et al., 2011) and find themselves in environments lacking in essential resources, such as grocery stores, day care, health clinics, and pharmacies.

Youth aged 11 to 18 years are uniquely situated to be aware of the challenges facing their family and may take on additional responsibilities during this period of transition, often helping parents care for siblings while parents are working jobs with nontraditional hours. Teens are of the age to continue their education but could face challenges when trying to catch up to peers if they had limited access to education during their premigration or migration period. Some teenagers may face pressure to go to work, forgoing their education to support their family through a minimum-wage job.

Although the challenges facing newly arrived refugees can be formidable, we have seen incredible resilience and hope in refugee populations across the country.[4] Additionally, despite some misconstrued information about who refugees are and what they can contribute to the countries that receive them, refugees entering the United States are the most vetted immigrants to enter

---

[4]Authors Hilado and Allweiss are mental health professionals in a refugee mental health program. Remarks reflect clinical observations across their cases.

the country and arguably pose the least risk to domestic terrorism. Moreover, much of the literature suggests that refugees provide substantial, concrete contributions to building strong civic communities. Many seek to contribute to society immediately, including the support of local economies through their trade skills and strong work ethic (Mason, 2018).

Statistics on refugee employment show that many are employed in various industries including manufacturing (20.3%), health care (14.2%), and general services (10%), representing the top three fields (New American Economy, 2017). Kallick and Mathema (2016) found that Burmese refugees had a higher percentage of professional capacities (24%) in areas such a teaching, social work, and the arts compared with U.S.-born employees (16%). According to Mason (2018),

> the shift into white collar work indicates that refugees not only make substantial investments in human capital, like education and English ability, but are also responsive to the changing labor demands of the economy. A study of refugees who arrived to the United States in 1980 found that ten years later these refugees earned 20% more than economic immigrants during the same time period. (Cortes, 2004, as cited in Mason, 2018, p. 1)

These statistics provide a mere snapshot of the economic contributions refugees can make in their resettlement country; positive contributions that need more attention because it could influence immigration policy in favor of increasing arrival quotas (National Immigration Forum, 2018).

## EFFECTS OF U.S. IMMIGRATION POLICY AND THE CURRENT SOCIOPOLITICAL CLIMATE

Current U.S. immigration policies and the polarizing rhetoric used to describe immigrants and refugees is yet another example of postmigration experiences that negatively impact refugee arrivals. U.S. immigration policy has changed its position on refugee resettlement. The executive orders under the Trump Administration implemented in January 2017 fundamentally changed the U.S. Refugee Program in ways that are still felt today. The orders dramatically reduced the number of refugee arrivals allowed in the country specifically from nations deemed as "high risk," often synonymous with Muslim-majority countries. Additional vetting requirements have bolstered these reductions by significantly lowering the chances for individuals to even be reviewed. The rhetoric used to describe refugees has also influenced policy, resulting in continued policies that limit refugee arrivals from certain regions. Thus, 2017 set the precedent for ongoing limitations on arrivals, newer and more restrictive review processes, and processing delays for those already identified as the most vulnerable and in need of resettlement (American Immigration Council, 2020).

There has been a rise in hate crimes against Arab populations post-9/11 (Disha et al., 2011; Hendricks et al., 2007), noting increased reports of verbal harassment of people perceived to be of Arab descent, damage to churches and mosques associated with Arab communities, and in some cases targeted physical assaults such as attacks, shootings, and murders (Hendricks et al., 2007). The escalating misinformation and fear of the "other" has galvanized those with existing prejudice against other identities of ethnicity, gender, sexual orientation, religion, and political opinion. According to Hilado and Lundy (2017):

> Unfortunately, major immigration policies globally are being informed by the wealth of misinformation and fear around terrorist groups, impacting those immigrants who are neither seeking opportunities to harm others nor those who would take advantage of the resources of a country. Many are simply wanting an opportunity to better themselves and their families while becoming productive, contributing members in their receiving country. This backdrop of fear mongering and hate has and will continue to have a long-lasting impact on the lives of native-born children of immigrants and new immigrants for decades to come. (p. 14)

The hostile rhetoric of immigration has shown negative impact on the well-being of arriving immigrant and refugee communities. Research suggests that when a receiving community is viewed as hostile, new arrivals have a harder time adjusting, experiencing higher levels of anxiety, sadness, and loneliness (Agbényiga et al., 2012; Dow, 2011); this has been noted in our own practices and across other refugee resettlement agencies and community and mental health programs. Broadly across immigration research, there has been an increase in preterm labors among immigrant populations in New York (Moreno, 2018), increased fear and anxiety among adolescent youth across Mid-Atlantic states (locations not identified to protect identity of participants; Moreno, 2018), and poor health care utilization among refugees due to feelings of disrespect and lack of understanding of one's culture (Boise et al., 2013). Some researchers have cited public health risks as the fear of identification and related repercussions have forced some communities to avoid health, mental health, or social services (Allweiss & Hilado, 2017). All these factors, although sometimes not specific to refugee status, nonetheless greatly influence refugee communities.

## CUMULATIVE IMPACT OF IMMIGRATION TRAUMA AND MENTAL HEALTH NEEDS

The American Psychiatric Association (2013) defines a *trauma* as an emotional response to an event that directly threatens an individual's physical safety and well-being, causing feelings of extreme emotional disturbance and psychological distress. Given the nature of the refugee experience and the migration story, traumatic experiences are virtually universal among refugee populations. Essential to note is the potential for multiple or cumulative traumas during each phase of movement, and the trauma may be chronic or long-lasting at each stage. As such, professionals must consider the cumulative impact of trauma threaded across a refugee's migration journey from fleeing one's country of origin, experiences in transit to a new country, and to postresettlement experiences.

Resettled refugee adults are likely to have adverse mental health symptoms due to the prolonged series of traumatic experiences throughout their journey to their final resettlement country (Kirmayer et al., 2011). Depression, generalized anxiety, and posttraumatic stress disorder are common mental health symptoms seen among refugees worldwide (Slewa-Younan et al., 2015). For resettled refugees, the resettlement process itself adds a compounding layer of challenges such as acculturating to a new culture, learning a new language, and experiencing social isolation as a result of losing one's home country and culture. These challenges can lead to adverse mental health symptoms such as hopelessness and distress (Yako & Biswas, 2014). There is also evidence indicating an elevated incidence of psychotic disorders after migration (Cantor-Graae, 2007). Moreover, some refugees even report psychological distress in the form of somatic symptoms (e.g., chronic headaches, tingling sensations in their extremities, and flulike symptoms; Aragona et al., 2005). Without proper attention to these mental health problems, refugees are likely to feel the adverse effects across all areas of life, including social relationships, integration into the workforce, and general functioning.

There is also specific attention to the needs of refugee children and youth. Burbage and Walker (2018) stated that

> refugee children and youth, specifically those who have experienced trauma and adverse childhood experiences (ACEs), have different developmental needs than their counterparts who are not refugees. ACEs are traumatic events experienced by children that shape their development and can lead to negative outcomes in adolescence and adulthood, including disruptive behavior, post-traumatic stress disorder, anxiety, and depression. (sect. 1)

Trends from the research indicate several factors that increase the stress of adjustment and can lead to poor youth mental health outcomes for youth.

These include having parents with low education who are working low-wage jobs and have limited English-language skills (Fuligni, 1998). Additionally, children face worse outcomes if their family has limited social supports, if they are living in poverty, and if they are facing prejudice in the country or resettlement. Youth often speak of helplessness to change their family's situation, and many internalize blame for their family's poor life circumstances and parental stress. Additionally, parents and children often adjust to life in their new country at differing rates due to the frequency of youth's exposure with the dominant culture in a school setting (Birman et al., 2005). This gap can cause shifting understandings of self, family, and the world, which can lead to increased conflict between generations.

Furthermore, we see trauma symptoms exacerbated when changes in family dynamics and developing a transnational identity place additional stressor on the family. Youth may lose capabilities in their native language while rapidly gaining skills in their new language. Roles may shift as parents become dependent on their children for translation and interpretation; youth may resent this role if their new culture values independence and individualism over familial ties and their communal identity. Researchers found that acculturation stress is mitigated by the maintenance of aspects of both identities, which become integrated into a positive and inclusive sense of self (Birman et al., 2005). The receiving country's receptivity to new immigrant populations impacts this identity formation, and if welcoming communities celebrate differences and tolerate bicultural backgrounds, identity formation can be positive. Not surprisingly, researchers found that a youth's sense of belonging was the single best indicator of a positive mental health outcome (Beirens et al., 2007; Hek, 2005; Kia-Keating & Ellis, 2007; O'Sullivan & Olliff, 2006). For parents of these bicultural youth or older adults who face greater challenges in navigating transcultural environments, the evidence is reflected in both parent and children or youth's general well-being and ability to adapt to their new home.

For families who do not have access to proper mental health care during the resettlement process, psychosocial deficits can impede entire families and communities from adjusting and integrating to life in a new country. As a result, there is growing focus on the intergenerational impact of trauma, culturally sensitive clinical approaches to working with refugee populations, and the importance of mental health supports for all refugees. The need is clear, and the action required must be immediate. As Burbage and Walker (2018) stated, "the level of trauma that refugees experience has a recognized effect on their mental health and well-being, but we have the opportunity to help them rebuild and change the trajectory of their futures." At the same time, practitioners need a deep understanding of the cultural stigma associated with the term "mental health" and the clear, formidable treatment barriers that exist. This includes adequate access to culturally and linguistically sensitive mental health services that reflect a balance between evidence-based practice that empowers individuals while honoring traditional methods of healing, the interdependent roles of family and community, and the intergenerational impact of immigration trauma.

To this end, this book is timely as a response to addressing the mental health needs of all resettled refugees—adults and youth—who have experienced complex trauma in their journeys to safety and who deserve access to appropriate mental health services that will help them heal, rebuild, and transform their lives. There is greater understanding on the complex nature of immigration trauma in the individual, the family, and the community. It seeks to introduce practitioners to a broad array of treatment models that have been proven effective in supporting refugee mental health, accounting for both the strengths and barriers for treatment to the refugee community. The efforts reflected in this book will support the building of a workforce in refugee mental health that can adequately support communities serving refugee populations worldwide. Moreover, the content highlights the importance of understanding best practices and using that knowledge to inform research and policies that could further support the mental well-being of refugee communities globally.

## CASE VIGNETTE

This case is a composite, and any confidential information has been disguised. Bushra is a Somali single mother of five children. Before being resettled in the United States as a refugee, she lived in Dadaab Refugee Camp in Kenya for 22 years. She has no schooling and is illiterate in her own language. She has limited work experience from the refugee camp, where she was mostly self-employed making and selling baskets, but she spent about a year working at a food stand in the camp. Bushra has lingering pain from a back injury she suffered in the camp and finds it hard to sit or stand for long periods of time.

Bushra's children, Mohamad (age 13), Amina (age 12), Ayaan (age 10), Ali (age 8), and Abderazak (age 6) were all born in Dadaab and have known no other home before their resettlement in the United States. Mohamad suffers from seizures as a result of traumatic brain injury and has had a hard time adjusting to school life. Ayaan is blind in one eye and has limited vision in the other, making it difficult for her to see in class. Abderazak is chronically ill and frequently misses school due to his illness.

To thrive in her new home country, Bushra needs to find a job to support her family but is afraid of taking a job because of the level of care her children need. She lives in an apartment complex that is home to other Somali refugees, but she does not know them well enough to depend on them for childcare on a regular basis. Additionally, she speaks no English and finds it hard to attend English as a Second Language classes routinely. When she does attend classes, she is easily frustrated because of the difficulty of learning the language.

**Case Vignette Reflective Questions:**

1. What components of Bushra's premigration experiences (i.e., experiences in her country of origin and postdisplacement) do you believe are of the greatest influence to her adjustment to life in the United States?

2. What supports does Bushra need postresettlement (i.e., experiences on arrival in the United States) to help her thrive in her new home?

3. Identify Bushra's strengths and resilience qualities that can be used to support her and her family moving forward.

## SUMMARY

To understand the refugee experience in the United States, it is critical for professionals to recognize the complex nature of migration and the breadth of its impact worldwide. To begin, current migration flows are ever increasing due to factors ranging from economic opportunities, to political and social conflict, to natural disasters. A record 70.8 million people were displaced in 2018, with an average of 37,000 people fleeing home every day. The majority of displaced people are hosted in developing nations like Turkey, Pakistan, and Uganda where instability and a lack of resources are prevalent, making it hard for migrants to be absorbed into society. As noted earlier in the chapter, the three main groups of refugees in the world right now are coming from ongoing conflict and unrest in Myanmar, the Democratic Republic of Congo, and Syria. People from these three nations represent some of the largest populations currently being resettled in the United States. Once a person is displaced, there are three options for them: repatriation to their home country, integration into their country of displacement, or resettlement to a third nation. Although resettlement is often the safest option for people, only 1% of refugees are ever resettled, waiting an average of 17 years in limbo.

Resettlement in the United States in particular is a long, complicated process consisting of many checks and screens that must all be in place before a person can be admitted. Once initiated, this process can take a minimum of 18 months to complete but often lasts upwards of 3 years. After refugees arrive in the United States, they are met by their assigned resettlement agency in their destination city. They receive financial support, housing, English classes, job placement, health care, and other public benefits for their first 8 to 10 months in the United States. Despite these benefits, the model of resettlement in the United States pushes self-sufficiency above everything else, encouraging refugee families to get on their feet as quickly as possible after arrival. This self-sufficiency approach does not always consider the needs of people being resettled. Refugees often arrive with immense physical and mental health needs, including chronic disease, depression, posttraumatic stress disorder, and generalized anxiety, while many refugee children arrive with adverse childhood experiences or traumatic events that can have lasting and profound impact on their development and lifelong success. To provide high-quality mental health services that support overall well-being, therapists must understand the full breadth of experiences that encompass the refugee resettlement journey. Building on this primer to the refugee experiences, the subsequent chapters support learning on the specific populations and effective best practice that we believe will meet our collective goal of supporting refugee mental health.

## REFERENCES

Agbényiga, D. F., Barrie, S., Djelaj, V., & Nawyn, S. (2012). Expanding our community: Independent and interdependent factors impacting refugees' successful community resettlement. *Advances in Social Work, 13*(2), 306–324. https://doi.org/10.18060/1956

Allweiss, S., & Hilado, A. (2017). Physical and mental health stabilization: The importance of wellbeing in the adjustment of new immigrants. In A. Hilado & M. Lundy (Eds.), *Models for practice with immigrants and refugees: Collaboration, cultural awareness and integrative theory* (pp. 57–76). Sage Publications.

American Immigration Council. (2020). *An overview of U.S. refugee law and policy.* https://www.americanimmigrationcouncil.org/research/overview-us-refugee-law-and-policy

American Psychiatric Association. (2013). *Diagnostic and statistical manual of mental disorders* (5th ed.). American Psychiatric Association Press.

APA Presidential Task Force on Immigration. (2013). Crossroads: The psychology of immigration in the new century. *Journal of Latina/o Psychology, 1*(3), 133–148. http://www.apa.org/topics/immigration.immigration-report.pdf

Aragona, M., Tarsitani, L., Colosimo, F., Martinelli, B., Raad, H., Maisano, B., & Geraci, S. (2005). Somatization in primary care: A comparative survey of immigrants from various ethnic groups in Rome, Italy. *International Journal of Psychiatry in Medicine, 35*(3), 241–248. https://doi.org/10.2190/2G8N-MNNE-PGGP-PJJQ

BBC News. (2017). *Myanmar: What sparked latest violence in Rakhine?* https://www.bbc.com/news/world-asia-41082689

Beehler, S., Birman, D., & Campbell, R. (2011). *The effectiveness of cultural adjustment and trauma services (CATS): Generating practice-based evidence on a comprehensive, school-based mental health intervention for immigrant youth.* University of Illinois Chicago and Ruth Campbell International Institute of New Jersey.

Beirens, H., Hughes, N., Hek, R., & Spicer, N. (2007). Preventing social exclusion of refugee and asylum seeking children: Building new networks. *Social Policy and Society, 6*(2), 219–229. https://doi.org/10.1017/S1474746406003484

Birman, D., Ho, J., Pulley, E., Batia, K., Everson, M. L., & Ellis, H. (2005). *Mental health interventions for refugee children in resettlement* [White paper]. Refugee Trauma Task Force, National Child Traumatic Stress Network. https://doi.org/10.1037/e315362005-001

Boise, L., Tuepker, A., Gipson, T., Vigmenon, Y., Soule, I., & Onadeko, S. (2013). African refugee and immigrant health needs: Report from a community-based house meeting project. *Progress in Community Health Partnerships, 7*(4), 369–378. https://doi.org/10.1353/cpr.2013.0045

Burbage, M. L., & Walker, D. K. (2018). A call to strengthen mental health supports for refugee children and youth [Commentary]. *NAM Perspectives.* National Academy of Medicine. https://nam.edu/a-call-to-strengthen-mental-health-supports-for-refugee-children-and-youth/

Cantor-Graae, E. (2007). Ethnic minority groups, particularly African-Caribbean and Black African groups, are at increased risk of psychosis in the UK. *Evidence-Based Mental Health, 10*(3), 95. https://doi.org/10.1136/ebmh.10.3.95

Cortes, K. E. (2004). Are refugees different from economic immigrants? Some empirical evidence on the heterogeneity of immigrant groups in the United States. *Institute for the Study of Labor* (IZA Discussion Paper 1063). IZA Institute of Labor Economics. http://ftp.iza.org/dp1063.pdf

Disha, I., Cavendish, J. C., & King, R. D. (2011). Historical events and spaces of hate: Hate crimes against Arabs and Muslims in post-9/11 America. *Social Problems, 58*(1), 21–46. https://doi.org/10.1525/sp.2011.58.1.21

Dow, H. D. (2011). An overview of stressors faced by immigrants and refugees: A guide for mental health practitioners. *Home Health Care Management & Practice, 23*(3), 210–217. https://doi.org/10.1177/1084822310390878

Friends of the Congo. (2018). Resource center. *Crisis in the Congo: Uncovering the truth.* http://congojustice.org/resource-center/

Fuligni, A. J. (1998). Adolescents from immigrant families. In V. C. McLoyd & L. Steinberg, (Eds.), *Studying minority adolescents: Conceptual, methodological, and theoretical issues* (pp. 127–143). Lawrence Erlbaum Associates.

Gelardi, C. (2018). Here's how many refugees the US has accepted in 2018. *Global Citizen.* https://www.globalcitizen.org/en/content/us-accepted-refugees-2018

Gilsinan, K. (2015). *The confused person's guide to the Syrian civil war.* https://www.theatlantic.com/international/archive/2015/10/syrian-civil-war-guide-isis/410746/

Hek, R. (2005). The role of education in the settlement of young refugees in the UK: The experiences of young refugees. *Practice, 17*(3), 157–171. https://doi.org/10.1080/09503150500285115

Hendricks, N. J., Ortiz, C. W., Sugie, N., & Miller, J. (2007). Beyond the numbers: Hate crimes and cultural trauma within Arab American immigrant communities.

*International Review of Victimology, 14*(1), 95–113. https://doi.org/10.1177/026975800701400106

Hilado, A., & Lundy, M. (Eds.). (2017). *Models for practice with immigrants and refugees: Collaboration, cultural awareness and integrative theory.* Sage Publications.

Huber, C., Reid, K., & Koenic, D. C. (2018). *Syrian refugee crisis: Facts, FAQs, and how to help.* World Vision. https://www.worldvision.org/refugees-news-stories/syrian-refugee-crisis-facts

International Migration Law. (2019). *Glossary on migration.* International Organization for Migration. https://publications.iom.int/system/files/pdf/iml_34_glossary.pdf

International Organization for Migration. (2020). *Who is a migrant?* https://www.iom.int/who-is-a-migrant

Kallick, D. D., & Mathema, S. (2016). *Refugee integration in the United States.* Center for American Progress and Fiscal Policy Institute. https://cdn.americanprogress.org/wp-content/uploads/2016/06/15112912/refugeeintegration.pdf

Kia-Keating, M., & Ellis, B. H. (2007). Belonging and connection to school in resettlement: Young refugees, school belonging, and psychosocial adjustment. *Clinical Child Psychology and Psychiatry, 12*(1), 29–43. https://doi.org/10.1177/1359104507071052

Kirmayer, L. J., Narasiah, L., Munoz, M., Rashid, M., Ryder, A. G., Guzder, J., Hassan, G., Rousseau, C., Pottie, K., & the Canadian Collaboration for Immigrant and Refugee Health (CCIRH). (2011). Common mental health problems in immigrants and refugees: General approach in primary care. *Canadian Medical Association Journal, 183*(12), E959–E967. https://doi.org/10.1503/cmaj.090292

Lysgaard, S. (1995). Adjustment in a foreign society; Norwegian Fulbright grantees visiting the United States. *International Social Science Bulletin, 7*, 45–51.

Mason, J. (2018). *Immigrants as economic contributors: Refugees are a fiscal success story for America.* National Immigration Forum.

Moreno, C. (2018, December 21). *Anti-immigrant rhetoric hurts the health of Latino families, even those here legally.* https://www.huffpost.com/entry/anti-immigration-health-latino-families_n_5c1938dee4b08db990586083

National Immigration Forum. (2018). *Immigrants as economic contributors: Refugees are a fiscal success story for America.* https://immigrationforum.org/article/immigrants-as-economic-contributors-refugees-are-a-fiscal-success-story-for-america/

New American Economy. (2017). *From struggle to resilience: The economic impact of refugees in America.* https://www.newamericaneconomy.org/wp-content/uploads/2017/06/NAE_Refugees_V5.pdf

O'Sullivan, K., & Olliff, L. (2006). *Settling in: Exploring good settlement for refugee young people in Australia.* Centre for Multicultural Youth Issues.

Office of Refugee Resettlement. (2020). *Refugees and ORR programs.* https://www.acf.hhs.gov/orr/refugees

Pope, A. (2015, November 20). *Infographic: The screening process for refugee entry into the United States.* https://obamawhitehouse.archives.gov/blog/2015/11/20/infographic-screening-process-refugee-entry-united-states

Porter, M., & Haslam, N. (2005). Predisplacement and postdisplacement factors associated with mental health of refugees and internally displaced persons: A meta-analysis. *JAMA, 294*(5), 602–612. https://doi.org/10.1001/jama.294.5.602

Radcliffe, R. (2018). *"Bombs are still falling": Syrian refugees at risk of forced return home.* https://www.theguardian.com/global-development/2018/feb/05/syrian-refugees-at-risk-of-forced-return-home

RefugeeOne. (2017). *RefugeeOne annual report fiscal year 2017.* http://www.refugeeone.org/uploads/1/2/8/1/12814267/refugeeone_fy2017_annual_report_1.pdf

Refugee Processing Center. (2020, January 3). *Refugee admissions report.* https://www.wrapsnet.org/admissions-and-arrivals/

Relief Web. (2018). *Dangerous ground—Syria's refugees face an uncertain future.* https://reliefweb.int/report/syrian-arab-republic/dangerous-ground-syria-s-refugees-face-uncertain-future

Russell, R. V., Frances, K., & Stage, F. K. (1996). Leisure as burden: Sudanese refugee women. *Journal of Leisure Research, 28*(2), 108–121. https://doi.org/10.1080/00222216.1996.11949764

Slewa-Younan, S., Uribe Guajardo, M. G., Heriseanu, A., & Hasan, T. (2015). A systematic review of post-traumatic stress disorder and depression amongst Iraqi refugees located in Western countries. *Journal of Immigrant and Minority Health, 17*(4), 1231–1239. https://doi.org/10.1007/s10903-014-0046-3

United Nations High Commissioner for Refugees. (2017). *Convention and protocol relating to the status of refugees.* https://www.unhcr.org/en-us/3b66c2aa10

United Nations High Commissioner for Refugees. (2018). *Global trends: Forced displacement in 2017.* http://www.unhcr.org/5b27be547.pdf

USA for UNHCR. (2018a). *DR Congo Emergencies.* http://www.unhcr.org/en-us/dr-congo-emergency.html

USA for UNHCR. (2018b). *What is a refugee?* https://www.unrefugees.org/refugee-facts/what-is-a-refugee

U.S. Department of State. (2018). *The refugee processing and screening system.* https://www.state.gov/documents/organization/266671.pdf

Yako, R. M., & Biswas, B. (2014). "We came to this country for the future of our children. We have no future": Acculturative stress among Iraqi refugees in the United States. *International Journal of Intercultural Relations, 38*, 133–141. https://doi.org/10.1016/j.ijintrel.2013.08.003

Zong, J., & Batalova, J. (2017). *Syrian refugees in the United States in 2017.* Migration Policy Institute. https://www.migrationpolicy.org/article/syrian-refugees-united-states-2017

# 3 ENGAGING REFUGEES WITH CULTURAL HUMILITY

LAURA E. CAPTARI, HADIDJA NYIRANSEKUYE,
JOLIE SHELTON ZAREMBA, MONICA GERBER,
JOSHUA N. HOOK, DON E. DAVIS, JESSE OWEN,
AND DARYL R. VAN TONGEREN

Every 2 seconds, somewhere in the world, a man, woman, or child is forced to flee for their lives. At least 44,000 people per day are added to the 70.8 million displaced worldwide due to war, life-threatening persecution, or other human rights violations (United Nations High Commissioner for Refugees [UNHCR], 2018a). More than 25 million of these individuals have received official refugee status through the United Nations, and some have the opportunity for resettlement. Three million refugees have been resettled in the United States since the formation of the Federal Refugee Resettlement Program in 1980 (Pew Research Center, 2017). Amid this cross-cultural transition, individuals with refugee status must navigate complex government systems, loss of social support, language learning, housing and transportation challenges, vocational shifts, and acculturative stress. Many refugees describe this process as "starting over from zero" as they seek to build a new life, identity, and home.

This research was supported by a grant from the John Templeton Foundation (grant 60622). The opinions expressed in this publication are those of the authors and do not necessarily reflect the views of the John Templeton Foundation.

https://doi.org/10.1037/0000226-003
*Refugee Mental Health*, J. D. Aten and J. Hwang (Editors)

What does it mean to be a refugee? What is it like to leave everything you know behind and enter a new country in search of safety? In this chapter, we take an experience-near approach to answering these questions, exploring the diverse and intersectional realities of refugees through the lens of cultural humility. As one therapist put it, "We need to really shift from this idea that we are the experts that are fixing the problems in other people's lives" (Hong, 2017). Rather than speaking *for* refugees, we incorporate their narratives throughout, drawing on in-depth qualitative interviews with refugees and service providers conducted as part of an ongoing participatory action research project in a southwestern urban metroplex. All names and identifying details have been altered to protect confidentiality.

We begin with an overview of cultural humility as it relates to thera- peutic work directly, as well as building relationships across cultures more broadly. Next, we offer an empowerment-focused model for conceptual- izing the refugee experience. We explore the therapist as a cultural being and discuss the roles of social location, stimulus value, and implicit biases on potential therapeutic ruptures. We include several specific case examples of therapeutic work informed by cultural humility and offer suggestions for community collaborations.

## COMPLEMENTARY LENSES FOR MULTICULTURAL WORK

The need for cultural competence has long been emphasized when working with diverse clients, including the development of cultural awareness, knowl- edge, and skills (Sue et al., 1982, 1992). A variety of multicultural scholars counterpoint *competence* language, which serves an important role in estab- lishing top-down standards, with *cultural humility* language, which empha- sizes a flexible, open, and responsive therapeutic stance and a commitment to lifelong learning. Cultural humility includes both personal and relational aspects (Davis et al., 2011). We envision cultural competence and humility as interconnected and complementary lenses promoting meaningful engage- ment with refugees, as described next.

### Cultural Competence

To build cultural competence in working with refugees, a therapist might attend a workshop on refugee mental health, review relevant research on evidence-based interventions, engage with refugee communities, or consult with a colleague who has expertise in this area. Although each of these steps is important, we believe they are not sufficient. Entering a session from a posture of competence—assuming we know how to best help refugees—we may miss the actual person sitting across from us. Unexamined biases, as well as our own social location of power and privilege as mental health professionals, could impede our ability to authentically connect. Transformational therapeutic work stems from a relationship of safety, trust, and collaboration based on the unique needs of each client (Norcross, 2011). This is especially true when engaging individuals with refugee status, as many have experienced significant trauma, oppression, and being mistreated and controlled by authority figures.

It is easy to talk about refugees as "them"—a homogeneous group of vulnerable individuals who have endured horrific losses, systemic traumas, and harsh environmental conditions and who desperately need help and support. Although these are unfortunate realities for many with refugee status, such overgeneralizations can be limiting. First, this narrative collapses much complexity and diversity of the refugee experience into a single mental image, one often highly influenced by negative media portrayals of refugees as threatening and dangerous on one extreme or victimized and powerless on the other (Esses et al., 2013). Second, therapists are much more likely to overlook individual and culturally embedded strengths, healing practices, and resilience factors (Walsh, 2016b). Third, this mindset creates a helper–victim dynamic by which well-meaning efforts to provide therapeutic and community support can result in further shame and stigmatization (Erden, 2017). Despite good intentions, empathy without empowerment can be othering.

### Cultural Humility

Cultural humility includes both personal and relational aspects (Davis et al., 2011). A truly humble therapeutic stance begins with an accurate view of oneself, including awareness of personal and professional limitations, as well as recognition what one does *not* know. This mindset necessitates an ongoing commitment to self-examination, inviting feedback from others, pursuing difficult conversations, and owning and working to alter implicit biases (Mosher et al., 2017). Interpersonally, humility involves being other-oriented rather than self-focused, embodying curiosity and a learning, rather than expert, stance about each client's unique experiences and perspectives Evidence suggests that cultural humility buffers against negative outcomes of conflict and helps restore a sense of connection and trust (Davis & Hook, 2013). Cultural humility functions like a "social oil." Much like an engine needs adequate oil to avoid overheating, humility orients people toward collaboration and repair following social ruptures in high-stakes social interactions (Davis & Hook, 2013).

Cultural humility constitutes the core value of a way of being while conducting therapy, rather than a way of doing, which is sometimes implied by competence language. It is an orientation, a lifelong commitment, and a therapeutic orientation to attend to the moment-by-moment interpersonal process in ways that prioritize, value, and prize diversity (Hook et al., 2013; Mosher et al., 2017). This shift to cultural humility language "primes therapists to focus all resources within their grasp toward optimizing attentiveness and responsiveness to the client's needs" (Davis et al., 2018, p. 91). Culturally humble therapists attend to power differences and work toward the development of mutual partnerships. According to the Multicultural Orientation Framework, culturally humble therapists move toward opportunities to explore clients' cultural identities and develop an increasing level of comfort and openness doing so (Davis et al., 2018).

## CONCEPTUALIZING THE REFUGEE JOURNEY

Engaging refugees with cultural humility necessitates consideration of their worldview, values, and unique lived experiences. Otherwise, therapists may unknowingly project a Western understanding of distress, symptomology, and coping onto someone of a very different cultural background and learning history. We encourage therapists to recognize their position as cultural foreigners and "focus on the whole person within her or his social and political ecology and on past as well as present traumatogenic experiences" (Kira & Tummala-Narra, 2015, p. 1). Notably, this systemic formulation may not fit neatly within the *Diagnostic and Statistical Manual of Mental Disorders* (American Psychiatric Association, 2013) diagnostic categories.

Here, we detail a cultural humility-informed model for understanding and working with refugees (see Figure 3.1), considering the context of systemic oppression in their home country, which was inherent in the decision to flee and is all too often replicated through well-meaning but ill-informed mental health interventions. This model can be helpful in (a) conceptualizing the complexity of refugee clients' lived experience, (b) thinking systemically about their current challenges and needs, and (c) practically applying cultural humility in therapeutic contexts. We have intentionally depicted the influences of oppression and empowerment as overlapping because many with refugee status experience these realities concurrently throughout the resettlement process. Furthermore, we acknowledge that cultivating mental health

**FIGURE 3.1. Cultural Humility-Informed Model of Refugee Experience**

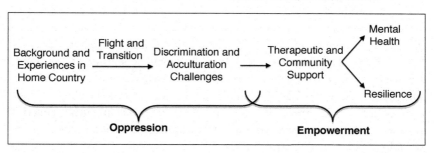

and resilience is an ongoing journey and that psychological difficulties frequently coexist with notable adaptive capacities and personal strengths. The therapist's role is to support clients in responding to ongoing oppression by fostering empowerment, growth, and resilience.

## Experiences in Home Country

Playing soccer in the street is a common childhood pastime, but imagine 7- and 8-year-olds vying for the ball and taking aim for a goal whose edges are marked not by orange cones but decapitated human heads (Aqrawy, 2016). While horrific, such scenes are tragically common in societies of ongoing war and violence, where children have never known a life without trauma. Refugees often subsisted in their home country amid systemic trauma and harsh environmental conditions, where government and community systems (e.g., police, health care, food sources) were compromised (Walsh, 2016b). For many, exposure to physical and sexual violence, instability, extreme fear, and ongoing risk of death were daily realities. Chronic stressors can have a profound negative impact on both physical and psychological health (Van der Kolk & McFarlane, 2012).

In countries such as Sudan, where civil war has dragged on for decades, multiple generations are growing up in a traumatized society. One study found depression in 63% of the sample, and rates of suicide 100 times greater than in the general population (Murthy, 2007). In Afghanistan, where a significant portion of the population has been displaced in recent years, 62% of individuals reported depression, 72% experienced anxiety, and 42% displayed posttraumatic stress disorder (PTSD) symptoms (Cardozo et al., 2004). A study in Kurdish refugee camps found that 87% of children displayed PTSD symptoms and 92% evidenced learning difficulties (Murthy, 2007). Although Western diagnostic categories fail to capture the entirety of the refugee experience, they highlight the legacy of trauma on the body and brain.

Considering these high rates of trauma exposure, well-meaning therapists may equate therapeutic work with trauma processing. Caution is warranted here. Refugees are already overwhelmed by language learning, parenting in a new culture, and navigating complexities of transportation, work, and daily subsistence. Thus, a culturally humble therapist prioritizes the client's beliefs about what is most important, which may focus on problem-solving, practical support, and facilitating community connections, rather than overt trauma work in the first year's post-resettlement. We acknowledge that this may feel challenging and perhaps at first not "therapeutic" in light of the more clearly defined step-by-step processes taught in graduate training programs or evidence-based models of trauma work. Cultural humility in therapy can, however, offer countless opportunities for moments of connection and healing outside the trauma narrative.

## Flight From Home and the Transition Period

Nyan, a refugee from Myanmar, remembers fleeing as a young boy to the jungle as military rebels overtook his village. "I looked back and saw our house burning and our rice fields destroyed," he described. "We couldn't go back. If they saw you, they would torture, rape, or kill you—because we were the enemy in their mind." There is significant diversity in the journeys of individuals who, like Nyan, experience forced migration. It is estimated that only 2.6 million refugees subsist in camps. Some may seek shelter with extended family or friends, whereas the vast majority live in urban areas, often in informal dwellings (UNHCR, 2018a). Refugees are usually not able to obtain formal employment in countries of asylum; thus, they rely on humanitarian aid and often live in extreme poverty. Education is not always available, with only 61% of refugee-status children attending primary school and 23% attending secondary school (UNHCR, 2016). Some families experience multiple relocations. Kalila's parents fled from Palestine to Lebanon, resettled there, and years later were forced to leave due to persecution. Growing up in a world constantly disrupted, Kalila reflects, "We never know what the future has for us."

The process of evaluation for resettlement is intensive and selective. In 2017, there were 1.19 million refugees in need of resettlement, with only 75,188 spots available worldwide (UNHCR, 2018b). Approval for resettlement may evoke complicated emotions. Aya, a young woman from Iraq, recalls feeling a surge of hope with the news. However, excitement was soon overshadowed by pain, as her father's visa was denied due to past military involvement. For Aya, her mother, and siblings, pursuing their dream would mean forced separation from their father until further notice. That same day, Aya recalls, she also received word that her uncle, who had been like a grandfather to her, was killed by the militia. Thus, while many refugees envision their country of resettlement as "just a few steps away from heaven," the journey of resettlement inherently involves loss and mourning, including recognition that returning home is impossible (Papadopoulos, 2002). Noting this diversity of responses, a culturally humble therapist seeks to understand what the label of refugee and the resettlement process mean to each particular client.

### Postmigration Discrimination and Acculturation

Refugees are impacted not only by governmental policies but also by implicit and explicit cultural messages about their legal status. "Any group acknowledged and proclaimed as 'the other' by prevailing *zeitgeist* and dominant social powers, and further dehumanized, may become the subject of discrimination" (Küey, 2017, p. 24). The social, political, and historical context of one's resettlement country adds to the burden of minority stress, influence postmigration psychological functioning, and can compound earlier traumatic experiences (George, 2010). Examining antirefugee bias in Western culture, Esses and colleagues (2013) found reoccurring themes of refugees as potential terrorists, likely to bring infectious diseases, taking away from citizens, and looking for free handouts. These messages incite fear, suspicion, and sometimes aggression in communities where refugees resettle. Amhad, who immigrated with his wife and children from Jordan, painfully recalls driving by a mosque soon after arriving in the United States and seeing people protesting outside, holding up signs and shouting, "Go back home!" Amhad tearfully recounted,

> We have no home—this was supposed to be our new home. . . . I have lived with the term refugee for 11 years. After I came to the U.S., I was given the term "alien" and an "alien number." It made me feel I was a person who came from a different planet, from Mars. As a permanent resident, I am now a "former refugee" . . . it did not change. I want people to see that my family and I—we are human beings.

Amhad's experience highlights the dehumanizing effect of post-resettlement discrimination on refugees' mental health. Internalized xenophobia can result in chronic psychological distress, perpetuating the social oppression and victimization that refugees moved across the world to escape

(Schmitt et al., 2014). In a study of resettled Somali adolescents, post-migration discrimination explained significant variance in PTSD symptoms, over and above premigration trauma experiences (Ellis et al., 2008). Among Afghan refugees, discrimination was found to be particularly psychologically damaging among those who held a strong intraethnic identity or had experienced higher pre-resettlement trauma (Alemi & Stempel, 2018). Due to biases about skin tone and religious practice, refugees who do not easily "blend in" with their community are more likely to be targeted. Many describe the experience of not fitting anywhere. In Layla's words, "Being a refugee means being a Baha'i who wasn't wanted in Iran and an Iranian who isn't wanted in America. It's like being in a stateless place." Layla's struggle highlights the profound influence that sociocultural context can have on one's identity and sense of self.

A culturally humble therapist listens for and works to disrupt systems of social oppression, which may be more insidious than premigration traumas (e.g., witnessing the murder of family members) and be experienced by resettled individuals in stark contrast from idealized expectations about what life in America would look like. Ongoing discrimination can fuel feelings of helplessness, fear, and acculturation challenges, and clients may be reticent to discuss such experiences due to feelings of shame or coping through minimization. Empowering refugees in the face of social oppression may include "working toward restoring collective self-efficacy, collective self-esteem, and perceived control through therapeutic and school- and community-based interventions" (Kira & Tummala-Narra, 2015, p. 457).

## Mental Health and Resilience

*Resilience* has been described as "an unfolding process in which new vulnerabilities and strengths emerge during developmental, societal, and cultural transitions throughout one's life and during periods of acute stress and trauma" (Tummala-Narra, 2007, p. 35). Through the lens of cultural humility, therapeutic engagement with refugees often uses an indirect approach to psychological intervention by exploring innate resources within a client, family, or community that can activate resilience processes, reclaim indigenous healing practices, and cultivate a sense of personal agency and dignity. A primary emphasis on psychopathology or symptom reduction may be counterproductive when working with refugees whose cultural background includes significant mental health stigma. Furthermore, in collectivistic contexts, psychological treatment focus on one identified client may not be well received. Family is central to many refugees' lives and identities, but relatively few psychological services in the United States are oriented collectively. Cultural sensitivity and ongoing consultation with leaders in refugee communities are needed to avoid neglecting real psychological needs on the one extreme or overpathologizing normative adjustment experiences on the other (Papadopoulos, 2002), as we discuss subsequently.

Psychological distress among refugees often presents somatically rather than through cognitive or emotional symptoms (Hollifield et al., 2005). This may include headaches, heart palpitations, feeling jittery, being unable to eat or sleep, physical weakness, and episodes of paralysis (Hobfoll, 2014). As such, unique approaches to both assessment and intervention must be taken. Depending on the culture, well-being is often best facilitated by embodied, rather than verbally mediated, practices. Researchers have called attention to cultural traditions, religious rituals, and indigenous wisdom within refugee communities that represent inherent strengths (Murray et al., 2010). Culturally humble therapists avoid reinventing the wheel and instead attend to and reinforce cultural resources that are already present. Developed out of a community program with Bosnian and Kosovar refugees, a systemic framework of resilience considers the influences of belief systems (e.g., meaning, hope, spirituality), organizational aspects (e.g., flexibility, connection, access to resources), and communication processes (e.g., emotional expression, empathy, problem-solving) in promoting refugee empowerment (Walsh, 2016a, 2016b).

Saul (2013) argued, on the basis of extensive work with torture survivors, that collective trauma often necessitates collective contexts for healing. Many cultures use art, theatre, dance, music, poetry, and other creative activities in therapeutic ways. Such interventions may fall in one of four broad areas: facilitating social connectedness and resource-sharing, creating safe contexts for storytelling and validation of suffering and loss, finding ways to reestablish culturally normative rhythms and routines to support a sense of belonging and identity, and envisioning and moving toward a new and hopeful future (Saul, 2013). Ultimately, empowerment helps refugees build social capital by creating a sense of connection and belonging with both fellow refugees and community stakeholders (Pittaway et al., 2016), as well as reinforcing the strengths and resources they have already used effectively in their survival and adaptation.

## THE THERAPIST AS A CULTURAL BEING

### Developing Mutual Recognition

Each of us comes to therapeutic work with refugees not only as a professional but also as a person with a unique life history, cultural identities (e.g., racial/ ethnic identification, gender, nationality, sexual orientation), social location, and worldview. Ongoing consideration of our own personal subjectivity, blind spots, and implicit biases is a vital aspect of culturally humble therapeutic work with individuals of refugee status. Ethical bracketing has been proposed as one way that therapists can manage differences in the counseling room (Kocet & Herlihy, 2014). From this perspective, therapists are encouraged to check their personal identities and values at the door, assuming a neutral professional stance to avoid potential conflicts over differences. Such an approach provides one strategy for seeking common ground. However, we strongly encourage therapists engaging refugee clients to go significantly further by acknowledging, reflecting on, and openly discussing—both in supervision/consultation and, when appropriate, with clients—how the therapeutic dyad may be prone to implicitly enact oppressive relational dynamics. For example, our internal pull toward an expert stance or the felt pressure to help, fix, or heal when working with refugee clients can serve as warning signals that our own vulnerabilities need to be explored, better understood, and effectively managed.

A two-person relational model provides a helpful framework for recognizing how refugee clients' identities, cultural backgrounds, relational patterns, and psychological vulnerabilities inevitably intersect with our own (Wachtel, 2010). Each client we meet and interact with is "being shaped by and inevitably embedded within a matrix of relationships with other people" (Mitchell, 1988, p. 3)—including us as their therapist and their community of resettlement. Mitchell (1988) encouraged a shift from "the individual as a separate entity whose desires clash with an external reality, [to] an interactional field within which the individual arises and struggles to make contact and to articulate himself" (p. 3). Never is this bidirectional flow of communication and implicit relational knowledge more vital to attend to than when working with clients—such as refugees—whose lived experience may be radically different from our own. Psychotherapy is a relational endeavor, coconstructed in moment-to-moment exchanges at the intersection of a therapist's and client's cultural identities. Thus, even when consciously bracketing aspects of the self, it is neither possible nor therapeutic to fully remove the therapist's self from clinical work with refugees.

On the contrary, it is our shared humanness that often is most connecting. From the first moment of meeting with a refugee client, building a therapeutic alliance requires negotiation of what is initially a radical separateness—two strangers sitting in a room with vastly different life experiences. Bracketing alone may be insufficient. Avoidance or compartmentalization of our reactions could inadvertently lead to a color-blind, religion-blind, or culture-blind approach, collapsing "difference to sameness" (Benjamin, 1994, p. 234). Cultural humility enables the development of an intersubjective space of mutual recognition (Benjamin, 2004), in which we can acknowledge, rather than trying to blot out, our subjective experience and cultural identities and important ways this might inform treatment, while simultaneously recognizing and privileging refugee clients' experiences and identities in the moment. Recognition of both therapist and client as cultural beings and the impact of this on treatment has been associated with greater levels of therapeutic change (Elvy, 2010) but requires a commitment to continual self-examination in the pursuit of professional growth. Thus, in addition to learning about refugee clients' cultures and belief systems, therapists must take initiative to consider how their own background and life experiences could influence the therapeutic encounter for good or ill.

### The Need for Critical Self-Examination

Empirical evidence suggests that implicit biases persist among presumably culturally competent professionals (Boysen & Vogel, 2008). Grouping objects, events, and people together based on similarities and differences is an automatic cognitive process that aids in organizing the vast amounts of information we take in on a daily basis. "Categories are the basis for normal prejudgment. We cannot possibly avoid this process. Orderly living depends on it" (Allport, 1954, p. 20). The problem is when we let these automatic categories "do the work," rather than engaging in the more time-intensive process of getting to know each client as a unique individual. Cultural humility facilitates critical self-evaluation of subconscious prejudices—subtle ways that we have each been shaped by historical sociocultural contexts—recognizing that this often seeps into conceptualization, diagnosis, and intervention approaches.

In a graduate seminar, I (LEC) was challenged to examine implicit biases when the professor wrote a long list of identity variables on the board (e.g., refugee, asylum seeker, undocumented immigrant, foreigner, American, Muslim, Buddhist, Hindu) as well as intersectional groupings of these identities and challenged us to write down the first words that came to mind, without censoring ourselves. I remember the significant discomfort I felt, not wanting to be presumed "racist" or any other pejorative term. However, this professor created a classroom environment that, albeit uncomfortable, was ultimately a safe space for critical self-reflection without spiraling into shame. As caring professionals, we are often motivated to push prejudicial attitudes aside, rather than adopting a self-compassionate and curious stance about why these things come to mind in the first place. We encourage readers to engage in self-reflective exercises to increase personal awareness of implicit beliefs about individuals with refugee status (see Exhibit 3.1 for an example).

**EXHIBIT 3.1. Examining Implicit Biases About Refugees: An Exercise to Develop Greater Cultural Humility**

We all have biases, and most of them are outside of our conscious awareness. As helping professionals, it is vital to examine and understand automatic reactions that might influence our therapeutic work with individuals of refugee status. Honestly acknowledging our prejudices without collapsing into shame and guilt frees us to expand on these incomplete and counterproductive schemas to engage more empathically and deeply with our clients. Either individually or with a group of trusted peers, set aside time to consider and expand on your implicit attitudes about refugees. Feel free to use the following instructions as a loose framework to guide you.

1. Use a whiteboard or blank piece of paper to write out various identities that individuals of refugee status might hold. Consider race/ethnicity, nationality, gender identity, sexual orientation, religion/spirituality, social location/socioeconomic status, educational background, employment/vocation, relationship status, ability, health, age, and so forth. You might also consider intersections between identity variables, based on the refugee groups you are working with (e.g., Christian Somali women who are single mothers or LGBTQ individuals within the Muslim Iraqi community).

2. Under each category, write out whatever words come to mind for you. Try to avoid filtering yourself. If you are pulled to write solely positive descriptors, reconsider what you've heard "in the air." How might the media portray this group inaccurately and harmfully? How have you heard them talked about before? Although it can be difficult to write out more negative descriptors, doing so should not be equated with fully endorsing these prejudices. Instead, it frees you to take a look at and consider what biases in the sociopolitical environment might be implicitly shaping you.

3. Take a few minutes to read over and silently reflect on these lists of words, labels, and descriptors. Pay attention to the emotions that come up for you. Do you feel sad? Angry? Ashamed? Emboldened? Something else? Process this as a group (or journal about it if you are going through this exercise individually). You will likely be relieved to realize you are not the only one who had strong emotional reactions to this exercise.

4. Reflect on and talk together (or write out) where you first heard these labels and ideas about each specific group. Was it within your family? At school? From friends or coworkers? Through mass media (e.g., TV, news, music, social networking)? Consider your own identities and cultural background and how this may have subtly shaped your perceptions of refugee groups. Tracing back and understanding where our narrow categorizing got started about any particular group can be enlightening, freeing, and rehumanizing, as we become more aware of and honor both diversity and shared humanity.

5. Take personal ownership for change. Pick one group you know the least about or have some problematic and incomplete views of. Identify a specific action step you can take to expand your understanding of that group, whether by reading, talking with a friend, visiting a local house of worship or community event, or taking a class. Consider how you can expand on automatic biases by intentionally seeking out ongoing relationships with individuals of refugee status.

*Note.* LGBTQ = lesbian, gay, bisexual, transgender, and queer.

Although self-examination is often uncomfortable in the moment, developing greater self-awareness will decrease the likelihood of engaging in microaggressions and enhance therapeutic ability to work effectively with refugee clients. None of us are immune to the harmful and incomplete messages in contemporary culture that privilege certain groups while scapegoating others. In *Racism Without Racists*, Bonilla-Silva (2017) highlighted the ongoing structural inequalities within American society that are often unconsciously internalized. Further, the U.S. sociopolitical climate often engenders fear, skepticism, and even hatred toward individuals who look different. Common stereotypes relevant to working with refugees include equating Americans with light skin and darker skin with foreigners, presuming that Muslims are more likely to participate in religious violence, associating dark-skinned individuals with less education, and linking women with family rather than career pursuits. However, there is a difference between knowing stereotypes and endorsing them (Banaji & Greenwald, 2016). Honest recognition of biases is the first step to developing new perspectives. Cultural humility has been associated with more positive attitudes toward refugees, controlling for religious and political beliefs (Captari et al., 2019). Thus, we encourage therapists working with refugees to engage in reflective practice, taking time to wonder about, own, process, and explore their personal reactions, both individually and with trusted colleagues.

### Awareness of Power and Privilege

The role of a helping professional imbues therapists with more power than we often realize, and this power differential can be experienced as an extension of structural racism and xenophobia (Washington, 2008). By the very nature of receiving refugee status, such individuals have been subjected to oppression and disenfranchisement. When engaging refugees, cultural humility is vital to recognize and process the interpersonal dynamic in the room. Each of us has a unique stimulus value based on gender, age, skin tone, build, and personality (Kelly, 2017). Therapists who hold majority identities, particularly those that are immediately observable, may experience an increased power differential in their work with refugees (Dottolo & Kaschak, 2018). This dynamic can be difficult to navigate, especially with clients whose collectivistic values prioritize agreeableness rather than assertiveness. Such individuals may be reticent to disclose to their therapist if the treatment approach is insensitive, unhelpful, or counterproductive. We encourage therapists to reflect on and, when clinically appropriate, process with refugee clients how they experience the therapeutic relationship. What might they expect of the therapist and the therapeutic process? What might they be afraid of? How can the therapist and client work toward the development of a mutual partnership in pursuit of the client's goals? Directly approaching such topics and using here-and-now processing necessitates the development of a strong therapeutic alliance.

Bearing witness to refugees' stories of horrific trauma and loss may elicit a sense of wishing to rescue or heal; furthermore, clients may "pull" for this dynamic (Herman, 1997). However, taking a dominant or expert role in the therapeutic dyad is likely to reinforce a client's sense of helplessness and external locus of control. In the words of a colleague, "Only victims need to be rescued" (A. Geerts-Perry, January 17, 2018, personal communication). There is a significant difference between "power over" and "power to" in relationships (Goodrich, 1991). Empowerment is a central consideration because refugees have often been dehumanized, tortured, and psychologically dismembered through manipulation and control. Joseph, a leader in a Rwandan refugee community, describes the impact of group therapeutic support: "After the genocide, many of us felt that we were completely dead inside. But when you came and sat with us—again and again—when you listened to us, you reminded us that we are alive."

Refugees often have no words to fully describe the traumas they have experienced. Therapeutic work may be slow and laborious. Cultural humility enables therapists to maintain a consistent stance of deep listening, patient attunement, and generous involvement. Pizer (2018) described the struggle to contain and metabolize clients' "rage, hopelessness, dread, or anguish, thus conveying a fundamental human respect, a willingness to [enter into another's] pain, confusion, and self-doubt" (p. 111). Offering oneself as an empathic witness—rather than an omnipotent rescuer—restores human dignity, felt safety, and personal agency thereby activating innate "power for self-healing" (Mollica, 2008). Research has found that clients' perception of their therapist's multicultural orientation—including cultural humility—is positively related to a strong working alliance, which predicts greater psychological improvement (Owen et al., 2011).

## Addressing Therapeutic Ruptures

Cultural humility aids in repairing therapeutic ruptures with refugee clients and thus decreases the likelihood of premature termination, while also increasing refugees' experience of feeling understood and supported. Therapists and individuals of refugee status may differ on multiple variables, including race/ethnicity, native language, social class, gender norms, religious or spiritual beliefs, worldview, and understanding of mental health, to name a few. Thus, the stage is set for misunderstandings, microinvalidations, and microaggressions. Considering this, it is vital to name and create space to talk about cultural differences from the very first session, expressing a genuine desire to understand and empower each refugee client while recognizing that even with the best intentions, we may "get it wrong" sometimes. Laying the groundwork to openly discuss misunderstandings and differences that arise in treatment can strengthen trust and rapport. Research suggests that minor strains on the therapeutic alliance generally occur every few sessions, often outside of a therapist's awareness (Safran & Muran, 2000). This is not cause for shame or self-doubt but a reminder that we are all human.

Attending to and repairing ruptures has been associated with more positive treatment outcomes, but such incidents can be easy to overlook or write off (Safran et al., 2011). Unintentional discrimination with refugee clients could include "brief and commonplace daily verbal, behavioral, and environmental indignities . . . that communicate hostile, derogatory, negative racial slights and insults to the target person or group" (Sue et al., 2007, p. 273). In one study, 81% of racial/ethnic minority clients reported at least one racial microaggression in counseling; however, clients who perceived their therapist to exhibit cultural humility experienced significantly less microaggressions (Hook et al., 2016). Unfamiliarity with one or more aspects of a refugee client's identity or culture could lead a therapist to avoid potentially "touchy" subjects, such as religion or ethnic heritage, yet this implicitly communicates these self-aspects are not relevant or important. For example, although many refugees have experienced significant trauma, one client noted, "When all you ask about is my trauma, it feels like nothing else about me is real." Clients' perception of missed opportunities to discuss cultural issues in session is associated with worse treatment outcomes (Owen et al., 2016). Both our refugee clients and we as therapists are cultural beings with manifold important experiences that have shaped us. Failing to acknowledge, address, and integrate any aspect of a refugee's experience in treatment is likely to have a deleterious impact.

Recognizing our position of inherent power, therapists can take initiative to (a) express ongoing curiosity about refugee clients' experience in treatment (e.g., what is helpful vs. not helpful); (b) invite feedback and check in when clients seem less engaged, overly compliant, or upset; (c) privilege refugee clients' culture and worldview in understanding both causes of distress and helpful means of coping and adaptation; and (d) forthrightly own our clinical mistakes and missteps. Working through impasses and transference–countertransference enactments requires a heavy dose of cultural humility, the ability to stay present with and be curious about difficult affects, and readiness to acknowledge when we have misspoken or missed something. Yet therapeutic ruptures have the potential to be incredibly impactful and healing when we harness them as opportunities to listen deeply to empower refugee clients.

## CULTURAL HUMILITY IN THERAPY

Effective engagement with refugees often requires deconstruction of Western counseling theories as generally defined. Therapeutic engagement may look quite different from two people sitting together in a professional office for an hour once a week. In some societies, it is unheard of, and perhaps even shameful to one's family, to talk with a stranger about personal problems. Further, admission of mental difficulty is often equated with weakness, "craziness," or even demon possession. As one refugee shared, "In my culture, if someone has a psychological problem, their family chains them up to a tree out back." Cultural mistrust, and suspicion of authority in particular, have been documented among refugees and should be honored as a protective strategy in light of past experiences of government corruption and betrayal (Ellis et al., 2011; Ní Raghallaigh, 2013).

Using the principles of cultural humility, we suggest that therapists explore the various ways in which healing might take place for the client, which may mean broadening the scope of therapeutic frame. This could include working alongside a translator rather than expecting a refugee client to communicate solely in English or meeting with refugee families at a location they know and trust (e.g., community agency, school, refugee resettlement office) rather than expecting them to come to the therapist's office. Both formal and informal mental health supports are needed, considering what each individual or family needs in the moment (Brar-Josan & Yohani, 2017). Additionally, understanding culture-based frameworks of communication within refugee communities aids in buffering therapist frustration at not receiving direct answers or linear accounts during interviews or interventions. Clients from high-context cultures use a communication style that relies more heavily on implicit cues, body language, and contextual factors, whereas those from low-context cultures prefer explicit and direct use of language (Hall, 1976). Considering these factors, we next detail several case examples of therapeutic work with refugees.

### Building Bridges Between Two Places

Akifa[1] was a shy 8-year-old when she began the third grade. Her family had resettled in the United States 2 years ago from Somalia, and the class was excited to welcome her. Although friendly and sweet, Akifa struggled to follow directions and frequently zoned out, doodling on her page or staring

---

[1] Composite case study.

off into space. As the year continued, her teacher became worried and referred her for educational testing. However, the results were puzzling. In some areas, Akifa scored at the level of a middle schooler, while in other aspects, she scored on par with first graders. There were definitely some academic weaknesses, but nothing pointed to a learning disability.

The school counselor suggested that maybe Akifa would benefit from emotional support and referred her to a therapy group at school for children whose parents were recently divorced. At this, Akifa's mother retorted, "This is a child who, in her very short life, has seen and heard and experienced things that many of you can't even dream of. She reacts according to what she has known." The evaluators expressed concerns over the themes of death prevalent in Akifa's narratives. "Do you talk to her about death at home? Is she watching violent movies?" they questioned the family. "Akifa has seen people die right in front of her," her father replied. "Of course we talk about it! It is important for us that she understand, that we prepare her for how to handle it if we were to die."

Reaching an impasse, the school referred this family to a local nonprofit that helps refugee parents navigate the complications of American educational systems. At intake, Akifa's parents were skeptical and guarded. Her father described being offered help that isn't helpful: "Whatever program they want us to put Akifa in to help her be 'normal' isn't a program for her." Frustration is evident in his voice. It seemed that, so far, the mental health and educational systems had done little to empower Akifa and her family, but rather had tried to force Western diagnostic categories on a child in transition.

Stepping out of the position of expert, the therapist began to explore the family's perspective. "Tell me about your family," he posed. They seemed surprised. As they talked, the therapist moved toward conversations that explored the family's Somalian cultural identity. He quickly became aware of how Akifa and her siblings live between two worlds. Akifa had integrated well into her classroom, making friends easily. But while her classmates were likely watching TV or playing, Akifa helped out substantially with cooking meals and caring for her younger siblings. "She helps us with English, too," her parents laughed. This is a common experience among refugee families, with children acculturating and acquiring conversational language at a faster level, which can result in substantial responsibility and parentification (Rousseau et al., 2004).

Akifa's assessment results do not seem to capture the full scope of her lived experience and current challenges. Refugee children are often over-represented in special education due to poor performance on standardized assessments (Peña et al., 2011); however, the English used for academic tasks "takes much longer to acquire than conversational (or oral) language proficiency" (Kaplan et al., 2016, p. 89). With this in mind, the therapist pursues a more systemic conceptualization of this child's difficulties. Even after 2 years in the United States, Akifa's family is still transitioning. Akifa often worries and asks about her cousins, who have not yet been approved for resettlement. Disrupted family relationships and uncertainty about members' safety and whereabouts has been associated with learning difficulties for refugee children (Kaplan et al., 2016).

Albeit with good intent, the professionals who initially sought to help Akifa experienced significant barriers engaging her family because they ignored important cultural nuances, taking a one-size-fits-all approach to academic support. The lens of cultural humility offers a broader perspective that places Akifa's academic difficulties in the context of the significant shifts she has experienced over the past several years—in place, language, culture, and expectations at home. Over the course of family therapy, listening to Akifa's parents and working collaboratively to support her success helped this young girl begin to develop a bicultural identity (Schwartz et al., 2010). Noticing Akifa's creative bent, the therapist referred her to an after-school art program. Providing family-based therapeutic support proved far more beneficial to Akifa's well-being and academic functioning than the school's original intervention plan. By the end of third grade, she was on par with her classmates, and painting profusely.

## Listening for Intersectionality

A Syrian refugee, Samira[2] displayed ongoing psychological distress after resettlement. Her caseworker discussed the possibility of meeting with a mental health professional, and Samira hesitantly agreed. She expected a cold and sterile doctor's office but was surprised when the therapist showed her a play space where her children could pass the time and offered her a cup of tea as they sat down in the counseling room. Initial aspects of the therapeutic encounter—from first contact by phone, to paperwork, to lighting, decoration, and atmosphere—can communicate cultural sensitivity in powerful ways. Although she has advanced degrees and experience in trauma work, the therapist is a beginner at working with Samira. In fact, she knows precious little. This honest recognition could lead her to self-consciousness, resulting in "trying harder," which would likely be therapeutically counterproductive.

---

[2]Fictional case study.

Instead, Samira's therapist seeks to recognize and accept the limitations of her awareness to be present and curious as she gets to know the unique lived experience of this client.

Samira is no stranger to interviews—the immigration process is stressful and invasive. But the culturally humble therapist seeks to do more than gather information about her symptoms. *What's it like to be Samira?* The therapist listens deeply and avoids rushing, remembering the words of a book she recently picked up:

> We listen to people in depth, over an extended period of time, with great intensity. We listen to what they say and don't say, to what they say in words and through their bodies and enactments. We listen to them by listening to ourselves, to our minds, our reveries, and our own bodily reactions. We listen to their life stories and to the story they live with us in the room. We attend to their past, present, and future. We listen to what they already know or can see about themselves, and for what they don't yet know or can't see in themselves. (Aron & Starr, 2013, p. 24)

A single mother of two children, Samira fled Aleppo amid civil war after her husband was killed. Samira's refugee status is just one of many intersecting vulnerable identities that she carries. She is also a woman, a Muslim, a widow, a mother, and a teacher. The theory of intersectionality explores how holding multiple minority identities often increases risk for oppression and violence (Cho et al., 2013). In the United States, Samira is at risk for discrimination because of her hijab and accent. She may be presumed to be uneducated or incompetent despite her well-established educational credentials, and she can't help but notice the stares at the grocery store and the pickup line at school. Samira also faces unique stressors as a single woman—and a mother—in an unfamiliar culture. Yet she is a woman of incredible strength and unwavering hope.

The therapist and Samira discuss her challenges negotiating these various identities. She worries about her children. Often, they crawl in her bed crying at night. As she holds their little bodies praying for comfort, Samira desperately misses her *habibi*. Images of his mangled body flood her mind. Tears well up in her eyes, recalling this. In an instant, therapist and client are transported back to that fateful day when she decided to flee. It was her husband's dying wish. Although her trauma is apparent, an intersectional therapeutic approach conceptualizes Samira as a multifaceted being, acknowledging "the complexity surrounding multiple axes or dimensions of social identity and how they intersect to influence the health of immigrant and refugee women" (Guruge & Khanlou, 2004, p. 32). Samira averts her gaze as she describes her job. She seems ashamed, struggling with the vocational shift from teacher to working in a manufacturing plant. She details—with pain—the gender and religious discrimination she regularly experiences. But Samira lights up when talking about her children; it is because of them that she perseveres.

Over the course of treatment, Samira began to find her footing and build a home. She developed collective self-efficacy by connecting with a religious community and eventually secured a new job. This shift enabled her to move her family from their cramped apartment to a small home near their mosque. In reengaging with her faith tradition, Samira found a welcoming community, yet another place where she was not defined by the legal status with which she entered the United States. Cultural humility enables us to listen deeply— and to listen for intersectionality, not just symptoms. By doing so, we help refugee clients and families recognize and cultivate the inherent strengths they already possess (Walsh, 2016b).

### Reclaiming Cultural Healing Practices

Seeking to engage the Rwandan community, a therapist collaborated with the local resettlement office to organize a trauma-focused group.[3] She invited a Rwandan community leader to serve as consultant and planned to use a narrative therapy approach. At the first weekly gathering, she welcomes group members and encourages them to share one aspect of their refugee journey. The women are somewhat guarded, making small talk and struggling to overtly discuss the horrors they have experienced. Raissa hesitantly describes how the rebels murdered her nine brothers. But her voice is flat and her body stiff, as if still huddled in the family cellar expecting her killers to burst in at any moment. Instead of engaging, other group members avoid eye contact and seem relieved when the session is over. *I'm missing something,* the therapist reflects. Adopting a learner stance, she asks her coleader, "In your culture, how do people deal with hardship and process trauma?"

"Before the genocide, everything was different," the woman replies. Her eyes light up. "Then, we used to dance and sing and chant together. This was how we held each other's suffering. We would weave baskets together . . . and talk and laugh and cry. But when the killings started, we ran for our lives. There was no time to grieve." The therapist listened, fascinated, as her coleader describes healing practices embedded within Rwandan culture. "Drums have a special meaning," the woman continues. "For thousands of years, our ancestors used them to send messages across distances. Some rhythms communicate joy, others embody anguish. Back in the village, beating

---

[3]Composite case study.

the *ngoma* was an invitation—the minute you hear it, you leave your house and go join in. A lead drummer starts a beat, and people begin to improvise. When someone starts a stanza and no one responds, this is a tragedy."

It takes humility for this therapist to recognize the significant gaps in her understanding of Rwandan culture. "Hmm . . . maybe these women don't need to talk. Maybe they need to dance!" she laughs. The women are surprised upon arriving at the next group to see *ngoma* drums lining the wall. The coleader steps up to the front and begins a beat, and the women respond with enthusiasm, as if a long-forgotten piece of home has been awakened in their midst. Some join in on the drumline, others take to the dance floor. The process unfolding is profound, the embodiment of longheld anguish. Figures once frozen in terror now writhe with energy. The women weep, they laugh, they remember. They say with their bodies what their minds cannot comprehend.

In subsequent weeks, a process of healing continues to spontaneously unfold. Each woman takes her turn—supporting the others, grieving herself. One night, Raissa begins a chant of longing and loss. She speaks in her native tongue, Kinyarwanda, remembering her 6-month-old infant who died in her arms. Her body gives way, and she is held in the elder women's grasp. Their tears mingle with her own. There is no way to manualize this process. It is free-flowing and improvised. As group members take more ownership for how their time will be spent, the therapist's role fades into the background. Only after the fact is anyone vaguely aware that what has occurred on Wednesday evenings is *therapy.* The women begin to report feeling less anxious, having more energy, and sleeping better. Nightmares that have plagued Raissa for years begin to melt away. In a modest office space in an unfamiliar city, these women are finding a way to metabolize their trauma, and the group continues to grow as women invite their friends.

In working with refugees, therapists' most important role is often to help individuals reclaim lost cultural practices that enable healing and transformation, not force assimilation to Western coping strategies. Ceremonies, festivals, and religious practices are powerful embodied experiences that can facilitate healing (McKenna Longacre et al., 2012; Monteiro & Wall, 2011). Considering underlying mechanisms of emotion and memory, Hinton and Kirmayer (2013) noted how

> healing rituals often have a playful, ludic, novelty-seeking aspect that tends to induce a positive mood state that may promote cognitive flexibility . . . [and] have the effect of increasing emotional and cognitive "flexibility" which is a major source of psychological resilience. (p. 615)

We encourage therapists to draw out each client's culture and heritage, asking about culturally consistent coping strategies. Let refugees teach you what they did in the past to manage stress, process grief, and find joy, and you are likely to tap into their existing sources of strength and resilience.

When working within agencies often bound by limited funding and pre-determined definitions of what therapy "should be," it can feel difficult to foster spaces for empowerment through creativity and connection. Some healing practices are not feasible or advisable in the direct context of treatment but can be discussed in sessions and incorporated in a client's lifestyle. Culturally humble therapists are always on the lookout for creative ways to incorporate clients' culture and heritage in the conversation. This could include creating a genogram together, exploring the role of a religious holiday in honoring the deceased, discussing a client's connection with a cultural myth or historical event, or learning the words for *suffering* and *healing* in their native language.

## CULTURAL HUMILITY IN COMMUNITY COLLABORATIONS

Refugee resettlement agencies act as a short-term "safety net," providing a small measure of financial support and helping newly arrived families orient to community resources, such as finding their first job, enrolling their children in school, and receiving food stamps (Fix et al., 2017). However, within 3 to 6 months, refugees are expected to be financially independent, culturally integrated, and able to fend for themselves. This is a weighty and unrealistic expectation, considering that refugees must navigate a new language, transportation system, health care network, community, and educational world—not to mention gaining full-time employment. Where is the nearest grocery store? How do I pay the electric bill? What is Medicaid, and are my children eligible? How can we get involved in a house of worship? Seemingly endless daily stressors can result in a cumulative burden that impedes resilience processes (Kira et al., 2014). Next, we identify five practical considerations that integrate cultural humility in building community collaborations to help meet these needs.

### Address Gaps in Services

Nongovernmental organizations and social service agencies provide some follow-up once a family's case is closed at the resettlement office, but case management and capacity building are two different things (Lenette & Ingamells, 2015). A significant gap exists between refugee needs and the current services available due to lack of funding (Edward & Hines-Martin,

2015). Too often, agencies focus on individual assistance (e.g., helping a single mother secure a minimum wage job) but fail to consider related family factors (e.g., early-morning childcare necessary to take the job, access to education to advance in a career). Although local agencies have inroads and trust within refugee communities, staff often lack training and time to facilitate mental health support services. "We listen to their stories of trauma, and often we become traumatized too," one caseworker describes. In contrast, therapists possess the expertise to intervene in culturally adapted ways but frequently lack access to and credibility with refugee communities.

Even if they are experiencing distress, a majority of refugees will not seek out therapy because it does not fit within their cultural framework of health (van der Boor & White, 2020). As one agency director shared, "Mental health comes up, but it's not direct. They wouldn't say, 'Oh, I need mental health services,' but might mention in passing, 'This baby died at 9 days old . . . and the mom hasn't stopped crying yet.'" Making inroads with refugee families will likely require leaving your office, building relationships with community leaders, and participating in relevant cultural activities. We note with dismay the responses of some to this assertion as constituting a professional boundary violation or not being "real therapy." When working with people who have been repeatedly tortured, psychologically manipulated, or otherwise violated, establishing yourself as a credible and trustworthy individual is a slow and relationship-intense process. Mental health stigma, financial and transportation limitations, and necessary prioritization of daily stressors are common barriers (Khan & Shafqat, 2017). Many refugee communities also inherently value group connections; small gestures of social engagement, such as greetings and learning about each other's families, necessitate a slower relationship-building process on top of which these additional barriers are laid. Despite this, collaborations between mental health professionals and local agencies hold tremendous potential to facilitate refugee mental health.

### Develop Mutual Partnerships

A collaborative model for refugee engagement requires cross-disciplinary and interfaith relationships (Vostanis, 2014). We encourage therapists to reach out to and meet with area refugee resettlement offices, nongovernment and social service agencies, and houses of worship. Conduct an informal needs assessment to better understand local gaps in services and barriers to connection. Take the stance of a learner and recognize that those on the "front lines" of refugee work in your community have much to teach you. From their perspective, what are the greatest needs facing refugees in the area? What outreach activities, events, programs, classes, or groups are they already conducting? What would they like to accomplish or do but lack the time, funding, or training to organize? Cultural humility is vital in this process to establish yourself as a partner working alongside area agencies toward mutually established goals, rather than an expert trying to start something "new." In addition to providing direct services, therapists' role may be one of providing training and support to social services staff who are exposed to vicarious trauma and at heightened risk for burnout (Lusk & Terrazas, 2015).

Whenever possible, directly involve the refugee community (e.g., religious leaders or those who resettled in the more distant past) in developing interventions. For example, English classes offered through a local agency could incorporate a psychoeducation component by discussing anxiety, depression, and acculturation challenges (Amri & Bemak, 2012). Children displaying problem behaviors may be more responsive to an after-school camp, including sports, art, and theatre activities that integrate positive coping skills throughout, rather than attempting to start a formal therapy group. Family conflicts and parenting challenges could be addressed through a weekly gathering involving food, sharing, and therapeutic support. Walsh (2002) offered a wonderful prototype in the Coffee and Family Education/Support (CAFES) and Tea and Family Education/Support (TAFES) groups, which use a "respectful, healing, and empowering" approach rather than treating "traumatized individuals" (p. 135–136). Community activities such as these can also help identify children or families who are at significant risk. Individuals exhibiting severe and chronic distress could be referred for ongoing therapy through a referral network of area therapists who each agree to take on one pro bono, long-term case.

## Proceed Slowly and Intentionally

Culture-blindness might encourage quick fix or one-size-fits-all approaches, resulting in help that is not helpful and programs that reinforce the perception of refugees as helpless victims. Humility bids therapists to tread with care, recognizing that we are cultural foreigners in refugee communities. Slow and intentional program development attends to the characteristics of specific refugee groups (e.g., Congolese vs. Syrian vs. Burmese), as the needs, customs, and cultural practices of differing communities vary widely. The CAFES/TAFES gatherings (Walsh, 2002) recognized the importance of coffee in Bosnian culture and tea among Kosovar families, adapting their name and therapeutic framework accordingly. In program development, culturally humble therapists also consider the influence of historic ethnic conflicts on interrelations between local refugees. For example, a well-intended Rwandan cultural celebration could incite tensions between Hutu and Tutsi refugees due to their respective roles in the Rwandan genocide.

Awareness of power and oppression also raises critical consciousness about language. Designations of "therapist" and "client" may need to be reframed using more culturally relevant terms. One community center decided, "We don't call people coming here 'clients,' we call them 'participants' because they choose to participate . . . so, we need to honor this choice" (Kagaba & Gagné, 2017, p. 676). These are just a few examples among many that highlight the vital importance of attending to cultural values, customs, and norms. No matter how critically reflective, any therapist working in isolation is ill-equipped to effectively engage refugee communities. Such work necessitates ongoing learning, consultation, and collaboration with "insiders" who are cultural experts.

### Empower Community Leaders

Religious communities and faith-based organizations are important liaisons in helping refugees feel welcomed and creating a sense of belonging (Bauman et al., 2016). Many offer mentoring programs through which arriving refugee families are paired with local parishioners to spend time together and get oriented to the community. Such programs can facilitate the development of relational networks and social capital, but care should be taken to honor refugees' religious/spiritual beliefs rather than imposing one's own. Therapeutic activities offered at mosques, synagogues, and churches where refugees attend, especially those cofacilitated by religious leaders, are much more likely to engender trust and participation. Trauma healing programs have been developed for explicitly Muslim (Zoellner et al., 2018) and Christian (Hill et al., 2016) contexts in a number of languages, integrating spiritual beliefs and faith practices as sources of resiliency.

From a long-term perspective, mental health needs may be most effectively addressed by empowering and training leaders within refugee communities. For example, mental health facilitation (MHF) offers "community-based mental health training that can be adapted to reflect the social, cultural, economic and political climate of any population, nation or region" (Hinkle, 2014, p. 1). So far, MHF has been adapted and used in 26 countries. After initial training, community and religious leaders could meet regularly for group supervision and consultation with local therapists. Culturally humble therapists recognize that former refugees carry within them tremendous cultural and experiential knowledge and that many therapeutic exchanges happen in the context of day-to-day living—around meals, on front porches, at the playground—not a professional office. Thus, systemic interventions promote therapeutic capacities and healing networks within refugee communities rather than importing Western interventions.

## CONCLUSION

This chapter has wrestled with the question "What does it mean to be a refugee?" By highlighting the lived experiences and narrative accounts of those who have endured forced migration, we have sought to spark the development of cultural humility in readers through an attitude of curiosity, an appreciation of complexity, and a recognition that each person with a refugee experience is truly unique. Despite frequently negative perceptions of refugees in media and politics, those who work with such clients on a day-to-day basis describe these individuals as hardworking, grateful to be alive, determined, brave, hospitable and loving and as assets to the community.

It is important to note that the perspectives discussed here are in large part representative of therapists who do not have a shared experience of diaspora and who practice within the United States. Ongoing work is needed to apply the lens of cultural humility in situations when the therapist and client have overlapping or shared experiences and in cultures around the world that are actively engaged with refugee mental health. By looking for and activating clients' inherent strengths, resilience factors, and health-promoting cultural practices, a therapeutic stance of cultural humility can facilitate mental health through a variety of creative interventions. We encourage therapists to think outside the box and work collaboratively toward refugee empowerment, in both the counseling room and the community.

## REFERENCES

Alemi, Q., & Stempel, C. (2018). Discrimination and distress among Afghan refugees in northern California: The moderating role of pre- and post-migration factors. *PLOS ONE*, *13*(5), e0196822. https://doi.org/10.1371/journal.pone.0196822

Allport, G. W. (1954). *The nature of prejudice*. Addison-Wesley Publishing.

American Psychiatric Association. (2013). *Diagnostic and statistical manual of mental disorders* (5th ed.). American Psychiatric Association Press.

Amri, S., & Bemak, F. (2012). Mental health help-seeking behaviors of Muslim immigrants in the United States: Overcoming social stigma and cultural mistrust. *Journal of Muslim Mental Health*, *7*(1), 43–63. https://doi.org/10.3998/jmmh.10381607.0007.104

Aqrawy, L. (2016, March). Plenary address. Humanitarian Health Conference, Kansas City, MO.

Aron, L., & Starr, K. (2013). *A psychotherapy for the people: Toward a progressive psycho-analysis*. Routledge. https://doi.org/10.4324/9780203098059

Banaji, M. R., & Greenwald, A. G. (2016). *Blindspot: Hidden biases of good people*. Bantam Books.

Bauman, S., Soerens, M., & Smeir, I. (2016). *Seeking refuge: On the shores of the global refugee crisis*. Moody Publishers.

Benjamin, J. (1994). The shadow of the other (subject): Intersubjectivity and feminist theory. *Constellations: An International Journal of Critical and Democratic Theory, 1*, 231–255.

Benjamin, J. (2004). Beyond doer and done to: An intersubjective view of thirdness. *The Psychoanalytic Quarterly, 73*(1), 5–46. https://doi.org/10.1002/j.2167-4086.2004.tb00151.x

Bonilla-Silva, E. (2017). *Racism without racists: Color-blind racism and the persistence of racial inequality in America*. Rowman & Littlefield.

Boysen, G. A., & Vogel, D. L. (2008). The relationship between level of training, implicit bias, and multicultural competency among counselor trainees. *Training and Education in Professional Psychology, 2*(2), 103–110. https://doi.org/10.1037/1931-3918.2.2.103

Brar-Josan, N., & Yohani, S. C. (2017). Cultural brokers' role in facilitating informal and formal mental health supports for refugee youth in school and community context: A Canadian case study. *British Journal of Guidance & Counselling, 47*(4), 512–523.

Captari, L. E., Hook, J. N., Aten, J. D., Davis, E. B., Ranter, J. M., Davis, D. E., Van Tongeren, D. R., & Shannonhouse, L. R. (2019). Prejudicial and welcoming attitudes toward Syrian refugees: The roles of cultural humility and moral foundations. *Journal of Psychology and Theology, 47*(2), 123–129. https://doi.org/10.1177/0091647119837013

Cardozo, B. L., Bilukha, O. O., Crawford, C. A., Shaikh, I., Wolfe, M. I., Gerber, M. L., & Anderson, M. (2004). Mental health, social functioning, and disability in postwar Afghanistan. *JAMA, 292*(5), 575–584. https://doi.org/10.1001/jama.292.5.575

Cho, S., Crenshaw, K. W., & McCall, L. (2013). Toward a field of intersectionality studies: Theory, applications, and praxis. *Signs: Journal of Women in Culture and Society, 38*(4), 785–810. https://doi.org/10.1086/669608

Davis, D. E., DeBlaere, C., Owen, J., Hook, J. N., Rivera, D. P., Choe, E., Van Tongeren, D. R., Worthington, E. L., & Placeres, V. (2018). The multicultural orientation framework: A narrative review. *Psychotherapy, 55*(1), 89–100. https://doi.org/10.1037/pst0000160

Davis, D. E., & Hook, J. N. (2013). Measuring humility and its positive effects. *APS Observer, 26*(8). https://www.psychologicalscience.org/observer/measuring-humility-and-its-positive-effects

Davis, D. E., Hook, J. N., Worthington, E. L., Jr., Van Tongeren, D. R., Gartner, A. L., Jennings, D. J., II, & Emmons, R. A. (2011). Relational humility: Conceptualizing and measuring humility as a personality judgment. *Journal of Personality Assessment, 93*(3), 225–234. https://doi.org/10.1080/00223891.2011.558871

Dottolo, A. L., & Kaschak, E. (Eds.). (2018). *Whiteness and White privilege in psychotherapy*. Routledge. https://doi.org/10.4324/9781315626444

Edward, J., & Hines-Martin, V. (2015). Exploring the provider's perspective of health and social service availability for immigrants and refugees in a southern urban community. *Journal of Immigrant and Minority Health, 17*(4), 1185–1191. https://doi.org/10.1007/s10903-014-0048-1

Ellis, B. H., MacDonald, H. Z., Lincoln, A. K., & Cabral, H. J. (2008). Mental health of Somali adolescent refugees: The role of trauma, stress, and perceived discrimination. *Journal of Consulting and Clinical Psychology, 76*(2), 184–193. https://doi.org/10.1037/0022-006X.76.2.184

Ellis, B. H., Miller, A. B., Baldwin, H., & Abdi, S. (2011). New directions in refugee youth mental health services: Overcoming barriers to engagement. *Journal of Child & Adolescent Trauma, 4*(1), 69–85. https://doi.org/10.1080/19361521.2011.545047

Elvy, M. M. (2010). *Therapist intersubjective negotiation as a predictor of therapeutic change* [Doctoral dissertation]. The New School for Social Research.

Erden, O. (2017). Building bridges for refugee empowerment. *Journal of International Migration and Integration, 18*(1), 249–265. https://doi.org/10.1007/s12134-016-0476-y

Esses, V. M., Medianu, S., & Lawson, A. S. (2013). Uncertainty, threat, and the role of the media in promoting the dehumanization of immigrants and refugees. *Journal of Social Issues, 69*(3), 518–536. https://doi.org/10.1111/josi.12027

Fix, M., Hooper, K., & Zong, J. (2017). *How are refugees faring? Integration at US and state levels.* Migration Policy Institute.

George, M. (2010). A theoretical understanding of refugee trauma. *Clinical Social Work Journal, 38*(4), 379–387.

Goodrich, T. J. (Ed.). (1991). *Women and power: Perspectives for family therapy.* W. W. Norton.

Guruge, S., & Khanlou, N. (2004). Intersectionalities of influence: Researching the health of immigrant and refugee women. *Canadian Journal of Nursing Research, 36*(3), 32–47.

Hall, E. T. (1976). *Beyond culture.* Anchor Books.

Herman, J. L. (1997). *Trauma and recovery: The aftermath of violence—from domestic abuse to political terror.* Basic Books.

Hill, H., Hill, M., Baggé, R., & Miersma, P. (2016). *Healing the wounds of trauma.* American Bible Society.

Hinkle, J. S. (2014). Population-based mental health facilitation (MHF): A grassroots strategy that works. *The Professional Counselor, 4*(1), 1–18. https://doi.org/10.15241/jsh.4.1.1

Hinton, D. E., & Kirmayer, L. J. (2013). Local responses to trauma: Symptom, affect, and healing. *Transcultural Psychiatry, 50*(5), 607–621. https://doi.org/10.1177/1363461513506529

Hobfoll, S. (2014). Resource caravans and resource caravan passageways: A new paradigm for trauma responding. *Intervention (Amstelveen, Netherlands), 12*, 21–32. https://doi.org/10.1097/WTF.0000000000000067

Hollifield, M., Eckert, V., Warner, T. D., Jenkins, J., Krakow, B., Ruiz, J., & Westermeyer, J. (2005). Development of an inventory for measuring war-related events in refugees. *Comprehensive Psychiatry, 46*(1), 67–80. https://doi.org/10.1016/j.comppsych.2004.07.003

Hong, A. (2017). Mental health services for immigrants and refugees in Philly must be reworked. *Generocity.org.* https://generocity.org/philly/2017/06/19/mental-health-services-immigrants-refugees-nonprofits/

Hook, J. N., Davis, D. E., Owen, J., Worthington, E. L., Jr., & Utsey, S. O. (2013). Cultural humility: Measuring openness to culturally diverse clients. *Journal of Counseling Psychology, 60*(3), 353–366. https://doi.org/10.1037/a0032595

Hook, J. N., Farrell, J. E., Davis, D. E., DeBlaere, C., Van Tongeren, D. R., & Utsey, S. O. (2016). Cultural humility and racial microaggressions in counseling. *Journal of Counseling Psychology, 63*(3), 269–277. https://doi.org/10.1037/cou0000114

Kagaba, T., & Gagné, P. (2017). Resettlement agency: The case of the welcome home community center. *International Relations, 5*(11), 671–686.

Kaplan, I., Stolk, Y., Valibhoy, M., Tucker, A., & Baker, J. (2016). Cognitive assessment of refugee children: Effects of trauma and new language acquisition. *Transcultural Psychiatry, 53*(1), 81–109. https://doi.org/10.1177/1363461515612933

Kelly, S. (2017). *Diversity in couple and family therapy: Ethnicities, sexualities, and socio-economics.* Praeger.

Khan, M., & Shafqat, A. (2017). 4.68 Barriers and facilitators to mental health service access among young refugees: A look at the literature. *Journal of the American Academy of Child & Adolescent Psychiatry, 56*(10, Suppl.), S252. https://doi.org/10.1016/j.jaac.2017.09.436

Kira, I. A., Omidy, A. Z., & Ashby, J. S. (2014). Cumulative trauma, appraisal, and coping in Palestinian and American Indian adults: Two cross–cultural studies. *Traumatology: An International Journal, 20*(2), 119–133. https://doi.org/10.1037/h0099397

Kira, I. A., & Tummala-Narra, P. (2015). Psychotherapy with refugees: Emerging paradigm. *Journal of Loss and Trauma, 20*(5), 449–467. https://doi.org/10.1080/15325024.2014.949145

Kocet, M. M., & Herlihy, B. J. (2014). Addressing value-based conflicts within the counseling relationship: A decision-making model. *Journal of Counseling and Development, 92*(2), 180–186. https://doi.org/10.1002/j.1556-6676.2014.00146.x

Küey, L. (2017). How to deal with growing racism and discrimination against refugees and asylum seekers in Europe? *European Psychiatry, 41*(Suppl. 1), S24. https://doi.org/10.1016/j.eurpsy.2017.01.130

Lenette, C., & Ingamells, A. (2015). Mind the Gap! The growing chasm between funding-driven agencies, and social and community knowledge and practice. *Community Development Journal: An International Forum, 50*(1), 88–103. https://doi.org/10.1093/cdj/bsu024

Longacre, M., Silver-Highfield, E., Lama, P., & Grodin, M. (2012). Complementary and alternative medicine in the treatment of refugees and survivors of torture: A review and proposal for action. *Torture, 22*(1), 38–57.

Lusk, M., & Terrazas, S. (2015). Secondary trauma among caregivers who work with Mexican and Central American refugees. *Hispanic Journal of Behavioral Sciences, 37*(2), 257–273. https://doi.org/10.1177/0739986315578842

Mitchell, S. (1988). *Relational concepts in psychoanalysis.* Harvard University Press.

Mollica, R. F. (2008). *Healing invisible wounds: Paths to hope and recovery in a violent world.* Vanderbilt University Press.

Monteiro, N. M., & Wall, D. J. (2011). African dance as healing modality throughout the diaspora: The use of ritual and movement to work through trauma. *The Journal of Pan African Studies, 4*(6), 234–252.

Mosher, D. K., Hook, J. N., Captari, L. E., Davis, D. E., DeBlaere, C., & Owen, J. (2017). Cultural humility: A therapeutic framework for engaging diverse clients. *Practice Innovations, 2*(4), 221–233. https://doi.org/10.1037/pri0000055

Murray, K. E., Davidson, G. R., & Schweitzer, R. D. (2010). Review of refugee mental health interventions following resettlement: Best practices and recommendations.

*American Journal of Orthopsychiatry, 80*(4), 576–585. https://doi.org/10.1111/j.1939-0025.2010.01062.x

Murthy, R. S. (2007). Mass violence and mental health—Recent epidemiological findings. *International Review of Psychiatry, 19*(3), 183–192. https://doi.org/10.1080/09540260701365460

Ní Raghallaigh, M. (2013). The causes of mistrust amongst asylum seekers and refugees: Insights from research with unaccompanied asylum-seeking minors living in the Republic of Ireland. *Journal of Refugee Studies, 27*(1), 82–100. https://doi.org/10.1093/jrs/fet006

Norcross, J. (Ed.). (2011). *Psychotherapy relationships that work: Evidence-based responsiveness*. Oxford University Press. https://doi.org/10.1093/acprof:oso/9780199737208.001.0001

Owen, J., Tao, K. W., Drinane, J. M., Hook, J. N., Davis, D. E., & Kune, N. F. (2016). Client perceptions of therapists' multicultural orientation: Cultural (missed) opportunities and cultural humility. *Professional Psychology, Research and Practice, 47*(1), 30–37. https://doi.org/10.1037/pro0000046

Owen, J. J., Tao, K., Leach, M. M., & Rodolfa, E. (2011). Clients' perceptions of their psychotherapists' multicultural orientation. *Psychotherapy, 48*(3), 274–282. https://doi.org/10.1037/a0022065

Papadopoulos, R. (2002). *Therapeutic care for refugees: No place like home*. Routledge.

Peña, E. D., Gillam, R. B., Bedore, L. M., & Bohman, T. M. (2011). Risk for poor performance on a language screening measure for bilingual preschoolers and kindergarteners. *American Journal of Speech-Language Pathology, 20*(4), 302–314. https://doi.org/10.1044/1058-0360(2011/10-0020)

Pew Research Center. (2017). *Key facts about refugees in the U.S.* http://www.pewresearch.org/fact-tank/2017/01/30/key-facts-about-refugees-to-the-u-s/

Pittaway, E. E., Bartolomei, L., & Doney, G. (2016). The glue that binds: An exploration of the way resettled refugee communities define and experience social capital. *Community Development Journal: An International Forum, 51*(3), 401–418. https://doi.org/10.1093/cdj/bsv023

Pizer, S. (2018). Deep listening/affective attunement. In R. E. Barsness (Ed.), *Core competencies of relational psychoanalysis* (pp. 104–120). Routledge.

Rousseau, C. C., Rufagari, M.-C., Bagilishya, D., & Measham, T. (2004). Remaking family life: Strategies for re-establishing continuity among Congolese refugees during the family reunification process. *Social Science & Medicine, 59*(5), 1095–1108. https://doi.org/10.1016/j.socscimed.2003.12.011

Safran, J. D., & Muran, J. C. (2000). *Negotiating the therapeutic alliance: A relational treatment guide*. Guilford Press.

Safran, J. D., Muran, J. C., & Eubanks-Carter, C. (2011). Repairing alliance ruptures. *Psychotherapy, 48*(1), 80–87. https://doi.org/10.1037/a0022140

Saul, J. (2013). *Collective trauma, collective healing: Promoting community resilience in the aftermath of disaster*. Routledge. https://doi.org/10.4324/9780203842188

Schmitt, M. T., Branscombe, N. R., Postmes, T., & Garcia, A. (2014). The consequences of perceived discrimination for psychological well-being: A meta-analytic review. *Psychological Bulletin, 140*(4), 921–948. https://doi.org/10.1037/a0035754

Schwartz, S. J., Unger, J. B., Zamboanga, B. L., & Szapocznik, J. (2010). Rethinking the concept of acculturation: Implications for theory and research. *American Psychologist, 65*(4), 237–251. https://doi.org/10.1037/a0019330

Sue, D. W., Arredondo, P., & McDavis, R. J. (1992). Multicultural counseling competencies and standards: A call to the profession. *Journal of Counseling and Development,* *70*(4), 477–486. https://doi.org/10.1002/j.1556-6676.1992.tb01642.x

Sue, D. W., Bernier, J. E., Durran, A., Feinberg, L., Pedersen, P., Smith, E. J., & Vasquez-Nuttall, E. (1982). Position paper: Cross-cultural counseling competencies. *The Counseling Psychologist, 10*(2), 45–52. https://doi.org/10.1177/0011000082102008

Sue, D. W., Capodilupo, C. M., Torino, G. C., Bucceri, J. M., Holder, A. M. B., Nadal, K. L., & Esquilin, M. (2007). Racial microaggressions in everyday life: Implications for clinical practice. *American Psychologist, 62*(4), 271–286. https://doi.org/10.1037/0003-066X.62.4.271

Tummala-Narra, P. (2007). Conceptualizing trauma and resilience across diverse contexts: A multicultural perspective. *Journal of Aggression, Maltreatment & Trauma, 14*(1–2), 33–53. https://doi.org/10.1300/J146v14n01_03

United Nations High Commissioner for Refugees. (2016). *Left behind: Refugee education in crisis.* http://www.unhcr.org/59b696f44.pdf

United Nations High Commissioner for Refugees. (2018a). *Global trends: Forced displacement in 2018.* https://www.unhcr.org/globaltrends2018/

United Nations High Commissioner for Refugees. (2018b). *Resettlement fact sheet: 2017.* http://www.unhcr.org/en-us/5a9d507f7

van der Boor, C. F., & White, R. (2020). Barriers to accessing and negotiating mental health services in asylum seeking and refugee populations: The application of the candidacy framework. *Journal of Immigrant and Minority Health, 22*(1), 156–174. https://doi.org/10.1007/s10903-019-00929-y

Van der Kolk, B. A., & McFarlane, A. C. (Eds.). (2012). *Traumatic stress: The effects of overwhelming experience on mind, body, and society.* Guilford Press.

Vostanis, P. (2014). Meeting the mental health needs of refugees and asylum seekers. *The British Journal of Psychiatry, 204*(3), 176–177. https://doi.org/10.1192/bjp.bp.113.134742

Wachtel, P. L. (2010). *Relational theory and the practice of psychotherapy.* Guilford Press.

Walsh, F. (2002). A family resilience framework: Innovative practice applications. *Family Relations, 51*(2), 130–137. https://doi.org/10.1111/j.1741-3729.2002.00130.x

Walsh, F. (2016a). *Strengthening family resilience* (3rd ed.). Guilford Press.

Walsh, F. (2016b, August). *Strengthening resilience in refugee families impacted by trauma and loss.* American Psychological Association National Conference, Denver, CO.

Washington, H. (2008). *Medical apartheid: The dark history of medical experimentation on Black Americans from colonial times to the present.* Doubleday.

Zoellner, L., Graham, B., Marks, E., Feeny, N., Bentley, J., Franklin, A., & Lang, D. (2018). Islamic trauma healing: Initial feasibility and pilot data. *Societies, 8*(3), 47. https://doi.org/10.3390/soc8030047

# 4 ETHICAL CONSIDERATIONS AND CHALLENGES IN WORKING WITH REFUGEES

RACHEL SINGER, RENEE DEBOARD-LUCAS, AND SOMBO PUJEH

Providing ethical mental health interventions for refugees necessitates a clear understanding of the systemic factors that impact this population. Individuals seeking safe haven within the United States face a plethora of challenges, ranging from obtaining coveted refugee or asylee status to navigating experiences of acculturation. Caps on the number of refugees allowed entry into the United States has fluctuated with changing political administrations. In 2016, 84,995 refugees resided in the United States. In 2018, U.S. President Donald Trump vowed to reduce the limit to 45,000 (BBC, 2018) and dramatically reduced the number actually admitted, with only 22,491 refugees admitted in the United States in the 2018 fiscal year (Hansler, 2018). Although these numbers may be diminishing, there is a marked need for sound clinical interventions due to high rates of mental health concerns among refugees and asylum seekers (Heeren et al., 2014). By the very nature of their flight from hardship, refugees experience high rates of mental health disorders, including depression, anxiety, and posttraumatic stress disorder (PTSD; American Psychological Association [APA], 2012; Heeren et al., 2014; Mahtani, 2003; Robjant et al., 2009). Mental health symptoms may develop as a result of the individual's initial reasons for fleeing their country of origin but may also be

https://doi.org/10.1037/0000226-004
*Refugee Mental Health*, J. D. Aten and J. Hwang (Editors)

amplified by the very process of seeking safe haven in a new country (Robjant et al., 2009). Recognizing the particular vulnerability of this population, it is imperative that therapists are adequately prepared to provide competent treatment using evidence-based interventions.

The United States is not alone in experiencing complex political climates related to immigration. As Sidhu (2017) noted, "Several election campaigns in Australia have been fought, and won, on the basis of 'turning back the boats'" (p. 294), advocating a position of zero tolerance for asylum seekers. Therapists can play a unique role in addressing the individual, family, and community mental health needs of refugees. Additionally, clinicians in the field of mental health may be called on to further question "how are repressive and violent measures normalized and what role might be played to challenge and subvert these practices by the many people who work within the refugee settlement ensemble?" (Sidhu, 2017, p. 294). Balancing the micro- and macrolevel needs of this population necessitates careful integration of ethical codes of conduct, such as the American Psychological Association's (2017a) *Ethical Principles of Psychologists and Code of Conduct* (hereinafter, APA Ethics Code) and the World Health Organization's (WHO; 2013) Comprehensive Mental Health Action Plan 2013–2020. Simply fostering awareness of these codes alone may not always suffice because at times, ethical codes of conduct may appear to clash with other systems of immigration, courts, and the police system (APA, 2012). In these instances, therapists must engage in an active practice of consultation, collaboration, and seek supervision where necessary (Schweitzer et al., 2015).

The present chapter provides an overview of specific guidelines for ethical practice and highlights particular areas in which therapists may experience challenges.

## ETHICAL CODES

Building on a foundation of clear ethical codes, both aspirational and practical, is a necessity when working with particularly vulnerable populations, including refugees and individuals seeking asylum. Kass (2017) defined *ethics* as "both a method—analyzing the ethical acceptability of a policy or program based on morally relevant criteria—and a set of moral values shared by a community" (p. 4). In this chapter, two specific ethical standards serve as guiding principles for providing treatment for refugees. The APA Ethics Code provides both general aspirational principles as well as specific recommendations for practice and research. In 2011, the APA created a specific Task Force on

Immigration to review research recommendations for immigrants, refugees, and asylees (APA, 2012). For the purposes of this chapter, the authors focus on APA's ethical codes as they may be particularly relevant to the readers of this chapter. Please consult other professional guidelines for more information on other fields. On a global scale, the *World Health Action Plan: 2013–2020* established international mental health standards for caring and protecting refugees (WHO, 2013).

In addition to understanding the underlying recommendations from these guiding ethical bodies, it is also essential to understand central factors that shape the mental health of this population. For example, it is pertinent to foster awareness of the context that led the individual to seek refuge in a foreign country, the migration experience, and ultimately experiences of acculturation (APA, 2012). Multiculturally competent interventions are a key component of ethical therapy (Singer & Fuentes, 2018). Therefore, understanding the complex and intersecting identities of the individual him or herself is paramount.

## APA Ethical Guidelines

The APA has established a code of ethics that guides the daily work of therapists. These ethical principles create expectations and a cohesive framework for holding therapists accountable to a high standard of practice in their interactions with patients. The APA Ethics Code consists of five general principles that are aspirational in nature and are not enforceable rules. However, they are intended to guide therapists toward making ethical decisions when dilemmas arise. There is also a set of 10 sections, each containing Ethical Standards that are enforceable and apply to the various domains in which a therapist may conduct their work. As a whole, the Ethics Code is intended to create best practices of care for therapists' professional conduct (APA, 2017a). For a summary of recommendations based on APA's ethical guidelines, see Table 4.1.

### General Principles
The five General Principles (A–E) in the APA Ethics Code are intended to create high standards for which therapists can strive in their ethical practice of mental health care. Principle A is *Beneficence and Nonmaleficence*, which inspires therapists to provide care that is in clients' best interest and does not cause them harm (APA, 2017a). Therapists seek to protect the rights and well-being of their patients, and when conflicts occur, they strive to resolve them in a way that avoids or minimizes potential harm to the patient.

**TABLE 4.1. Summary of the Application of Ethical Principles to Psychological Practice With Refugees**

| APA principle | Recommendations for therapists |
|---|---|
| Beneficence and Nonmaleficence | Peer consultation to maintain neutrality<br>Check value systems<br>Reflexivity, particularly for culturally sensitive topics |
| Fidelity and Responsibility | Learn about clients' value systems<br>Seek ongoing relevant professional trainings |
| Integrity | Review benefits and drawbacks of any treatment<br>No false promises of guarantees<br>Recognize potential mistrust of authorities |
| Justice | Recognize potential biases<br>Ensure adequate norms for evidence-based treatment<br>Identify boundaries of competence |
| Respect for People's Dignity | Understand intersectionality of identities<br>Protect vulnerable populations |

*Note.* Originally presented in *Ethical Interventions With Immigrant, Refugee, and Asylee Clients*, by R. R. Singer and A. Ricks, March 2019. Symposium presented at the Maryland Psychological Association Essential Requirements Conference, Timonium, MD.

In adhering to this particular principle, therapists must be aware of and provide protections against factors that may potentially negatively affect their patients' care. These factors may be personal, financial, social, organizational, or political. For example, a therapist who is working with a patient who is a refugee may find that their own values or political views differ from those of their patient. For this therapists in this situation to operate in accordance with the principle of Beneficence and Nonmaleficence, they must recognize that this difference exists and implement therapy in a way that is unbiased toward their own views and that recognizes the client's worldview as valid. Therapists may benefit from seeking peer consultation to discuss potential conflicts and recognize the bounds of their neutrality to prevent a negative impact on the therapy or the therapeutic relationship (Singer & Tummala-Narra, 2013).

Therapists will need to engage in adequate reflexivity of their own cultural values to provide multiculturally competent and sensitive interventions for refugee clients (Singer & Tummala-Narra, 2013). In specific instances, such as working with refugee clients who have experienced female genital mutilation (FGM), therapists may find it difficult to be objective. Strong reactions to clients' experiences in these areas may influence therapists' abilities to form a clear relational bond in treatment or may cause rifts in trust. Balancing clients' safety with their preferences for clinical interventions is essential on potentially emotionally charged topics, including FGM (Vissandjée et al., 2014).

This area in particular may warrant careful consultation and supervision with colleagues with specific background and training in supporting these clients (APA, 2017a; Schweitzer et al., 2015).

Personal factors that can hamper a therapist's ability to practice Beneficence and Nonmaleficence may include the therapist's own physical and/or mental health concerns. Therapists who have difficulty managing their own personal needs or stress levels may consequently suffer from "professional burnout" that may affect their ability to provide care. For clinicians who may share background with their clients, including their own history of migration or trauma, they may find it difficult to properly convey empathy or understanding of the patient's concerns in the face of potentially retriggering clinical content.

Principle B is *Fidelity and Responsibility*, which indicates that therapists establish relationships with their clients and colleagues based on trust and accountability (APA, 2017a). Therapists seek to understand and clarify their professional roles and obligations as they work to maintain professional standards of conduct. Under the principle of fidelity and responsibility, any conflicts that may arise are dealt with in a manner that avoids exploiting or harming the client. Therapists understand the limits of their competence and seek appropriate consultation from or refer to colleagues who have a particular area of expertise. Therapists working with refugee clients may not be familiar with values or social preferences from their client's country of origin. To provide the best care for their client, therapists might pursue further professional training or consultation from providers or religious figures who have a more in-depth understanding of the customs or values typical of their home country because these may influence the client's functioning or response to stressful situations.

This focus on competence also includes an assessment of therapists' understandings of and background in working with spoken language interpreters (Wright, 2014). In keeping with Principle B, therapists strive to familiarize themselves with working with interpreters to facilitate ethical and more accessible treatment for their clients. In further promoting accessibility, therapists are encouraged to conduct some of their work on a pro bono or reduced fee basis or in situations that do not provide them with personal benefit (APA, 2017a). Refugee clients may not be able to afford a therapist's regular rates because the migration process may have resulted in a significant loss in status, income, and means to make ends meet.

Principle C pertains to *Integrity* in all aspects of a therapist's work (APA, 2017a). Therapists are expected to provide clinical services and represent the field accurately, honestly, and truthfully. This would include presenting the pros and cons of a particular treatment to a patient and taking into consideration the stresses that a refugee may experience, whether they are newly arrived or have had more time to adjust. It is often helpful for therapists to acknowledge that symptoms can increase before they improve and not make false promises or guarantee particular outcomes. In working with refugee clients, therapists might find a healthy mistrust for authority figures developed out of necessity (Whaley, 2001). Refugee clients may have a history of torture by those in positions of authority (Mahtani, 2003). Further, clients may have doubts about whether therapists' stated claims about potential benefits of a treatment modality are actually in their own best interest (APA, 2012). Therapists should work collaboratively with their clients to offer options for treatment and enable their clients to ask questions to help them determine their preferred course of action. This may include integrating healing methods requested by the client or working collaboratively with a religious or spiritual leader to provide integrated care.

When maintaining integrity, therapists should follow through on their professional agreements and avoid entering into commitments that may be ill-advised or have unclear parameters. A therapist would not, for example, agree to see a particular patient and then fail to schedule regular appointments due to an overly full clinical caseload. A refugee client may also experience an unpredictable schedule due to the necessity of managing various life stressors. They may also need to move frequently due to lack of resources or other logistical challenges. Therapists thus may need to exert additional caution in ensuring continuity of care in treatment.

Principle D focuses on *Justice*. Under this principle, therapists recognize that it is fair and just for all people to have access to clinical services that are of equal high quality (APA, 2017a). All patients are entitled to use the same types of services through the same processes. For example, patients who are refugees are entitled to the same compassionate, evidenced-based treatment that is available to persons of a different status. Patients would not be expected to settle for subpar treatment based on limited funds or citizenship status. Another aspect of the principle of justice calls for therapists to exercise reasonable judgment, recognize their own biases, and respect the limits of their expertise and competence. Failure to recognize or observe these biases and limits does not condone provision of unjust services or practices. APA's multicultural guidelines suggest that therapists should take in to consideration whether a particular treatment has been shown to be effective with diverse populations and cultures and, if it has not, to determine whether they can make reasonable modifications without compromising care (APA, 2017b). Similarly, a therapist who comes from a culture that values independence should be aware of the biases they may bring to the table when treating an individual from a culture that holds more collectivist values. Without recognizing their own personal biases, they may incorporate unfair and inaccurate interpretations of their client's decision to move in with their parents versus to live on their own.

The final aspirational principle of the APA Ethics Code is Principle E, which refers to *Respect for People's Rights and Dignity* (APA, 2017a). A central component of this principle is showing respect for the value and worth of all people and the autonomy they have in decision making. All individuals are entitled to privacy and confidentiality in their therapeutic services. It is a therapist's duty to be aware of the need to protect the rights and well-being of people and communities who may be constrained in their ability to make truly autonomous decisions. For example, refugees may have worries about the status of visas, the welfare of family members at home, or their own well-being in an often hostile political environment. These concerns may limit their ability to make autonomous decisions about employment or living situations, which will likely influence their stress levels and clinical presentation in therapy.

Therapists should be aware of and respect the multitude of differences among and within their clients. These may be cultural, individual, or role differences that pertain to age, gender, gender identity, race, ethnicity, country of origin, religion, sexual orientation, disability, language, and socioeconomic status. In demonstrating respect for these differences, therapists must also work to minimize and remove the impact that their own biases and backgrounds may have on the therapeutic relationship. For example, therapists who do not hold religious beliefs should be aware of the biased lens through which they may view their patient who is a refugee based on religious persecution. Similarly, a therapist would not knowingly participate in or condone activities that tolerate or promote prejudices based on the differences just noted.

### Standards

Beyond the general aspirational principles, the APA Ethics Code also includes 10 sections that contain standards to guide clinicians' mental health, research, and community interventions (APA, 2017a). These sections are (1) Resolving Ethical Issues, (2) Competence, (3) Human Relations, (4) Privacy and Confidentiality, (5) Advertising and Other Public Statements, (6) Record Keeping and Fees, (7) Education and Training, (8) Research and Publication, (9) Assessment, and (10) Therapy. Although all standards may include some applicability to the experiences of immigrants, this chapter highlights specific areas that might be most likely to address ethical dilemmas pertinent to refugee clients.

Section 1: Resolving Ethical Issues includes a specific focus on identifying potential discrepancies between ethical codes and legal regulations. Specifically, "if psychologists' ethical responsibilities conflict with law, regulations, or other governing legal authority, psychologists clarify the nature of the conflict, make known their commitment to the APA Ethics Code, and take reasonable steps to resolve the conflict" (APA, 2017a). A legal body that addresses immigrants' documentation status, the U.S. Immigration and Customs Enforcement agency, includes the Department of Homeland Security's Homeland Security Investigations division. A primary purpose of this agency is to "investigate cross-border criminal activity" (U.S. Department of Homeland Security, 2019). Therapists' primary goals in providing treatment to clients who identify as refugees is to support their mental health functioning. At times, it may appear as though these are conflicting goals because individuals seeking refugee status may have entered the United States without legal documentation and may not follow legal protocol for seeking asylum status. In the case of conflicts between the law and ethical codes, therapists are advised to "take reasonable steps to resolve the conflict consistent with the General Principles and Ethical Standards of the Ethics Code" (APA, 2017a). This may include providing information regarding the mental health impact of testifying in a court case regarding a refugee's client and further documenting the ways in which a breach of confidentiality may impair individual functioning. Consulting with a malpractice attorney with experience representing mental health clinicians may provide additional support regarding legal expectations for therapists asked to testify in court.

A key component of therapeutic practice is to ensure that clinicians are practicing within the scope of their competence. Section 2 refers to therapists' *competence*. Within the purview of Standard 2.01, clinicians are expected to develop an awareness of the *boundaries of competence*. When it comes to working with refugee clients, it may not be possible for a therapist to have previous experience in working with refugees from every country of origin. There is an expectation to identify potential sources of training, such as education, supervision, and professional study, that may provide a solid foundation for providing competent interventions (APA, 2017b). Boundaries of competence here may also refer to language. Familiarity with a language does not equate to adequate ability to conduct therapeutic treatment or assessment in that language. Therapists should be aware of their own language limitations and use trained interpreters as necessary (Wright, 2014).

There may be times when the best course of treatment is to provide an external referral. However, the ethical codes recognize that this may not always be an option. For example, at times, a therapist may be the best source of clinical support for that particular individual or family. If therapists have "closely related prior training," they may "provide such services in order to ensure that services are not denied if they make a reasonable effort to obtain the competence" (APA, 2017a). For example, a therapist who is trained to provide asylum evaluations but has not worked with clients from a particular country of origin might seek specific supervision or consultation to ensure that their existing methods are appropriately adapted to that individual's cultural presentation (APA, 2017b). A clear recommendation for competence involves actively working to maintain appropriate levels of competence. This may include focusing continuing education trainings on building skills for treating refugees effectively.

Issues related to therapist burnout and secondary trauma also falls under the purview of competence, specifically, Standard 2.06, Personal Problems and Conflicts. Working with clients with high rates of trauma can be emotionally draining for therapists. The APA Ethics Code advises that "psychologists refrain from initiating an activity when they know or should know that there is a substantial likelihood that their personal problems will prevent them from performing their work-related activities in a competent manner" (APA, 2017a). As Schweitzer et al. (2015) found, sometimes therapists are aware of the boundaries of their competence when it comes to burnout. One participant in their study noted, "I wasn't working as effectively and I could feel I wasn't, because that client was feeling very hopeless and I would be drawn into the feeling of hopelessness, which sort of sucked my energy out" (p. 114). Therapists should take careful steps to bolster their own mental health, including seeking consultation, supports, practicing adequate self-care, and referring clients to other services if their own professional abilities are impaired.

Other complications may arise in working with refugee clients. Section 3 focuses on recommendations for *human relations* (APA, 2017a). Standard 3.05 discourages therapists from engaging in multiple relationships if these many roles would impair the therapist's ability to be objective. Individuals who are refugees may also be seeking asylum within their new host country. There are questions about whether therapists can effectively provide both therapy and objective asylum evaluations. Meffert et al. (2010) highlighted the importance of objectivity in cases of legal court testimony on behalf of an asylum seeker. Should the attorney representing the asylum-seeking individual request follow-up mental health support from the therapist, Meffert et al. (2010) suggested the following:

> A request from an attorney to help stabilize or treat a client may best be responded to by referral to [a different] treatment provider Ultimately, this referral may be more beneficial to asylum seekers, as they will gain an identified

mental health care provider with whom they can continue, if needed, after the conclusion of the case. (p. 487)

There may be times when dual roles are unavoidable. In this instance, Standard 3.05 suggests that the therapist must make efforts to clarify "role expectations and the extent of confidentiality and thereafter as changes occur" (APA, 2017a). This clarification would be essential both for the refugee client but also for any judicial body, law enforcement, or other external system.

Additional planning and clarification may be helpful in the case of Standard 3.12, *Interruptions of Psychological Services*. As previously noted, refugee clients may be particularly transient because of their unique needs. This issue is also addressed by Standard 10.09, *Interruption of Therapy*. Should the therapist become aware of the client's need to move or discontinue services, the therapist must take reasonable steps to ensure continuity of care. It might behoove any therapist working with this population to foster a professional network of colleagues who are trained to provide mental health supports to refugee clients in a wide range of geographic locations.

The fourth standard of the APA ethical code highlights mandates on *Privacy and Confidentiality* (APA, 2017a). As with all clinical relationships, therapists working with refugees must discuss any limits on confidentiality as early as possible in the therapeutic relationship (APA, 2017a). This standard is particularly salient for working with refugee populations and subsequently collaborating with spoken language interpreters (Wright, 2014). It is essential to ensure that clients understand the roles of the interpreters and potential limits or threats to confidentiality (APA, 2017b). Conversely, therapists must ensure that the interpreting services with whom they are working have adequate training in the imperative to ensure a client's confidentiality. At times, the interpreters themselves may also be refugees. Therapists may need to assess for secondary trauma among their interpreters, ensure that these professionals receive supports, and assess for potential impact on the quality of care (Wright, 2014).

This Standard, 4.02, includes discussion with legal representatives—in this case, potentially immigration attorneys. There may be very salient fears within the immigrant population regarding whether the information that they tell a therapist is secure or whether sharing information in treatment would result in negative ramifications (e.g., deportation, family separation; WHO, 2013). Any fears about confidentiality may stem from valid mistrust based on their experiences in their country of origin or lack of accurate information regarding Western mental health care policies (WHO, 2013). Standard 4.04 also indicates the importance of limiting information in any written reports about a client to only the salient or necessary information. Refugee clients may experience real safety concerns if their personal or identifying information is shared with those who wish them harm.

Along a similar vein, Standard 6, *Record Keeping and Fees* (APA, 2017a), may have a few key areas of note for refugee individuals. Due to the sensitive nature of confidentiality in working with this population, therapists may need to take extra precautions for Standard 6.02, *Maintenance, Dissemination, and Disposal of Confidential Records of Professional and Scientific Work*. In creating a professional will, therapists may ensure the secure transfer of any pertinent records related to their work with a refugee client to a trusted colleague who can follow up with that individual as need or to securely destroy any non-essential documents with identifying information. Often asylum cases may drag on for years, indicating the importance of careful and secure record keeping even after the retirement or death of a therapist who provided clinical supports for a refugee or asylee client.

In keeping with ethical codes of conduct while simultaneously incorporating culturally sensitive interventions, refugee clients may not be able to afford a full fee for clinical services. Some cultures include a specific expectation of barter or trade in exchange for services. Standard 6.05, *Barter With Clients/ Patients* allows for the possibility of these alternative means of payment "only if (1) it is not clinically contraindicated, and (2) the resulting arrangement is not exploitative" (APA, 2017a). The therapist must therefore be aware of the client's financial means and seek consultation regarding appropriate methods of assessing fair value for bartered goods.

Therapists may serve other roles in treating refugee clients outside of the traditional therapeutic context, including conducting *Assessments*. Standard 9.01 focuses on the underlying *Bases for Assessments*. Under this principle, any assessment conducted by a therapist must be "sufficient" or "substantiate their findings" (APA, 2017a). In other words, any evaluation must be thorough and adequate. In the case of an asylum assessment, it may be difficult to corroborate the report of a refugee individual describing their experiences of persecution related to their reasons for fleeing their home country. As Meffert et al. noted, clients bear the "burden of proof" to provide evidence behind their story and may often need to do so with little additional evidence due to a hasty flight from their home. It is not the therapist's duty to confirm or disconfirm the occurrence of maltreatment, and thus therapists may need to elicit information that established the credibility of their client. Therapists may also need to provide psychoeducation to the court system that seemingly bizarre demeanor (e.g., remaining calm while recounting an experience of trauma, or conversely high emotional arousal while discussing similarly triggering content) are actually normative responses for an individual recovering from a traumatic experience.

There may be additional challenges with Standard 9.02, Use of Assessment, and Standard 9.09, Test Scoring and Interpretation Services, when it comes to application for immigrant clients. To ensure that tests are appropriate for diverse populations, therapists understand the norms of validity. Has this particular test been demonstrated to be the most relevant and appropriate tool for individuals from a particular cultural background? There may be alternative assessments that are better suited for that particular client base. In reporting any results, therapists should also note any potential limitations of their assessments, including cultural factors that may affect the validity of their results.

The final section in the APA ethical Codes, Section 10, focuses on ethical issues related to therapy (APA, 2017a). As previously noted, informed consent is a crucial element of ethical practice. Standard 10.01, Informed Consent to Therapy, focuses on the mandates of informing clients as early as possible in the therapeutic relationship about all aspects of treatment. This may include a discussion of the scope of treatment, methods for payment and the cost of various services, and any limitations to confidentiality (APA, 2017a). This process also involves careful discussion and ample opportunities for clients' questions, concerns, and clarification. Therapists should ensure that any written consent forms are translated into the preferred language of their refugee clients. Not all clients may have the capacity to read (APA, 2012), so clinicians must also be able to provide alternative means of reviewing consent (e.g., discussing it verbally). The use of interpreters here may enable clients to fully access the material and enter into treatment sufficient information to determine whether they wish to initiate treatment.

Particular challenges may arise with Standard 10.02, Therapy Involving Couples or Families. Refugee individuals may come from countries that endorse more collectivistic family structures than Westernized clients. Therapists must ensure that they do "clarify at the outset (1) which of the individuals are clients/patients and (2) the relationship the psychologist will have with each person" (APA, 2017a). However, multiple individuals from the same refugee family may have experienced extensive psychological and emotional trauma, and these shared experiences may warrant the use of creative interventions. Involving client's significant others, parents, community elders, or other social support systems may allow for a more thorough and therefore more effective treatment (Singer & Fuentes, 2018).

Because this extended system approach may also lead to concerns regarding confidentiality of client's private health information, Standard 10.03, Group Therapy, may come with similar concerns about confidentiality.

Therapists should pay particular attention to this challenge and carefully review the necessity for group members, family members, or community members to limit their conversations about each other outside of therapy. Doing so may ensure an added layer of protection for refugee clients whose safety may be in jeopardy if others find out about their location or specific experiences.

## World Health Action Plan Guidelines

The APA provides recommendations for psychologists working within the United States, whereas the WHO highlights global recommendations for international health issues. The WHO is a specialized agency of the United Nations that has served as the directing and coordinating authority for international health matters and public health since being established in 1948. Working with 194 Member States across six regions and from more than 150 offices, WHO staff are united in a shared commitment to achieve better health for everyone, everywhere. One of WHO's constitutional functions is to provide reliable and objective information and advice in the field of human health. It fulfills this responsibility in part through its publications programs, which seek to support countries in making policies that benefit public health and address their most pressing public health concerns (WHO, 2013). The definition of health in the of the WHO Constitution is "a state of complete physical, mental and social well-being and not merely the absence of disease or infirmity" (WHO, 2013).

The WHO published a series of guidelines on addressing mental health services through a comprehensive plan. These recommendations suggest that the best approach to mental health interventions is one that integrates multidisciplinary approaches (WHO, 2013). These guidelines are intended for use by international, national, and local agencies. Further, the guidelines assessment strategies for monitoring outcomes from interventions. The 2013–2020 Global Mental Health Action Plan includes a proposed vision, objectives and a set of recommended actions which, when performed collectively by Member States, international partners and the WHO Secretariat, will reduce the mortality and disability for people with mental health conditions, prevent mental disorders and promote mental health and well-being. The action plan has, at its core, the globally accepted principle that there is "no health without mental health" (WHO, 2013).

### Mental Health Plan 2013–2020
According to the WHO report, mental health is an integral part of all health and is furthermore a right of all people. However, mental health access may

be limited for individuals in lower resource settings. WHO guidelines use the diagnostic classifications from the *International Statistical Classification of Diseases and Related Health Problems*, 10th revision *(ICD-10)*.

This plan includes six core principles:

1. Universal health coverage: Regardless of age, sex, socioeconomic status, race, ethnicity or sexual orientation and following the principle of equity, persons with mental disorders should be able to access, without the risk of impoverishing themselves, essential health and social services that enable them to achieve recovery and the highest attainable standard of health.

2. Human rights: Mental health strategies, actions and interventions for treatment, prevention and promotion must be compliant with the Convention on the Rights of Persons with Disabilities and other international and regional human rights instruments.

3. Evidence-based practice: Mental health strategies and interventions for treatment, prevention and promotion need to be based on scientific evidence and/or best practice, taking cultural considerations into account.

4. Life course approach: Policies, plans and services for mental health need to take account of health and social needs at all stages of the life course, including infancy, childhood, adolescence, adulthood and older age.

5. Multisectoral approach: A comprehensive and coordinated response for mental health requires partnership with multiple public sectors such as health, education, employment, judicial, housing, social and other relevant sectors as well as the private sector, as appropriate to the country situation.

6. Empowerment of persons with mental disorders and psychosocial disabilities: Persons with mental disorders and psychosocial disabilities should be empowered and involved in mental health advocacy, policy, planning, legislation, service provision, monitoring, research and evaluation. (WHO, 2013)

Ultimately, the plan aims to achieve equity through universal health coverage and stresses the importance of prevention to reach the highest attainable standard of health (WHO, 2013). Its overall goal is to promote mental well-being; prevent mental disorders; provide care; enhance recovery; promote human rights; and reduce the mortality, morbidity, and disability for persons with mental disorders. More specifically, the plan calls for greater collaboration with informal mental health care providers, religious leaders, faith healers, traditional healers, schoolteachers, police officers, local nongovernmental organizations, and even family members. The plan also proposes certain actions member states can take around policy and law, resource planning, stakeholder collaboration, and empowerment of people with mental disorders to implement the mental health action plan. For example, there is an emphasis on the need to integrate and coordinate holistic prevention, rehabilitation, promotion, care, and support that aims at meeting both mental and physical health care needs. This integrated and responsive care will help facilitate the recovery of persons of all ages with mental disorders within and across general health and social services through service user-driven treatment and recovery plans and, where appropriate, with the input of families.

**Mental Health Plan Proposed Actions**
This plan includes markers of progress, including information that Member States can use to monitor their own progress. These goals are intended to be both aspirational and voluntary, with acknowledgment that each Member State may achieve different levels of the goals. The plan highlights the following proposed objectives:

1. To strengthen effective leadership and governance for mental health. Commitment of government is a key factor for developing effective policies and plans to address mental health. The creation of a central system for organization within the country's health ministry and integration of mental health services into general health can generate stronger and more effective responses. Further, strengthening and empowering people with mental disorders and psychosocial disabilities and their organizations should remain central to leadership efforts. This may include involving clients into review and monitoring of mental health services or in delivery of mental health interventions.

2. To provide comprehensive, integrated, and responsive mental health and social care services in community-based settings. To improve access to care and service quality, WHO recommends the development of comprehensive community-based mental health and social care services; the integration of mental health care and treatment into general hospitals and primary care; continuity of care between different providers and levels of the health system; effective collaboration between formal and informal care providers; and the promotion of self-care—for instance, through the use of electronic and mobile health technologies. The establishment of interdisciplinary teams and work with faith-based organizations is suggested to provide general wellness information and careening.

3. To implement strategies for promotion and prevention of mental health. Because poor mental health is strongly influenced by a range of social and

economic determinants across the life course, there is a need to build in access to mental health care within larger primary care and medical-based interventions services because these may be first lines of defense for interventions. For example, for programs that focus on children particularly, integrating these interventions within a school-based context may increase access to care. It is important to provide services and programs to children and adults who have experienced adverse life events that address their trauma, promote recovery and resilience, and avoid retraumatizing those who seek support.

4. To strengthen information systems, evidence, and research for mental health. Routine surveillance/information systems for mental health in most low-income and middle-income countries are rudimentary or absent, making it difficult to understand the needs of local populations and to plan accordingly. There is also a scarcity of evidence-based research around mental health promotion, prevention, treatment, recovery, care, policy, and service evaluation, particularly in low and middle-income countries. If collected, this crucial mental health information could be used to ensure culturally appropriate and cost-effective strategies are tailored to respond to mental health needs and priorities that exist.

The WHO (2013) plan also calls for mental health in humanitarian emergencies through collaboration with committees that focus on emergency preparedness and the assessment of existing application of emergency procedures. Furthermore, the need to build interventions that are sustainable to address long-term supports rather than solely focusing on immediate crisis stabilization is highlighted as an effective strategy.

## WHO Mental Health Plan and Refugees

Although the WHO identifies gaps in existing evidence and develops tools to support future actions and decisions; at present, there are no global or region-wide indicators or standards for refugee and migrant health. Furthermore, there is no global or regional framework currently implemented for the standardized and routine collection of data. This leads to a shortage of scientifically valid and comparable health data on refugee and migrant populations. Collecting such reliable and comparable records is challenging because of the mobile nature of the population, uncoordinated or nonexistent information exchange, and administrative and cultural barriers in accessing services and providing information (WHO, 2013).

Given the heightened risk of psychiatric morbidity among minority populations, refugees, persons caught up in conflict or disasters and other vulnerable groupings, targeted application of this policy instrument to these identified groups is warranted. The comprehensive mental health plan addresses disparities and encourages member states to proactively identify and provide appropriate support for groups at particular risk of mental illness who have poor access to services. It also highlights governments' important role in using information on risk and protective factors for mental health to put in place actions to prevent mental disorders and to protect and promote mental health at all stages of life. Refugees often have unique mental health needs that stem from the migration to a new country, acculturative stressors and living difficulties that typically accompany resettlement, and previous experiences of trauma. These migration factors can significantly impact mental and physical health, functioning, and quality of life among these individuals. This plan emphasizes the need for evidence-based practice that builds in appropriate standards of cultural competence. For example, the plan calls for the building of supportive groups for individuals with similar areas of concern. Refugees who are experiencing displacement may particularly benefit from this increased access to long-term community support and leave those clients with tools for maintaining social supports. This level of support for this vulnerable population allows for more tailored and relevant interventions to address the mental health needs that arise.

To address the varying stages in which countries are in developing and implementing a comprehensive response in the area of mental health, the WHO provides a specific action plan. Given the uniqueness of each Member State, the plan is considered to be a set of guidelines that can be adapted, as appropriate, to national priorities and specific national circumstances. As the plan notes,

> The vision of the action plan is a world in which mental health is valued, promoted and protected, mental disorders are prevented and persons affected by these disorders are able to exercise the full range of human rights and to access high quality, culturally-appropriate health and social care in a timely way to promote recovery. In turn, individuals will be able to attain the highest possible level of health and participate fully in society and at work, free from stigmatization and discrimination around mental health. (WHO, 2013, p. 9)

## RECOMMENDATIONS

Within the many roles that therapists play in working with refugees, there may also be less traditional options for supporting this population. Expertise in evidence-based treatment combined with background in working with diverse clients can create a perfect backdrop for additional opportunities, such as informing research and policy.

## Policy: Therapists as Advocates

Traditional roles for therapists often center around individual treatment. This identity may be somewhat constricting for therapists working with refugee clients. Working with refugees steeped in a complex web of stressors mandates a more comprehensive model than conventional therapeutic methods. Atkinson et al. (1993) suggested that identifying the specific role a therapist should take in working with diverse clients depends on three dimensions related to clients *locus of control, level of acculturation*, and *goals of helping*. The degree of control that clients have over their lived experience may depend on a variety of factors, including external stressors and internal behaviors. For refugee clients, there may be a wide range of environmental challenges that impede their personal well-being. It is also critical to consider their internal resilience, strategies, and responses to difficult situations and the ways in which their cultural values influence their worldview.

The second dimension of this model, acculturation, represents the manner in which an immigrant responds to, integrates, or rejects the culture from their country of origin and the culture in their new host country (Berry, 2005). High levels of acculturation may result in rejection of their original culture, whereas lower levels of acculturation may entail limited integration of new cultural practices. The third dimension, goals of helping, ranges from preventative strategies to remediation, or retroactively responding to stressors.

Depending on where clients fall of each of these three scales, Atkinson et al. (1993) recommended that therapists should alter their intervention strategies. For refugee clients who have already lived through likely multiple traumatic stressors, specific roles may include advocacy and facilitation of indigenous healing for low acculturation clients versus serving as an agent of change or therapist for clients with higher levels of acculturation. The role of the advocate may be particularly salient for clients experiencing a high level of oppression in their new country.

> In the advocate role, the counselor may literally need to speak for the client because limited English-speaking may preclude self-representation. In some cases, this may mean demanding services that are being withheld without justification. In others it may mean advising people in power of the impact that their actions, whether intentional or not, are having on the client. (Atkinson et al., 1993, p. 266)

This imperative to advocate for vulnerable refugee clients overlays on the ethical tenet of beneficence (APA, 2017a). Specific immigration practices intended to deter refugees from seeking safe haven in the United States may ultimately cause irreparable levels of distress in this population. As Kass (2017) noted,

> The values emblematic of our country are often thought to include deep commitments to individual liberties and to entrepreneurship, but also empathy for others, care for the sick, and broad interests—regardless of how we get there—in lifting the tide for all. (p. 5)

Psychologists may serve a unique role providing psychoeducation to government officials, journalists, and the general public on this issue.

## Research

Under APA Principle D: Justice (APA, 2017a) and the WHO's (2013) recommendations, providing effective treatment entails using evidence-based methods for interventions. Many existing therapies rely on convenience samples, meaning that subsequent concerns arise about the generalizability of this data to diverse populations. Clinicians working industriously to apply evidence-based protocol will likely note significant gaps in research. Engaging in active research portfolios or collaborating with researchers allows opportunities to expand understanding about research outcomes of existing interventions. Additionally, therapists' and immigrant clients' voices must be a part of any research that examines actual application of theoretical interventions as they may be able to note potential resources, hurdles, or practical strategies for applying these tools. Although some research exists in this area, there is always a need for clear research on the efficacy of specific treatment approaches (Nicholl & Thompson, 2004).

Any research on this topic should include careful discussion of consent/assent forms and of therapeutic treatment approaches (Ellis et al., 2007). There may be a fear from refugee research participants that their responses will influence their process of obtaining legal immigration documentation, so researchers should clearly delineate the bounds of confidentiality and the specific uses for any data from a research study with this population. One way to highlight this process and to gain participation from the refugee community is to work collaboratively with a leader within this community to share information regarding a research study and to build trust with community members. Building trust may also entail developing an understanding of any historical context, responsiveness to feedback shared by the community, and clear discussion about any research intentions (Christopher et al., 2008).

Beyond assessing existing measures, Ellis et al. (2007) also highlighted the need to disseminate this information within the refugee community as well.

Eliciting feedback from the individuals an intervention is intended to serve allows them to make informed decisions about their preferred treatment modalities and to further weigh in on potential benefits or drawbacks to particular approaches.

## Practice

Therapists observe the effects of the often traumatic journeys on their clients who are refugees. In their clinical work together, therapists have the opportunity to apply the ethical principles and standards discussed here (Singer & Fuentes, 2018). There are often aspects of a refugee client's experience that must be considered in the context of these ethical guidelines to avoid harm to the client and to maximize the intended benefit. Björn and Björn (2004) delineated four aspects that are important to consider in a refugee's experience to provide the most ethically sound care: (a) traumatic life events that the person has experienced, (b) the client's preferences for and access to coping strategies, (c) placement in a hierarchy within their family and between the client and the therapist, and (d) the client's feelings about repatriation.

The traumatic life events that sadly are commonplace for many refugee clients are often outside the scope of what most people can imagine or that therapists typically encounter in their everyday work (APA, 2012). Events such as war, sexual violence, and torture are extremely emotionally charged events and involve details that are likely difficult for providers to hear about (McDonnell et al., 2013). In considering their own self-care, providers may feel the urge to create distance from the situations their client has experienced. However, to provide the best and most ethical care, therapists must be willing to listen fully to their clients' stories and learn about the experiences and contexts in which they occurred. It is critically important for therapists to consider empathically that their clients may have been both a victim and a perpetrator of violence or other acts (Björn & Björn, 2004; Stenmark et al., 2014). In these situations, the authors recommend that the therapist view the client as a victim of a nonfunctioning, brutally damaging society who is currently in need of the therapist's professional care.

A therapist who is mindful of ethical dilemmas pertinent to their refugee clients will also consider the individual's preference for, or reliance with, coping strategies that may differ from the host society (APA, 2012). For example, people originating from a collectivist society may place a higher value on coping within the context of a group rather than individually (Björn & Björn, 2004; Engelbrecht & Jobson, 2016). This individual may make decisions that to an individualistic therapist may seem to benefit the client's family or social group more than the client and may be perceived as undervaluing the client's well-being. However, this interpretation would stem from a cultural bias toward coping as an individual and valuing the individual's needs above the group. Therapists can provide the most effective and ethical care when they become familiar with their client's culture and values, fully appreciate the worth these practices have for the client, and refrain from viewing differences in coping as abnormal (Bemak & Chung, 2017; Björn & Björn, 2004).

In providing the most effective and ethical care, it is imperative for therapists to consider their own placement in a hierarchy between themselves and the refugee patient, as well as the patient's position within their own family hierarchy (Björn & Björn, 2004; Singer & Tummala-Narra, 2013). The therapist is already viewed as being in a position of power for a person or family who may not understand or feel comfortable with the values and customs in their new residence. For example, it could be offensive for a therapist to recommend that a child receive treatment if the parents have not expressed concern about this issue. The therapist must consider the benefit of the child accessing early treatment against the risk of alienating the parents and minimizing their expertise in raising their child.

Therapists must also consider that family hierarchies are often at risk of changing as a result of the various stressors and changes associated with relocating to a new country with potentially different values and practices (APA, 2012; Björn & Björn, 2004; Singer & Tummala-Narra, 2013). Parents are considered the heads of the family. However, when they are refugees in a new society, their position often changes due to the absence of key people in their family and community who typically provide support. Furthermore, parents have to address logistical issues such as learning new skills, jobs, and languages. Children often learn new customs and languages at a faster pace, which can advance their position above the parents. Providing therapeutic support to the child without also serving the family or without considering the impact on the family's sense of balance could be disruptive and damaging.

Using children as interpreters is complicated and often problematic (Hsieh, 2016). To further maintain the family hierarchy, therapists should never ask children to serve as interpreters because it is harmful to the child and puts them in a position of power over their parents (Björn & Björn, 2004). Therapists should also consider differences in parenting practices between the host country and the country of origin. Culture influences societal expectations for appropriate behavior. Indeed, what is considered abuse in one country may not be in another and may be viewed as typical practices in the country of origin (Kelly et al., 2019). Therapists should seek consultation as they attempt to strike a balance between protecting the child and following the mandated reporting laws in the host country and avoiding continued disruption to the family hierarchy. Restoring the family hierarchy by keeping a family together has the potential for long-term benefits to the child that may be disrupted by reporting a behavior as abuse that is considered to be typical in the country of origin.

Related to the idea of family hierarchy is the fact that many women are often considered as supports to children or wives accompanying husbands. Therapists should allow women to speak about needs and concerns that are specific to them, not just in their roles as wives and mothers. Many women are not given the opportunity to speak about their separate concerns and traumas that may include abuse, rape, or female genital mutilation (Humphries, 2006). Therapists should allow women the opportunity to disclose these traumatic experiences and the impact they have had on them as individuals, while also understanding that women may be reluctant to focus on their needs as an individual above the needs their family may have.

Björn and Björn (2004) provided specific questions that can help therapists consider four domains and guide them in their efforts to provide the most ethical treatment when working with an individual who is a refugee: (a) What is the right thing to do at this moment from an ethical point of view? (b) Which consequences will the decision have for the person in the future? and (c) Where can we get more information to understand the problem better? In asking these questions, the goal is for therapists to continuously examine their approach and challenge their existing cultural and societal biases that could inadvertently influence treatment.

## SUMMARY

Providing competent care to refugee clients requires a clear grasp of ethical standards and multicultural recommendations for therapists' codes of conduct. The APA provides clear guidelines through the ethical codes (APA, 2017a), Multicultural Guidelines (APA, 2017b), and the Taskforce on Immigration report (APA, 2012). The WHO's (2013) report extends these strategies to a larger macro level. Integrating these tenets into clinical interventions must also include careful reflexivity on behalf of clients themselves (Singer & Tummala-Narra, 2013), as well as thoughtful utilization of supervision, consultation, and training.

## REFERENCES

American Psychological Association. (2017a). *Ethical principles of psychologists and code of conduct* (2002, Amended June 1, 2010, and January 1, 2017). Retrieved from http://www.apa.org/ethics/code/index.aspx

American Psychological Association. (2017b). *Multicultural guidelines: An ecological approach to context, identity, and intersectionality.* http://www.apa.org/about/policy/multicultural-guidelines.pdf

American Psychological Association, Presidential Task Force on Immigration. (2012). *Crossroads: The psychology of immigration in the new century.* http://www.apa.org/topics/immigration/report.aspx

Atkinson, D. R., Thompson, C. E., & Grant, S. K. (1993). A three-dimensional model for counseling racial/ethnic minorities. *The Counseling Psychologist, 21*(2), 257–277. https://doi.org/10.1177/0011000093212010

BBC. (2018, September). *U.S. slashes number of refugees to 30,000.* https://www.bbc.com/news/world-us-canada-45555357

Bemak, F., & Chung, R. C. (2017). Refugee trauma: Culturally responsive counseling interventions. *Journal of Counseling and Development, 95*(3), 299–308. https://doi.org/10.1002/jcad.12144

Berry, J. W. (2005). Acculturation: Living successfully in two cultures. *International Journal of Intercultural Relations, 29*(6), 697–712.

Björn, G. J., & Björn, A. (2004). Ethical aspects when treating traumatized refugee children and their families. *Nordic Journal of Psychiatry, 58*(3), 193–198. https://doi.org/10.1080/08039480410006298

Christopher, S., Watts, V., McCormick, A. K., & Young, S. (2008). Building and maintaining trust in a community-based participatory research partnership. *American Journal of Public Health, 98*(8), 1398–1406. https://doi.org/10.2105/AJPH.2007.125757

Ellis, B. H., Kia-Keating, M., Yusuf, S. A., Lincoln, A., & Nur, A. (2007). Ethical research in refugee communities and the use of community participatory methods. *Transcultural Psychiatry, 44*(3), 459–481. https://doi.org/10.1177/1363461507081642

Engelbrecht, A., & Jobson, L. (2016). Exploring trauma associated appraisals in trauma survivors from collectivistic cultures. *SpringerPlus, 5*(1), 1565. https://doi.org/10.1186/s40064-016-3043-2

Hansler, J. (2018, October). *US admits lowest number of refugees in more than 40 years.* CNN. https://www.cnn.com/2018/10/02/politics/us-refugees-fy18/index.html

Heeren, M., Wittmann, L., Ehlert, U., Schnyder, U., Maier, T., & Müller, J. (2014). Psychopathology and resident status—comparing asylum seekers, refugees, illegal migrants, labor migrants, and residents. *Comprehensive Psychiatry, 55*(4), 818–825. https://doi.org/10.1016/j.comppsych.2014.02.003

Hsieh, E. (2016). *Working with interpreters in cross-cultural care.* Routledge. https://doi.org/10.4324/9781315658308

Humphries, B. (2006). Supporting asylum seekers: Practical and ethical issues for health and welfare professionals. *Irish Journal of Applied Social Studies, 7*(2), 75–86.

Kass, N. E. (2017). Ethics, refugees, and the president's executive order. *The American Journal of Bioethics: Ajob, 17*(5), 4–5. https://doi.org/10.1080/15265161.2017.1301139

Kelly, L., Magalhaes, M. J., Meysen, T., & Garner, M. (2019). The contested concept of culture: Encounters in policy and practice (pp. 121–133). In C. Hagemann-White,

L. Kelly, & T. Meysen (Eds.), *Interventions against child abuse and violence against women: Ethics and culture in practice and policy*. Verlag Barbara Budrich. https://doi.org/10.2307/j.ctvr7fcsw.10

Mahtani, A. (2003). The right of refugee clients to an appropriate and ethical psychological service. *International Journal of Human Rights, 7*(1), 40–57. https://doi.org/10.1080/714003784

McDonnell, M., Robjant, K., & Katona, C. (2013). Complex posttraumatic stress disorder and survivors of human rights violations. *Current Opinion in Psychiatry, 26*(1), 1–6. https://doi.org/10.1097/YCO.0b013e32835aea9d

Meffert, S. M., Musalo, K., McNiel, D. E., & Binder, R. L. (2010). The role of mental health professionals in political asylum processing. *The Journal of the American Academy of Psychiatry and the Law, 38*(4), 479–489.

Nicholl, C., & Thompson, A. (2004). The psychological treatment of post-traumatic stress disorder (PTSD) in adult refugees: A review of the current state of psychological therapies. *Journal of Mental Health, 13*(4), 351–362. https://doi.org/10.1080/09638230410001729807

Robjant, K., Hassan, R., & Katona, C. (2009). Mental health implications of detaining asylum seekers: Systematic review. *The British Journal of Psychiatry, 194*(4), 306–312. https://doi.org/10.1192/bjp.bp.108.053223

Schweitzer, R., Wyk, S., & Murray, K. (2015). Therapeutic practice with refugee clients: A qualitative study of therapist experience. *Counselling & Psychotherapy Research, 15*(2), 109–118. https://doi.org/10.1002/capr.12018

Sidhu, R. (2017). Navigating unfreedoms & re-imagining ethical counter-conducts: Caring about refugees & asylum seekers. *Educational Philosophy and Theory, 49*(3), 294–305. https://doi.org/10.1080/00131857.2016.1225558

Singer, R., & Fuentes, M. (2018). Ethical issues associated with mental health interventions for immigrants and refugees. In M. Leach & L. Welfel (Eds.), *Cambridge handbook of applied psychological ethics* (pp. 384–405). Cambridge University Press.

Singer, R., & Tummala-Narra, P. (2013). White clinicians' perspectives on working with racial minority immigrant clients. *Professional Psychology, Research and Practice, 44*(5), 290–298. https://doi.org/10.1037/a0034299

Singer, R. R., & Ricks, A. (2019, March 8). Ethical interventions with immigrant, refugee, and asylee clients. In R. R. Singer (Chair), Maryland Psychological Association Essential Requirements Conference [Symposium]. Timonium, MD, United States.

Stenmark, H., Guzey, I. C., Elbert, T., & Holen, A. (2014). Gender and offender status predicting treatment success in refugees and asylum seekers with PTSD. *European Journal of Psychotraumatology, 5*(1), 20803. Advance online publication. https://doi.org/10.3402/ejpt.v5.20803

U.S. Department of Homeland Security. (2019). *Homeland Security investigations*. https://www.ice.gov/hsi

Vissandjée, B., Denetto, S., Migliardi, P., & Proctor, J. (2014). Female genital cutting (FGC) and the ethics of care: Community engagement and cultural sensitivity at the interface of migration experiences. *BMC International Health and Human Rights, 14*, 13. https://doi.org/10.1186/1472-698X-14-13

Whaley, A. L. (2001). Cultural mistrust and mental health services for African Americans: A review and meta-analysis. *The Counseling Psychologist, 29*(4), 513–531. https://doi.org/10.1177/0011000001294003

World Health Organization. (2013). *Mental health action plan 2013–2020.* https://apps.who.int/iris/bitstream/handle/10665/89966/9789241506021_eng.pdf;jsessionid=0C4FD50F9A852D7DDB2C965CFB03B4EC?sequence=1

Wright, C. (2014). Ethical issues and potential solutions surrounding the use of spoken language interpreters in psychology. *Ethics & Behavior, 24*(3), 215–228. https://doi.org/10.1080/10508422.2013.845532

# 5

# A CULTURALLY RESPONSIVE INTERVENTION FOR MODERN-DAY REFUGEES

## A Multiphase Model of Psychotherapy, Social Justice, and Human Rights

FRED BEMAK AND RITA CHI-YING CHUNG

In the past several years, refugee migration worldwide has escalated. Although this is reviewed in Chapter 2 of this volume, a brief synopsis to begin the current chapter is important to fully understand the context for presenting a culturally responsive treatment model that takes into account historical, sociopolitical, cultural, and ecological perspectives.

The growing number of refugees is a result of ongoing and recent civil conflicts, violence, terrorism, persecution (related to race, religion, nationality, political opinion, or membership in a particular social group), natural disasters, and global warming. These factors have forced refugees to involuntarily leave their home countries, fleeing to safety. This may involve crossing international borders because returning to one's home country may be unsafe (Bemak & Chung, 2017a, 2017b). There are approximately 70.8 million refugees worldwide, the highest number of refugees since World War II (United Nations High Commissioner for Refugees [UNHCR], 2019). In the United States, more than 3 million refugees have resettled since 1975 (U.S. Department of State, 2018). The ongoing increase in refugee mass migration has become a political quandary for many Western countries, involving heated political debates on how to effectively respond to this catastrophic situation.

https://doi.org/10.1037/0000226-005
*Refugee Mental Health*, J. D. Aten and J. Hwang (Editors)

The volume of refugees fleeing across international borders is overwhelming, causing difficulty in receiving and processing them. This situation has resulted in racial and ethnic tensions and xenophobia with citizens in relocation countries who harbor fear and negativity toward refugees, worried that the refugees will absorb limited resources and opportunities and consequently have a deleterious impact on the economy and safety in their communities (Bemak & Chung, 2017b).

With the increasing and interminable refugee migration to the U.S. and worldwide, this group continues to encounter psychosocial challenges (Bemak & Chung, 2017a, 2017b). Pre- and postmigration experiences impact their psychological well-being and mental health, requiring psychologists to be aware of the distinctive nature of this population. This chapter describes the multiphase model (MPM) of psychotherapy, social justice, and human rights. The MPM is a culturally responsive multifaceted clinical intervention model that addresses the refugee experience from an ecological, holistic, social justice, and human rights perspective.

## OVERVIEW OF MODERN-DAY REFUGEE ISSUES

To fully understand and appreciate the refugee experience, the chapter begins with an overview of modern-day challenges encountered by refugees, a description of factors impacting refugee mental health, followed by a description of the MPM.

### Contemporary Refugees: Changing Faces

Contemporary refugees are living in a complex world fraught with local, regional, national, and global politics that fosters strong disagreement about their circumstances and status. Today's refugees are faced with hostilities, aggression, persecution, and violence that is underscored by massive casualties, losses, and mass migration. Migration is riddled with turmoil and threats that promotes frightening concerns about safety before, during, and after flight from dangerous situations, all of which impacts psychological well-being (Achiume, 2014; Bemak & Chung, 2017a, 2017b; Furtak, 2015). Refugee admittance to the United States, similar to other countries, is related to global conflicts and events (Igielnik & Krogstad, 2017).

#### Environmental, Climate, or Eco-Refugees
Due to global warming, deforestation, and desertification, refugees known as climate, environmental, or eco-refugees are an emergent refugee group

(Taylor, 2017). This population is forced to relocate due to sudden, long-lasting, and marked environmental disruption (natural or people-made) that changes their local and regional environments and threatens their livelihoods, compromising quality of life and physical and psychological well-being (International Organization for Migration [IOM], 2018). Between 2008 and 2015, disasters displaced 203.4 million people (Internal Displacement Monitoring Centre, 2015) leading to a mass migration of climate refugees. According to January 15, 2020 National Oceanic and Atmospheric Administration data 2010 to 2019 is the hottest decade ever recorded. Furthermore, United Kingdom Met Office reported that 2019 was one of the top-three hottest years on record, and the World Meteorological Organization offsite link also ranked 2019 second warmest for the globe. With increasing natural disasters (i.e., hurricanes, tsunamis, and earthquakes), increasing effects of global warming (i.e., rising sea levels, droughts, and disruption of seasonal weather patterns), and people triggering environmental changes (i.e., desertification and deforestation) eco-refugees are the fastest growing refugee group, with speculation that by 2050, they may reach one billion (IOM, 2018). In fact, new language that describes the psychological well-being of eco-refugees underscores mental health risks and implications of escalating climate change. Psychoterratic conditions include "ecoanxiety" (anxiety individuals encounter due to constant threatening situations associated with climate change); "ecoparalysis" (complex feelings of helpless and hopelessness of not being able to effectively act to diminish climate change risks); and "solastalgia," which is anxiety and distress caused by displacement because of a climate change weather occurrence (Albrecht, 2011; Albrecht et al., 2007). Even so, this group does not fall under the 1951 United Nations Refugee Convention definition because environmental refugees, according to the UN, do not necessarily experience the fear of persecution. Despite the UN Convention not recognizing the environment (natural or people-made) as a persecuting agent, we have included climate refugees in this chapter based on the fact that (a) they are the fastest growing refugee group; (b) many of eco-refugees do fit within the UN definition based on other experiences; (c) all refugees, regardless of legal definition, have similar experiences of trauma, loss, displacement, and disruption to their quality of life and physical and psychological well-being and feelings of hopelessness and helplessness; and (d) the MPM has relevance to all refugee populations regardless of the formal definition.

**Techfugees**
Historically, refugees abruptly left their homes with little planning, preparation, or clarity about their destination or dangers they may encounter during migration (Bemak & Chung, 2016, 2017b). Many of today's refugees are

technologically savvy, relying on technology throughout the migration process by using smart phones, social media, and the Internet and are therefore labeled "techfugees" (Bemak & Chung, 2017b; Graham, 2015; Murphy et al., 2016). Illustrating the technological infusion into refugees' lives is the 85% of Syrian youth in refugee camps with smartphones, underscoring the financial means to afford the technology (Ram, 2015). Techfugees have access to updated information about local, regional, national, and global politics, helping them predict and anticipate political turmoil in their home countries and enabling them to be proactive and intentional about fleeing their home countries. Techfugees obtain updated information about which countries are sympathetic, open, and welcome their arrival and later use technology to navigate safe escape routes and access resources upon their arrival (Bemak & Chung). Using technological applications ("apps"), such as Google Maps, GPS, WhatsApp, Skype, Facebook, and Viber, enables greater odds for a safe and successful migration, and, when problems are encountered, authorities can be alerted through these applications (Ram, 2015). An example of this was seen when a refugee's boat sank and the individual used WhatsApp to alert the Greek coastguard, while simultaneously using the phone's GPS to ensure swimming in the right direction (Graham, 2015). Techfugees also share their exact GPS coordinates with others who anticipate making similar journeys, alerting them about potential dangers, such as border guards or human traffickers, making technological devices essential during flight (Bemak & Chung, 2017b; Ram, 2015).

Many techfugees are fully equipped with smartphones, chargers, and extra cell phones. When they arrive at their destination country, unlike past refugees whose first concern is food, shelter, and safety, techfugees' first question is to ask for Wi-Fi services and charging stations (Graham, 2015; Murphy et al., 2016). Through free messaging services, techfugees are able to communicate with friends and family back home, sometimes taking selfies to let their families know they have arrived safely (Graham, 2015). Once in their destination countries, techfugees again rely on technology to access resources using apps that assist them with language translations; finding refugee centers, shelter, and food; managing money; currency exchange; and other social services; they also get updates on political changes in their host and neighboring countries (Ram, 2015). For techfugees, almost all the information they need is accessible on their mobile devices with the touch of a screen (Bemak & Chung, 2017b). In addition, technologically savvy techfugees fully understand the power of social media for humanitarian appeals to both people and governments, thus documenting their grueling journey with selfies, photos, and videos that are uploaded in various mainstream and social media outlets.

This highly effective technological tool gains immediate global attention, outcry, assistance, and support to their plight, as was seen with videos of paltry meals, holding residential pens, drinking water in toilets, and unsanitary refugee camps (Bemak & Chung, 2017b).

Realizing techfugees' heavy reliance on technology, international and humanitarian aid organizations have developed apps, such as, appsforrefugees.com, to assist refugees with migration adaptation and adjustment by providing updated location-specific logistical and registration information about where and how to register with local authorities. Other examples include the UNHCR, which disseminates information via SMS (short message service or text message); the Gherbtna (the Arabic word for "exile" or "loneliness") app, which provides resources about residency and opening a bank account, for example; and a Red Cross site that allows people to upload photos to locate missing family members (Bemak & Chung, 2017b). Thus, technology is playing an integral role in refugee migration and resettlement, making smartphones and technological devices a valued commodity for refugees. However, it should be mentioned that not everyone has mobile devices or technological knowledge, requiring us to remember we must also support non-techfugees who may fall through the cracks and be forgotten, abandoned, and dismissed.

### Political and Media Impact on Refugee Xenophobia and Racism

Although politics plays a major role in refugee resettlement, the widespread use of mainstream and social media adds a new dimension in the political landscape of the refugee experience. To support their political agenda, contemporary politicians rely on media outlets to influence public perception of refugees by correlating refugees with personal safety and job security. For example, recent terrorist attacks in Europe were conducted by terrorists disguised as refugees, resulting in the promotion of widespread fear, racism, and xenophobia toward refugees. This culture of fear (Chung et al., 2008) has been reinforced by some politicians, such as Ben Carson, U.S. Secretary of Housing and Urban Development, who stated: "[terrorists] sneak into the country as refugees" and made reference to the Paris attack, stating, "The Paris terrorist attacks have demonstrated that terrorists will pose as refugees to enter our land. We must do our utmost to thwart the terrorists' ambitions" (Scott, 2015). In addition, framing the issue as "keeping the U.S. safe" on January 27, 2017, U.S. President Donald Trump signed an executive order that suspended all refugee admissions, an indefinite ban of Syrian refugees, and a travel ban, often called the Muslim Ban, of individuals from seven majority Muslim countries (Iran, Iraq, Libya, Somalia, Sudan, Syria, and Yemen). Notably, priority for admissions was given to religious minorities (Christians) in Syria who were facing persecution in their countries (De Luce & Ainsley, 2018). The Muslim Ban further extended to individuals with permanent residence (green-card holders) and those with dual citizenship with the United Kingdom and Canada, creating widespread confusion and disruptions for universities, hospitals, and public and private organizations and companies (De Luce & Ainsley, 2018). In response to the chaos and intensified culture of fear created by the executive order, the president added to the confusion by stating, "To be clear, this is not a Muslim ban, as the media is falsely reporting . . . this is not about religion—this is about terror and keeping our country safe" (BBC, 2017). Justifying his actions and fueling the culture of fear, the president recalled the September 11, 2001, attacks, despite the fact that none of the 19 hijackers on 9/11 came from any of the seven countries named in the Muslim ban but rather were from Saudi Arabia, the United Arab Emirates, Egypt, and Lebanon (De Luce & Ainsley, 2018).

Mainstream and social media outlets are a powerful mechanism for influencing individual opinions about refugees, creating a 24/7 opportunity to view "live" regional, national, and global minute-by-minute coverage of refugee related situations. Simultaneously, provocative media headlines imply that refugees are a security threat, portraying refugees as hostile, suspicious, and dangerous. Through mainstream and social media, the general public has been inundated with xenophobic fear of refugee violence and threats that refugees will take the hard-earned and limited resources, jobs, and opportunities to which some U.S. citizens feel they alone are entitled (Bemak & Chung, 2017a). These negative attitudes and beliefs prompted UN Secretary-General Ban Ki-moon to state, "Xenophobic and racist responses to refugees and migrants seem to be reaching new levels of stridency, frequency, and public acceptance" (Wulfhorst, 2016). The combination of political rhetoric and media is highly effective in influencing public opinion of refugees, with polls revealing that U.S. citizens are opposed to admitting large numbers of refugees who are fleeing war and oppression (Krogstad & Radford, 2017). For example, in 2016, 54% of registered voters stated that it is not the United States' responsibility to accept Syrian refugees (Krogstad & Radford, 2017). The result of promoting antirefugee sentiment is further perpetuation of the culture of xenophobic fear that exacerbates individual's strongly held negative, racist, and intolerant sentiments toward this group (Bemak & Chung, 2017a, 2017b; Chung et al., 2008).

In contrast, the media has also been instrumental in educating the public about human rights and social justice violations encountered by refugees.

For example, the Muslim ban was contested by various states, resulting in dozens of lawsuits as well as nationwide public protests and demonstrations (BBC, 2017). However, what is not reported are refugees' longer term contributions to the economy, which according to the U.S. Department of Health and Human Services (USDHHS) adds $63 billion more in government revenue than it costs to resettle these individuals (Tharoor, 2018). Despite protests and lawsuits filed on behalf of refugees, the combination of politics and media are indeed a powerful influence on individuals' reactions, perceptions, and beliefs about refugees, producing and reinforcing racist and xenophobic fear and negative attitudes and behaviors toward this group (Bemak & Chung, 2017a).

## POSTMIGRATION TRANSITION AND RESETTLEMENT PSYCHOSOCIAL CHALLENGES

The disruptive and frightening experiences of refugees who are forced to flee their homes because of life-threatening circumstances, migration, relocation, and resettlement result in a multitude of psychosocial challenges. This section discusses these adjustment and adaptation challenges.

### Impact of Premigration Trauma on Postmigration Resettlement

Once refugees arrive at their resettlement location, psychological support and interventions often focus on postmigration adjustment without considering premigration experiences. It is essential that psychologists are aware of, recognize, and understand the impact of premigration trauma on postmigration resettlement adaptation and adjustment (Bemak & Chung, 2017b; Chung & Kagawa-Singer, 1993). With sudden flight from their home communities, refugees may face serious, traumatic, life-threatening issues, such as witnessing or being subjected to violence, rape, and killing, that remain psychologically troubling during postmigration (Bemak & Chung, 2017a). These traumatic experiences, which are often unresolved, may manifest once there is stability in resettlement. Research has found that refugees are more at risk than other populations for developing serious mental health problems as a result of their premigration trauma (American Psychological Association [APA], 2010; Bemak & Chung, 2016; Kinzie, 2005). Refugee mental health problems include depression, dissociation, anxiety, posttraumatic stress disorder (PTSD), and psychosis and higher rates of psychopathology compared with the general population (APA, 2010; Hollander et al., 2016; Vickers, 2005).

Furthermore, specific refugee subgroups have been identified as being at greater risk for developing serious mental health disorders. Older refugees experience greater challenges and feelings of helplessness adjusting to a new environment and learning a new language and new routines (Strong et al., 2015), whereas single men younger than 21 who lack familial and social support may experience greater isolation (Bemak & Chung, 2016). Unaccompanied children and adolescents are highly vulnerable to being exploited and victims of human trafficking (Brannan et al., 2016; Unterhitzenberger & Rosner, 2016). In addition, rape, sexual assault, abuse, and violence have become byproducts of war, making women and girls, in particular, susceptible to mental health problems. These violations can occur in their home country, during the escape, in refugee camps or facilities and also during postmigration. Finally, women whose husbands were killed during war are another risk group (Chung & Bemak, 2002b; Morash et al., 2007; Shakil, 2016).

Recently in the Australian detention facility in Nauru, an island near Australia, refugee children as young as 8 to 10 years old have attempted suicide and committed horrific acts of self-harm (Harrison, 2018). They have been diagnosed with traumatic withdrawal syndrome (TWS). TWS or resignation syndrome is a rare mental health condition that can be life-threatening. TWS is a response to severe trauma, feelings of hopelessness and helplessness, living in unsafe conditions without hope for a change, psychological and physical withdrawal from life by disengaging from any activities, inability to eat and drink, and eventually being unresponsive and unable to speak so that their body begins to shut down. Treatment for TWS, which can take months, requires access to pediatric intensive care (Harrison, 2018).

## Acculturation

Various models of acculturation describe the adjustment process and challenges in adapting to a new foreign country (Berry, 2002). For refugees to successfully adjust to a new country, it is important that there is a sense of belonging and security. Berry's model describes the different phases of the acculturation process: assimilation, integration or biculturalism, rejection, and deculturation. Refugees successful acculturation depends on how they accept, integrate, or reject new norms and worldviews of the resettlement country (Berry, 2002). Biculturalism is the most psychologically healthy acculturation phase because the individual is successful at adjusting and adapting in the new country and simultaneously integrating traditional values and beliefs (Berry, 2002). Although biculturalism is ideal, a major challenge for refugees is navigating the differences, and at times conflicts, between their values, beliefs, worldviews, and attitudes and those of the host country. Formal and informal rules of behavior and ways of doing things, such as childrearing and discipline, may differ and require a relearning or unlearning of old habits and behaviors.

Compounding the challenges in acculturation is when refugees move from a collectivistic, group-orientated sociocentric culture to an individualistic egocentric culture. Adding to the change in sociocultural perspectives are refugees' premigration trauma experiences, where healing from these traumas can play a crucial role in acculturation and psychosocial adjustment (Bhugra, 2004). Without extended family and community support to assist with the healing, acculturation may become even more difficult (Bemak & Chung, 2016). Compounding problems in psychological adjustment and acculturation to new resettlement country is the racism and xenophobia that is common in some host countries, triggering ongoing pain, hurt, guilt, and sadness, all of which may inhibit psychological well-being and acculturation. Finally, survivor's guilt may hinder acculturation. Survivor's guilt has taken on new forms due to technology because refugees are now able to ascertain immediate information about their home country and world events and maintain constant contact with family and friends through Skype, Whatsapp, Facebook, or Viber. Access to technology may create intense stress and survivor's guilt, impacting successful acculturation (Bemak & Chung, 2017a).

**Language, Education, and Employment**

A primary aim of host countries and the UNHCR is for refugees to secure employment and become economically self-sufficient. Language proficiency in the host country is crucial for successful adjustment, economic independence, and educational training. Lack of language proficiency significantly reduces refugees' navigational and social capital and creates major challenges to finding gainful employment and housing, accessing resources and educational training, and attending to general everyday activities, such as shopping, transportation, and doctor's appointments (Bemak & Chung, 2013, 2016, 2017a, 2017b; Bemak et al., 2003; Goldenberg, 2008). Compounding this is the criticism of U.S. English as a second language programs for not attending to psychological issues related to both learning and to not knowing a new language (Bemak & Chung, 2016; Bemak et al., 2003).

In addition, refugee resettlement policies can be a barrier to attaining economic self-sufficiency. For example, the U.S. policy, unlike other resettlement countries, requires refugees to pay back airfare costs (Bemak & Chung, 2017a). Thus, refugees fleeing from their home countries, many of whom were traumatized during premigration, arrive in the U.S. struggling with language and finding employment, while at the same time having to repay transportation costs. This intensifies existing stress, culture shock, adjustment, acculturation, and mental health issues. Furthermore, refugees' educational qualifications may not be equivalent, transferable, or recognized or may not meet employment requirements in the host country; other refugees may lack skills necessary to join the workforce. All of this may lead to downward socioeconomic mobility, added stress, and heightened anxiety as refugees are forced to "start from scratch" or "begin again," resulting in under- or unemployment. A consequence of the underemployment or unemployment of refugee men may force women to find work, contributing to the upward social mobility of women and impacting traditional gender roles and family dynamics (Bemak et al., 2003; Chung & Bemak, 2002b; Delara, 2016; Yakushko et al., 2008).

The educational systems in the host country may differ significantly from educational system in the refugees' home country. School policies, expectations, behaviors, extracurricular activities, mixed gender classes, and the American emphasis on test scores and advanced career preparation may be dramatically different (Bemak & Chung, 2016; Bemak et al., 2003). Refugee students may encounter discrimination from peers and school staff due to lack of language proficiency, dress, habits, and food, which may be viewed as strange and foreign. Without knowledge about school culture and without peer support, refugee students may also be targets of physical and emotional abuse, verbal harassment, assault, or robbery, which may contribute to alienation and isolation (Bemak & Chung, 2017b).

## Changes in Family Dynamics

A challenge in psychosocial adjustment for refugees is the dramatic change in family structure and dynamics (Bemak & Chung, 2016; Bemak et al., 2003). Refugee parents and caretakers may be confronted and confused by host countries' rules and behaviors that may be different from their traditional childrearing and discipline practices, some of which may even be illegal in the host countries. Caretakers may feel powerless, undermined, and unsupported trying to employ traditional methods of childrearing. At the same time, children typically adjust and adapt to the new culture and learn the language faster than adults, creating a major shift in family dynamics (Bemak & Chung, 2017a). Thus, parents and caretakers often rely and become dependent on their children to be cultural and language interpreters (Bemak & Chung, 2016; Bemak et al., 2003). Concurrently, children may question their parents'/ caretakers' well-established traditional cultural norms, wanting to adapt and "fit in" to the new culture by participating in school and social activities, sleepovers, and sports activities and challenging views on marriage, dating, and curfews, for example. This creates intergenerational conflict within the family structure and may result in a loss of adult authority, power, and control over their children (Bemak et al., 2003). These conflicts and role changes redefine family relationships and may cause family dysfunction, conflict, role confusion, and painful social restructuring (Bemak & Chung, 2017b). Refugee youth may witness the transformation of their parents/caretakers from autonomous and culturally competent providers to depressed, overwhelmed, and dependent individuals who lack confidence as they grapple with language and customs, lacking navigation skills to access cultural and social capital that results in anxiety, depression, anger, frustration, and confusion over the loss of authority in and control of their lives (Bemak & Chung, 2017b; Chung & Bemak, 2002b).

Given refugees' premigration and postmigration trauma experiences and the psychosocial challenges in adjusting to resettlement countries, this population has a great need for mental health services. Psychologists need to be aware of multiple variables that influence effective, culturally responsive mental health services for refugees. The next section discusses these factors, followed by a discussion of a culturally responsive mental health intervention, the MPM of psychotherapy, social justice, and human rights.

## FACTORS INFLUENCING REFUGEE MENTAL HEALTH INTERVENTIONS

Many variables influence effective culturally responsive therapeutic interventions for refugees. This section first discusses cultural belief systems and its impact on refugee mental health and psychological well-being, followed by a discussion on political countertransference and the culture of fear that may influence psychotherapists' ability to provide culturally responsive services. The section concludes by presenting the MPM model as a culturally responsive intervention that incorporates human rights and social justice.

### Cultural Belief Systems and Mental Health

To provide effective services, it is critical for psychologists to understand how the refugees' culture influences the conceptualization of health and mental health, symptomatology, help-seeking behaviors, and treatment expectations and outcomes (Chung & Lin, 1994; Chung & Singer, 1995; Gielen et al., 2004; Kirmayer, 1989; Kleinman, Eisenberg, & Good, 1978;

USDHHS, 2001). Individualistic Western paradigms of psychotherapy focusing on independent functioning and coping is in direct contrast to refugees from collectivistic cultural healing perspectives that emphasize relationships, social networks, and a holistic approach to therapy (Kirmayer, 1989; Kleinman et al., 1978). Providing culturally responsive psychological services for refugees requires assessment and treatment methodologies consistent with refugees' cultural values and beliefs, while understanding and accepting the impact of culture on the various aspects of mental health problems. Lack of awareness or ignoring the influence of culture on mental health may result in misdiagnosis or overdiagnosis and subsequently cause psychological harm to refugee clients (Chung & Lin, 1994; Chung & Singer, 1995; Kirmayer, 1989; Kleinman et al., 1978). For example, in Syria many people believe in *jinn*—evil spirits—as the cause of their problems. Syrian refugees may describe being attacked, taken over, or even hit by jinn. Western psychologists might view someone with these symptoms as psychotic, prescribing medication and therapeutic interventions to treat the "delusion." In contrast, culturally responsive interventions might consider jinn as an expression of faith and combine treatment interventions with spiritually oriented practices to eliminate the presence of evil spirits. This example illustrates how to reconceptualize the presenting problem, treat the symptomology in a culturally responsive manner, use culturally responsive help-seeking behaviors, and redefine treatment and outcome expectations.

## Cultural Influence on the Utilization of Mainstream Mental Health Services

Although refugee trauma results in a high need for mental health services in resettlement countries, there is often an underutilization and reluctance to seek help from mainstream mental health services (Chung & Lin, 1994; de Anstiss et al., 2009). Research has found that refugees, consistent with their cultural practices, will often initially explore traditional healing methods with elders, families, friends, herbal medicines, and religious and spiritual leaders (Chung & Lin, 1994). Only after failing to receive help from these traditional healing practices, as a default, some refugees seek out mainstream professional mental health treatment as their last option. Even so, some refugees may concurrently use traditional methods and mainstream treatment (Bemak et al., 2003; Chung & Lin, 1994). As a result of delaying seeing mainstream mental health providers refugees may present with intensified problems. Contributing to postponement of accessing mainstream services is the cultural stigma of mental illness on the entire family, the lack of cultural responsiveness by mainstream service providers, accessibility and transportation to services, and language barriers (Chung & Lin, 1994; de Anstiss et al.,

2009; Fung & Wong, 2007; Kim et al., 2011). Research has found that lack of cultural sensitivity may result in low utilization, high dropout rates, and premature termination from mainstream services (Bemak & Chung, 2017b; Sue et al., 1991).

## Political Countertransference and the Culture of Fear

The deep-seated political view that refugees are synonymous with terrorists has created significant concerns about how many and which refugee groups will be admitted in resettlement countries (Bemak & Chung, 2017a). Under the pretext of keeping resettlement countries safe from terrorism, politics shapes how we view refugee resettlement. The inability to separate refugees from those who participate in terrorist acts has created a culture of fear that has had significant negative influence on the public's perceptions of refugees (Chung et al., 2008). The mainstream and social media help propagate a culture of fear of refugees and reinforce myths that large numbers of refugees are potential terrorists. As psychologists, we are exposed to these messages, making it essential that we are not only aware of our countertransference but also understand what we have termed *political countertransference* (Chung et al., 2008). Self-awareness of one's countertransference and its effect on the therapeutic process is well established in mental health. We have extended this to include political countertransference, referring to psychologists' exposure to political messages via media outlets (e.g., television, newspapers, social media, websites), which can be internalized overtly, covertly, and subliminally into our viewpoints regarding our clients and our safety. This heightened message of fear and safety related to refugees may be transferred to our clients (Chung et al., 2008) and influence our clinical work. Thus, with continuing terrorist attacks and threats throughout the world and in the United States and the ongoing political rhetoric about keeping "America safe" from terrorism, psychologists must be aware of their reactions to politically charged issues, especially as they relate to refugees and political countertransference (Bemak & Chung, 2017a).

## Language Translators and Cultural Interpreters

Language barriers have been identified as obstacles to seeking help from mainstream mental health services (Chung & Lin, 1994; Bemak et al., 2003; Resera et al., 2015). In contrast to a majority of U.S. psychologists (83.6%) who identify as White and monolingual English speakers (Lin et al., 2015), there is significant cultural and language diversity within the refugee population. The wide range of refugees' language and culture makes it is essential

116 • Bemak and Chung

for psychologists to work in partnership with individuals who can provide not only language translation but also cultural interpretation (Bemak et al., 2003; Tribe & Lane, 2009). It has been our experience that literal language translation by itself is inadequate to understand the cultural context of psychological problems. Without understanding the cultural intricacies and nuances that go with the verbal language, such as tone, speech cadence and pitch, and changes in posture, psychologists may miss deeper meanings derived from cultural perspectives. In addition, some words may not be translatable and if literally translated make no sense (Bemak et al., 2003; Chung et al., 1997; Resera et al., 2015), making it important for translators to also interpret the cultural context.

It is important that psychologists establish partnerships with the interpreters that define clear boundaries, roles, expectations, and relationships (Resera et al., 2015). Without this clarification, interpreters may answer for the client because they feel they know the answer; modify, edit, or censor the translation because of embarrassment about what is being said by the client; change the client's response because they think it is an incorrect answer; be overly helpful by providing the client with additional information or clarity on what the psychologist stated (Bemak et al., 2003; Chung et al., 1997); or view the client as an ally (Resera et al., 2015). The following are other important considerations we recommend that clinicians keep in mind: (a) not using children and other family members as interpreters because it disrupts traditional roles, relationships, and dynamics in the family (Bemak et al., 2003); (b) using interpreters who may result in sessions running longer than usual; (c) attempting to ensure long-term consistency with interpreters (Resera et al., 2015); (d) checking in regularly with interpreters because they may experience secondary trauma, transference, and countertransference (Tribe & Keefe, 2009; Tribe & Lane, 2009); and (e) acknowledging the presence of a third person in the room and its effects on the therapeutic dynamic. The triad relationship should be discussed with clients so that they clearly understand the role of the interpreter and do not feel reliant on the interpreter to speak for them (Tribe & Keefe, 2009).

## MULTIPHASE MODEL OF PSYCHOTHERAPY, SOCIAL JUSTICE, AND HUMAN RIGHTS

Given the growing number of global refugees, it is vital that psychologists adapt clinical intervention strategies to be culturally responsive while specifically addressing the distinctive and unique refugee experience. To provide effective refugee mental health services, it is important to understand the historical, cultural, and sociopolitical context of the refugee experience that includes profound issues of transition, loss, change, trauma, and displacement (Bemak & Chung, 2017a, 2017b). Furthermore, we would suggest that it is essential to incorporate human rights and social justice as an embedded aspect of clinical interventions given the human rights violations encountered by refugees. Considering these factors, we developed the MPM of psychotherapy, social justice, and human rights as a culturally responsive intervention for refugees that responds specifically to the complexity of the refugee experience from displacement to postmigration psychosocial adjustment and challenges. The MPM was constructed using constructs from various models and guidelines, including the APA's (2017) *Multicultural Guidelines: An Ecological Approach to Context, Identity, and Intersectionality*; cross-cultural empathy (Chung & Bemak, 2002a; Draguns, 2007); humanistic trauma interventions (Briere & Scott, 2015); exposure therapy (McLean & Foa, 2013); clinical practice guidelines developed by the U.S. Department of Veteran Affairs & Department of Defense (2010); the three-phase trauma therapy (triphasic) model (Herman, 1997); and group cognitive behavior therapy (Beck et al., 2009). Essential in using the MPM is understanding the interaction between pre- and postmigration, refugee cultural identity and acculturation, cross-cultural empathy (Chung & Bemak, 2002a; Draguns, 2007), and political countertransference (Bemak & Chung, 2016; Chung et al., 2008). Lack of awareness and understanding of these issues may lead to damaging treatment, premature client termination, and promote *psychological colonialism* (Bemak & Chung, 2011), imposing mainstream or Western beliefs and values on refugees without considering cultural, psychosocial, psychopolitical, and history experiences and perspectives.

The MPM psychosocial therapeutic model incorporates individual, group, and family interventions through the integration of cultural responsiveness, social and community processes, and personal and social empowerment. The incorporation of these issues promotes greater responsiveness to psychotherapy, improved accuracy in diagnosis, and more responsive and effective treatment. Employing the MPM requires a reconceptualization of the therapist's role and does not require additional time, funding, or resources. The MPM has five phases that can be used in any sequence as determined by the psychologist: Phase I: Mental Health Education; Phase II: Individual, Group and Family Psychotherapy; Phase III: Cultural Empowerment via Social and Navigational Capital; Phase IV: Indigenous Healing; and Phase V: Social Justice and Human Rights (see Figure 5.1). A brief summary of the five phases follows.

**FIGURE 5.1. Multiphase Model of Psychotherapy, Social Justice, and Human Rights**

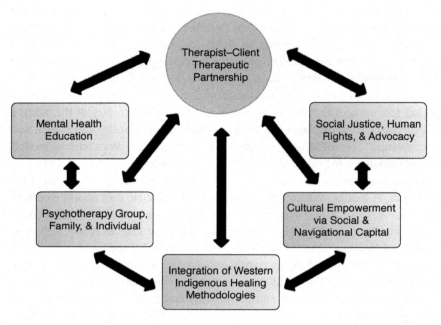

## Phase I: Mental Health Education

Often refugees are unfamiliar with mainstream mental health interventions. Phase I, Mental Health Education, introduces refugee clients to the therapeutic relationship, educating the client about what happens, what to expect, and respective roles of the client and psychologist during the therapeutic process. During this orientation to relationships in therapy, constructs (which may be new for refugees) such as the following are presented: confidentiality, time boundaries, self-disclosure, expectations for interpersonal dynamics and therapeutic interactions, and the role of the interpreter. This is particularly important because the history of displacement and trauma may cultivate mistrust and uncertainty (Majumder et al., 2015; Ní Raghallaigh, 2014), making it important to promote both a safe and trusting therapeutic alliance and empathy (Bemak & Chung, 2016; Chung & Bemak, 2002a; Kruse et al., 2009). Although this is explained when therapy commences, the roles and expectations may be revisited in future sessions as needed. This phase can also educate psychologists about the cultural influence on refugees' conceptualization of the problem, manifestation and symptom expression, mental health help-seeking behavior, and treatment expectations (Chung & Lin, 1994; Chung & Singer, 1995).

## Phase II: Individual, Group, or Family Psychotherapy

Phase II incorporates individual, group, and family therapy interventions that use healing processes based on cultural norms and beliefs. Similar to Phase I in which refugees are unacquainted with Western psychotherapeutic practices, they are also unfamiliar with Western therapeutic techniques and intervention methodologies. An example was when a family from the Democratic Republic of Congo came for counseling. Critical was the psychologist's knowledge about family structure and dynamics and absence of the extended family system. Traditional customs dictate that the father's role is that of provider and protector, and mother's role is that of caring for the children and home. When implementing the MPM, it is important to acknowledge these roles, responding first to the father, then mother, as the family sorts out role conflicts in the new culture. Western psychotherapy emphasizes self-sufficiency, individuation, and independence, which contradicts the reliance, support, and strength many refugees rely on from their families and communities (Bemak & Chung, 2016; Hong & Domokos-Cheng Ham, 2001).

During Phase II, it is important to remember that clients may be reluctant to share personal and private feelings and thoughts given premigration traumatic experiences and social stigma. An example of this can be seen with a Sudanese refugee who very reluctantly described being raped in Sudan to a psychologist. She shared how fearful she was to share, believing it may bring back the bad feelings, as well as concern that others would see them speaking together and call her *majnoon* (crazy), which would stigmatize her in the Sudanese community. Similarly, it is important to remember that refugee lives are rooted in cultural interdependence and in expectations for directedness and solutions from both clinicians and indigenous healers (Bemak & Chung, 2016, 2017a; Kinzie et al., 1988). Interventions that have been found to be useful include psychological first aid, cognitive restructuring therapy, existential counseling, storytelling, role-playing, trauma-focused cognitive-behavioral therapy, imagery, dream work, projective drawing, narrative therapy, gestalt therapy, relaxation, using metaphor, play therapy, critical incident stress debriefing, critical incident stress management, and interpersonal group therapy.

Three key factors are important to keep in mind when implementing MPM Phase II. First, a large majority of refugees come from collectivistic cultures (see UNHCR, 2014, which identifies the top 10 countries of origin for refugees, who all come from collectivistic cultures), where cooperation, group identity, and social connectivity within the framework of the family, group, and community are more valued than individual well-being (Hofstede, 2001; Triandis, 2001). Consequently, the MPM emphasizes healing within the context of collectivistic cultures, stressing the value of interdependence and adjustment within one's social context as a foundation for healing. Hence group and family therapy, social support, and sharing experiences have been recognized as efficacious psychological interventions with refugees (e.g., Akinsulure-Smith, 2009; Bemak & Chung, 2013; Ehntholt et al., 2005; Goodkind et al., 2011; Lacroix & Sabbah, 2011).

An example of deep family connections was evident when a 15-year-old Syrian refugee described to the psychologist how, when escaping to Turkey, his family was attacked. He and his two younger sisters became separated from their parents and were terrified. It was essential that the psychologist fully understood the depth of this boy's Syrian family context and relationships and subsequent meaning of the young man's terror.

Second, clinicians must understand refugees' sociopolitical background in relationship to their current life circumstances and psychological functioning. Many refugees were subjected to physical and psychological infringements by authority figures that resulted in hypersensitivity about sharing personal information and trusting others (Bemak & Chung, 2016). Understanding the reasons for hesitation to engage intimately in the therapeutic relationship is important for psychologists.

Third, psychologists should maintain a keen awareness of the need to ensure that interventions are culturally responsive. Essential cross-cultural therapeutic skills to work with refugees would include the following:

- Understand the correlation between psychological distress and somatization for refugees. An example of this can be seen with a Bhutanese 56-year-old male refugee who had been tortured. He described significant stomach pain that caused difficulty sleeping and eating despite numerous tests that found no evidence of a medical problem. The psychologist believed it was a somatoform pain disorder, similar to a number of other Bhutanese refugees.

- Consider the verbal and nonverbal context of cross-cultural communication.

- Be aware and appreciate the quality and nature of cross-cultural verbal interactions between client and psychologist.

- Interpret refugees' behavior, feelings, thoughts, and experiences from a cultural perspective.

- Integrate culturally responsive healing methodologies, such as dream-work, storytelling, metaphor, cognitive behavior therapy, narrative therapy, imagery, ritual, myth, role-playing, psychodrama, gestalt, existential counseling, and psychodrama (Bemak & Chung, 2016; 2017a; Duarté-Vélez et al., 2010; Parthasarthi et al., 2004; Schottelkorb et al., 2012).

## Phase III: Cultural Empowerment via Social and Navigational Capital

The term *cultural empowerment* is more than 40 years old, first used by Solomon (1976) to describe African American clients connecting with their own power to self-advocate across cultural barriers. Cultural empowerment can be linked to obtaining social and navigational capital and is closely associated with the refugee experience of gaining environmental mastery that contributes to psychological healing and psychosocial adjustment and adaptation (Bemak, 1989). Many refugee clients face daunting circumstances during postmigration that require mastering skills to exist and adapt to their new communities as a first step in psychological well-being. It is important, as an element of psychotherapy, to first resolve practical problems that negate the frustration of language barriers, social services, education, medical care, employment, housing, and transportation (Bemak & Chung, 2013). Implementing Phase III requires psychologists' familiarity with acculturation challenges and combining case-management type assistance in accessing social and navigational capital and subsequently cultural empowerment.

It is important to make the distinction that helping refugee clients locate relevant information and supporting their adjustment is not being a case manager but rather a *cultural systems information guide* (Bemak & Chung, 2017a, 2017b). Obtaining social and navigational capital is a critical element in moving forward to become culturally empowered, acculturated, and successfully adjusted. Phase III may be revisited as needed during psychological interventions and may be particularly relevant as refugee clients become better acclimated to new communities and face barriers that require novel environmental mastery skills while gaining social and navigational capital. For example, refugees from homogeneous societies may experience racism and discrimination and have little or no experience with handling these issues in their home countries (Dietz, 2010). Thus, psychologists should stay up-to-date on changing political and economic policies related to refugees to gauge and help them prepare for public responses that may promote increasing hostility and discrimination toward them. Phase III might also include preparing for job interviews; becoming familiar with public transportation costs, schedules, and routes; accessing social services; reviewing policies on holidays and vacations; and connecting with support groups. An example of using MPM Phase III as an aspect of the counseling can be seen with a Burmese refugee community leader who experienced helplessness stopping repression when he lived in Burma. He came for counseling eager to help other Burmese refugees. Phase III may consist of helping him develop strategies to use his leadership skills and assume a more prominent helping role in the Burmese community.

## Phase IV: Indigenous Healing

Integrating Western and indigenous healing practices has been identified by the World Health Organization (WHO; 2008) as conducive to better mental health outcomes. Phase IV, consistent with the WHO's findings, combines Western psychotherapy with indigenous healing practices that originate in refugees' homelands. The integration of traditional healing requires that psychologists are receptive to alternative forms of treatment, many of which are beyond the scope of Western psychological training and practice. Thus, Phase IV underscores the importance of integrating racial, ethnic, and cultural healing practices with Western-based psychotherapy. Note, however, that not all indigenous healing practices are effective, nor are all indigenous healers authentic, so psychologists must assess traditional healers' legitimacy and credibility before forging "treatment partnerships." An example was when we were working with refugees who were rape victims from Myanmar. We approached a Buddhist monk and asked him if he could develop a healing ritual for rape victims. He did so, which was a tremendous boost and addition to the psychological work we were doing with the women.

## Phase V: Social Justice and Human Rights

Historically, refugees, who involuntarily flee their homes, encounter human rights violations. Phase V, Social Justice and Human Rights, addresses how psychologists can infuse social justice and human rights into psychological treatment. Similar to the other MPM phases, Phase V can be used during any of the other MPM phases. Attending to social injustice and human rights violations as part of the psychological interventions that assist in healing and changing life conditions is an important contribution to refugees' psychological well-being and mental health (Chung & Bemak, 2012). Incorporating social justice and human rights may involve advocacy while addressing issues such as health care, employment discrimination, unfair access of services, housing access, or discriminatory treatment in the legal and educational systems (Chung & Bemak). For example, a Somalian refugee was being treated unfairly at work. Using the MPM, the psychologist discussed coping strategies not only to respond more effectively to the situation and fear but to also understand the legality and the client's rights. Psychologists may use Phase V to (a) ensure that refugee clients are aware of and knowledgeable about their rights; (b) provide information to colleagues and professionals about the historical, sociopolitical, and cultural influences on refugees' lives during pre- and postmigration; (c) become active in changing public policy by researching, speaking at public hearings, and writing to legislators (APA, 2017); (d) provide assistance to refugee clients and their families as well as refugee communities to encourage public advocacy for equal treatment and access to opportunities and resources; and (e) ensure that social justice and human rights work is an integral part of mental health treatment and a core component in the psychological healing of refugees.

The next sections provide two case studies illustrating the use of the MPM. Please note that the two case studies have been developed from a compilation of numerous refugees' lives. At the time of writing this chapter, Afghanistan and Syria have the highest number of fleeing refugees in the world and so were chosen as the countries of origin for the case studies. The case studies presented here are composites, so names and identities have been disguised and confidentiality maintained for all client composites described in the case studies.

## CASE STUDY OF MATEEN

Mateen is a 23-year-old Afghan refugee who arrived in the United States 2 years ago from a refugee village in Pakistan. In Afghanistan, Mateen had been studying business, hoping to be the first in his family to create a local farming business in his hometown. When he was 18, his house was bombed, killing his parents and two younger siblings.

Immediately after the bombing, he fled to Pakistan and settled in a refugee village, where he struggled to establish social connections given the chaotic atmosphere in the village and his deep feelings of hurt and sadness of losing his family. After a few weeks, Mateen met an imam living in the refugee village who began to offer him religious teachings. The imam was able to help Mateen start to feel better and gain a sense of belonging in the camp, connecting with others who were also studying Islamic teachings. Mateen spoke with the imam about his strong family values and his grief losing his family. Three years later, sponsored by a nonprofit agency, Mateen migrated to the United States and settled in at a boarding house. The sponsoring agency helped him continue his business education and find a job as custodial staff at the local community college where he would be studying. Despite having housing, a job, and studying, Mateen felt lonely without family and friends.

## Critical Incident

Mateen's loneliness grew over the next 6 months. He wanted to reconnect with the imam in Pakistan for religious guidance but could not find a way to contact him. Being on his own again, he thought about his family "all the time," experiencing "overwhelming sadness." Mateen began missing some of his classes and even missing an occasional shift at work. Adding to his difficulties were antiimmigration policies and growing bigotry related to foreigners in the United States. A few times Mateen was harassed and even called a terrorist when he went shopping, making him hesitant to venture out of his boarding house.

## Sequence of Events

One of Mateen's college peers, whom he occasionally spoke with, noticed his increasing absence from class. He asked him if there was anything wrong. For the first time, Mateen shared how lonely and sad he was, missing his family, the imam, and his home. His friend recommended he see someone at the college counseling center to speak about his difficulties. Mateen rejected this suggestion, but after a few more weeks of difficulty and a failed exam, he decided to talk with someone at the center. Speaking with the therapist, Mateen shared feelings of loneliness, having no one to care for him, and desperately missing his family. He also talked about his fear of deportation and "starting over" again. He even cried one day, talking about how he missed friends, family, and home, where he never experienced discrimination.

Even so, Mateen remained hesitant to talk much about his life in Afghanistan, increasingly speaking more about his time in the refugee camp. When asked by the therapist about why he left Afghanistan, Mateen casually mentioned that his family died and that he was not there with them when the bombing happened, then quickly started talking about the differences in climate between Afghanistan and the United States. The therapist suggested that Mateen join a therapy group with other refugees with similar losses of loved ones.

## Key Clinical Questions

1. Who constitutes Mateen's support system at the moment? Can he identify people that he considers trustworthy or potentially trustworthy in the United States?

2. What is behind Mateen's avoidance to talk about his life in Afghanistan? What would be helpful in supporting him to become more open about his pain and the loss of his family and community?

3. How important is the Muslim faith for Mateen?

4. What link might the Muslim faith have with healing for Mateen?

5. How have past experiences influenced his feelings about starting over again in his new life?

6. What was Mateen's relationship with his parents and siblings like in Afghanistan?

7. How does he feel about being the sole surviving member of his family?

8. What is the effect of discrimination and racism on Mateen?

### Applying the MPM of Psychotherapy, Social Justice, and Human Rights

### Phase I: Mental Health Education
Only recently did Mateen begin speaking to the therapist at the college while becoming familiar with how therapy works. It would be helpful for the therapist to clearly explain the purpose and process of how group therapy works so that Mateen has a clear understanding of expectations and norms for participation and involvement in group therapy.

### Phase II: Individual, Group, and Family Therapy
The individual therapeutic process has created beginning levels of trust, openness, and healing. Joining a group of refugees where others share the experience of loss and trauma will be a critical next step for Mateen, particularly given his coming from a collectivistic culture. In a group, he could meet others with similar experiences and receive and provide support for other group members. A group has the potential to be empowering for Mateen, helping him find his own voice and ways to become more open with his pain by sharing about the profound loss of his family and difficulties transitioning to a new and very different country.

### Phase III: Cultural Empowerment via Social and Navigational Capital
Given the short amount of time Mateen has been in the United States, there may be confusion about available services and resources. The therapist could help locate culturally responsive resources within the Islamic community, such as finding an imam who could continue to provide religious guidance and a mosque where he could go for prayer and teachings, as he had done

in Pakistan. It may also be helpful to ascertain what college and community resources are available that might be of interest to Mateen. For example, a Business Majors Club or College Diversity Office racial/ethnic/cultural/ religious support group could help him expand his social network and activities. There may also be a number of community activities supportive of the refugee community, such as speakers and dance performances that the therapist could help identify. Once located, the therapist could help Mateen with bus timetables to access those events. Finally, it would be helpful to explain migration and deportation policies and laws that apply to Mateen's situation, thus alleviating some of his concerns.

### Phase IV: Indigenous Healing

It will be important to explore Mateen's spirituality. Moreover, it will be crucial to explore his relationship with the imam in the Pakistan refugee camp. With Mateen's permission, it may be helpful for the therapist to attempt to contact the imam in Pakistan to better understand Mateen's time in the camp, how the imam was helpful in Mateen's healing, and what recommendations the imam might have for Mateen's continued healing. In conjunction, as mentioned previously, it may be helpful to locate a mosque and religious teacher nearby so that Mateen could continue his spiritual healing in conjunction with psychological counseling, allowing the therapist and imam to become partners in the healing.

### Phase V: Social Justice and Human Rights

The contemporary political atmosphere has an impact on Mateen. Helping him clearly understand the issues and his legal rights is important. Alleviating his anxiety about deportation and discrimination may reduce stress and help Mateen feel more secure about his rights and what he could do if faced with discrimination related to employment, housing, or education. Understanding his rights and the law could be discussed in therapy and play an essential role in reducing stress and anxiety.

## CASE STUDY OF FARIDA

Farida is a 42-year-old refugee from Syria who has been in the United States for 4 years. She came to the United States with her husband and three children (two sons, ages 8 and 10, and one daughter, age 15). Her left arm was severely injured in her hometown during the infighting in Syria. In their escape from their home country Farida recalls struggling to feed her entire family and remembers being afraid that her children would die. She also remembers trying to shield her children from the violence she witnessed while leaving Syria.

Farida and her husband are very religious and live by the precepts of Islam as practicing Muslims. They have been raising their children to be faithful and practicing Muslims. As the years have gone by in the United States, their daughter has been questioning their Muslim faith, recently stating that she thinks she is no longer a believer. Farida is scared that her children are becoming "Americanized," feeling that the cohesiveness of the family is threatened. In addition, neither Farida nor her husband are fluent in English, making them somewhat dependent on their three children for translation. The family often speaks about how the United States is so different from the way life was in Syria, even with the war. While Farida and her husband reminisce about Syria, their children talk about how wonderful their lives are in the United States and how they never want to return to Syria. This difference of connection to Syria has Farida worried, feeling like the family is growing apart and that her daughter will be lost without a strong connection to her faith or family.

The small city in the United States where Farida's family lives has few Syrians but does have a strong Muslim community. Farida and her husband are involved in the Muslim community, trying to maintain a strong connection for their children as well. Even so, Farida has noticed that her children have increasingly asked to spend time with friends from school, lacking enthusiasm for religious family activities. This has caused tension in the family.

The recent struggles between Farida and her children are causing tensions with her husband. She often finds herself arguing with him, accusing him of not helping to keep the family together. Farida typically stays at home and is often overprotected by her husband because of her injury. Because she rarely leaves her home, she has little knowledge of her surrounding community except for the local grocery store and the mosque. Her isolation, coupled with family tensions, has led Farida to begin questioning her importance to the family. She is increasingly nervous, reporting pain in her injured arm, and has difficulties sleeping. She has also heard that her husband is telling friends that his wife is very irritable nowadays.

## Critical Incident

Approximately 2 months ago there was a huge blowup between Farida and her daughter. One day when the children came home from school Farida asked if they could help prepare meals for a religious community gathering.

Farida's daughter refused, saying that she would not help prepare meals for a religious event. This escalated into a heated argument ending with the daughter telling her mother that she was a horrible mother and that she wished Farida had injured her head rather than her arm in Syria. The confrontation shocked Farida, triggering memories of violence from Syria. That afternoon Farida's husband came home to find Farida sobbing in the bedroom. Farida just lay on the ground, scared and crying. He described to his closest friends how this day was a turning point in her life.

## Sequence of Events

Farida feels that since coming to the United States, her family has been "falling apart." Although she does acknowledge that life is safer, she is increasingly confused about her purpose and role in this new life. Seeing her children and husband adapt so quickly and flourish has really affected her emotionally. She finds herself reliving the horrors she experienced in Syria more frequently, seeing death, destruction, rape, and robbery. She has never told the full story regarding the injury of her arm to anyone and, after the confrontation with her daughter, has contemplated removing herself from the family picture that sits in the living room.

Some community friends have asked Farida to talk to one of the elders in the community about her family troubles, but she reports that it would honestly be easier if she were no longer here. She says that her children don't need her and that her husband is fine without her, so why does she even need to be around. Her husband has begun to worry and reached out to the elder about this situation. After speaking with her, the elder recommended that she see a local mental health agency that is known to help with this type of problem with refugees.

## Key Clinical Questions

1. What happened to Farida during the escape from Syria?
2. What are Farida's feelings about her injury and the limitations it has placed on her?
3. How does Farida view the influence of U.S. culture and values on her children?
4. What is happening to Farida as a result of the tensions and conflicts in her family?
5. What would it look like to Farida if she "were no longer here"?
6. How did Farida envision life being in the United States before escaping from Syria?

7. Currently, what role does she think she plays within her family? Does she really think she is expendable? How so?
8. How do Farida's thoughts align with her Muslim faith?
9. In her mind, what would "fix" Farida's relationship with her husband and her children?

### Applying the MPM of Psychotherapy, Social Justice, and Human Rights

#### Phase I: Mental Health Education

Even though the recommendation for seeking mental health services came from the local elder, it is essential that Farida and her family understand that psychotherapy is confidential. It is also important for Farida to understand how individual, group, and family therapy could help her and the family with the struggles they are facing. Thus, Farida should be given a clear description of how therapy works.

#### Phase II: Individual, Group, and Family Therapy

The falling out with her daughter was a catalyst for Farida's remembering the dangerous escape from Syria. The family's flight from Syria was a major transition, fraught with trauma, to their new lives. Given the family-based nature of the Syrian community, family therapy may be helpful to explore communication patterns, evolving roles, and adaptive roles in a new culture.

It is suggested that family therapy begin with a focus on adjustment and acculturation. How is the family as a unit adjusting? How is each individual in the family adjusting? How can the family coexist more harmoniously in the new culture? What is life in the United States like for the entire family? What are some difficulties of adapting to a new country? How is the U.S. culture affecting the children and parents? The psychologist can begin to untangle the stressors associated with acculturation and identifying the areas of trauma, building a foundation to later work on more painful issues. It is important to hear family members' stories about their experience in Syria. This must be done patiently and with care because there is deep pain associated with this experience. The consideration and influence of the Muslim faith must also be considered in the exploration of memories, given that both parents have used religion as a guideline for their lives.

It may also be helpful for Farida to participate in group therapy with other refugee members who have experienced violence or abuse. This could prove to be highly beneficial because it may provide Farida with a connection to members of the community who may share the similar experiences and feelings of loss. It may be helpful for the therapist to establish links with the community to develop a community-based support group that would explore trauma and the effects of acculturation on the family unit.

### Phase III: Cultural Empowerment and Social and Navigational Capital

To understand herself and her role in the family in this new phase of her life, Farida must find a way to heal. Part of this healing incorporates mastery and access to Farida's new environment (e.g., cultural empowerment). Having greater involvement in the community may help Farida establish a better social network and navigate her way around the city without being so dependent on her family. Helping Farida find culturally and socially appropriate support groups, activities, events, and celebrations is essential in moving her beyond the confines of her home.

### Phase IV: Indigenous Healing

Given the importance attributed to her Muslim faith, a connection with the local imam is vital. The imam may be able to assist with religious guidance and healing and could partner with the therapist, enhancing the therapeutic work done in family and group therapy. In addition, meetings between the imam and the children may be helpful to ascertain how the imam may be of help in their acceptance or questioning of faith.

### Phase V: Social Justice and Human Rights

Given the injury to her arm, Farida may be entitled to various resources that would support her disability. Educating her about her rights as someone who is disabled is essential for future medical treatment or employment. In addition, as refugees living in a culture where there is growing antimigrant sentiment, it is important for the family to understand policies, practices, and rights that relate to refugees. This might include educational support, discrimination at employment sites, and disability rights, for example. Educating the family members about their rights is an essential component of the therapy.

## SUMMARY

The increasing worldwide refugee population is dramatically changing the global landscape. Given the unique refugee experience and higher rates of mental health concerns compared with the general population, it is essential that psychologists have a comprehensive understanding of the cultural, historical, sociopolitical, psychological, ecological, and economic factors that shape refugees' lives, as well as an understanding of human rights as they pertain to refugees. Displacement and involuntary flight from their homes and refugee camp experiences, coupled with postmigration resettlement, present momentous challenges in maintaining psychological well-being. To this end, we have described a culturally responsive model of intervention, the multiphase model of psychotherapy, social justice and human rights, a five-phase intervention approach that integrates culturally responsive Western psychotherapy with cultural empowerment via social and navigational capital, psychosocial interventions, indigenous healing methods, and social justice/human rights. The MPM takes into account cultural belief systems, acculturation and acclimation, the influence of public policy and economics, human rights, and psychological and social adaptation, offering a holistic framework and strategy to meet the complex issues facing refugees.

## REFERENCES

Achiume, E. T. (2014). Beyond prejudice: Structural xenophobic discrimination against refugees. *Georgetown Journal of International Law, 45*(3), 323–381.

Akinsulure-Smith, A. (2009). Brief psychoeducational group treatment with re-traumatized refugees and asylum seekers. *Journal for Specialists in Group Work, 34*(2), 137–150. https://doi.org/10.1080/01933920902798007

Albrecht, G. (2011). Chronic environmental change: Emerging "psychoterratic" syndromes. In *Climate change and human well-being* (pp. 43–56). Springer Publishing Company.

Albrecht, G., Sartore, G. M., Connor, L., Higginbotham, N., Freeman, S., Kelly, B., Stain, H., Tonna, A., & Pollard, G. (2007). Solastalgia: The distress caused by environmental change. *Australian Psychiatry, 15*(1, Suppl.), S95–S98. https://doi.org/10.1080/10398560701701288

American Psychological Association. (2010). *Resilience and recover after war: Refugee children and families in the United States.* http://www.apa.org/pi/lgt/resources/guidelines.aspx

American Psychological Association. (2017). *Multicultural guidelines: An ecological approach to context, identity, and intersectionality.* http://www.apa.org/about/policy/multicultural-guidelines.pdf

BBC. (2017, February). *Trump's executive order: Who does travel ban affect?* https://www.bbc.com/news/world-us-canada-38781302

Beck, J. G., Coffey, S. F., Foy, D. W., Keane, T. M., & Blanchard, E. B. (2009). Group cognitive behavior therapy for chronic posttraumatic stress disorder: An initial randomized pilot study. *Behavior Therapy, 40*(1), 82–92. https://doi.org/10.1016/j.beth.2008.01.003

Bemak, F. (1989). Cross-cultural family treatment with Southeast Asian refugees. *Journal of Strategic & Systemic Therapies, 8*(Bonus issue), 22–27. https://doi.org/10.1521/jsst.1989.8.bonus.22

Bemak, F., & Chung, R. C.-Y. (2011). Post-disaster social justice group work and groups supervision. *Journal for Specialists in Group Work, 36*(1), 3–21. https://doi.org/10.1080/01933922.2010.537737

Bemak, F., & Chung, R. C.-Y. (2013). Immigrants and refugees. In F. T. L. Leong, L. Comas-Díaz, G. Nagayama Hall, & J. Trimble (Eds.), *APA handbook of multicultural psychology* (pp. 503–517). American Psychological Association.

Bemak, F., & Chung, R. C.-Y. (2016). Counseling immigrants and refugees. In P. B. Pedersen, J. Draguns, W. Lonner, J. Trimble, & M. Scharron del Rio (Eds.), *Counseling across cultures* (7th ed., pp. 323–346). Sage Publications. https://doi.org/10.4135/9781483398921.n16

Bemak, F., & Chung, R. C.-Y. (2017a). Psychological impact of terrorism on refugees. In C. Stout (Ed.), *Terrorism, political violence, and extremism: New psychology to understand, face, and defuse the threat* (pp. 260–284). Praeger.

Bemak, F., & Chung, R. C.-Y. (2017b). Refugee trauma: Culturally responsive counseling interventions [Special issue on traumatology]. *Journal of Counseling and Development, 95*(3), 299–308. https://doi.org/10.1002/jcad.12144

Bemak, F., Chung, R. C.-Y., & Pedersen, P. B. (2003). *Counseling refugees: A psychological approach to innovative multicultural interventions*. Greenwood Press.

Berry, J. W. (2002). Conceptual approaches to acculturation. In K. M. Chun, P. B. Organista, & G. Marin (Eds.), *Acculturation: Advances in theory, measurement and applied research* (pp. 17–38). American Psychological Association.

Bhugra, D. (2004). Migration and mental health. *Acta Psychiatrica Scandinavica, 109*(4), 243–258. https://doi.org/10.1046/j.0001-690X.2003.00246.x

Brannan, S., Campbell, R., Davies, M., English, V., Mussell, R., & Sheather, J. C. (2016). The Mediterranean refugee crisis: Ethics, international law and migrant health. *Journal of Medical Ethics, 42*(4), 269–270. https://doi.org/10.1136/medethics-2016-103444

Briere, J. N., & Scott, C. (2015). *Principles of trauma therapy: A guide to symptoms, evaluation, and treatment* (2nd ed.). Sage Publications.

Chung, R. C.-Y., & Bemak, F. (2002a). The relationship of culture and empathy in cross-cultural counseling. *Journal of Counseling and Development, 80*(2), 154–159. https://doi.org/10.1002/j.1556-6678.2002.tb00178.x

Chung, R. C.-Y., & Bemak, F. (2002b). Revisiting the California Southeast Asian mental health needs assessment data: An examination of refugee ethnic and gender differences. *Journal of Counseling and Development, 80*(1), 111–119. https://doi.org/10.1002/j.1556-6678.2002.tb00173.x

Chung, R. C.-Y., & Bemak, F. (2012). *Social justice counseling: The next steps beyond multiculturalism*. Sage Publications.

Chung, R. C.-Y., Bemak, F., & Okazaki, S. (1997). Counseling Americans of Southeast Asian descent: The impact of the refugee experience. In C. Lee (Ed.), *Multicultural issues in counseling* (2nd ed., pp. 207–231). American Counseling Association.

Chung, R. C.-Y., Bemak, F., Ortiz, D. P., & Sandoval-Perez, P. A. (2008). Promoting the mental health of migrants: A multicultural-social justice perspective. *Journal of Counseling and Development. Multicultural and Diversity Issues in Counseling, 38*(Special issue), 310–317.

Chung, R. C.-Y., & Kagawa-Singer, M. (1993). Predictors of psychological distress among southeast Asian refugees. *Social Science & Medicine, 36*(5), 631–639. https://doi.org/10.1016/0277-9536(93)90060-H

Chung, R. C.-Y., & Lin, K. M. (1994). Help seeking-behavior among Southeast Asian refugees. *Journal of Community Psychology, 22*(2), 109–120. https://doi.org/10.1002/1520-6629(199404)22:2<109::AID-JCOP2290220207>3.0.CO;2-V

Chung, R. C.-Y., & Singer, M. K. (1995). Interpretation of symptom presentation and distress. A Southeast Asian refugee example. *Journal of Nervous and Mental Disease, 183*(10), 639–648. https://doi.org/10.1097/00005053-199510000-00005

de Anstiss, H., Ziaian, T., Procter, N., Warland, J., & Baghurst, P. (2009). Help-seeking for mental health problems in young refugees: A review of the literature with implications for policy, practice, and research. *Transcultural Psychiatry, 46*(4), 584–607. https://doi.org/10.1177/1363461509351363

De Luce, D., & Ainsley, J. (2018, September). *Trump admin rejected report showing refugees did not pose major security threat.* https://www.nbcnews.com/politics/immigration/trump-admin-rejected-report-showing-

Delara, M. (2016). Social determinants of immigrant women's mental health. *Advances in Public Health, 2016*, 1–11. https://doi.org/10.1155/2016/9730162

Dietz, J. (2010). Introduction to the special issue on employment discrimination against immigrants. *Journal of Managerial Psychology, 25*(2), 104–112. https://doi.org/10.1108/02683941011019320

Draguns, J. G. (2007). Empathy across national, cultural, and social barriers. *Baltic Journal of Psychology, 8*, 5–20.

Duarté-Vélez, Y., Bernal, G., & Bonilla, K. (2010). Culturally adapted cognitive-behavior therapy: Integrating sexual, spiritual, and family identities in an evidence-based treatment of a depressed Latino adolescent. *Journal of Clinical Psychology, 66*(8), 895–906. https://doi.org/10.1002/jclp.20710

Ehntholt, K. A., Smith, P. A., & Yule, W. (2005). School-based cognitive-behavioural therapy group intervention for refugee children who have experienced war-related trauma. *Clinical Child Psychology and Psychiatry, 10*(2), 235–250. https://doi.org/10.1177/1359104505051214

Fung, K., & Wong, Y.-L. R. (2007). Factors influencing attitudes towards seeking professional help among East and Southeast Asian immigrant and refugee women. *The International Journal of Social Psychiatry, 53*(3), 216–231. https://doi.org/10.1177/0020764006074541

Furtak, F. T. (2015). The refugee crisis: A challenge for Europe and the world. *Journal of Civil & Legal Sciences, 5*(1), 1–2.

Gielen, U. P., Fish, J. M., & Draguns, J. G. (Eds.). (2004). *Handbook of culture, therapy and healing.* Lawrence Erlbaum Associates.

Goldenberg, C. T. (2008). Teaching English language learners: What the research does—and does not—say. *American Educator.* http://www.aft.org/pdfs/americaneducator/summer2008/goldenberg.pdf

Goodkind, J., Githinji, A., & Isakson, B. (2011). Reducing heath disparities experienced by refugees resettled in urban areas: A community based transdisciplinary intervention model. In M. Kirst, N. Schaefer-McDaniel, S. Hwang, & P. O'Campo (Eds.), *Converging disciplines* (pp. 41–55). Springer-Verlag. https://doi.org/10.1007/978-1-4419-6330-7_4

Graham, L. (2015, September). *How smartphones are helping refugees in Europe.* CNBC. http://www.cnbc.com/2015/09/11/how-smartphones-are-helping-refugees-in-europe.html

Harrison, V. (2018, September). *Nauru refugees: The island where children have given up on life.* https://www.bbc.com/news/world-asia-45327058

Herman, J. L. (1997). *Trauma and recovery.* Basic Books.

Hofstede, G. (2001). *Culture's consequences: Comparing values, behaviors, institutions, and organizations across nations.* Sage Publications.
Hollander, A.-C., Dal, H., Lewis, G., Magnusson, C., Kirkbride, J. B., & Dalman, C. (2016). Refugee migration and risk of schizophrenia and other non-affective psychoses: Cohort study of 1.3 million people in Sweden. *British Medical Journal, 352,* i1030. https://doi.org/10.1136/bmj.i1030
Hong, G. K., & Domokos-Cheng Ham, M. (2001). *Psychotherapy and counseling with Asian American clients: A practical guide.* Sage Publications.
Igielnik, R., & Krogstad, J. M. (2017, February 3). *Where refugees to the U.S. come from.* https://www.pewresearch.org/fact-tank/
Internal Displacement Monitoring Centre. (2015, May). *Global overview 2015: People internally displaced by conflict and Violence.* http://www.internal-displacement.org/publications/global-overview-2015-people-internally-displaced-by-conflict-and-violence
International Organization for Migration. (2018). *World migration report 2018.* https://www.iom.int/definitional-issues
Kim, G., Aguado Loi, C. X., Chiriboga, D. A., Jang, Y., Parmelee, P., & Allen, R. S. (2011). Limited English proficiency as a barrier to mental health service use: A study of Latino and Asian immigrants with psychiatric disorders. *Journal of Psychiatric Research, 45*(1), 104–110. https://doi.org/10.1016/j.jpsychires.2010.04.031
Kinzie, J. D. (2005). Some of the effects of terrorism on refugees. *Journal of Aggression, Maltreatment & Trauma, 9*(3–4), 411–420. https://doi.org/10.1300/J146v09n03_12
Kinzie, J. D., Leung, P., Bui, A., Ben, R., Keopraseuth, K. O., Riley, C., Fleck, J., & Ades, M. (1988). Group therapy with Southeast Asian refugees. *Community Mental Health Journal, 24*(2), 157–166. https://doi.org/10.1007/BF00756658
Kirmayer, L. J. (1989). Cultural variations in the response to psychiatric disorders and emotional distress. *Social Science & Medicine, 29*(3), 327–339. https://doi.org/10.1016/0277-9536(89)90281-5
Kleinman, A., Eisenberg, L., & Good, B. (1978). Culture, illness, and care: Clinical lessons from anthropologic and cross-cultural research. *Annals of Internal Medicine, 88*(2), 251–258. https://doi.org/10.7326/0003-4819-88-2-251
Krogstad, J. M., & Radford, J. (2017, January). *Key facts about refugees to the U.S.* http://www.pewresearch.org/fact-tank/2017/01/30/key-facts-about-refugees-to-the-u-s/
Kruse, J., Joksimovic, L., Cavka, M., Wöller, W., & Schmitz, N. (2009). Effects of trauma-focused psychotherapy upon war refugees. *Journal of Traumatic Stress, 22*(6), 585–592. https://doi.org/10.1002/jts.20477
Lacroix, M., & Sabbah, C. (2011). Posttraumatic psychological distress and resettlement: The need for different practice in assisting refugee families. *Journal of Family Social Work, 14*(1), 43–53. https://doi.org/10.1080/10522158.2011.523879
Lin, L., Nigrinis, A., Christidis, P., & Stamm, K. (2015). *Demographics of the U.S. psychology workforce: Findings from the American Community Survey.* Center for Workforce Studies, American Psychological Association. https://www.apa.org/workforce/publications/13-demographics/report.pdf
Majumder, P., O'Reilly, M., Karim, K., & Vostanis, P. (2015). "This doctor, I not trust him, I'm not safe": The perceptions of mental health and services by unaccompanied

refugee adolescents. *The International Journal of Social Psychiatry, 61*(2), 129–136. https://doi.org/10.1177/0020764014537236

McLean, C. P., & Foa, E. B. (2013). Dissemination and implementation of prolonged exposure therapy for posttraumatic stress disorder. *Journal of Anxiety Disorders, 27*(8), 788–792. https://doi.org/10.1016/j.janxdis.2013.03.004

Morash, M., Bui, H., Zhang, Y., & Holtfreter, K. (2007). Risk factors for abusive relationships: A study of Vietnamese American immigrant women. *Violence Against Women, 13*(7), 653–675. https://doi.org/10.1177/1077801207302044

Murphy, A., Woodman, M., Roberts, B., & McKee, M. (2016). The neglected refugee crisis. *British Medical Journal, 352*, i484. https://doi.org/10.1136/bmj.i484

National Oceanic and Atmospheric Administration. (2020, January 15). 2019 was 2nd hottest year on record for Earth say NOAA, NASA. https://www.noaa.gov/news/2019-was-2nd-hottest-year-on-record-for-earth-say-noaa-nasa#:~:text=NASA%20also%20found%20that%202010,second%20warmest%20for%20the%20globe

Ní Raghallaigh, M. (2014). The causes of mistrust amongst asylum seekers and refugees: Insights from research with unaccompanied asylum seeking minors living in the Republic of Ireland. *Journal of Refugee Studies, 27*(1), 82–100. https://doi.org/10.1093/jrs/fet006

Parthasarthi, M. S., Durgamba, V. K., & Murthy, N. S. (2004). Counseling migrant families in Southern India. *International Journal for the Advancement of Counseling, 26*(4), 363–367. https://doi.org/10.1007/s10447-004-0171-0

Ram, A. (2015, December). Smartphones bring solace and aid to desperate refugees. *Wired.* http://www.wired.com/2015/12/smartphone-syrian-refugee-crisis

Resera, E., Tribe, R., & Lane, P. (2015). Interpreting in mental health, roles and dynamics in practice. *International Journal of Culture and Mental Health, 8*(2), 192–206. https://doi.org/10.1080/17542863.2014.921207

Schottelkorb, A., Doumas, D., & Garcia, R. (2012). Treatment for childhood refugee trauma: A randomized controlled trial. *International Journal of Play Therapy, 21*(2), 57–73. https://doi.org/10.1037/a0027430

Scott, E. (2015, November). *Ben Carson compares some refugees to "rabid" dogs.* CNN. http://www.cnn.com/2015/11/19/politics/ben-carson-rabid-dogs-refugees/

Shakil, M. (2016). Gender based violence: A paradoxical analysis. *Journal of the Humanities and Social Sciences, 23*(2), 118–125.

Solomon, B. (1976). *Black empowerment.* Columbia University Press.

Strong, J., Varady, C., Chahda, N., Doocy, S., & Burnham, G. (2015). Health status and health needs of older refugees from Syria in Lebanon. *Conflict & Health, 9*(1), 12. https://doi.org/10.1186/s13031-014-0029-y

Sue, S., Fujino, D. C., Hu, L. T., Takeuchi, D. T., & Zane, N. W. (1991). Community mental health services for ethnic minority groups: A test of the cultural responsiveness hypothesis. *Journal of Consulting and Clinical Psychology, 59*(4), 533–540. https://doi.org/10.1037/0022-006X.59.4.533

Taylor, M. (2017). Climate change "will create world's biggest refugee crisis." *The Guardian.* https://www.theguardian.com/environment/2017/nov/02/climate-change-will-create-worlds-biggest-refugee-crisis

Tharoor, I. (2018, September 14). *How Trump has sunk the hopes of refugees.* https://www.washingtonpost.com/world/2018/09/14/how-trump-has-sunk-hopes-refugees/?wpisrc=nl_az_most&wpmk=1

Triandis, H. C. (2001). Individualism-collectivism and personality. *Journal of Personality, 69*(6), 907–924. https://doi.org/10.1111/1467-6494.696169

Tribe, R., & Keefe, A. (2009). Issues in using interpreters in therapeutic work with refugees. What is not being expressed? *European Journal of Psychotherapy and Counselling, 11*(4), 409–424. https://doi.org/10.1080/13642530903444795

Tribe, R., & Lane, P. (2009). Working with interpreters across language and culture in mental health. *Journal of Mental Health (Abingdon, England), 18*(3), 233–241. https://doi.org/10.1080/09638230701879102

United Nations. (1951). *The 1951 refugee convention.* http://www.unhcr.org/en-us/1951-refugee-convention.html

United Nations High Commissioner for Refugees. (2014). *Global trend report 2013.* http://www.unhcr.org/5399a14f9.html

United Nations High Commissioner for Refugees. (2019). *Figures at a glance June 2019.* https://www.unhcr.org/figures-at-a-glance.html

Unterhitzenberger, J., & Rosner, R. (2016). Case report: Manualized trauma-focused cognitive behavioral therapy with an unaccompanied refugee minor girl. *European Journal of Psychotraumatology, 7*(1), 29246. https://doi.org/10.3402/ejpt.v7.29246

U.S. Department of Health and Human Services. (2001). *Mental health: Culture, race, and ethnicity—A supplement to mental health. A Report of the Surgeon General.* Public Health Service, Office of the Surgeon General.

U.S. Department of State. (2018). *Refugee admissions.* https://www.state.gov/j/prm/ra/index.htm

U.S. Department of Veteran Affairs & Department of Defense. (2010). *VA/DoD clinical practice guidelines. Management of posttraumatic stress.*

Vickers, B. (2005). Cognitive model of the maintenance and treatment of post-traumatic stress disorder applied to children and adolescents. *Clinical Child Psychology and Psychiatry, 10*(2), 217–234. https://doi.org/10.1177/1359104505051212

World Health Organization. (2008). *Fact sheet no. 134: Traditional medicine.* http://www.who.int/inf-fs/en/fact134.html

Wulfhorst, E. (2016). The UN is planning to campaign against xenophobia and racism amid the refugee crisis. *Business Insider.* http://www.businessinsider.com/the-un-is-planning-to-campaign-against-xenophobia-and-racism-amid-the-refugee-crisis-2016-5

Yakushko, O., Backhaus, A., Watson, M., Ngaruiya, K., & Gonzalez, J. (2008). Career development concerns of recent immigrants and refugees. *Journal of Career Development, 34*(4), 362–396. https://doi.org/10.1177/0894845308316292

# 6 CULTURALLY ADAPTED THERAPEUTIC APPROACHES

*The Healing Environment and Restorative Therapy Model*

RICHARD F. MOLLICA, EUGENE F. AUGUSTERFER,
AND NINA CAMPANILE

It is extremely challenging to discuss psychological healing in the care and cure of the major health and mental health damage caused by the refugee experience. The number of persons and communities affected by mass violence and displacement is enormous. The traumatic life experiences of refugees can range from fleeing home to the experience of violent events of unspeakable horror. The resulting physical and emotional impact of the refugee experience has been revealed to occur not only over the lifetime of individuals and communities impacted by traumatic experience but is also passed along to future generations. Unfortunately, for years, until very recently, the mental health problems of refugees were largely ignored—even denied—by international policy makers responsible for the protection and humanitarian aid to refugees. As illustrated in this chapter, the "invisible wounds" of mass violence and displacement, either due to human-made or natural disaster, are no longer "invisible" (Mollica, 2006). Policy makers are struggling with the challenge of bringing refugee mental health into the mainstream of humanitarian relief (Mollica, 2000).

This chapter focuses on the major psychological healing approaches that are emerging as evidence-based and culturally valid therapies for the care

https://doi.org/10.1037/0000226-006
*Refugee Mental Health*, J. D. Aten and J. Hwang (Editors)

of refugee populations. As Dr. Stanley Jackson (1992), the late historian of medicine from Yale, stated, "healing" refers historically to those "various measures that have been employed by their social functionaries who can be classified as healers and who have made efforts to cure, to restore health, or to bring about recovery from sickness" (p. 1623). He went on to say that "psychological healing" includes those practices and processes that serve to resolve or ease the psychological burdens of human suffering and illness (Jackson, 1992). Jackson would likely agree that in the refugee field, psychological healing has been used to describe an enormous range of psychological, social, cultural, and economic practices, including religious, spiritual, and traditional healing. Psychological healing is offered by a vast array of healing practitioners that have been previously referred to as "indigenous healers." They include primary care practitioners/family doctors, mental health counselors, humanitarian aid workers, spiritual and religious clergy, teachers, community elders, and traditional healers. These healers are "indigenous" because they work at the local community level. The diverse practices of these indigenous healers and their relative efficacy are not the focus of this chapter. Instead, an emphasis will be placed on evaluating the best practices emerging out of mainstream Western mental health traditions as well as those practices described by the term *complementary medicine*. Additionally, this chapter also offers a new healing model called Healing Environment and Restorative Therapy (HEART), which builds on Maslow's (1943) hierarchy of needs and Mollica et al.'s (2015) H-5 model. The new H-5 model builds on the basic model of humanitarian relief used universally by humanitarian aid policy makers and practitioners.

This chapter is also timely because the impact of violence on local communities and citizens is at an all-time high. There are now more than 70.8 million forcibly displaced persons worldwide, including millions of persons displaced by climate change and millions of persons in communities affected by natural disasters (United Nations High Commissioner for Refugees [UNHCR], 2019). The UN prediction is that all of these numbers will be increasing over the next decade. Concurrent with this awareness of the huge numbers of persons affected by human-made and natural disasters is the advent and expansion of the trauma-informed care movement (TICM). Over the past 30 years, there has been increasing awareness of the devastating impact of violence on the health, mental health, and wellness of affected individuals, families, and communities. This awareness of the importance of the recognition, diagnosis, treatment, and prevention of human-made human suffering and natural disasters is secondary to the demand for a revolution in the mental health care of traumatized persons at all levels of health care.

This chapter reviews refugee trauma and mental health as an area in need of a new therapeutic framework and practice. The human rights violations affecting all refugee populations are in urgent need of a different model of therapy that moves beyond the traditional mainstream conventional therapies. Specifically, this chapter

- reviews the magnitude of the mental health problem for traumatized refugee populations;

- assesses the known scientific and cultural efficacy of mainstream therapies in refugee communities and patients;

- assesses the scientific and cultural efficacy of new and complimentary healing approaches, such as meditation and yoga; and

- presents the new HEART, building on the theoretical foundations and principles of Maslow's (1943) hierarchy of needs and Mollica et al.'s (2015) H-5 model.

## MAGNITUDE OF THE PROBLEM

Natural disasters and armed conflict have marked human existence from time immemorial, but in recent times, the scale and scope of these events have increased markedly. Between 2009 and 2018, natural disasters have affected about 184.7 million people every year (Centre for Research on the Epidemiology of Disasters, 2020). Mental health is an issue of global importance, with an estimated 264 million people worldwide suffering from depression, and depression is a leading cause of disability worldwide and is a major contributor to the overall global burden of disease (World Health Organization [WHO], 2020). Depression affects more women than men, and left untreated, it can lead to suicide. Globally, close to 800,000 people die from suicide every year, and suicide is the second leading cause of death in 15- to 29-year-olds (WHO, 2020). The rates of mental health illness in human-made and natural disasters are dramatically increasing against an existing baseline. The World Bank (2016) reported that in conflict situations, the psychiatric literature estimates an increase in disorder prevalence explained by high levels of stress that can prompt psychosocial or psychiatric disorders that were previously nonexistent or dormant.

Disasters, natural and human-made, including armed conflict, have triggered one of the largest migrations of people the world has ever experienced. As stated earlier, disasters affect millions of people around the world every year. The UNHCR reported that as of June 2019, there were 70.8 million forcibly displaced people worldwide, 86% of whom were from low- and middle-income countries. Additionally, hundreds of millions of persons have been displaced by climate change in recent years (UNHCR, 2019). The need for health and mental health services to address the problems caused by disasters and displacement is well documented. Mollica et al. (2004) reported that mental health is becoming a central issue for the public health of complex emergencies. Although temporary symptoms tend to be common in the acute phase of disaster recovery, psychological sequelae can persist for 3 to 5 years after a natural disaster. Therefore, it is important that we review the most frequently used methods of treatment for refugee populations to ensure that those therapies methods meet the highest standard for efficacy and culture attunement.

## MENTAL HEALTH IMPACT

The mental health impact of violence on traumatized populations due to posttraumatic stress disorder (PTSD) and major depression can be significant (Cheung et al., 2018). The general rule of thumb across culturally diverse refugee populations is that the prevalence of depression can be as high as 66% and the prevalence of PTSD as high as 33% (Cheung et al., 2018; Morina et al., 2018). These two psychiatric diagnoses are usually comorbid in the acute and chronic phase. A recent study of Syrian refugees in Turkey, for example, revealed high levels of horrific trauma with associated rates of PTSD of 33.5% (Alpak et al., 2015). Schoenbaum et al. (2009) analyzed the mental health impact of natural disasters over time and found that at 6 months postdisaster, rates of mild to moderate mental health problems were 25% for adults and 30% for children; rates of severe refugee mental health problems for adults were 5% and 10% for children. Longitudinal studies by Mollica and his colleagues (1999, 2001) revealed that although initial high rates of PTSD and depression and related social disability declined over time, few initially asymptomatic individuals became symptomatic, and few symptomatic individuals become asymptomatic. Suicidality has only recently been studied in refugee populations and those communities exposed to natural disasters (Refugee Health Technical Assistance Center, 2011). Meyerhoff et al. (2018) found that suicidal behavior and death by suicide are significant and pressing problems in the Bhutanese refugee community; currently, Bhutanese refugees are dying by suicide at a rate nearly 2 times that of the general U.S. population.

The major risk factors associated with mental health sequela in traumatized refugee communities include the following:

- gender;

- age;

- direct impact of the traumatic life events versus witnessing and hearing about traumatic life events;

- type of traumatic event, with murder or unnatural death of a child and disappearance of a loved one being the most traumatizing;

- number and frequency of traumatic life experiences (dose–effect relationships between traumatic life experiences and mental health symptoms have been consistently demonstrated and replicated);

- gender-based violence;

- torture—being a victim of torture as well as witnessing torture or living in an environment where torture is still occurring (see Steel et al., 2009);

- lack of food, water, and a home or shelter;

- lack of social support and work opportunities; and

- ongoing lack of safety and security (Kim, 2016; Mollica et al., 2014; Steel et al., 2009).

Reunification studies on the risk and resiliency factors associated with people returning home to their countries of origin are almost nonexistent. The few studies that exist reveal that forced repatriation and poor health lead to an increase in psychiatric disorders upon return. Mollica et al. (1999, 2001), in their Bosnia study, found a number of repatriated elderly who died without known medical problems. These researchers speculated this was the "giving-up–given-up" syndrome described by Engel (1968) years ago. Although research studies on resiliency are limited, altruistic behavior, work or school, and spirituality are factors highly associated with resiliency in the face of mental health problems (Mollica et al., 2002; Reed et al., 2012; Rousseau & Guzder, 2008).

## MAINSTREAM WESTERN THERAPIES

Assessing the cultural validity and efficacy of mainstream therapies for marginalized populations is extremely complex. First, it must be determined who is the focus of the mental health intervention. Second, what is the goal of treatment? Third, is the intervention effective for relieving mental health problems in diverse cultures and sociopolitical situations? This chapter cannot review the history of psychological mental health interventions in Western society. Similarly, a vast and extensive scientific literature on mental health care in non-Western societies exists (see van der Veer, 1992). Current modern trends in psychological healing have emphasized the role of psychotropic drugs, psychodynamic psychotherapy, and cognitive behavior therapy (CBT) in caring for traumatized patients. In addition to these approaches, eye-movement desensitization and reprocessing (EMDR), narrative exposure therapy (NET), and exposure therapy (ET) have been widely used in the trauma field. However, none of these approaches have been widely studied in the mental health care of refugees and other patients exposed to mass violence and natural disaster (Satcher, 2001). A review of the mental health interventions or "therapies" for refugees reveals that Mollica (1988) was the first to describe the use of listening to the patient's traumatic life history. He called this narrative approach the *trauma story*. The four major domains of the trauma story are described in his book *Healing Invisible Wounds: Paths to Hope and Recovery in a Violent World* (Mollica, 2000). The trauma story approach is used extensively in the trauma-informed care movement; it is also embedded in the extensive groundbreaking research of Pennebaker (1997) and his colleagues on the physical and emotional benefits provided by emotional disclosure. The important salutary impact of emotional disclosure in written form or sharing in conversation with a therapist has been extensively demonstrated in diverse settings, including storytelling using native oral histories by African Americans to care for refractory hypertension, narrative reconstruction of the potentially emotionally devastating impact of being a patient in an intensive care unit, and non-Western use of storytelling in aboriginal Australia (Atkinson, 2002; Garrouste-Orgeas et al., 2014; Houston et al., 2011).

## SPECIALIZED MENTAL HEALTH THERAPIES FOR REFUGEES

This section provides a review of the scientific literature on the efficacy of mental health therapies—CBT, EMDR, meditation and yoga, and narrative exposure therapy (NET)—with refugee populations follows. A Cochrane review of torture survivors suggests that narrative exposure therapy (NET) and other forms of CBT offer moderate benefits in reducing distress and PTSD but evidence was of low quality (Patel et al., 2014).

### Cognitive Behavior Therapy

CBT has gained popularity in the United States for the treatment of various disorders, particularly depression and anxiety. However, research on its treatment efficacy with refugees is not widely published. Kar (2011) reviewed the literature on the use of CBT for treatment of PTSD and reported that studies of CBT with refugees suggest its effectiveness. In a study of Vietnamese refugees with pharmacology-resistant PTSD and panic attacks, CBT led to significant improvement in all outcomes as measured by the Harvard Trauma Questionnaire (HTQ), Anxiety Sensitivity Index, and the Hopkins Symptom Checklist–25. Sijbrandij et al. (2017) examined how best to strengthen mental health care systems for Syrian refugees in Europe and the Middle East, integrating scalable psychological interventions in eight countries. They reviewed various interventions, including CBT, and reported that refugees who had resettled in high-income countries showed a reduction in symptoms of PTSD and depression after treatment with CBT and NET, with the strongest evidence base seen for NET (Sijbrandij et al., 2017).

In a study of flexible CBT and antidepressants in 217 refugees with war-related PTSD, Buhmann et al. (2016) showed no effect on PTSD symptoms with CBT and antidepressants and a small-to-moderate effect of antidepressants and psychoeducation on depression in the traumatized refugees. In a follow-up study of trauma-affected refugees, Buhmann and colleagues examined the long-term treatment effects of CBT and antidepressants on trauma-affected refugees. They reported that despite the limited decline in symptom scores and treatment effects immediately after treatment, the condition of the treated trauma-affected refugees was significantly improved 6 and 18 months after treatment (Buhmann et al., 2018).

### Eye-Movement Desensitization and Reprocessing

EMDR has been used in the treatment of trauma for a long time. However, the use of EMDR with refugees who have suffered significant and complex trauma is limited. In a pilot study, Acarturk et al. (2015) examined Syrian refugees with PTSD to determine the effectiveness of using EMDR to reduce PTSD and depression symptoms. The study included 29 adult participants (EMDR group = 15, wait-list group = 14). They reported that the EMDR group had lower PTSD scores after treatment compared with the wait-list group and had lower depression scores than did the wait-list group. They concluded that the pilot randomized controlled trial (RCT) indicated that EMDR may be effective in reducing PTSD and depression symptoms among Syrian refugees.

In a follow-up study, Acarturk et al. (2016) examined the use of EMDR for treatment of PTSD and depression in an RCT of Syrian refugees ($n = 37$ in the EMDR treatment group and $n = 33$ in the wait-list group). Using the HTQ and the Impact of Event Scale—Revised, they reported that the EMDR therapy group showed a significantly larger reduction of PTSD symptoms as assessed with the HTQ than did the wait-list group (Buhmann et al., 2018). Yurtsever et al. (2018) examined an EMDR Group Intervention for 47 adult Syrian Refugees with PTSD. Using the Impact of Event Scale, Beck Depression Inventory–II, and International Neuropsychiatric Interview (MINI) at pre-, post-, and 4-week follow-up, the researchers found that the EMDR group had significantly lower PTSD and depression symptoms after the intervention (Gallegos et al., 2017).

### Meditation, Mindfulness, and Yoga

Meditation and yoga have a rich tradition dating back millennia. However, the use of meditation and yoga for treatment of psychological trauma is relatively recent. Gallegos et al. (2017) did a meta-analytic review of RCTs using meditation and yoga for PTSD. The studies included were 19 RCTs with data on 1,173 participants. In this meta-analytic review, complementary mind and body health approaches for the treatment of PTSD showed small to moderate effects of yoga on PTSD, which were comparable to mindfulness and meditation approaches. Telles et al. (2010) examined stress symptoms and heart rate variability in survivors of the Bihar flood in north India. Twenty-two volunteers (group average age $\pm$ *SD*, 31.5 $\pm$ 7.5 years; subjects were all male) were randomly assigned to two groups, a yoga and a no-yoga wait-list control group. The yoga group practiced yoga for an hour daily, while subjects in the control group participated in their routine activities. The authors reported a significant decrease in sadness in the yoga group compared with an increase in anxiety in the control group. Thus, Telles et al. concluded that a week of yoga can reduce feelings of sadness and possibly prevent an increase in anxiety in flood survivors a month after the disaster.

In another systematic review and meta-analysis, Cramer et al. (2018) examined the data on yoga for PTSD. Cochrane Library, Medline/PubMed, PsycInfo, Scopus, and IndMED were searched through July 2017 for RCTs assessing the effects of yoga on symptoms of PTSD. After reviewing the studies, they concluded that only a weak recommendation for yoga as an adjunctive intervention for PTSD could be made. Regarding meditation for PTSD, Agger (2015) reported on the use of meditation for healing after the mass atrocity in Cambodia. We know that after catastrophic events in which people's survival has been threatened, as happened during the Khmer Rouge regime in Cambodia (1975–1979), some continue to suffer from painful mental symptoms (Mollica et al., 2014). Cambodia lacks a developed mental health care system. To address this need, Western psychological approaches to managing the effects of trauma were therefore introduced to Cambodia in the 1990s (Agger, 2015). However, there exists a range of indigenous practices that Cambodians can call on to help calm the distressed mind, and indeed, elements of these practices, particularly meditation and mindfulness, have helped inform Western psychological practice. The author concluded that in the Khmer context, practicing mindfulness is inextricably linked to other cultural notions, particularly that of merit-making, and its objectives are both to bring psychological benefit to individuals and to support cultural regeneration. Nickerson and Hinton (2011) examined anger regulation in traumatized Cambodian refugees. They interviewed six Cambodian monks living in Massachusetts on their opinions about the causes, phenomenology, and appropriate intervention strategies for anger among Cambodian refugees living in Massachusetts. Given their understanding of the Cambodian culture, the monks recommended strategies including studying Buddhist teachings, and meditation/mindfulness.

Kalmanowitz and Ho (2017) examined the impact of art therapy and mindfulness on 12 participants (nine women and three men), aged 18 to 45, all of whom reported fearing for their lives and having experienced multiple traumatic events. The participants attended art therapy and mindfulness studio workshops for 4 full days over a 9-day period. Between the workshops, they attended a focus group to identify cultural and religious factors that helped them cope with adversity. The participants reported that the experience helped them see what they had previously not seen, regulate their emotions, express themselves in a safe way, gain emotional distance, become aware of triggers, and achieve clarity of thought.

Rees et al.'s (2014) important study examined the role of transcendental meditation on reducing PTSD in Congolese refugees. Eleven participants living in temporary shelters in Kampala, Uganda, chose to learn transcendental meditation (TM). The participants had been exposed to extreme trauma, including sexual assault, torture, and being forced to witness abuse or killing of loved ones. The participants learned TM and practiced on a daily basis. After 10 days of practice, scores on the Longitudinal PTSD Checklist–Civilian decreased significantly, and at postintervention 30 days after the training, it had dropped significantly more (Rees et al., 2014).

In another study of refugees and survivors of torture, Longacre et al. (2012) examined the role of meditation and other complementary treatments as part of an integrated treatment plan. Specifically, they examined published studies on the use of meditation in the literature. Their review confirmed meditation as a safe and easily implemented modality, even when practiced among vulnerable populations. The authors concluded that meditation and other complementary treatments are promising and that the use of these techniques with vulnerable populations warrants further study (Longacre et al., 2012).

## Narrative Exposure Therapy

NET has been used widely for PTSD and those exposed to psychological trauma. In a systematic review and meta-analysis of psychological interventions for PTSD in refugees and asylum seekers, Thompson et al. (2018) reviewed 525 trials, including 16 RCTs. They found evidence to support the use of EMDR and NET for those with PTSD symptoms.

Neuner et al. (2004) demonstrated the effectiveness of NET in an RCT of Sudanese refugees living in a Ugandan refugee settlement. Forty-three Sudanese refugees received either four sessions of NET, four sessions of supportive counseling, or one session of psychoeducational therapy. One year after treatment, only 29% of NET participants met criteria for PTSD, while 70% of supportive counseling participants met criteria for PTSD, and 80% of psychoeducational participants met criteria for PTSD. The NET treatment consisted of the participant constructing a detailed chronological account of their story with the therapist (Neuner et al., 2004).

Tribe and colleagues (2019) conducted a systematic review of psychosocial interventions for adult refugees and asylum seekers. The aim of the review was to provide an exhaustive summary of the current literature on psychosocial interventions, both trauma- and nontrauma-focused, for refugee populations experiencing PTSD, depressive, or anxiety symptoms and to produce recommendations for future research and current clinical practice. The review found medium- to high-quality evidence supporting the use of NET. A lack of culturally adapted treatments was apparent, and there was less evidence to support standard CBT, EMDR, and multidisciplinary treatments (Tribe et al., 2019).

In a study of complex PTSD and phased treatment in refugees, ter Heide et al. (2016) found that asylum seekers and refugees often have an increased risk of developing complex PTSD. They examined treatment modalities and reported that trauma-focused treatment should be offered to all refugees who seek treatment for PTSD. They stated that such treatments, especially NET and culturally adapted CBT, have consistently been found to be high in efficacy. Robjant and Fazel (2010) echoed this statement: "Emerging evidence suggests that NET is an effective treatment for PTSD in individuals who have been traumatized by conflict and organized violence, even in settings that remain volatile and insecure" (p. 1).

As documented in the preceding review, it is our opinion of the authors that the most promising treatments for those who have suffered significant trauma are culturally adapted meditation and NET, especially NET that allows survivors to recount their story in the presence of a trained empathic interviewer, listener, or therapist. Although these treatment modalities are indeed promising, the magnitude of the refugee problem does not allow Western-based mental health therapies to be universally applied in large-scale community settings. The cultural validity and efficacy of CBT, EMDR, and NET in non-Western settings is at the earliest stages of research. It may be found, however, that the small percentage of those refugees and displaced persons with severe mental illness may benefit greatly from these specialized treatment modalities.

## MASLOW'S HIERARCHY OF NEEDS

The therapies mentioned in the preceding section are often available for only a small percentage of symptomatic refugees, and the purpose of refugee mental health is also to advocate for the broader need to improve the well-being of refugees and cultivate a preventative approach in a population of people who have known history of traumatic experiences. There is a great need for large-scale refugee mental health interventions that can be economically applied at the community and individual levels that are culturally effective in diverse sociocultural settings. One starting point for extending this search is with a reappraisal of Maslow's hierarchy of needs (Maslow, 1943, 1954). Maslow's brilliant analysis of the hierarchy of needs has been a primary organizing principle of the humanitarian aid community in its approach to disaster relief. Figure 6.1 illustrates Maslow's pyramid of basic human needs. The pyramid is built on a base of basic human needs for survival: food, water, and shelter. All disaster relief work in times of natural disaster, civil strife, or war build on this model by first ensuring safety and security for the affected populations. The humanitarian aid community attempts to protect the traumatized population by first and foremost providing food, water, shelter, and protection from ongoing violence or danger. Mixed into this equation is the requirement that all humanitarian emergencies protect populations from infectious diseases and other public health hazards by providing clean water

**FIGURE 6.1. Maslow's Hierarchy of Needs**

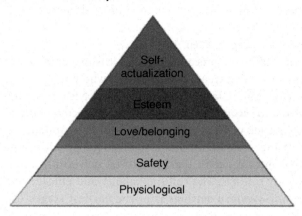

and sanitation. Over time, once these two basic levels of needs are secured (see Figure 6.1), higher levels of needs can be met. Maslow, one of America's great humanistic psychologists, ultimately believed that as individuals moved up the pyramid of needs, they eventually achieve self-actualization. According to Maslow and his humanistic colleagues, such as Viktor Frankl in his *Man's Search for Meaning*, all human beings try to achieve meaning in their lives. At the end of his life, Maslow went as far as to state that his hierarchy of needs led to not only self-actualization but also self-transformation on a spiritual level.

## THE MASLOW MODEL: IMPLICATION FOR REFUGEE EXPERIENCES

The hierarchy of needs was first described by Maslow in his 1943 paper "A Theory of Human Motivations" in *Psychological Review*. Maslow strove for a universal set of principles that affect all people's regardless of their ethnicity, social class, or national identity. The hierarchy of needs is generally depicted as a five-layered pyramid. Maslow considered these goal-directed needs to start at the base, with the most pressing and basic human needs lying at the bottom of the pyramid. His system was linear because he believed that the basic needs must be met first before higher needs can be achieved (Maslow, 1971). A brief description of each level of need follows.

## Physiological Needs

Physiological needs are the most basic needs for human existence and survival. These include food, water, housing, and sanitation. All of the needs directly affect refugees during the emergency phase (Mollica et al., 2004). Responding to the basic needs of highly traumatized communities is fundamental to the work of UNHCR, the U.S. Federal Emergency Management Agency, and other disaster relief agencies.

## Safety Needs

Safety and security are a fundamental basic need for traumatized communities affected by natural disaster and human violence. In the absence of physical safety, individuals cannot stabilize themselves socially, culturally, economically, and politically. This level includes protection from war and civil strife within safe environments, freedom from sexual and other forms of gender-based violence within refugee camps, and the protection of children from domestic violence, bullying, and discrimination. Access to adequate health care is also a priority. Similarly, access to mental health care is necessary but rarely seen as a priority by international humanitarian relief agencies.

## Social Belonging

After basic needs are met, the third level in this hierarchy is interpersonal support and social belonging. This includes family reunification, school and sports for children, access to religious and community activities.

## Self-Esteem Needs

Maslow (1954) described *self-esteem* as the mechanism of desire, achievement, strength, adequacy, confidence in the face of the world, and independence and freedom. He regarded this as a longing to be "someone," to be respected and valued within the family and the community. Maslow classified a lower version of self-esteem as the need for respect from others and a higher version as the need for self-respect (Maslow, 1954).

## Self-Actualization

At the top of the pyramid is the achievement of self-actualization. Maslow summarized this dramatically in his famous phrase "What a man can be, he must be"—that is, the desire of every being is to realize their full potential. Later in his development of this model, Maslow added the need for *transcendence*. This refers to the highest levels of human achievement found in altruistic behaviors and spirituality.

## Critiques of the Hierarchy of Needs in the Humanitarian Context

The hierarchy of needs remains a major influence on humanitarian relief despite the many limitations that have pointed out by his followers and critics (Geller, 1982; Neher, 1991). However, this approach faces many problems in the context of refugees or asylum seekers. The average stay of a refugee in a refugee camp is 28 years. As the years progress, the initial emergency phase is long over, and refugees have not moved up the pyramid through jobs and education. Further, Maslow and the humanitarian aid community have never been able to define what is concretely meant by the other levels (e.g., esteem). How do you define "esteem," and how do you promote it? How do you measure it? The Maslow self-actualization model also failed to recognize that self-actualization may not occur by only moving up the pyramid. Resiliency and posttraumatic growth studies reveal that self-actualization through reflection and personal transformation can occur at each level of the pyramid. In fact, psychological and physical self-healing occurs as soon as violence occurs (Mollica, 2000). As Mollica and his colleagues revealed in the Cambodian refugee camps in Thailand in the 1980s and 1990s, refugees will fight to work, practice their religion, and develop good communities and family relationships despite the many barriers set up to prevent this (Mollica et al., 1993). Even in a "hopeless" environment, traumatized people can find hope. Certainly, his theory is culturally limited to individualistic Western communities; his concept of self-actualization neglected the significant and varying needs of women and children; and linear advancement up the pyramid has not proven to be valid. In fact, self-actualization may and does occur at each level of the pyramid as revealed by the resiliency and posttraumatic growth literature (Koltko-Rivera, 2006). Maslow was not able to describe those factors that are necessary to assist a person in achieving self-actualization. The two basic needs levels are clearly defined and can (and are) operationalized by international relief agencies, but higher need levels are hard to define and measure. Maslow's model has not found a place for mental health and is not capable of identifying the needs of individuals severely damaged by traumatic life experiences. A revised model based on the human subjective experience of violence is therefore needed (Gold, 2013; Henwood et al., 2015).

Where does therapy fit into the Maslow model of humanitarian relief (Lonn & Dantzler, 2017; Mitschke et al., 2017; Slobodin & de Jong, 2015)? Clearly, at the field level, not all refugees and survivors of violence can receive CBT or other forms of conventional Western therapy. Humanitarian aid policy has tried to skirt this dilemma by attempting to replace "one-to-one" therapies with psychological interventions that can act indirectly on physical and emotional distress by providing generic interventions at the social, cultural, community, and family levels of care. Unfortunately, generic psychosocial approaches may not work for individuals who have been severely physically and mentally damaged by violence, such as torture or gender-based violence. In a general population of traumatized refugees, the types of intervention must be tailored to the severity of the illness. Research studies unfortunately have failed to indicate the type of therapy needed to address the higher levels of the hierarchy (Tol et al., 2011). Most important, depending on the severity of mental illness, all members of the population may not need an intensive therapy. Identifying those in need of specific mental health interventions, including complementary therapies, has not been determined. There is an urgent need to establish these criteria for specific mental health treatments.

## HEART: COMBINING THE H-5 MODEL AND MASLOW'S HIERARCHY OF NEEDS

Maslow's hierarchy of needs model can be and has been applied to the entire population at risk by the international humanitarian aid community. However, a new approach is needed that combines clinical insights with Maslow's model to produce effective healing of traumatized survivors. This new therapy model is called HEART—*healing environment and restorative therapy* (see Appendix 6.1). Like Maslow's model, HEART applies to the entire refugee population. The HEART model uses the term *restorative*, which means to reestablish health, strength, and a feeling of well-being. All traumatized persons at the field level are found to experience some emotional and physical distress due to their traumatic life situation. According to the new HEART model, the goal of humanitarian aid is to *restore* the traumatized person to *wellness*.

## H-5 MODEL

The H-5 model adds clinical mental health insights to Maslow's model to create the new HEART Model. As noted earlier, the H-5 model is a bottom-up model, in contrast to Maslow's top-down model (Maslow, 1943). The H-5 model attempts to address the urgent need of the millions of people worldwide who are displaced due to war, civil strife, natural disaster, or climate change. The H-5 model privileges the need to focus on the health and mental health problems and treatment of those suffering from traumatic life experiences. In contrast to Maslow's model, the H-5 model focuses on the human experience of traumatized persons. It is a dynamic model in which the five elements are occurring simultaneously and are linked and overlapping. Although each of the five elements are intrinsic to the human healing process, their capacity to aid recovery and return a traumatized person to wellness can be assisted by clinicians and policy makers. The H-5 model will be welded to Maslow's approach to maximize the recovery and restoration of traumatized individuals and communities to a state of wellness.

Maslow's model is a motivation-driven model, which postulated that the needs of individuals are driven within the individuals themselves. Not surprisingly, Maslow derived his theory from the study of healthy and successful people. In contrast, the H-5 model tries to determine the emotional and physical impact of violence on human beings. The H-5 model identifies the emotional, physical, and spiritual forces that are contributing to the suffering of a survivor of violence. The H-5 model does not privilege human self-actualization over and above the restoration of traumatized human being's restoration to wellness and a stage of physical and emotional well-being. These two models, if wedded together, can lead to a powerful, culturally and scientifically new approach to the care of highly traumatized persons and communities. Recently, there have been numerous published presentations of the H-5 model for the care of refugees and other traumatized persons and communities (Mollica et al., 2015; Suárez-Orozco, 2019). The five overlapping areas of the H-5 model are illustrated in Figure 6.2.

The H-5 model is an empirical approach based on the actual impact of traumatic life experiences on the health and mental health of refugee populations. At the core of the H-5 model is the trauma story, described earlier (Mollica, 2006). All five dimensions of the H-5 model are anchored in a common thread to the trauma story—the personal life story and narrative of the survivor of disaster and human violence. Listening to the trauma story is a key component of healing. A brief summary of the five elements follows.

## H-1 Human Rights Violation

All refugees and survivors of mass violence by definition have suffered human rights violations. This includes human-inflicted suffering due to loss of home; physical violence, including gender-based violence and torture; killing of

**FIGURE 6.2. Core Elements of the H-5 Model**

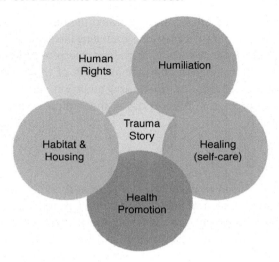

family and community members, spouse, or child; and a host of other often unspeakable atrocities. Acknowledging and responding to human rights violations are essential therapeutic aspects of healing that are associated with social justice.

## H-2 Humiliation

In most refugee situations, the primary goal of violence is the cultural and physical annihilation of the individual, family, and community. Acts of humiliation are major instruments of violence used to achieve this goal. This includes torture, gender based violence, destruction of homes, killing of health care professions and clergy, and the destruction of hospitals, clinics, and places of worship (Mollica, 2000).

## H-3 Healing (Self-Care)

Self-healing is a natural process. As soon as violence strikes, a self-healing process is activated at the physical, mental, and spiritual levels (Mollica, 2006). In many studies of refugees, work, education (for children), spirituality, and altruistic behavior have been associated with increased resiliency to violence and displacement (Mollica et al., 2002). Humanitarian aid must work to build on and support the self-healing process.

## H-4 Health Promotion

Numerous epidemiological studies have revealed the negative health impact of violence on refugees many decades after traumatic life events have occurred (Mollica et al., 2015). Extensive scientific evidence has revealed the long-term impact of violence on the health and mental health of traumatized people, including chronic disease, diabetes, stroke, drug addiction, suicide, and chronic depression. Health promotion is necessary at the earliest stages of a violent experience.

## H-5 Habitat

The word *habitat* is used in place of *housing* to address the total environmental and cultural context of refugees and other traumatized persons. It is derived from the Latin *habitare*, meaning the natural environment of a person or the place where an organism dwells. This element implies a reciprocal and positive relationship between the physical and natural world and the human beings living within that world. Habitat is a major, foundational concept in the HEART model that is fully described by the term *built environments*, discussed shortly. This concept is relevant to refugees because they often face abysmal living conditions many years after they have fled their country of origin, causing social disruption, emotional damage, psychological stress (De Bruijn & Klijn, 2009).

## THE NEW HEART MODEL

The new HEART model began with the research of Mollica and his colleagues in the Cambodian refugee camps in Thailand, called Site 2, in the early 1990s. In these camps, hundreds of thousands of refugees experienced poor housing and extreme deprivation under the international's community's policy of "humane deterrence" for displaced persons (Mollica et al., 1993). The recent Ghata Project (n.d.) in Lebanon for Syrian refugee children demonstrated how young people in primary school can be helped to build a safe and beautiful school environment for themselves. This is despite continuing to live in tent-based refugee housing that harkens back to the Cambodian living experience in Site 2 (Mollica et al., 1993). The HEART healing environment pyramid that integrates Maslow's hierarchy of needs and the H-5 model is illustrated in Figure 6.3. This new pyramid begins with the *built environment* at the foundation level (Parsons & Hartig, 2000; Zborowsky & Kreitzer, 2008). For example, when refugees are fleeing from mass violence, they enter a new

**FIGURE 6.3. The HEART (Healing Environment and Restorative Therapy) Model**

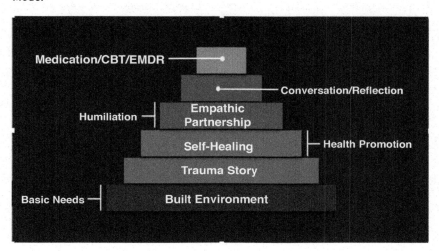

*Note.* CBT = cognitive behavior therapy; EMDR = eye-movement desensitization and reprocessing.

*habitat* for food, water, shelter, and safety and protection. International care-takers have done an excellent job providing these security measures. But here problems arise: The housing structures of humanitarian aid have not advanced over the past 50 years. In the HEART pyramid, the *built environments* are the actual material housing structures that provide a safe and secure retreat to the refugees from violence and disease in the emergency phase and beyond (Ulrich, 1991; van den Berg et al., 2003). Restoration of wellness needs to occur the moment the humanitarian aid worker meets a traumatized person and community. A small number of innovative and concerned architects have tackled this problem by designing and building refugee homes and schools that (a) are inexpensive; (b) use easily available recyclable materials; (c) can be easily built by refugees themselves, including school-age children; (d) can be transported home upon repatriation; (e) use plants, animals, and local arts to create a beautiful living and educational environment; and (f) are cheaper than standard UN tents. In addition, solar power can be added to provide low-cost energy for heating and lighting. Lighting is especially needed to prevent the ongoing sexual violence that is rampant in refugee camps worldwide (UNHCR, 2017).

The four basic principles of the *built environments*—the foundation of HEART—are illustrated in Figure 6.4.

**FIGURE 6.4. The Built Environment**

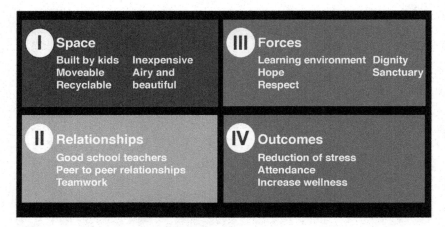

Principle 1: *Space* is the actual physical space itself. Space provides the living rooms where all human activities occur. It can be an overcrowded tent or a culturally beautiful environment, like those that have been pioneered in Lebanon and Sudan. The quality and aesthetics of the space provide the promise and opportunity of recovery. The health benefits of the presence of plants and animals have been well-established in assisting human beings in recovering from physical and emotional distress and illness (Ulrich, 1999; Zborowsky & Kreitzer, 2008). After the Italian earthquake devastated central Italy, many people refused to leave their animals because they were "family." Syrian refugees spent their precious money to have songbirds live with them in their refugee-camp homes. Lebanese architects have planted vegetables and fruits, including tomatoes and grapes, and often beautiful plants in Palestinian refugee camps in every available pot and abandoned sink they could find, creating a virtual garden of beauty on every corner and street. In most refugee scenarios, refugees can design and build their own spaces for living, school, and recreation.

Principle 2: *Relationships* refers to the reality that space relates to the quality and condition of relationships. An overcrowded tent where adults and children have to sleep on top of each other will foster one type of family life. A spacious school built by refugee kids will foster a different quality of education than a tent school. Humanitarian relief agencies have done a poor job of defining the quality of human relationships they want to foster in the refugee camps they have wanted.

Principle 3: *Forces* defines the physical, spiritual, and psychosocial forces that promote, sustain, and nurture traumatized persons, families, and communities. For example, in a refugee camp, a well-built marketplace facilitates communication, sharing, and support among the shoppers. A well-designed school creates feelings of safety and security that promotes education and the opportunity for sacred and religious spaces in the home and the community creates opportunity for spiritual forces that includes prayer, reflection, and meditation.

Principle 4: *Outcomes* defines the evaluation work that needs to occur to monitor over time whether the desired outcomes of the HEART model are being achieved. The health and mental health impact of the built environment needs to be fully evaluated based on these principles.

Unfortunately, the current habitats of refugee camps have not been evaluated in an integrative holistic matter using the principles of the built environment. Almost no research exists on the impact of tent life and temporary housing on health and wellness over time. Yet even without this research, mental health practitioners and aid workers know that these are important conditions shaping the wellness recovery pathways of refugees. In the HEART model, it can be appreciated that the built environment meets the basic physiological, safety, and security needs of refugees combined with the social, relational, and mental health needs. The built environment not only can foster self-actualization but, more important, it becomes the framework in which all the other elements of the healing and recovery can occur. HEART provides the structure, context, and secure base from which all healing and restorative activities can become manifest amid experiences of trauma. When traumatized persons flee their homes, they need to enter an ecologically friendly and safe environment that not only meets their basic needs (physiological and safety needs) but also provides a physically and emotionally secure living space. Typically, however, refugees enter a physical environment of confinement and extreme poverty. The basic "temporary" UN tents set up during the emergency phase often become refugees' permanent living spaces for many years (De Bruijn & Klijn, 2009).

The next levels of HEART, illustrated in Figure 6.3, are briefly described in the following sections.

## Trauma Story

The traumatic life narratives of all survivors are an intimate part of their daily lives. All traumatized persons can benefit by telling their story to an interested and engaged listener (Mollica, 1988). The built environment is a nurturing place that may include not only a home, but also schools, marketplaces, and areas for sport; in such spaces, families and communities can share their stories and support each other. Encouraging storytelling in individual therapy or at community events is an essential aspect of recovery. Traumatized individuals universally feel isolated and need a place and encouragement to engage with others in a meaningful way.

## Self-Healing

Self-healing begins after a human being experiences violence. All structures and individual therapy must acknowledge and build on the self-healing power of the survivor. Research has consistently shown that the four major areas of resiliency related to trauma include social connectedness, altruism, work (education for poor), and spirituality (Mollica, 2006; Mollica et al., 2002). Each of these resiliency supports can be enhanced by the built environment and by projects aimed at education, work, and skilled-based training. In The Liberia Women's Health Project (Mollica, 2017), 15 areas of women's health, including approaches to addressing and improving mental health, were taught successfully to Liberian women who had been affected by civil war, poverty, and the Ebola crisis. These women were able to successfully train hundreds of other Liberian women in their local communities. Overall, the Liberian women revealed a decrease in emotional distress and an increase in wellness and self-efficacy.

## Empathic Partnership

Empathy is an essential element in the healing and recovery process. A major clinical slogan guides clinical care: Healing occurs when two people work together in a shared empathic partnership in a community to create a new worldview (Mollica, 2006). This is a relational model of recovery. Traumatized persons have lost their world and are searching for meaning in their lives. An empathic relationship is a key to helping survivors create a rich and meaningful new life. Through an empathic partnership, the deep wounds of humiliation can be overcome. Out of an empathic partnership, self-actualization can truly blossom. Maslow never discussed the interpersonal relational forces that are necessary for self-actualization and transformation. Unfortunately, humanitarian aid agencies have little understanding of the latter and therefore can neglect implementing policies and projects that are empirically based on the real-life situation of the people they are assisting. This leads to a considerable amount of empathic failure at the policy level.

Empathic policies and therapies maximize the synergy to create positive community outcomes. Paradoxically, Carl Rogers, Maslow's close colleague, realized in his therapy the capacity of human beings to arrive at self-actualization through empathy (Rogers, 1951).

### Conversation and Reflection

Conversation and reflection are opposite sides of the same coin. On the reflective side, complementary therapies such as meditation, yoga, and prayer have been demonstrated to have remarkable benefits for the reduction of suffering in traumatized persons. On the conversation side, not only individual and community storytelling but also everyday talking and listening to others in the marketplace, at places of worship, or on the sports field are essential to meaningful human existence. At this level of the HEART model, meditation and other forms of complementary medicine enter into healing as empathic practices. The place of conversation and in-depth listening with empathy is a crucial element in healing and recovery. Medical historian Stanley Jackson (1992) stated the following:

> Among other things, a healer in a community is commonly a person to whom a sufferer tells things; and out of his or her listening, the healer develops the basis for therapeutic interventions. The psychological healer, in particular, is one who listens in order to learn and understand, and, from the fruits of this listening, he or she develops the basis for reassuring, advising, consoling, comforting, interpreting, explaining, or otherwise intervening. (p. 1623)

Jackson was highlighting the powerful potential of the shared empathic dialogue that leads to recovery in therapy. The HEART model privileges the importance of the built environment creating spaces for reflection (e.g., small prayer and meditation rooms) and conversations (e.g., coffeeshops and private counseling rooms). Jackson (1992) went on to say, "One author [W. Johnson], an authority on communication, has said—'To be human is to speak. To be abundantly human is to speak freely and fully'" (p. 1623). Although Maslow revealed little on how to achieve self-actualization, he would have accepted the idea that a good listener is the best agent for helping one achieve both wellness and transformation (Mollica et al., 2001; Rousseau & Guzder, 2008). At the top of the HEART are individual therapies and other specialized forms of mental health care; the peak of the pyramid is not the pinnacle to be achieved by moving up from each lower layer. Each level builds to the top level where a small number of persons need specialized mental health care, such as medication, NET, or EMDR. These interventions are most useful to those who are severely damaged and cannot fully recover from a more general intervention.

## CONCLUSION

The HEART model integrates the H-5 model and Marlow's hierarchy of needs into a unitary system of care. While each model has related and overlapping goals that include the healing of human suffering and self-actualization, respectively, the HEART model serves to integrate these two goals into a holistic approach of restoration and wellness. In this model, the goals of both healing and self-actualization are privileged as legitimate ends. The latter is captured in the restorative slogan "The same, different, but better." The HEART model uses Marlow's model not only to influence humanitarian aid policies and projects, but also for individual, group, and family therapy. Although deep empathic listening is generic to all good health and mental health care, this might be the first time these general elements of healing have been embodied within a built environment. For the first time, a framework that is both culturally effective and realistic is available for the pursuit of healing and self-actualization.

---

### APPENDIX 6.1

### HEART MODEL: HEALING ENVIRONMENT AND RESTORATIVE THERAPY

A simple rubric to follow in implementing the HEART model. As a policy planner and a healer, you can help restore traumatized persons to wellness, enhance resiliency, and achieve self-actualization.

1. *Assess* the quality of the built environment, including home, school, sports fields, marketplaces, and places of spirituality.
2. *Identity* lack of basic needs: safety, security, food, water sanitation, and lighting.
3. *Obtain* the trauma story, acknowledging past and ongoing human rights violations, ostracism, and bullying.
4. *Promote* self-healing through social connectedness, altruism, work, education, and spirituality.
5. *Reinforce and teach* health promotion concepts and practices.
6. *Listen deeply and establish* empathic partnerships.
7. *Address* humiliating experiences and feelings.
8. *Engage* in therapeutic conversations.
9. *Recommend* through reflection, meditation, prayer, yoga, nature experiences, and reflective writing, and the arts.

10. *Identify and provide* specialized mental health services such as CBT, EMDR, NET, and medication for serious emotional suffering.
11. *Promote* posttraumatic growth and self-actualization at each level of care (1–10 above).
12. *Evaluate and monitor* whether wellness, resiliency, and self-actualization are being achieved.

## REFERENCES

Acarturk, C., Konuk, E., Cetinkaya, M., Senay, I., Sijbrandij, M., Cuijpers, P., & Aker, T. (2015). EMDR for Syrian refugees with posttraumatic stress disorder symptoms: Results of a pilot randomized controlled trial. *European Journal of Psychotraumatology*, 6(1), 27414. https://doi.org/10.3402/ejpt.v6.27414

Acarturk, C., Konuk, E., Cetinkaya, M., Senay, I., Sijbrandij, M., Gulen, B., & Cuijpers, P. (2016). The efficacy of eye movement desensitization and reprocessing for posttraumatic stress disorder and depression among Syrian refugees: Results of a randomized controlled trial. *Psychological Medicine*, 46(12), 2583–2593. https://doi.org/10.1017/S0033291716001070

Agger, I. (2015). Calming the mind: Healing after mass atrocity in Cambodia. *Transcultural Psychiatry*, 52(4), 543–560. https://doi.org/10.1177/1363461514568336

Alpak, G., Unal, A., Bulbul, F., Sagaltici, E., Bez, Y., Altindag, A., Dalkilic, A., & Savas, H. A. (2015). Post-traumatic stress disorder among Syrian refugees in Turkey: A cross-sectional study. *International Journal of Psychiatry in Clinical Practice*, 19(1), 45–50. https://doi.org/10.3109/13651501.2014.961930

Atkinson, J. (2002). *Trauma trails, recreating song lines: The transgenerational effects of trauma in Indigenous Australia.* Spinifex Press.

Buhmann, C. B., Nordentoft, M., Ekstroem, M., Carlsson, J., & Mortensen, E. L. (2016). The effect of flexible cognitive-behavioural therapy and medical treatment, including antidepressants on post-traumatic stress disorder and depression in traumatised refugees: Pragmatic randomised controlled clinical trial. *The British Journal of Psychiatry*, 208(3), 252–259. https://doi.org/10.1192/bjp.bp.114.150961

Buhmann, C. B., Nordentoft, M., Ekstroem, M., Carlsson, J., & Mortensen, E. L. (2018). Long-term treatment effect of trauma-affected refugees with flexible cognitive behavioural therapy and antidepressants. *Psychiatry Research*, 264, 217–223. https://doi.org/10.1016/j.psychres.2018.03.069

Centre for Research on the Epidemiology of Disasters. (2020). *Natural disasters 2019.* https://www.cred.be/publications

Cheung, M. C., AlQarni, N., AlMazrouei, M., Al Muhairi, S., Shakra, M., Mitchell, B., Al Mazrouei, S., & Al Hashimi, S. (2018). The impact of trauma exposure characteristics on post-traumatic stress disorder and psychiatric co-morbidity among Syrian refugees. *Psychiatry Research*, 259, 310–315. https://doi.org/10.1016/j.psychres.2017.10.035

Cramer, H., Anheyer, D., Saha, F. J., & Dobos, G. (2018). Yoga for posttraumatic stress disorder—a systematic review and meta-analysis. *BMC Psychiatry*, 18(1), 72. https://doi.org/10.1186/s12888-018-1650-x

De Bruijn, K. M., & Klijn, F. (2009). Risky places in the Netherlands: A first approximation for floods. *Journal of Flood Risk Management*, 2(1), 58–67.

Engel, G. L. (1968). A life setting conducive to illness: The giving-up–given-up complex. *Annals of Internal Medicine, 69*(2), 293–300. https://doi.org/10.7326/0003-4819-69-2-293

Gallegos, A. M., Crean, H. F., Pigeon, W. R., & Heffner, K. L. (2017). Meditation and yoga for posttraumatic stress disorder: A meta-analytic review of randomized controlled trials. *Clinical Psychology Review, 58*, 115–124. https://doi.org/10.1016/j.cpr.2017.10.004

Garrouste-Orgeas, M., Périer, A., Mouricou, P., Grégoire, C., Bruel, C., Brochon, S., Philippart, F., Max, A., & Misset, B. (2014). Writing in and reading ICU diaries: Qualitative study of families' experience in the ICU. *PLOS ONE, 9*(10), e110146. https://doi.org/10.1371/journal.pone.0110146

Geller, L. (1982). The failure of self-actualization theory: A critique of Carl Rogers and Abraham Maslow. *Journal of Humanistic Psychology, 22*(2), 56–73. https://doi.org/10.1177/0022167882222004

Ghata Project. (n.d.). *Ghata: Bringing education to informal tented settlements.* https://www.aub.edu.lb/ccecs/srrp/Pages/Ghata-Bringing-Education-to-Informal-Tented-Settlements.aspx

Gold, J. M. (2013). Spirituality and self-actualization: Considerations for 21st-century counselors. *The Journal of Humanistic Counseling, 52*(2), 223–234. https://doi.org/10.1002/j.2161-1939.2013.00044.x

Henwood, B. F., Derejko, K. S., Couture, J., & Padgett, D. K. (2015). Maslow and mental health recovery: A comparative study of homeless programs for adults with serious mental illness. *Administration and Policy in Mental Health and Mental Health Services Research, 42*(2), 220–228. https://doi.org/10.1007/s10488-014-0542-8

Houston, T. K., Allison, J. J., Sussman, M., Horn, W., Holt, C. L., Trobaugh, J., Salas, M., Pisu, M., Cuffee, Y. L., Larkin, D., Person, S. D., Barton, B., Kiefe, C. I., & Hullett, S. (2011). Culturally appropriate storytelling to improve blood pressure: A randomized trial. *Annals of Internal Medicine, 154*(2), 77–84. https://doi.org/10.7326/0003-4819-154-2-201101180-00004

Jackson, S. W. (1992). The listening healer in the history of psychological healing. *The American Journal of Psychiatry, 149*(12), 1623–1632. https://doi.org/10.1176/ajp.149.12.1623

Kalmanowitz, D. L., & Ho, R. T. H. (2017). Art therapy and mindfulness with survivors of political violence: A qualitative study. *Psychological Trauma: Theory, Research, Practice, and Policy, 9*(Suppl. 1), 107–113. https://doi.org/10.1037/tra0000174

Kar, N. (2011). Cognitive behavioral therapy for the treatment of post-traumatic stress disorder: A review. *Neuropsychiatric Disease and Treatment, 7*, 167–181. https://doi.org/10.2147/NDT.S10389

Kim, I. (2016). Beyond trauma: Post-resettlement factors and mental health outcomes among Latino and Asian refugees in the United States. *Journal of Immigrant and Minority Health, 18*(4), 740–748. https://doi.org/10.1007/s10903-015-0251-8

Koltko-Rivera, M. E. (2006). Rediscovering the later version of Maslow's hierarchy of needs: Self-transcendence and opportunities for theory, research, and unification. *Review of General Psychology, 10*(4), 302–317. https://doi.org/10.1037/1089-2680.10.4.302

Longacre, M., Silver-Highfield, E., Lama, P., & Grodin, M. (2012). Complementary and alternative medicine in the treatment of refugees and survivors of torture: A review and proposal for action. *Torture, 22*(1), 38–57.

Lonn, M. R., & Dantzler, J. Z. (2017). A practical approach to counseling refugees: Applying Maslow's hierarchy of needs. *Journal of Counselor Practice, 8*(2), 61–82.

Maslow, A. H. (1943). A theory of human motivation. *Psychological Review, 50*(4), 370–396. https://doi.org/10.1037/h0054346

Maslow, A. H. (1954). *Motivation and personality.* Prabhat Prakashan.

Maslow, A. H. (1971). *The farther reaches of human nature.* Arkana/Penguin Books.

Meyerhoff, J., Rohan, K. J., & Fondacaro, K. M. (2018). Suicide and suicide-related behavior among Bhutanese refugees resettled in the United States. *Asian American Journal of Psychology, 9*(4), 270–283. https://doi.org/10.1037/aap0000125

Mitschke, D. B., Praetorius, R. T., Kelly, D. R., Small, E., & Kim, Y. K. (2017). Listening to refugees: How traditional mental health interventions may miss the mark. *International Social Work, 60*(3), 588–600. https://doi.org/10.1177/0020872816648256

Mollica, R. F. (1988). The trauma story: Psychiatric care of refugee survivors of violence and torture. In F. M. Ochberg (Ed.), *Brunner/Mazel psychosocial stress series, No. 11. Post-traumatic therapy and victims of violence* (pp. 295–394).

Mollica, R. F. (2000). Invisible wounds. Waging a new kind of war. *Scientific American, 282*(6), 54–57. https://doi.org/10.1038/scientificamerican0600-54

Mollica, R. F. (2006). *Healing invisible wounds: Paths to hope and recovery in a violent world.* Harcourt, Inc.

Mollica, R. F. (2017). *Liberian Women's Health Promotion manual* [Unpublished manuscript].

Mollica, R. F., Brooks, R. T., Ekblad, S., & McDonald, L. (2015). The new H-5 model of refugee trauma and recovery. In J. Lindert & I. Levav (Eds.), *Violence and mental health.* Springer. https://doi.org/10.1007/978-94-017-8999-8_16

Mollica, R. F., Brooks, R., Tor, S., Lopes-Cardozo, B., & Silove, D. (2014). The enduring mental health impact of mass violence: A community comparison study of Cambodian civilians living in Cambodia and Thailand. *International Journal of Social Psychiatry, 60*(1), 6–20. https://doi.org/10.1177/0020764012471597

Mollica, R. F., Cardozo, B. L., Osofsky, H. J., Raphael, B., Ager, A., & Salama, P. (2004). Mental health in complex emergencies. *The Lancet, 364*(9450), 2058–2067. https://doi.org/10.1016/S0140-6736(04)17519-3

Mollica, R. F., Cui, X., McInnes, K., & Massagli, M. P. (2002). Science-based policy for psychosocial interventions in refugee camps: A Cambodian example. *Journal of Nervous and Mental Disease, 190*(3), 158–166. https://doi.org/10.1097/00005053-200203000-00004

Mollica, R. F., Donelan, K., Tor, S., Lavelle, J., Elias, C., Frankel, M., & Blendon, R. J. (1993). The effect of trauma and confinement on functional health and mental health status of Cambodians living in Thailand–Cambodia border camps. *Journal of the American Medical Association, 270*(5), 581–586. https://doi.org/10.1001/jama.1993.03510050047025

Mollica, R. F., McInnes, K., Sarajlić, N., Lavelle, J., Sarajlić, I., & Massagli, M. P. (1999). Disability associated with psychiatric comorbidity and health status in Bosnian refugees living in Croatia. *Journal of the American Medical Association, 282*(5), 433–439. https://doi.org/10.1001/jama.282.5.433

Mollica, R. F., Sarajlić, N., Chernoff, M., Lavelle, J., Vuković, I. S., & Massagli, M. P. (2001). Longitudinal study of psychiatric symptoms, disability, mortality, and emigration among Bosnian refugees. *Journal of the American Medical Association, 286*(5), 546–554. https://doi.org/10.1001/jama.286.5.546

Morina, N., Akhtar, A., Barth, J., & Schnyder, U. (2018). Psychiatric disorders in refugees and internally displaced persons after forced displacement: A systematic review. *Frontiers in Psychiatry, 9*, 433. https://doi.org/10.3389/fpsyt.2018.00433

Neher, A. (1991). Maslow's theory of motivation: A critique. *Journal of Humanistic Psychology, 31*(3), 89–112. https://doi.org/10.1177/0022167891313010

Neuner, F., Schauer, M., Klaschik, C., Karunakara, U., & Elbert, T. (2004). A comparison of narrative exposure therapy, supportive counseling, and psychoeducation for treating posttraumatic stress disorder in an African refugee settlement. *Journal of Consulting and Clinical Psychology, 72*(4), 579–587. https://doi.org/10.1037/0022-006X.72.4.579

Nickerson, A., & Hinton, D. E. (2011). Anger regulation in traumatized Cambodian refugees: The perspectives of Buddhist monks. *Culture, Medicine and Psychiatry, 35*(3), 396–416. https://doi.org/10.1007/s11013-011-9218-y

Parsons, R. J., & Hartig, T. (2000). Environmental psychophysiology. In J. T. Cacioppo, L. G. Tassinary, & G. G. Berntson (Eds.), *Handbook of psychophysiology* (pp. 815–846). Cambridge University Press. https://doi.org/10.1017/CBO9780511546396.032

Patel, N., Kellezi, B., & Williams, A. C. (2014). Psychological, social and welfare interventions for psychological health and well-being of torture survivors. *Cochrane Database of Systematic Reviews, 2014*(11), CD009317. https://doi.org/10.1002/14651858.CD009317.pub2

Pennebaker, J. W. (1997). *Opening up: The healing power of expressing emotions.* Guilford Press.

Reed, R. V., Fazel, M., Jones, L., Panter-Brick, C., & Stein, A. (2012). Mental health of displaced and refugee children resettled in low-income and middle-income countries: Risk and protective factors. *The Lancet, 379*(9812), 250–265. https://doi.org/10.1016/S0140-6736(11)60050-0

Rees, B., Travis, F., Shapiro, D., & Chant, R. (2014). Significant reductions in posttraumatic stress symptoms in Congolese refugees within 10 days of transcendental meditation practice. *Journal of Traumatic Stress, 27*(1), 112–115. https://doi.org/10.1002/jts.21883

Refugee Health Technical Assistance Center. (2011). *Suicide.* https://refugeehealthta.org/physical-mental-health/mental-health/suicide

Robjant, K., & Fazel, M. (2010). The emerging evidence for narrative exposure therapy: A review. *Clinical Psychology Review, 30*(8), 1030–1039. https://doi.org/10.1016/j.cpr.2010.07.004

Rogers, C. R. (1951). *Client-centered therapy: Its current practice, implications and theory.* Houghton Mifflin.

Rousseau, C., & Guzder, J. (2008). School-based prevention programs for refugee children. *Child and Adolescent Psychiatric Clinics of North America, 17*(3), 533–549, viii. https://doi.org/10.1016/j.chc.2008.02.002

Satcher, D. (2001). *Mental health: Culture, race, and ethnicity. A supplement to Mental Health: A Report of the Surgeon General.* Substance Abuse and Mental Health Services Administration.

Schoenbaum, M., Butler, B., Kataoka, S., Norquist, G., Springgate, B., Sullivan, G., Duan, N., Kessler, R. C., & Wells, K. (2009). Promoting mental health recovery after hurricanes Katrina and Rita: What can be done at what cost. *Archives of General Psychiatry, 66*(8), 906–914. https://doi.org/10.1001/archgenpsychiatry.2009.77

Sijbrandij, M., Acarturk, C., Bird, M., Bryant, R. A., Burchert, S., Carswell, K., de Jong, J., Dinesen, C., Dawson, K. S., El Chammay, R., van Ittersum, L., Jordans, M., Knaevelsrud, C., McDaid, D., Miller, K., Morina, N., La Park, A., Roberts, B., van Son, Y., . . . van Ittersum, L. (2017). Strengthening mental health care systems for Syrian refugees in Europe and the Middle East: Integrating scalable psychological interventions in eight countries. *European Journal of Psychotraumatology*, *8*(Suppl. 2), 1388102.

Slobodin, O., & de Jong, J. T. (2015). Mental health interventions for traumatized asylum seekers and refugees: What do we know about their efficacy? *International Journal of Social Psychiatry*, *61*(1), 17–26. https://doi.org/10.1177/0020764014535752

Steel, Z., Chey, T., Silove, D., Marnane, C., Bryant, R. A., & van Ommeren, M. (2009). Association of torture and other potentially traumatic events with mental health outcomes among populations exposed to mass conflict and displacement: A systematic review and meta-analysis. *JAMA*, *302*(5), 537–549. https://doi.org/10.1001/jama.2009.1132

Suárez-Orozco, M. (Ed.). (2019). *Humanitarianism and mass migration: Confronting the world crisis*. University of California Press. https://doi.org/10.1525/9780520969629

Telles, S., Singh, N., Joshi, M., & Balkrishna, A. (2010). Post traumatic stress symptoms and heart rate variability in Bihar flood survivors following yoga: A randomized controlled study. *BMC Psychiatry*, *10*(1), 18. https://doi.org/10.1186/1471-244X-10-18

ter Heide, F. J., Mooren, T. M., & Kleber, R. J. (2016). Complex PTSD and phased treatment in refugees: A debate piece. *European Journal of Psychotraumatology*, *7*(1), 28687. https://doi.org/10.3402/ejpt.v7.28687

Thompson, C. T., Vidgen, A., & Roberts, N. P. (2018). Psychological interventions for post-traumatic stress disorder in refugees and asylum seekers: A systematic review and meta-analysis. *Clinical Psychology Review*, *63*, 66–79. https://doi.org/10.1016/j.cpr.2018.06.006

Tol, W. A., Barbui, C., Galappatti, A., Silove, D., Betancourt, T. S., Souza, R., Golaz, A., & van Ommeren, M. (2011). Mental health and psychosocial support in humanitarian settings: Linking practice and research. *The Lancet*, *378*(9802), 1581–1591. https://doi.org/10.1016/S0140-6736(11)61094-5

Tribe, R. H., Sendt, K. V., & Tracy, D. K. (2019). A systematic review of psychosocial interventions for adult refugees and asylum seekers. *Journal of Mental Health (Abingdon, England)*, *28*(6), 662–676. https://doi.org/10.1080/09638237.2017.1322182

Ulrich, R. S. (1991). Effects of interior design on wellness: Theory and recent scientific research. *Journal of Health Care Interior Design*, *3*(1), 97–109.

Ulrich, R. S. (1999). Effects of gardens on health outcomes: Theory and research. In C. C. Marcus & M. Barnes (Eds.), *Healing gardens: Therapeutic benefits and design recommendations* (pp. 27–86). Wiley.

United Nations High Commissioner for Refugees. (2017). *How night-time street lighting affects refugee communities*. https://www.unhcr.org/5b3cb5bb7.pdf

United Nations High Commissioner for Refugees. (2019). *Figures at a glance*. https://www.unhcr.org/en-us/figures-at-a-glance.html

van den Berg, A. E., Koole, S. L., & van der Wulp, N. Y. (2003). Environmental preference and restoration: (How) are they related? *Journal of Environmental Psychology*, *23*(2), 135–146. https://doi.org/10.1016/S0272-4944(02)00111-1

van der Veer, G. (1992). *Counselling and therapy with refugees: Psychological problems of victims of war, torture and repression.* John Wiley & Sons.

The World Bank. (2016). *Psychosocial support in fragile and conflict-affected settings.* https://www.worldbank.org/en/topic/fragilityconflictviolence/brief/psychosocial-support-in-fragile-and-conflict-affected-settings.

World Health Organization. (2020). *Depression.* https://www.who.int/news-room/fact-sheets/detail/depression

Yurtsever, A., Konuk, E., Akyüz, T., Zat, Z., Tükel, F., Çetinkaya, M., Savran, C., & Shapiro, E. (2018). An eye movement desensitization and reprocessing (EMDR) group intervention for Syrian refugees with post-traumatic stress symptoms: Results of a randomized controlled trial. *Frontiers in Psychology, 9,* 493. https://doi.org/10.3389/fpsyg.2018.00493

Zborowsky, T., & Kreitzer, M. J. (2008). Creating optimal healing environments in a health care setting. *Minnesota Medicine, 91*(3), 35–38.

# 7

# SCREENING AND ASSESSING REFUGEE MENTAL HEALTH NEEDS

ALVIN KUOWEI TAY AND DERRICK SILOVE

Mental health professionals and trainees from a range of service settings, including clinics, hospitals, and nonprofit organizations, are increasingly required to assess and treat persons of refugee background. There is a pressing need to train mental health professionals to be conversant in key issues and challenges when assessing the wide array of mental health and psychosocial needs among refugees, including premigration history and stressors and postmigration living difficulties, mental health, and psychosocial needs. Refugees typically present with a complex history of persecution, migration, displacement, and resettlement. Investigating these key issues and integrating the findings in the process of assessment and case formulation may appear to be a daunting task for mental health practitioners, particularly those with limited exposure to and familiarity with refugee mental health.

This chapter summarizes the contemporary research on refugee mental health, focusing on the key domains of inquiry of relevance to refugee mental health assessments. The objective is to assist clinicians and service providers in formulating an evidence-based approach to undertaking a comprehensive assessment of the precipitating, perpetuating, and maintaining factors underlying refugee psychopathology. In particular, the key areas of assessment include eliciting a trauma history, assessing postmigration stressors and living

https://doi.org/10.1037/0000226-007
*Refugee Mental Health*, J. D. Aten and J. Hwang (Editors)

difficulties, assessing the adaptive stress arising from the overall psychosocial context, and assessing comorbid mental disorders in refugees. This chapter is intended to provide practical steps and recommendations to assist mental health practitioners in understanding the key issues of relevance to refugees and how standardized assessment tools can be applied through a culturally sensitive systematic inquiry into these issues within the context of basic principles of clinical practice.

## AN OVERVIEW OF MODERN REFUGEE MENTAL HEALTH RESEARCH

The history of refugee mental health research commenced in earnest in the 1980s with a series of systematic epidemiological investigations of survivors of mass persecution and genocide under repressive regimes (e.g., the Khmer Rouge of Cambodia, the Pinochet regime in Chile). Before this period, there were only a few systematic studies regarding the mental health of refugees (Kinzie & Fleck, 1987), the main body of earlier studies being based on either clinic-based reports and case histories or on observations of clinicians working with survivors of World War II concentration camps. The early clinical and epidemiological research until the 1990s conducted amongst refugees tended to focus on identifying common forms of mental distress, most prominently symptoms of depression and anxiety. The formulation of posttraumatic stress disorder (PTSD) as a mental disorder in the 1980s and its inclusion in the third edition of the American Psychiatric Association's (1980) *Diagnostic and Statistical Manual of Mental Disorders (DSM-III)*, led to a burgeoning of research in general psychiatric traumatology that greatly influenced the refugee field. In parallel, a major advance was the development and psychometric testing of measures of trauma and PTSD, particularly the Harvard Trauma Questionnaire (HTQ), which, while drawing on the *DSM* symptom profile of PTSD, was adapted to the language and culture of major refugee groups of the time from Southeast Asia (Vietnamese, Cambodians, Laotians; Mollica et al., 1992). The instrument, now updated to be consistent with the formulation of PTSD in the fifth edition of the *DSM (DSM-5*; American Psychiatric Association, 2013), has remained the most widely applied measure in the field, used in both community and clinical settings (Berthold et al., 2018).

### Assessing Exposure to Traumatic Events

Refugees typically present with a long history of trauma and abuse, including gross human rights violations, torture, witnessing murders and atrocities, interpersonal abuse, and sexual and gender-based violence. Ethical concerns have been raised about the risk of retraumatizing asylum seekers and refugees, particularly during the process of obtaining testimonies involving direct exposure to traumatic experiences for purposes of asylum application (Meffert et al., 2010). Eliciting a trauma history requires a careful and sensitive approach that minimizes the risk of retraumatization, a task typically undertaken by trained clinicians or therapists within the strict confines of privacy and confidentiality (Mollica, 2001). Brief trauma inventories (e.g., the HTQ) comprising the commonly experienced or witnessed trauma events can be applied to screen for trauma histories in a way that minimizes distress and potential risk of traumatization. Female (and male) refugee survivors of gender-based violence should be assessed by trained clinicians or practitioners who are attuned to the cultural issues and challenges associated with people exposed to sexual trauma. Furthermore, a multisectoral, multidisciplinary approach involving specialist agencies or service providers is needed to address the gender-specific needs and safety issues arising from the assessment within a collaborative care model (Mollica & Son, 1989).

## Postmigration Stressors and Living Difficulties

A further development was the recognition that although premigration trauma exposure was a major source of ongoing mental distress among refugees, postmigration living difficulties added to the risk of mental health problems (Schweitzer et al., 2006; Steel et al., 2011). Examples of this research included a series of epidemiological surveys conducted to assess trauma exposure, acculturative stress, ongoing deprivations, and the living conditions of Southeast Asian refugees resettled in Australia (Silove et al., 1998; Sinnerbrink et al., 1997). Further studies were then undertaken with asylum seekers from Sri Lanka, Iraq, and Afghanistan, in that setting using the newly developed Post-Migration Living Difficulty Checklist (PMLD), which covered a range of issues and challenges, including acculturation difficulties, discrimination, socioeconomic hardships, worries about the safety of family members left behind, being unable to return to the homeland in times of emergency, lack of legal rights and permission to undertake employment, detention, limited familiarity with immigration procedures, insecurity, and fear of repatriation (Silove et al., 2007; Steel et al., 1999). The PMLD remains a widely used index for assessing an array of postmigration issues in asylum seekers and resettled refugees (Jakobsen et al., 2011). In a principal component analysis of PMLD items on Tamil asylum seekers undergoing refugee status determination in Australia (Steel et al., 1999), the five dimensions identified include (a) access to health care (poor access to emergency medical care),

(b) residency determination (delays in processing visa application, conflict with immigration officials), (c) perceived threat to family members (worries about family left behind, separation from family), (d) acculturation or adaptation difficulties (communication difficulties, not being able to find work), and (e) loss of culture and support (loneliness and boredom, isolation).

## The Broader Psychosocial Environment

There is now general consensus in the field that the psychosocial environment plays a critical role in the adaptation and recovery from traumatic stress in refugees. Several contemporary ecological theories of posttraumatic adaptation have been subject to varying degrees of empirical investigation in the refugee field. One of the most widely studied models is Hobfoll's conservation of resources theory, which postulates that extensive losses (interpersonal, material, existential) overwhelm survivors' innate resources and their capacities to cope with the consequences and restore their mental health (Hobfoll, 1989; Hobfoll et al., 2007). Miller and Rasmussen (2010) posited that apart from traumatic events, daily stressors play a pathogenic role in precipitating and perpetuating mental distress in refugees. Examples of daily stressors include insecure environments, a lack of access to basic survival needs (e.g., food, water, shelter, health care), limited employment opportunities, a lack of traditional social support systems, and isolation.

The adaptation and development after persecution and trauma (ADAPT) model postulates that five psychosocial systems that support stable societies are fundamentally disrupted among refugee populations, including systems that support safety and security, justice, identities and roles, and a sense of meaning, whether political, social, cultural, ideological, or religious (Silove, 2013; Tay & Silove, 2017). The five domains reflect the cumulative experiences of refugees as they progress through the continuum of social disruptions spanning the phases of conflict, displacement, and resettlement. In contrast, traumatic events and stressors (i.e., postmigration living difficulties) represent discrete and proximate events or conditions that directly affect the individual at the microcosmic level (Tay et al., 2015b).

A key postulate of the ADAPT model is that the extent to which individuals and collectives are able to adapt to discrete events such as traumas and to ongoing conditions of deprivation depends largely on the integrity or disintegration of these fundamental psychosocial foundations of society. Furthermore, the more effectively the ADAPT pillars are restored, the less need there will be for individual-focused treatments for traumatic stress reactions, although a minority will need such interventions. In this way, the model allows for a systematic examination of the transition points leading from normative responses to psychopathology (Silove, 2013). For instance, recurring threats posed by conditions of persecution and insecurity undermine the safety/security pillar, generating adaptive posttraumatic reactions (e.g., hypervigilance, security seeking) that can, under particular circumstances, result in a pathological reaction, that is, PTSD. Similarly, direct exposure to gross human rights violations (e.g., interpersonal trauma, torture, rape) may precipitate and perpetuate feelings of injustice, manifesting as anger, frustration, and a sense of suspicion, which, if sufficiently compounded and not mitigated by corrective experiences such as access to justice, may lead to pathological forms of anger (Rees et al., 2013; Tay et al., 2017).

Although highlighted in theoretical formulations, comparatively less research attention has been given to measuring the longer term adaptive stressors that refugees experience, influences that arise from disruptions to key psychosocial support structures which in stable societies maintain mental health and functioning. Although several past studies have aimed to assess the more general psychosocial needs of postconflict and refugee populations, the measures used (Betancourt et al., 2014; Jordans et al., 2009) tended to be broad based and symptom oriented and assessed nonspecific psychosocial factors that indicated the overall level of threat in the society at the time. The Adaptive Stress Index (ASI) is a new psychosocial assessment tool formulated to assess the universal stressors refugees encounter in adapting to the postmigration environment within the specific context in which they reside (Tay, Rees, et al., 2019b). The ASI, partly validated in epidemiological samples (Tay et al., 2015b) and now being tested in ongoing psychotherapy trials of refugee groups (including the West Papuan, Burmese ethnic, and Rohingya refugees), may prove to be a culturally sensitive, contextually relevant measure of adaptive stressors universally experienced by refugees. Importantly, there is now a well-established literature outlining a clear mixed-method procedure for adapting the ASI, as well as other psychometric tools to each culture and context (Tay, Rees, et al., 2019b). For example, confirmatory factor analyses followed by item response theory modeling produced a refined and abbreviated set of 25 ADAPT-specific items. The approach undertaken to develop, adapt, and test the ASI is unique in that it applies a universal model—the ADAPT theory—to the specificities of the culture and context (Tay, Rees, et al., 2019b).

## Complexities in the Psychiatric Presentations of Refugees

Although contemporary research now supports a complex interplay among trauma exposure, postmigration living difficulties, and long-term psychosocial or adaptive stressors, accumulating evidence suggests that these factors play a contributing and perpetuating role in a wide range of psychological comorbidity beyond the commonly studies categories of PTSD and depression.

Meta-analyses and systematic reviews of the existing epidemiological studies in the field estimate that a minimum of 15% of refugees experience PTSD or depression, or both disorders (Charlson et al., 2016; Steel et al., 2009). In relation to PTSD, the prevalence is 10-fold higher in war-affected populations than populations not exposed to mass trauma or displacement (Creamer et al., 2001; Kessler et al., 1995; Steel et al., 2009). Nevertheless, PTSD is frequently comorbid with other diagnoses (Palic & Elklit, 2011) such as depression (Steel et al., 2009), anxiety (including the adult form of separation anxiety disorder; Silove et al., 2010; Tay et al., 2015c; Tay, Rees, Kareth, & Silove, 2016), prolonged or complicated bereavement (Boehnlein, 1987; Momartin et al., 2004; Nickerson et al., 2011; Tay, Rees, Chen et al., 2016), explosive forms of anger (including intermittent explosive disorder; Oruc et al., 2008; Rees & Silove, 2011; Rees et al., 2013; Tay et al., 2015a), somatic symptom disorder (Lin et al., 1985; Van Ommeren et al., 2002; Westermeyer et al., 1989), psychotic symptoms (Nygaard et al., 2017; Soosay et al., 2012), and, in some instances, drug and alcohol abuse (Ezard et al., 2011). These observations suggest that a broader approach is needed when assessing the mental health needs of refugees, one that extends beyond the commonly studied categories, such as PTSD and depression. In recent years, there has been growing consensus in the field that the scope of mental health epidemiology should be broadened to include all other relevant categories (Silove, Ventevogel, et al., 2017). At the same time however, the task of assessing for all possible comorbid disorders introduces a degree of diagnostic complexity and poses undue burden on refugees, particularly in a clinical context. Thus, for practical purposes, it is important for clinicians to be familiar, at minimum, with the key relevant categories—PTSD, complex PTSD (CPTSD), complicated bereavement, and explosive anger—conditions that are widely recorded in refugees. The following section focuses on these key mental health issues.

## Key Mental Health Issues in Refugees

### Posttraumatic Stress Disorder and Complex PTSD

PTSD remains the most widely studied disorder in refugees. Early observations among survivors of concentration camps and prisoners of war during World War II first described the core symptoms of posttraumatic stress, spanning somatic, cognitive, and affective disturbances (Eitinger, 1980). Although the introduction of PTSD in the *DSM-III* represents a turning point in the field (American Psychiatric Association, 1980), many critics at the time expressed concerns about extending the diagnosis to survivors of prolonged interpersonal abuse who commonly exhibited a symptom constellation (e.g., dissociation, somatization, affective dysregulation, distorted sense of self) not included in the classic definition of PTSD (Herman, 1992). Several attempts have been made to achieve consensus on a formal diagnosis of a complex form of PTSD. The category of Enduring Personality Change After Catastrophic Experiences was adopted by the *International Classification of Diseases* (10th revision [*ICD-10*]; World Health Organization [WHO], 2010) but received little clinical or research attention (Beltran et al., 2009, 2011). In the United States, the category of Disorder of Extreme Stress Not Otherwise Specified was proposed but omitted from the final draft of *DSM-IV* (van der Kolk et al., 1996) after field trials failed to support its validity. For the first time, the *ICD-11* adopted a category of complex PTSD (CPTSD) defined by, in addition to the classic hallmarks (i.e., reexperiencing, avoidance, hyperarousal) of PTSD, three additional domains: emotional dysregulation, interpersonal difficulties, and negative self-concept, collectively referred to as a disturbance of self-organization (Maercker et al., 2013; WHO, 2018a). Preliminary research in the refugee field has provided some support for the six-factor structure of CPTSD (Silove, Tay, Kareth, et al., 2017; Tay et al., 2015d, 2018). Importantly, one study indicated that only a small percentage of refugees manifested PTSD alone—that is, without the additional elements of CPTSD (Silove, Tay, Kareth, et al., 2017; Tay, Rees, Chen, et al., 2016). Past studies show that CPTSD is strongly associated with high levels of exposure to human rights abuses and results in severe impairment in functioning (Silove et al., 2018). Together, these findings raise important implications for refugee mental health assessment, and further investigation into the extensive adaptive difficulties incorporated in the diagnosis of CPTSD is warranted in refugees exposed to complex forms of interpersonal abuse (e.g., torture, childhood adversities, sexual violence, gender-based and intimate partner violence; Silove et al., 2018).

**Complicated Bereavement**
An important yet understudied condition in refugees is complicated bereavement, or prolonged grief. There has been a long period of controversy about medicalizing grief reactions, particularly in traditional societies where the process of grief can be prolonged and complicated and does not necessarily conform to a universal linear trajectory. Increasingly however, there is a body of research conducted with refugees that has identified a subpopulation that

exhibits chronic symptoms of grief after traumatic losses, resulting in extensive impairment of their functioning and mental health (Momartin et al., 2004; Tay, Rees, Chen, et al., 2016; Tay, Rees, et al., 2019a). In contemporary times, there has been growing agreement on the nosology of complicated bereavement, reflected in the inclusion of a category of complicated bereavement in the *DSM-5* (American Psychiatric Association, 2013) and a diagnosis of prolonged grief disorder in the *ICD-11* classifications (Maercker et al., 2013; WHO, 2018b), respectively. The changes to the classification systems were supported by an accumulative body of evidence from both epidemiological and clinical studies. For example, a recent meta-analysis of 14 studies among bereaved adults from high-income countries recorded a pooled prevalence of prolonged grief disorder of 9.8% (Lundorff et al., 2017). Several confirmatory factor analyses of grief symptoms have identified a two-factor structure comprising separation distress (yearning, searching, and loneliness) and traumatic or emotional distress (numbness, disbelief, distrust, anger, emptiness, and sense of futility about the future; Tay, Rees, Chen, et al., 2016). These studies also demonstrated that complicated grief is distinguishable from symptom constellations of depression and anxiety (Boelen et al., 2010; Morina et al., 2011; Tay, Rees, et al., 2019a). Other studies, however, have revealed a diversity of symptoms comprising the emotional distress domain, including numbness, feeling stunned, emptiness, mistrust, bitterness over the loss, difficulty accepting the loss, identity confusion, avoidance, and difficulty moving on with life (Shear et al., 2011). Two recent confirmatory factor analyses of *DSM-5*–consistent complicated bereavement symptoms conducted on two separate samples of West Papuan refugees found two analogous six-factor models of complicated bereavement comprising dimensions of anger/negative appraisal, avoidance/giving up, estrangement from others, and confusion and diminished identity (Tay, Mohsin, et al., 2019; Tay, Rees, Chen, et al., 2016). In both instances, although the symptoms of complicated bereavement reported by the refugees appear to be consistent with that of *DSM-5*, additional culturally specific features were accentuated among West Papuans, including anger/negative appraisal, behavioral changes, estrangement, and identity confusion. These findings suggest that culture and exposure to persecution and displacement may shape the content and configuration of the complicated bereavement reaction, an issue that requires recognition in international classification systems and clinical practice.

From a clinical perspective, many refugees are likely to be exposed to extensive traumatic losses, including the death of family members or loved ones arising from murder, starvation, disease, disappearances, and forced separations. Furthermore, research shows that there may be a close nexus between traumatic losses and a sense of identity confusion such that feelings of alienation, isolation, and identity confusion may be intensified in refugees who belong to collective cultures in which personal identity is strongly bound up with the sense of belonging to the ancestral land, the family, and wider kinship groups. For many resettled refugees, it is plausible that the combination of past losses compounded by the stress of confronting the myriad challenges that occur in the postmigration environment may contribute to increased vulnerability to pathological grief. Finally, research with refugees shows that anger and mistrust may feature in the presentation of complicated bereavement after traumatic losses (Rees et al., 2017; Silove, Tay, Steel, et al., 2017; Tay, Rees, Chen, et al., 2016). It is therefore important that clinicians screen for symptoms of complicated bereavement and investigate these interrelated issues in the process of case formulation.

**Explosive Anger**
There has been a large body of research on anger undertaken with clinical and nonclinical populations exposed to persecution, warfare, and other forms of psychological trauma (DiGiuseppe & Tafrate, 2006; Hawkins & Cougle, 2011). Previous studies conducted with combat veterans in the United States and Israel supported a strong link between traumatic exposure and explosive anger manifesting in loss of control, verbal or physical aggression (or both), interpersonal conflict, and functional impairment (Jakupcak & Tull, 2005; Lavi & Solomon, 2005). Clinic studies undertaken with trauma survivors from high-income countries indicate that explosive anger is frequently accompanied by depression and anxiety (Bryan et al., 2016; de Azevedo et al., 2010). With the exception of several investigations with refugees resettled in high-income countries (Hinton et al., 2003), there is relatively less focus on explosive anger in research in the refugee field. For example, culturally distinct idioms of distress have been described among Southeast Asian refugees attending a clinic in the United States (Hinton & Lewis-Fernández, 2010) and West Papuan refugees relocated to Australia (Rees & Silove, 2011). A series of epidemiological and clinical investigations conducted in postconflict Timor-Leste identified a high prevalence of explosive anger related to a combination of a persisting sense of injustice, political instability, and conditions of deprivation that corresponded broadly to the key epochs of occupation, persecution, displacement, and stabilization (Brooks et al., 2011).

A key related area of research is the focus on of intermittent explosive disorder (IED). IED is recognized as a psychiatric category in the *DSM-5* under "Disruptive, Impulse-Control, and Conduct Disorders." The disorder is characterized by impulsivity and explosive outbursts of anger (not premeditated) triggered by a disproportionate reaction to real or perceived provocations (American Psychiatric Association, 2013). Epidemiological data from national population studies show that the prevalence of IED tends to vary widely across countries and contexts, and a consistent finding is that exposure to interpersonal trauma is strongly associated with IED across populations (McLaughlin et al., 2012; Yoshimasu et al., 2011).

In a clinic-based treatment study conducted with trauma-affected persons who met criteria for IED ($n = 78$) from Timor-Leste, compared with a wait-list control, there was a marked reduction in IED (from 100% to 0) and symptoms of PTSD and psychological distress from baseline to follow-up among members of the treatment group who received a trauma-focused cognitive behavioral treatment for IED (Hewage et al., 2017). These observations support the cross-cultural validity and coherence of IED in refugee groups and raise important implications for clinical assessments. It is likely that a minority of survivors of trauma with severe explosive anger—in particular, those who exhibit the full constellation of IED—may warrant clinical attention. In general, persons manifesting severe explosive anger may be at risk of perpetuating a cycle of violence caused by legitimate frustrations (e.g., continuing occupation of the homeland, insecure residency) within the home (manifesting as domestic violence), or in the community (as inappropriate aggression toward neighbors or others in response to minor provocations; Rees et al., 2015). From a clinical perspective, the data underscore the need to widen the focus of mental health assessments and interventions for refugees beyond PTSD and depression. Failure to assess for IED symptoms risks overlooking a key reaction pattern of anger and aggression that may have adverse, far-reaching consequences on not only the individual but the family and the community as a whole.

### Cultural Models of Mental Distress and International Psychiatric Nosologies

Despite the acceleration of research in global mental health, for many resettled refugees, the notion of distress and healing is deeply rooted in their language, history, culture, traditions, and worldviews. Broadly, there is a lack of knowledge or familiarity with Western notions of trauma and counseling among refugees, and distress frequently manifests in somatic complaints, the source of which is attributed to preternatural forces. Furthermore, the monothetic biomedical models of psychiatry generally do not conform to the concepts and understanding of psychological problems in refugees (Good, 1996; Lewis-Fernández & Kleinman, 1995). In many traditional societies, there are often no clearly demarcated boundaries between the body and mind, and that there is no equivalence between the symptoms defined in the diagnostic systems (e.g., *DSM-5, ICD-11*) and the concepts of, for example, depression, PTSD, and anxiety disorders. Many previous studies conducted with refugees in clinical and community settings have identified culturally salient idioms of distress (Hinton & Lewis-Fernández, 2010). For many refugee groups, there are no recognized lexicons for terms that are equivalent to the *DSM-5* definitions of depression or PTSD.

Taken together, the research suggests at least three models of conceptualizing mental disorders in refugees. The first is a multi-comorbidity model in which common mental disorders (e.g., mood, anxiety, trauma-related, and somatic disorders) overlap with each another to a substantial degree that are not accounted for by any theoretical models per se. A second possibility is an idiographic model characterized by differing patterns of experiences that shape specific symptom outcomes that cross conventional categorical boundaries in an experientially meaningful manner, an idiographic perspective akin to the approach adopted by the RDoC (Research Domain Criteria) initiative in conceptualizing mental disorders (Akram & Giordano, 2017). For example, among West Papuan refugees, *sakit hati* (sick heart), an indigenously recognized term, refers to overwhelming feelings of resentment and injustice associated with persecution of families and communities in the homeland, manifesting as symptoms of withdrawal, brooding, distress, hostility, and angry outbursts (Rees & Silove, 2011). The convergence between the collective suffering of the population as a consequence of long-standing political persecution and the response pattern of individual's overwhelmed by these events is widely recognized within the community. A third possibility is a hierarchical/gradation model in which there is a stepwise increase in risk to mental disorders with moderate levels of exposure to trauma and stressors leading to CMDs and higher levels leading to a complex symptom constellation including complex PTSD (Silove et al., 2018). Further research is needed, however, to understand how and to what extent cultural models of distress overlaps with Western nosologies in influencing the form and expression of mental disorders.

## TOWARD AN EVIDENCE-BASED MULTILEVEL APPROACH TO REFUGEE MENTAL HEALTH ASSESSMENT

From a clinical perspective, the scope of refugee mental health assessment should be expanded to encompass the key issues related to refugee mental health outlined earlier. At the same time, however, a pragmatic approach is needed to balance efforts to conduct a comprehensive assessment of these interrelated issues with established principles of clinical practice in mental health. For example, a semistructured interview could be conducted to assess the key domains of inquiry outlined in this book—trauma history, postmigration stressors, the psychosocial context, and psychological comorbidity—supplemented by standardized international measures of trauma exposure, postmigration stress, adaptive stress, and common mental disorders adapted and tested in refugee populations from diverse backgrounds (see the case vignette that follows). The research described in this chapter presents a systematic, multilevel procedure for adapting and testing these assessment tools that can be applied with appropriate modifications for use in a clinical context.

For example, the HTQ for *DSM-5* (HTQ-5; Berthold et al., 2018) and its companion measure the Hopkins Symptom Checklist (HSCL-25; Mollica et al., 1996) can be used to assess exposure to traumatic events, PTSD, and depression. The symptom measures can be supplemented with the other relevant modules of the Refugee Mental Health Assessment Package (RMHAP; Tay, Rees, Chen, Kareth, Mohsin, et al., 2015) to assess other relevant categories for example, complicated bereavement and explosive anger. The PMLD can be used to assess the common postmigration stressors confronted by refugees. The ASI (Tay, Rees, et al., 2019b) may assist in measuring the longer term adaptive stressors arising from disruptions to key psychosocial support structures that refugees experience—that is, systems that support safety and security, attachment, access to justice, roles and identities, and existential meaning.

In relation to assessing psychological comorbidity, a more flexible approach may assist clinicians in defining culture-specific symptom constellations that extend beyond rigid diagnostic boundaries and correspond to specific trajectories of trauma and adversity experienced by refugees. When assessing comorbidity in this population, the three possible conceptual models of refugee psychotypology outlined in this chapter may assist clinicians in clarifying the complex relationships among the antecedents, perpetuating and maintaining factors, and the meaning underlying the presenting symptom constellations. For example, a refugee presented with chronic symptoms of grief (manifesting, for example, in preoccupations with and ruminations about the deceased, anger and bitterness, interpersonal difficulties, hopelessness, confusion, and loss of purpose and direction) with a background of extensive traumatic losses (arising from atrocities, loss of family, culture, and land) may experience a persisting sense of injustice, which in turn engenders a form of complicated grief in which extreme anger is a prominent feature (Tay, Rees, Chen, et al., 2016, 2017).

## CASE VIGNETTE

Ahmed is a 52-year-old Rohingya asylum seeker awaiting refugee status determination in Sydney, Australia.[1] A comprehensive mental health, cultural, and psychosocial assessment was requested by a solicitor on behalf of a legal service representing refugees to be submitted to the Refugee/Migration Review Tribunal for consideration for asylum. The 1-hour assessment was conducted by a clinical psychologist via an interpreter, the aim being to document the mental health and psychosocial effects of trauma, persecution, and ongoing stressors. A detailed clinical and psychosocial assessment was conducted to assess the following concerns.

### Current Situation and Support

Ahmed is currently on a temporary visa awaiting refugee status determination and lives in government-supported housing with a friend. He has been receiving ongoing financial support from the government. He has no family in Australia and has had limited involvement in community activities.

The following international measures were applied:

• The HTQ-5 was used to asses trauma exposure and PTSD and the HSCL was used to assess symptoms of depression and anxiety.

• The PMLD was used to assess postmigration stressors.

• The ASI was used to assess adaptive/psychosocial stressors.

• Relevant modules of the Refugee-Mental Health Assessment Package (R-MHAP) were used to assess complicated bereavement and explosive anger following a semistructured interview.

### Developmental and Personal History

Ahmed, a refugee of Rohingya descent, lived in the Rakhine state of Myanmar for the last 4 decades until 2014. He reported an unremarkable childhood during which he had completed primary education at a local Madrassa in the Maungdaw township of Rakhine but was prohibited from pursuing further education given his stateless status as a Rohingya. Ahmed reported a history of systematic discrimination and oppression: His wife was barred from giving

---

[1]This is a fictionalized composite case.

birth at a local hospital because of her ethnicity, and he was not allowed to build a new house on land that belongs to his family. He recalled numerous occasions when he had been stopped at checkpoints by police authorities for no apparent reason. In addition, he was not allowed to form any groups or organizations or to vote.

### Trauma History and Psychosocial Factors

The assessment revealed an extensive history of persecution and human rights violations. According to Ahmed, many military operations had been conducted by the Burmese army since the 1960s, aimed at exterminating the Rohingya people. He recalled several occasions (dating back to 1991) when trucks carrying Burmese soldiers arrived and began rounding up Rohingya from each village in the town and summarily executing them all. According to Ahmed, he saw soldiers burning down villages and throwing infants and children into fires or disemboweling them. He saw gang rapes and murders of Rohingya women and girls. In August 2016, he paid smugglers USD $4,000 to help him travel to Australia. His wife and son later went to Cox's Bazaar, Bangladesh. He recalled that it took 3 weeks to arrive in Australia. During his journey, he reported that he had little food and water and was confined to a small space on a vessel with hundreds of other people. He also saw a few people commit suicide by jumping off the boat.

### Presenting Problems

Ahmed showed ongoing symptoms of depression, including depressed mood, anhedonia (loss of interest in general activities), a strong sense of worthlessness, severe concentration impairment, insomnia, and reduced appetite. He reported that had "lost interest or energy to fish or read," felt "worthless," and that he was "wasting his life" because he could not work legally in Australia while awaiting outcome on his refugee status. Of particular concern was his impaired concentration, which, in combination with insomnia, appeared to play a key role in precipitating and perpetuating his depression.

Notably, Ahmed showed acute symptoms of explosive anger (consistent with the clinical presentation of IED), characterized by extreme anger and aggression, often manifesting in verbal and physical acts of violence. For example, he reported having "lost his temper" several times in public over "small things." Such a disproportionate response to triggering stressors is the hallmark of IED and is common among trauma-affected individuals. It is likely that his IED symptoms began around 2017 and worsened over recent years, as a result of ongoing living difficulties (being unable to work, being separated from his family, living under threats of forced repatriation) as well as the effects of past trauma he had experienced in Myanmar (for which he continued to report symptoms of posttraumatic stress, including nightmares about the trauma, exaggerated startle response, insomnia, and anger outbursts since 1990s).

## Mental State Examination

Ahmed was neatly dressed at the interview. He was eloquent and appeared agitated and angry at times, as evidenced in his pressured speech when discussing his current predicament and issues related to his residency. His affect was flat and his mood labile (alternating between sadness and anger). He expressed a strong sense of worthlessness and hopelessness. There was no evidence of thought disorder. His thoughts were rational. There was no evidence of perceptual abnormalities. He was able to recall details of past events in chronological order with reasonable accuracy. He was able to focus during the interview and oriented to space and time. He had good insight into his condition.

## Findings From Standardized Assessment Tools

Ahmed endorsed the majority of the trauma items on the HTQ, including, for example, torture, physical assault, imprisonment, interpersonal abuse, witnessing murders and atrocities, shortage of shelter and food, and not being able to access medical care in times of emergency. In relation to the PMLD, he endorsed a range of stressors, including fear of repatriation, insecure residency, discrimination, poverty, no access to health care and other basic services, delay in asylum application, and communication difficulties. On the ASI, he reported elevated levels of adaptive stress arising from the safety and security, attachment, justice, and meaning domains. With regard to mental health outcomes, he reported a mean score of 3.2 on the PTSD scale (exceeding the 2.5 clinical threshold) and mean scores of 2.2 and 2.4 on the depression and anxiety subscales of the HSCL, respectively. In addition, according to the R-MHAP modules, he met criteria for depression and IED.

## Formulation and Clinical Impression

Findings from both the semistructured interview and screening tools revealed chronic and ongoing symptoms of depression, explosive anger, and posttraumatic stress (dating back to 2015). Of particular concern is Ahmed's acute anger reactions and the depressive symptoms of anhedonia, worthlessness, and concentration impairment, which, in combination with his posttraumatic stress symptoms, may be related to both his ongoing circumstances and his traumatic history. Ahmed's clinical presentation is consistent with survivors of interpersonal trauma.

The onset of his posttraumatic stress and depressive symptoms appeared to be linked to the traumatic events that occurred in the 1990s. He reported that since then, these symptoms had remained constant at times but had deteriorated over recent months within the context of his forthcoming immigration hearing. His anger reactions appeared to have commenced in recent times, possibly due to extreme frustration concerning the ongoing circumstances and lack of control over his life since his arrival in Australia. Feelings of insecurity associated with his residency status appear to play a key role in contributing to his current mental health problems and impairment.

## Recommendations

Ahmed showed ongoing mental health and functioning impairment with signs of deterioration over recent months within the context of his pending immigration hearing. It is important that Ahmed is able to access culturally appropriate psychological treatment (e.g., cognitive behavior therapy, schema therapy), focusing on his anger reactions, depression, and posttraumatic stress symptoms. An additional challenge in addressing these issues relates to the ongoing conditions of threat and insecurity that Ahmed faces due to his residency status. It is therefore important that these interrelated factors be addressed simultaneously to strengthen his adaptive capacity if he is granted permanent residency in Australia.

## CONCLUSION

This chapter described a science-based, multilevel approach to refugee mental health assessment, drawing on contemporary research with a focus on the key issues and challenges commonly confronted by persons of refugee background. Specifically, we outlined the key domains of inquiry to guide assessment and case formulation, including prior trauma exposure, postmigration stressors or living difficulties, longer term adaptive stress arising from the psychosocial context, and psychological comorbidity. Furthermore, we described the steps involved in eliciting relevant key information in a comprehensive assessment and integrating findings obtained from the assessment into case formulation to inform clinical practice. The case vignette illustrated a systematic process of eliciting key information to reveal a complex interplay among premigration trauma, postmigration stress, the psychosocial context, and mental health issues in refugees who present with a long history of persecution and interpersonal abuses.

## REFERENCES

Akram, F., & Giordano, J. (2017). Research Domain Criteria as psychiatric nosology. *Cambridge Quarterly of Healthcare Ethics, 26*(4), 592–601. https://doi.org/10.1017/S096318011700010X

American Psychiatric Association. (1980). *Diagnostic and statistical manual of mental disorders* (3rd ed.). American Psychiatric Association Press.

American Psychiatric Association. (2013). *Diagnostic and statistical manual of mental disorders* (5th ed.). American Psychiatric Association Press.

Beltran, R. O., Silove, D., & Llewellyn, G. M. (2009). Comparison of *ICD-10* diagnostic guidelines and research criteria for enduring personality change after catastrophic experience. *Psychopathology, 42*(2), 113–118. https://doi.org/10.1159/000204761

Beltran, R. O., Silove, D., & Llewellyn, G. (2011). Enduring personality change after catastrophic experience: A review. In A. M. Columbus (Ed.), *Advances in psychology research* (pp. 75–106). Nova Press.

Berthold, S. M., Mollica, R. F., Silove, D., Tay, A. K., Lavelle, J., & Lindert, J. (2018). The HTQ-5: Revision of the Harvard Trauma Questionnaire for measuring torture, trauma and *DSM-5* PTSD symptoms in refugee populations. *European Journal of Public Health, 29*(3), 468–474.

Betancourt, T. S., Yang, F., Bolton, P., & Normand, S. L. (2014). Developing an African youth psychosocial assessment: An application of item response theory. *International Journal of Methods in Psychiatric Research, 23*(2), 142–160. https://doi.org/10.1002/mpr.1420

Boehnlein, J. K. (1987). Clinical relevance of grief and mourning among Cambodian refugees. *Social Science & Medicine, 25*(7), 765–772. https://doi.org/10.1016/0277-9536(87)90034-7

Boelen, P. A., van de Schoot, R., van den Hout, M. A., de Keijser, J., & van den Bout, J. (2010). Prolonged grief disorder, depression, and posttraumatic stress disorder are distinguishable syndromes. *Journal of Affective Disorders, 125*(1–3), 374–378. https://doi.org/10.1016/j.jad.2010.01.076

Brooks, R., Silove, D., Steel, Z., Steel, C. B., & Rees, S. (2011). Explosive anger in postconflict Timor Leste: Interaction of socio-economic disadvantage and past human rights-related trauma. *Journal of Affective Disorders, 131*(1–3), 268–276. https://doi.org/10.1016/j.jad.2010.12.020

Bryan, C. J., Bryan, A. O., Anestis, M. D., Anestis, J. C., Green, B. A., Etienne, N., Morrow, C. E., & Ray-Sannerud, B. (2016). Measuring moral injury: Psychometric properties of the Moral Injury Events Scale in two military samples. *Assessment, 23*(5), 557–570.

Charlson, F. J., Flaxman, A., Ferrari, A. J., Vos, T., Steel, Z., & Whiteford, H. A. (2016). Post-traumatic stress disorder and major depression in conflict-affected populations: An epidemiological model and predictor analysis. *Global Mental Health (Cambridge, England), 3*, e4. https://doi.org/10.1017/gmh.2015.26

Creamer, M., Burgess, P., & McFarlane, A. C. (2001). Post-traumatic stress disorder: Findings from the Australian National Survey of Mental Health and Wellbeing. *Psychological Medicine*, *31*(7), 1237–1247. https://doi.org/10.1017/S0033291701004287

de Azevedo, F. B., Wang, Y. P., Goulart, A. C., Lotufo, P. A., & Benseñor, I. M. (2010). Application of the Spielberger's State–Trait Anger Expression Inventory in clinical patients. *Arquivos de Neuro-Psiquiatria*, *68*(2), 231–234. https://doi.org/10.1590/S0004-282X2010000200015

DiGiuseppe, R., & Tafrate, R. (2006). Anger treatment for adults: A meta-analytic review. *Clinical Psychology: Science and Practice*, *10*(1), 70–84. https://doi.org/10.1093/clipsy.10.1.70

Eitinger, L. (1980). The concentration camp syndrome and its late sequelae. In J. E. Dimsdale (Ed.), *Survivors, victims, and perpetrators: Essays on the Nazi Holocaust* (pp. 127–162). Hemisphere Publishing Corporation.

Ezard, N., Oppenheimer, E., Burton, A., Schilperoord, M., Macdonald, D., Adelekan, M., Sakarati, A., & van Ommeren, M. (2011). Six rapid assessments of alcohol and other substance use in populations displaced by conflict. *Conflict and Health*, *5*(1), 1. https://doi.org/10.1186/1752-1505-5-1

Good, B. J. (1996). Culture and *DSM-IV*: Diagnosis, knowledge and power. *Culture, Medicine and Psychiatry*, *20*(2), 127–132. https://doi.org/10.1007/BF00115857

Hawkins, K. A., & Cougle, J. R. (2011). Anger problems across the anxiety disorders: Findings from a population-based study. *Depression and Anxiety*, *28*(2), 145–152. https://doi.org/10.1002/da.20764

Herman, J. L. (1992). Complex PTSD: A syndrome in survivors of prolonged and repeated trauma. *Journal of Traumatic Stress*, *5*(3), 377–391. https://doi.org/10.1002/jts.2490050305

Hewage, K., Zachary, S., Mohamed, M., Tay, A. K., De Oliveira, J. C., Da Piedade, M., Natalino, T., & Silove, D. (2017). A wait-list control study of a trauma-focused cognitive behavioural treatment for intermittent explosive disorder (IED) in Timor-Leste. *American Journal of Orthopsychiatry*, *88*(3), 282–294.

Hinton, D., Hsia, C., Um, K., & Otto, M. W. (2003). Anger-associated panic attacks in Cambodian refugees with PTSD; a multiple baseline examination of clinical data. *Behaviour Research and Therapy*, *41*(6), 647–654. https://doi.org/10.1016/S0005-7967(02)00035-9

Hinton, D. E., & Lewis-Fernández, R. (2010). Idioms of distress among trauma survivors: Subtypes and clinical utility. *Culture, Medicine and Psychiatry*, *34*(2), 209–218. https://doi.org/10.1007/s11013-010-9175-x

Hobfoll, S. E. (1989). Conservation of resources. A new attempt at conceptualizing stress. *American Psychologist*, *44*(3), 513–524. https://doi.org/10.1037/0003-066X.44.3.513

Hobfoll, S. E., Watson, P., Bell, C. C., Bryant, R. A., Brymer, M. J., Friedman, M. J., Friedman, M., Gersons, B. P., de Jong, J. T., Layne, C. M., Maguen, S., Neria, Y., Norwood, A. E., Pynoos, R. S., Reissman, D., Ruzek, J. I., Shalev, A. Y., Solomon, Z., Steinberg, A. M., & Ursano, R. J. (2007). Five essential elements of immediate and mid-term mass trauma intervention: Empirical evidence. *Psychiatry*, *70*(4), 283–315. https://doi.org/10.1521/psyc.2007.70.4.283

Jakobsen, M., Thoresen, S., & Johansen, L. E. E. (2011). The validity of screening for post-traumatic stress disorder and other mental health problems among asylum seekers from different countries. *Journal of Refugee Studies, 24*(1), 171–186. https://doi.org/10.1093/jrs/feq053

Jakupcak, M., & Tull, M. T. (2005). Effects of trauma exposure on anger, aggression, and violence in a nonclinical sample of men. *Violence and Victims, 20*(5), 589–598. https://doi.org/10.1891/0886-6708.2005.20.5.589

Jordans, M. J., Komproe, I. H., Tol, W. A., & De Jong, J. T. (2009). Screening for psychosocial distress amongst war-affected children: Cross-cultural construct validity of the CPDS. *Journal of Child Psychology and Psychiatry, 50*(4), 514–523. https://doi.org/10.1111/j.1469-7610.2008.02028.x

Kessler, R. C., Sonnega, A., Bromet, E., Hughes, M., & Nelson, C. B. (1995). Posttraumatic stress disorder in the National Comorbidity Survey. *Archives of General Psychiatry, 52*(12), 1048–1060. https://doi.org/10.1001/archpsyc.1995.03950240066012

Kinzie, J. D., & Fleck, J. (1987). Psychotherapy with severely traumatized refugees. *American Journal of Psychotherapy, 41*(1), 82–94. https://doi.org/10.1176/appi.psychotherapy.1987.41.1.82

Lavi, T., & Solomon, Z. (2005). Palestinian youth of the Intifada: PTSD and future orientation. *Journal of the American Academy of Child & Adolescent Psychiatry, 44*(11), 1176–1183. https://doi.org/10.1097/01.chi.0000177325.47629.4c

Lewis-Fernández, R., & Kleinman, A. (1995). Cultural psychiatry. Theoretical, clinical, and research issues. *Psychiatric Clinics of North America, 18*(3), 433–448.

Lin, E. H., Carter, W. B., & Kleinman, A. M. (1985). An exploration of somatization among Asian refugees and immigrants in primary care. *American Journal of Public Health, 75*(9), 1080–1084. https://doi.org/10.2105/AJPH.75.9.1080

Lundorff, M., Holmgren, H., Zachariae, R., Farver-Vestergaard, I., & O'Connor, M. (2017). Prevalence of prolonged grief disorder in adult bereavement: A systematic review and meta-analysis. *Journal of Affective Disorders, 212*, 138–149. https://doi.org/10.1016/j.jad.2017.01.030

Maercker, A., Brewin, C. R., Bryant, R. A., Cloitre, M., van Ommeren, M., Jones, L. M., Humayan, A., Kagee, A., Llosa, A. E., Rousseau, C., Somasundaram, D. J., Souza, R., Suzuki, Y., Weissbecker, I., Wessely, S. C., First, M. B., & Reed, G. M. (2013). Diagnosis and classification of disorders specifically associated with stress: Proposals for *ICD-11*. *World Psychiatry, 12*(3), 198–206.

McLaughlin, K. A., Green, J. G., Hwang, I., Sampson, N. A., Zaslavsky, A. M., & Kessler, R. C. (2012). Intermittent explosive disorder in the National Comorbidity Survey Replication Adolescent Supplement. *Archives of General Psychiatry, 69*(11), 1131–1139. https://doi.org/10.1001/archgenpsychiatry.2012.592

Meffert, S. M., Musalo, K., McNiel, D. E., & Binder, R. L. (2010). The role of mental health professionals in political asylum processing. *Journal of the American Academy of Psychiatry and the Law, 38*(4), 479–489.

Miller, K. E., & Rasmussen, A. (2010). War exposure, daily stressors, and mental health in conflict and post-conflict settings: Bridging the divide between trauma-focused and psychosocial frameworks. *Social Science & Medicine, 70*(1), 7–16. https://doi.org/10.1016/j.socscimed.2009.09.029

Mollica, R. F. (2001). The trauma story: A phenomenological approach to the traumatic life experiences of refugee survivors. *Psychiatry, 64*(1), 60–63. https://doi.org/10.1521/psyc.64.1.60.18242

Mollica, R. F., Caspi-Yavin, Y., Bollini, P., Truong, T., Tor, S., & Lavelle, J. (1992). The Harvard Trauma Questionnaire: Validating a cross-cultural instrument for measuring torture, trauma, and posttraumatic stress disorder in Indochinese refugees. *Journal of Nervous and Mental Disease, 180*(2), 111–116. https://doi.org/10.1097/00005053-199202000-00008

Mollica, R. F., & Son, L. (1989). Cultural dimensions in the evaluation and treatment of sexual trauma: An overview. *Psychiatric Clinics of North America, 12*(2), 363–379. https://doi.org/10.1016/S0193-953X(18)30437-4

Mollica, R. F., Wyshak, G., De Marneffe, D., Tu, B., Yang, T., & Khuon, F. (1996). Hopkins Symptom Checklist (HSCL-25): Manual for Cambodian, Laotian and Vietnamese versions. *Torture, 6*, 35–42.

Momartin, S., Silove, D., Manicavasagar, V., & Steel, Z. (2004). Complicated grief in Bosnian refugees: Associations with posttraumatic stress disorder and depression. *Comprehensive Psychiatry, 45*(6), 475–482. https://doi.org/10.1016/j.comppsych.2004.07.013

Morina, N., von Lersner, U., & Prigerson, H. G. (2011). War and bereavement: Consequences for mental and physical distress. *PLOS ONE, 6*(7), e22140. https://doi.org/10.1371/journal.pone.0022140

Nickerson, A., Bryant, R. A., Brooks, R., Steel, Z., Silove, D., & Chen, J. (2011). The familial influence of loss and trauma on refugee mental health: A multilevel path analysis. *Journal of Traumatic Stress, 24*(1), 25–33. https://doi.org/10.1002/jts.20608

Nygaard, M., Sonne, C., & Carlsson, J. (2017). Secondary psychotic features in refugees diagnosed with post-traumatic stress disorder: A retrospective cohort study. *BMC Psychiatry, 17*(1), 5. https://doi.org/10.1186/s12888-016-1166-1

Oruc, L., Kapetanovic, A., Pojskic, N., Miley, K., Forstbauer, S., Mollica, F. R., & Henderson, D. C. (2008). Screening for PTSD and depression in Bosnia and Herzegovina: Validating the Harvard Trauma Questionnaire and the Hopkins Symptom Checklist. *International Journal of Culture and Mental Health, 1*(2), 105–116. https://doi.org/10.1080/17542860802456620

Palic, S., & Elklit, A. (2011). Psychosocial treatment of posttraumatic stress disorder in adult refugees: A systematic review of prospective treatment outcome studies and a critique. *Journal of Affective Disorders, 131*(1–3), 8–23. https://doi.org/10.1016/j.jad.2010.07.005

Rees, S., & Silove, D. (2011). Sakit Hati: A state of chronic mental distress related to resentment and anger amongst West Papuan refugees exposed to persecution. *Social Science & Medicine, 73*(1), 103–110. https://doi.org/10.1016/j.socscimed.2011.05.004

Rees, S., Silove, D., Verdial, T., Tam, N., Savio, E., Fonseca, Z., Thorpe, R., Liddell, B., Zwi, A., Tay, K., Brooks, R., & Steel, Z. (2013). Intermittent explosive disorder amongst women in conflict affected Timor-Leste: Associations with human rights trauma, ongoing violence, poverty, and injustice. *PLOS ONE, 8*(8), e69207. https://doi.org/10.1371/journal.pone.0069207

Rees, S., Thorpe, R., Tol, W., Fonseca, M., & Silove, D. (2015). Testing a cycle of family violence model in conflict-affected, low-income countries: A qualitative study from Timor-Leste. *Social Science & Medicine, 130*, 284–291. https://doi.org/10.1016/j.socscimed.2015.02.013

Rees, S. J., Tay, A. K., Savio, E., Maria Da Costa, Z., & Silove, D. (2017). Identifying a combined construct of grief and explosive anger as a response to injustice amongst survivors of mass conflict: A latent class analysis of data from Timor-Leste. *PLOS ONE, 12*(4), e0175019. https://doi.org/10.1371/journal.pone.0175019

Schweitzer, R., Melville, F., Steel, Z., & Lacherez, P. (2006). Trauma, post-migration living difficulties, and social support as predictors of psychological adjustment in resettled Sudanese refugees. *Australian and New Zealand Journal of Psychiatry, 40*(2), 179–187. https://doi.org/10.1080/j.1440-1614.2006.01766.x

Shear, M. K., Simon, N., Wall, M., Zisook, S., Neimeyer, R., Duan, N., Reynolds, C., Lebowitz, B., Sung, S., Ghesquiere, A., Gorscak, B., Clayton, P., Ito, M., Nakajima, S., Konishi, T., Melhem, N., Meert, K., Schiff, M., O'Connor, M. F., Sareen, J., Bolton, J., Skritskaya, N., Mancini, A. D., & Keshaviah, A. (2011). Complicated grief and related bereavement issues for *DSM-5*. *Depression and Anxiety, 28*(2), 103–117. https://doi.org/10.1002/da.20780

Silove, D. (2013). The ADAPT model: A conceptual framework for mental health and psychosocial programming in post conflict settings. *Intervention, 11*(3), 237–248. https://doi.org/10.1097/WTF.0000000000000005

Silove, D., Momartin, S., Marnane, C., Steel, Z., & Manicavasagar, V. (2010). Adult separation anxiety disorder among war-affected Bosnian refugees: Comorbidity with PTSD and associations with dimensions of trauma. *Journal of Traumatic Stress, 23*(1), 169–172. https://doi.org/10.1002/jts.20490

Silove, D., Rees, S., Mohsin, M., Tam, N., Kareth, M., & Tay, A. K. (2018). Differentiating *ICD-11* complex post-traumatic stress disorder from other common mental disorders based on levels of exposure to childhood adversities, the traumas of persecution and postmigration living difficulties among refugees from West Papua. *BJPsych Open, 4*(5), 361–367. https://doi.org/10.1192/bjo.2018.49

Silove, D., Steel, Z., McGorry, P., & Mohan, P. (1998). Trauma exposure, postmigration stressors, and symptoms of anxiety, depression and post-traumatic stress in Tamil asylum-seekers: Comparison with refugees and immigrants. *Acta Psychiatrica Scandinavica, 97*(3), 175–181. https://doi.org/10.1111/j.1600-0447.1998.tb09984.x

Silove, D., Steel, Z., Susljik, I., Frommer, N., Loneragan, C., Chey, T., Brooks, R., le Touze, D., Ceollo, M., Smith, M., Harris, E., & Bryant, R. (2007). The impact of the refugee decision on the trajectory of PTSD, anxiety, and depressive symptoms among asylum seekers: A longitudinal study. *American Journal of Disaster Medicine, 2*(6), 321–329. https://doi.org/10.5055/ajdm.2007.0041

Silove, D., Tay, A. K., Kareth, M., & Rees, S. (2017). The relationship of complex post-traumatic stress disorder and post-traumatic stress disorder in a culturally distinct, conflict-affected population: A study among West Papuan refugees displaced to Papua New Guinea. *Frontiers in Psychiatry, 8*, 73. https://doi.org/10.3389/fpsyt.2017.00073

Silove, D., Ventevogel, P., & Rees, S. (2017). The contemporary refugee crisis: An overview of mental health challenges. *World Psychiatry, 16*(2), 130–139. https://doi.org/10.1002/wps.20438

Silove, D. M., Tay, A. K., Steel, Z., Tam, N., Soares, Z., Soares, C., Dos Reis, N., Alves, A., & Rees, S. (2017). Symptoms of post-traumatic stress disorder, severe psychological distress, explosive anger and grief amongst partners of survivors of high levels of trauma in post-conflict Timor-Leste. *Psychological Medicine, 47*(1), 149–159. https://doi.org/10.1017/S0033291716002233

Sinnerbrink, I., Silove, D., Field, A., Steel, Z., & Manicavasagar, V. (1997). Compounding of premigration trauma and postmigration stress in asylum seekers. *The Journal of Psychology, 131*(5), 463–470. https://doi.org/10.1080/00223989709603533

Soosay, I., Silove, D., Bateman-Steel, C., Steel, Z., Bebbington, P., Jones, P. B., Chey, T., Ivancic, L., & Marnane, C. (2012). Trauma exposure, PTSD and psychotic-like symptoms in post-conflict Timor Leste: An epidemiological survey. *BMC Psychiatry, 12*(1), 229. https://doi.org/10.1186/1471-244X-12-229

Steel, Z., Chey, T., Silove, D., Marnane, C., Bryant, R. A., & van Ommeren, M. (2009). Association of torture and other potentially traumatic events with mental health outcomes among populations exposed to mass conflict and displacement: A systematic review and meta-analysis. *JAMA, 302*(5), 537–549. https://doi.org/10.1001/jama.2009.1132

Steel, Z., Momartin, S., Silove, D., Coello, M., Aroche, J., & Tay, K. W. (2011). Two year psychosocial and mental health outcomes for refugees subjected to restrictive or supportive immigration policies. *Social Science & Medicine, 72*(7), 1149–1156. https://doi.org/10.1016/j.socscimed.2011.02.007

Steel, Z., Silove, D., Bird, K., McGorry, P., & Mohan, P. (1999). Pathways from war trauma to posttraumatic stress symptoms among Tamil asylum seekers, refugees, and immigrants. *Journal of Traumatic Stress, 12*(3), 421–435. https://doi.org/10.1023/A:1024710902534

Tay, A. K., Mohsin, M., Rees, S., Tam, N., Kareth, M., & Silove, D. (2018). Factor structures of complex posttraumatic stress disorder and PTSD in a community sample of refugees from West Papua. *Comprehensive Psychiatry, 85*, 15–22. https://doi.org/10.1016/j.comppsych.2018.05.001

Tay, A. K., Mohsin, M., Rees, S., Tam, N., Kareth, M., & Silove, D. (2019). The structure and psychosocial correlates of complicated bereavement amongst refugees from West Papua. *Social Psychiatry and Psychiatric Epidemiology, 54*(6), 771–780. https://doi.org/10.1007/s00127-019-01666-1

Tay, A. K., Rees, S., Chen, J., Kareth, M., Mohsin, M., & Silove, D. (2015). The Refugee-Mental Health Assessment Package (R-MHAP); rationale, development and first-stage testing amongst West Papuan refugees. *International Journal of Mental Health Systems, 9*(1), article 29. https://doi.org/10.1186/s13033-015-0018-6

Tay, A. K., Rees, S., Chen, J., Kareth, M., & Silove, D. (2015a). The coherence and correlates of intermittent explosive disorder amongst West Papuan refugees displaced to Papua New Guinea. *Journal of Affective Disorders, 177*, 86–94. https://doi.org/10.1016/j.jad.2015.02.009

Tay, A. K., Rees, S., Chen, J., Kareth, M., & Silove, D. (2015b). Examining the broader psychosocial effects of mass conflict on PTSD symptoms and functional impairment amongst West Papuan refugees resettled in Papua New Guinea (PNG). *Social Science & Medicine, 132*, 70–78. https://doi.org/10.1016/j.socscimed.2015.03.020

Tay, A. K., Rees, S., Chen, J., Kareth, M., & Silove, D. (2015c). Pathways from conflict-related trauma and ongoing adversity to posttraumatic stress disorder symptoms amongst West Papuan refugees: The mediating role of anxiety and panic-like symptoms. *Comprehensive Psychiatry, 63*, 36–45. https://doi.org/10.1016/j.comppsych.2015.08.005

Tay, A. K., Rees, S., Chen, J., Kareth, M., & Silove, D. (2015d). The structure of post-traumatic stress disorder and complex post-traumatic stress disorder amongst

West Papuan refugees. *BMC Psychiatry*, *15*(1), 111. https://doi.org/10.1186/s12888-015-0480-3

Tay, A. K., Rees, S., Chen, J., Kareth, M., & Silove, D. (2016). Factorial structure of complicated grief: Associations with loss-related traumatic events and psychosocial impacts of mass conflict amongst West Papuan refugees. *Social Psychiatry and Psychiatric Epidemiology*, *51*(3), 395–406. https://doi.org/10.1007/s00127-015-1099-x

Tay, A. K., Rees, S., Kareth, M., & Silove, D. (2016). Associations of adult separation anxiety disorder with conflict-related trauma, ongoing adversity, and the psychosocial disruptions of mass conflict among West Papuan refugees. *American Journal of Orthopsychiatry*, *86*(2), 224–235. https://doi.org/10.1037/ort0000126

Tay, A. K., Rees, S., Liddell, B., Tam, N., Nickerson, A., Steel, C., & Silove, D. (2017). The role of grief symptoms and a sense of injustice in the pathways to post-traumatic stress symptoms in post-conflict Timor-Leste. *Epidemiology and Psychiatric Sciences*, *26*(4), 403–413.

Tay, A. K., Rees, S., Tam, N., Kareth, M., & Silove, D. (2019a). Defining a combined constellation of complicated bereavement and PTSD and the psychosocial correlates associated with the pattern amongst refugees from West Papua. *Psychological Medicine*, *49*(9), 1481–1489.

Tay, A. K., Rees, S., Tam, N., Kareth, M., & Silove, D. (2019b). Developing a measure of adaptive stress arising from the psychosocial disruptions experienced by refugees based on a sample of displaced persons from West Papua. *International Journal of Methods in Psychiatric Research*, *28*(1), e1770. https://doi.org/10.1002/mpr.1770

Tay, A. K., Rees, S., Tam, N., Savio, E., Da Costa, Z. M., & Silove, D. (2017). The role of trauma-related injustice in pathways to posttraumatic stress symptoms among conjugal couples: A multilevel, dyadic analysis in postconflict Timor-Leste. *SAGE Open*, *7*(3), 1–10. https://doi.org/10.1177/2158244017723688

Tay, A. K., & Silove, D. (2017). The ADAPT model: Bridging the gap between psychosocial and individual responses to mass violence and refugee trauma. *Epidemiology and Psychiatric Sciences*, *26*(2), 142–145.

van der Kolk, B. A., Pelcovitz, D., Roth, S., Mandel, F. S., McFarlane, A., & Herman, J. L. (1996). Dissociation, somatization, and affect dysregulation: The complexity of adaptation of trauma. *The American Journal of Psychiatry*, *153*(7, Suppl.), 83–93. https://doi.org/10.1176/ajp.153.7.83

Van Ommeren, M., Sharma, B., Sharma, G. K., Komproe, I., Cardeña, E., & de Jong, J. T. V. M. (2002). The relationship between somatic and PTSD symptoms among Bhutanese refugee torture survivors: Examination of comorbidity with anxiety and depression. *Journal of Traumatic Stress*, *15*(5), 415–421. https://doi.org/10.1023/A:1020141510005

Westermeyer, J., Bouafuely, M., Neider, J., & Callies, A. (1989). Somatization among refugees: An epidemiologic study. *Psychosomatics*, *30*(1), 34–43. https://doi.org/10.1016/S0033-3182(89)72315-X

World Health Organization. (2010). Neurotic, stress-related and somatoform disorders. In *International classification of diseases* (10th rev.). http://apps.who.int/classifications/icd10/browse/2010/en#/F40-F48

World Health Organization. (2018a). Complex post traumatic stress disorder. In *International classification of diseases* (11th rev.). https://icd.who.int/browse11/l-m/en#http%3a%2f%2fid.who.int%2ficd%2fentity%2f585833559

World Health Organization. (2018b). Prolonged grief disorder. In *International classification of diseases* (11th rev.). https://icd.who.int/browse11/l-m/en#/ http://id.who.int/icd/entity/1183832314

Yoshimasu, K., Kawakami, N., & the WMH-J 2002–2006 Survey Group. (2011). Epidemiological aspects of intermittent explosive disorder in Japan; prevalence and psychosocial comorbidity: Findings from the World Mental Health Japan Survey 2002–2006. *Psychiatry Research*, *186*(2–3), 384–389. https://doi.org/ 10.1016/j.psychres.2010.07.018

# 8

# SCHOOL-BASED MENTAL HEALTH INTERVENTIONS AND OTHER THERAPIES TO HELP REFUGEE CHILDREN EXPLORE PREVIOUS EXPOSURE TO TRAUMA

MINA FAZEL

In this chapter, readers are introduced to some specific school-based mental health interventions along with expressive therapies, narrative exposure therapy (NET), and cognitive–behavioral approaches and the ways in which they have been used to reduce distressing symptoms and enhance psychological and social well-being in refugee children. The chapter addresses the potential benefits of these therapies and discusses how the evidence base remains limited for their use. Throughout the chapter, case studies and empirical evaluations of the interventions are provided.

Many and numerous opportunities can be taken to support refugee children arriving in new host country environments (Fazel & Betancourt, 2018). However, few interventions have been implemented to scale to support these children (Tyrer & Fazel, 2014). This therefore provides us with an important opportunity because there is good evidence that these children can be supported, and through this support, their mental health and educational attainment can be enhanced. Refugees under age 18 years comprise the largest global group of refugees, and thus it is important to ensure that these children, who have often experienced multiple potential stressors, are supported with the best available interventions. They are likely to have

https://doi.org/10.1037/0000226-008
*Refugee Mental Health*, J. D. Aten and J. Hwang (Editors)

experienced disruptions in their education, if indeed they have had previous educational experience. The sheer act of arriving in a new school can be incredibly stressful for any child, but for this transition to be coupled with new cultural, linguistic, and social contexts, with the additional complexities of potential family disruption and financial, housing, and immigration uncertainties, can be difficult for even the most resilient child. Refugee children, on top of all this, have a higher prevalence of mental health problems and, compared with host populations, higher rates of posttraumatic stress disorder (PTSD; Fazel et al., 2012).

Schools can provide stability and a pathway into community integration that might be difficult for refugee children and their parents to access in other environments (Fazel, 2015; Fazel & Betancourt, 2018; Fazel et al., 2016). Schools may be perceived as safe and trusting institutions by many (Fazel, Hoagwood, et al., 2014), and if properly supported, the school environment can be the key structure that assists refugee children in addressing the many complicated tasks that they now have to perform alongside learning (Fazel et al., 2016). A note of caution needs to be made: Although it is clear that schools have the potential to play a key role in supporting refugee children, particularly helping to address not only their educational and social needs but also their mental health needs, one has to be fully aware of the reality that refugee children might also experience harsh difficulties and cruel victimization in host country school contexts as well. It is in school that many refugee children acutely experience bullying and isolation. Given the many varied and difficult journeys these children might have experienced, alongside the reasons that might have propelled them and their families to seek refuge in another country, prevention of further stressful experiences within the school environment needs to be prevented as a priority for all schools receiving refugee children.

Little is known or has been studied about host country interventions to enhance refugee well-being; for example, we need a greater understanding of what structures and learning can take place for all those in a school community before the arrival of any refugee child, as well as what can then be done to ensure that the child's sense of belonging at the school is supported and enhanced. Feeling a sense of belonging in the school is a strong positive predictive factor in mental health for refugee children; thus, finding ways to enhance this in both structured and unstructured school contexts and for the refugee families as a whole, should not be underestimated. Numerous schools have found innovative and thoughtful ways to address this issue that can positively support not only refugee families but also other migrant groups and children arriving at nontraditional points of entry. Finding ways to share examples of good practice can be key to disseminating these thoughtful and useful examples and have included the following: broadening the range and availability of school clubs and extracurricular activities; introducing cultural sharing opportunities, such as world food days and themed school assemblies; and incorporating a broader global perspective within academic curricular so that examples utilized for subjects across the spectrum, including geography, history, art, science, and music, can include content from other continents and cultures.

The context of helping refugee children manage their mental health within schools, and in particular the importance of addressing previous traumatic experiences, needs to be done within a broader school environment that is cognizant of the potential ways that the prevention of mental health problems for refugee children can be conceptualized and addressed (Fazel & Betancourt, 2018). Schools that have good mental health therapies for traumatized refugee children must be able to provide such services within a whole-school environment that is supportive of all of mental health—not only for refugee children, but for all children within schools. This requires several basic areas of support:

- First is the ability of schools, potentially alongside health professionals, to conduct a thorough assessment of the refugee child, especially given the linguistic and cultural differences that can make this a particularly complex task (Fazel, 2018a, 2018b). Various physical and developmental milestones need to be assessed alongside social communication and peer and family relationships. Refugee children might, for example, be more likely to have experienced closed head injuries that have the potential to have an impact on a range of educational, emotional, and behavioral skills, but some of these might present in a similar manner to a child on the autism spectrum or a refugee child who has experienced multiple potentially traumatic events with withdrawn and socially removed behaviors. Proper determination of the cause of the problem will inform what type of intervention is appropriate because these can be very different depending on the cause. Conducting a thorough assessment, with the involvement of family members, is essential and likely to require an investment of time and resources, including having interpreters present.

- Second is the need for all agencies to work together with schools. Although schools can play a key role in supporting the mental health of refugee children and families, it can only do so if it is perceived by all relevant agencies as providing an important and acceptable location for refugee children and families to access care. This is not to say that school staff provides this therapeutic support alone but that the location of the school and the opportunity to work together with school staff, who often know these children well, is utilized by agencies as a particularly powerful place to locate support and provision. Therefore, schools need to feel fully supported if they are to extend their role and facilitate different organizations in working together. Schools cannot, however, be expected to manage the accountability and governance of other agencies involved, so clear agreements need to be made.

• Third, there needs to be an understanding between agencies as to where the responsibility for provision of therapeutic services lies. If the argument is being made for the increase of trauma-addressing therapies to lie within the school context, then it may be difficult to determine who holds the responsibility to provide these services and where funding for them should come from. Is this something health care systems should provide? Does it fall within the remit of education or even social care? The navigation of these questions can be so difficult at times that provision can falter in the process of answering them, potentially holding a clue as to why so few service innovations have been implemented to scale. Although there is no blueprint as to how this question should and can be addressed, it is likely that the principle of shared care and responsibility is likely to hold the most long-term promise. Improving the mental health of refugee children is likely also to help them access their educational opportunities; providing better mental health support within education is likely to improve access to therapy for refugee (and all vulnerable) children, and better outcomes in health and education are likely to improve the social and occupational outcomes of this population. Therefore, the connections are inextricable from responsibility across the health, education, immigration, and social care sectors.

• Finally, a renewed commitment to the research agenda is needed to ensure that only interventions that carry an evidence base indicating their effectiveness are promoted. Support across statutory and nonstatutory sectors can be strong in some regions for refugee children. This has led to a plethora of interventions that have been introduced to help address the needs of refugee children in schools and the community. In a systematic review of these school- and community-based interventions, it was evident that many types of interventions have been tried (Figure 8.1; adapted from Tyrer & Fazel, 2014). These include interventions addressing past traumatic events and current resettlement problems. They have been delivered to address individual, family, school, and group needs and have comprised a

**FIGURE 8.1. Diagram Showing the Range of School- and Community-Based Mental Health Interventions Studied for Refugee Children**

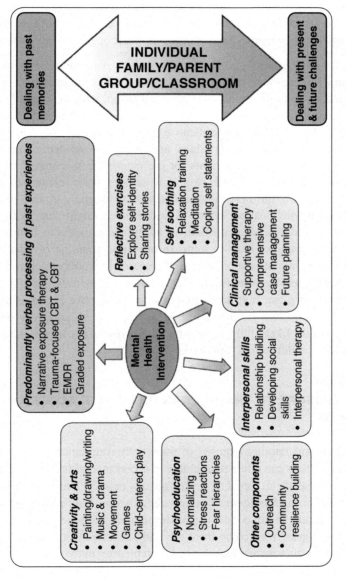

*Note.* CBT = cognitive behavior therapy; EMDR = eye movement desensitization and reprocessing. Adapted from "School and Community-Based Interventions for Refugee and Asylum Seeking Children: A Systematic Review," by R. A. Tyrer and M. Fazel, 2014, *PLoS ONE, 9*(2), p. 8 (https://doi.org/10.1371/journal.pone.0089359). CC BY-NC.

range of creative and expressive modalities. The evidence base, however, remains limited despite the many interventions that have been trialed. The strongest evidence base clearly lies in the cognitive therapies addressing past traumatic events, but it could be that other types of interventions could be demonstrated to be of benefit, but the evidence for these remains lacking. This is primarily because they have not been properly evaluated.

There are many barriers to conducting proper evaluations of service and therapeutic innovations. Among these are the need for financial resources to be directed away from clinical care into evaluation, which can feel inappropriate when the clinical need is perceived to be great. Funding to conduct small-scale evaluations can be difficult to secure, and this, coupled with the requirements to obtain relevant ethical approvals from academic institutions and basic governance requirements for the consent from parents, children, and schools can be a formidable task. Furthermore, basic research questions on how to identify the best measures, conduct the analysis, and write up the findings for publication, which in and of itself might carry a financial restriction to publish, all contribute to additional barriers to building the much-needed evidence base to improve our understanding of what might help these populations. Simplification of research procedures and consensus among researchers as to useful, freely available measures might enable this area to develop given that much potential good practice is lost as a result of these barriers. This is frustrating because this is an area where better evidence would likely help focus and direct resources to the maximum benefit of the children and families involved.

## HOW EXPOSURE TO TRAUMA CAN INFLUENCE ACCESSING THERAPY

For children and families exposed to potentially traumatic events, multiple additional barriers can affect their ability to access mental health services and therapies. These are on top of those that already exist for many in overcoming the stigma that hinders them from accessing mental health support. Stigma related to mental health concerns is widespread in high-income nations, but for many refugees, who come from low- and middle-income countries, the stigma surrounding mental health needs can be even more pernicious. Exposure to potentially traumatic events, and in particular multiple such events, can place a child at increased risk of developing mental health difficulties, of which PTSD lies at the more severe end of the spectrum of responses (Connor et al., 2015) and can present in a number of ways (Cook et al., 2017). Risk factors for the development of clinically significant problems include exposure to multiple types of trauma in the context of compromised family and social support systems (e.g., chronic poverty, parental mental illness, interpersonal isolation; Connor et al., 2015). As the cumulative burden of childhood adversity increases, the likelihood of developing emotional and behavioural problems that persist into adulthood increases in a dose–response manner. Therefore, refugee children, who have an estimated prevalence of PTSD at approximately 15% to 30%, are likely to experience multiple difficulties related to their trauma exposure that are important to consider in the context of developing therapies to address their needs (Blackmore et al., 2020).

The core symptoms of PTSD according to both the *Diagnostic and Statistical Manual of Mental Disorders* (fifth edition [*DSM-5*]) and the *International Classification of Diseases* (11th revision [*ICD-11*]) are clustered into three areas: (a) those around reexperiencing the original traumatic events (usually through flashbacks and nightmares); (b) avoidance of any reminders or associations with the traumatic event; and (c) increased levels of arousal, which can present with symptoms such as sleep difficulties and agitation. In addition, the *DSM-5* uses a four-factor model for PTSD and includes a cognitions and mood cluster because low mood and heightened levels of anxiety are common (Connor et al., 2015; La Greca et al., 2017). With these symptom clusters in mind, if one of the core symptoms of PTSD is avoidance of any reminder of the original traumatic exposure, it can be especially difficult for individuals to even consider therapy to address PTSD because most sufferers would be aware (or expect) that treatment might include some "exposure" to the traumatic memory. Avoidance is such an integral component of some people's presentation that accessing care can be even more challenging when they feel so strongly that they must "avoid" memories of past traumatic experiences.

Furthermore, for refugee populations, there is a relatively high correlation between child PTSD and parental PTSD because parents have likely had similar experiences. Parents with PTSD might be less able to recognise PTSD in their children and can find some of the tasks of parenting particularly challenging, which may result in increased intrafamiliar discord and aggression. If young people are dependent on their parents to access care, this becomes yet another barrier to their accessing treatment, (Fazel & Betancourt, 2018). If parents are also experiencing symptoms that they feel they must "avoid," they might feel they can best protect and care for their children by also not exposing their children to therapeutic support that might lead their child to reexperience past traumatic events. This is why psychoeducation must play such an important role in any component of care for those who have experienced mental health problems due to traumatic events because explanations about the different presentations of traumatic sequelae, the ubiquitous role that avoidance plays, and how difficult it might be to access care needs to be explained, addressed, and discussed.

Furthermore, if the young person has come from an area where those in positions of authority were perpetrators of human rights abuses, or even where schools were targeted either for destruction or for recruitment into armies, then those who have gone through these experiences might have difficulty trusting those in positions of authority and might find it difficult to feel safe at school (Fazel, Patel, et al., 2014). Providing therapies within the school context might therefore be inappropriate for this subgroup, especially in the first instance. For many other refugee children, however, accessing care in the context of an environment they are familiar with and feel safe in and where they have additional support from school staff might be an important way to facilitate care (Fazel et al., 2016).

Research conducted with refugee children who had received mental health support within United Kingdom school settings highlighted some interesting principles that are relevant for those providing services to consider (Fazel, 2015; Fazel et al., 2009, 2016; Fazel & Stein, 2003). First, refugee children had rates of mental health difficulties that were much higher than other ethnic minority children and White native-born children in their classes, with almost a third of children experiencing clinical levels of difficulties, compared with one in 10 White children. Second, the refugee children who were seen by school-based mental health services preferred to be seen in the school setting than other environments, with 71% stating that they preferred to access mental health services at school (Fazel et al., 2009). They valued being seen in the school primarily because it felt safe and was convenient, as the following comments reflect:

- I don't know why I just get this sense of feeling free when I'm around this school . . . more at ease.

- Maybe it [therapy in the mental health clinic] would be more complicated or something . . . maybe just to find it and maybe she doesn't know who you are, where you come from, like . . . I don't know, it's just different. I think in the school is better.

- Outside you don't know who you can trust.

- Because I think my English is not really good and I don't like to go [to mental health services].

- Children feel more protected because they are in a place that they know.

Furthermore, the research has shown how isolated many of the young people felt and that one of their main concerns and wishes was to integrate better with the other children at their school. They valued therapies being made available and mostly trusted their teachers in helping them access care.

## PRINCIPLES OF WORKING IN SCHOOLS TO ADDRESS TRAUMATIZED POPULATIONS

Experience from a range of contexts are all of relevance in enhancing our understanding of how to work with refugee children in schools. A systematic review of PTSD interventions in schools highlighted how the familiarity and safety often experienced in school environments is important to harness to deliver interventions for children, especially children who are from minority groups that rarely access care (Rolfsnes & Idsoe, 2011). The most comprehensive model to explore is one that adopts a multitiered approach to supporting children who have experienced trauma in the school setting. This would ensure that interventions are available at all levels and for all children, not just those who are refugees. The first level of care needed in schools is of the lowest intensity and tier, usually involving universal interventions that should be tailored to improving understanding of the varied impacts of trauma on any person experiencing such an event. The value of such psychoeducation cannot be underestimated, especially given that, as discussed earlier, the pervasiveness of avoidance in preventing access to care can be so profound that ensuring as many people as possible are aware of how trauma can affect themselves and others is essential. This level of work also ensures that those working with children in the school—be they teachers, teaching support staff, or other school staff—are aware of the how trauma can affect the children with whom they work. This increase in awareness will then potentially inform the manner in which the school plans its activities and manages those children who might be experiencing difficulties. For example, how school staff conceptualize and raise concerns about children who might internalize a problem can be assisted with better understanding of the impact of trauma—for example, with presentations of nonengagement with schoolwork or peers. Alternatively, those children who might externalize more and present with aggression might experience potential triggers within the school system. A refugee child in one of the schools I worked with would jump each time a door banged because it would remind him of a previous traumatic association. This led him to cower throughout the school day. Another child found it difficult to talk or engage with others—so much so that the school was worried he might have intellectual impairments and wanted to provide remedial learning support for him. At times, finding places to work that are away from the hustle and bustle of normal school environments can be supportive as long as they are not perceived to further isolate the child.

The second level of care within the school is to think about whether an intervention can prevent the development of a mental health problem in those children who are perceived to be at higher risk because of past trauma experiences. This stage might involve targeted screening and then prevention or early interventions. Although there is much desire to try and develop interventions to prevent the development of, for example, PTSD, there remains little evidence to support the broader implementation of any particular model across schools. Nonetheless, schools are likely to be an ideal location for providing preventive interventions for refugee children because they can facilitate access to care in a potentially nonstigmatizing environment. This area of work can also include early intervention, for which there is good support across the range of mental health problems that young people experience (Kieling et al., 2011).

The final component of care in schools to consider for children who have been exposed to potentially traumatic events is that of specific interventions to treat children with PTSD or psychologically disabling posttraumatic symptoms, either in individual or group settings (Pfefferbaum et al., 2014, 2017; Rolfsnes & Idsoe, 2011; Tyrer & Fazel, 2014). The range of interventions that have been described are vast (see Figure 8.1); however, the strongest evidence base lies in those that involve cognitive and verbally descriptive approaches, which are described in more detail shortly. Other therapeutic modalities that have been used include practical "here and now" approaches to address current problems and postmigration difficulties, relaxation techniques, psychoeducation, and better approaches to supported case management, primarily to help navigate the complexities of accessing health care in the postmigration environment. It is important to bear in mind that outcomes for children with persistent or even episodic PTSD can vary widely. However, risk factors for chronic PTSD, including poverty, exposure to cumulative stressors, and difficulties within the family, are often more prevalent among refugee children; thus, treatment of those with PTSD must be made available for these populations (Connor et al., 2015).

An example of these different levels is demonstrated by a description and evaluation of the California Trauma Informed School Systems Approach, based broadly on the Substance Abuse and Mental Health Services Administration's (2014) Concept of Trauma and Guidance for a Trauma-Informed Approach (see also Kataoka et al., 2018). The principles that inform this approach are depicted in its trauma-informed principles (see Figure 8.2). Although this was not developed for refugee children per se, it highlights the components necessary to consider in any system wanting to address the needs of its traumatized populations. The framework proposed encapsulates both the school itself and the school district to best ensure that the perspective that has been developed understands how violence and trauma can disrupt the social, emotional, and cognitive growth of students (Kataoka et al., 2018). School leadership, policies, and procedures often play a key role in the services being provided, and so aligning service outcomes with those relevant to educational progress can facilitate working together to support implementation of any trauma-focused service.

Providing a positive climate can promote a feeling of safety in the school and improve student engagement. For example, having clear antibullying

**FIGURE 8.2. Factors That Can Ensure That School Systems Are Trauma-Informed**

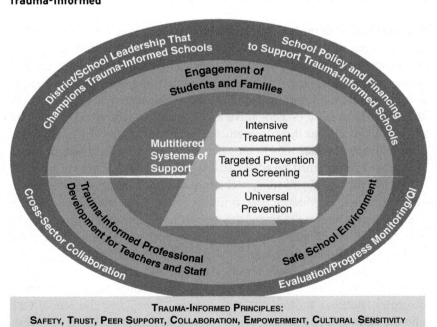

*Note.* QI = quality improvement. From "Applying a Trauma Informed School Systems Approach: Examples From School Community-Academic Partnerships," by S. H. Kataoka, P. Vona, A. Acuna, L. Jaycox, P. Escudero, C. Rojas, E. Ramirez, A. Langley, and B. D. Stein, 2018, *Ethnicity & Disease*, 28(Suppl. 2), p. 419 (https://doi.org/10.18865%2Fed.28.S2.417). Copyright 2018 by Ethnicity & Disease Inc. Reprinted with permission.

processes and an ongoing commitment to professional development for staff on the broad reaches of trauma-informed practices can be key components of longer term sustainable services. As part of this, teachers need to maintain their own self-care.

The final component of care, which is individual or group treatments, can then be provided in this multitiered system of support. The cases studies used by the authors describe different components, including the leveraging of school policies and financing to sustain trauma-informed practices, the promotion of a safe school environment through restorative practices, and the role of school leadership in engaging and empowering families, communities, and school staff to address neighborhood and school violence (Kataoka et al., 2018).

## EVIDENCE FOR SCHOOL-BASED MENTAL HEALTH INTERVENTIONS FOR REFUGEE CHILDREN

The evidence base on how to support traumatized children in schools has been growing substantially over the past decade. This section focuses on the expressive therapies and other school mental health therapies for trauma. The expressive therapies include a range of modalities, including art therapy, psychodrama, and music therapy, but the strongest evidence base lies in those that have more of a cognitive focus, involve a structured component of verbalization, and include cognitive behavior therapy (CBT) and NET. These therapies include a focus on a narration of a previous traumatic event. A note of caution must be made at this point: although a wide range of expressive therapies with refugee children in schools has been described in the literature, the evidence base is not as strong as in other areas of child mental health because many of the models have not been evaluated. The majority of the evaluations, and thus the evidence base, lies primarily with CBT and NET (Rolfsnes & Idsoe, 2011; Tyrer & Fazel, 2014).

For example, a systematic review of school-based intervention programs for PTSD, not limited to refugee children, included only 19 studies from nine countries (Rolfsnes & Idsoe, 2011). Of these, 16 explored the role of CBT, and the other studies included eye movement desensitization and reprocessing (EMDR), play-art, and mind–body skills. Many included multilevel components and had effect sizes in the medium to large range. They showed how school professionals were good delivery agents for these interventions, consistent with more general findings about school-based mental health interventions across the globe (Murphy et al., 2017). The review highlighted the difficulties with study quality, noting that many lacked randomization and had small sample sizes, wide participant age ranges, and lack of independent assessors and follow-up assessments, to name a few concerns (Rolfsnes & Idsoe, 2011). These results were comparable to those of another review, which also highlighted that the greatest evidence lies in supporting the use of trauma-focused therapies (Keeshin & Strawn, 2014). Another systematic review of school-based interventions for refugee children highlighted the broad range of expressive and cognitive therapies that have been used in schools for a range of mental health presentations. This review identified 11 studies conducted in school settings; the overall quality of the studies was low, and the strongest evidence base was for CBT or some form of verbal processing of previous traumatic events. The studies predominantly saw children in groups or classrooms; three conducted group creative therapies (including psychodrama and exposure through writing), and three used group CBT (Tyrer & Fazel, 2014). Other reviews have highlighted the importance of the school setting in delivering many components of the interventions and also parental involvement, although most of this involvement was related to psychoeducation rather than participation in the actual expressive or cognitive therapy (Pfefferbaum et al., 2017, 2014). Of interest, some evidence shows that children who participate in group approaches, rather than individual therapy, might be more likely to remain engaged in interventions. (Pfefferbaum et al., 2014). This was also observed in services developed in Oxford, where a group-based approach comprising a range of creative arts seemed the best way to engage a number of isolated unaccompanied refugee minors (Fazel et al., 2016). The following subsection describe several specific interventions in detail to highlight the evaluation and implementation challenges that have arisen.

## Expressive Therapies

There are compelling reasons why the range of expressive therapies (including the visual and performance arts) might lend themselves well to working with refugee children who have experienced traumatic events. First migrant populations such as refugees often come from low- and middle-income countries, so when they then come to reside in high-income settings, they often have to manage considerable linguistic and cultural change. Therefore, the expressive therapies can help overcome some of the limitations placed on those with poor host-country language proficiency. Second is the nature of working with children who have experienced potentially traumatic events. These experiences can be particularly difficult to verbalize, either because children can lack some of the necessary verbal dexterity that is needed or else because the memory can be too difficult to express because of the emotional processes that accompany memories that have been encoded (often poorly) in the midst of a traumatic event (Robjant & Fazel, 2010; Sullivan & Simonson, 2016). Expressive therapies, such as those that employ drama, music, and drawing, can not only traverse the linguistic barriers but also be meaningful across cultural divides and enable expression in a more universally accessible medium. The majority of papers written about the use of these therapies have focused on the process of working rather than on evaluating the evidence, however, so only a few have been robustly evaluated (van Westrhenen & Fritz, 2014).

Rousseau and colleagues in Canada have conducted a series of interventions using the expressive therapies for refugee and migrant children in classroom settings (Rousseau et al., 2005, 2007, 2014; Rousseau & Heusch, 2000). Over a series of trials that have been developed according to the data and experience gathered, they have introduced interventions into the classroom setting. They conducted sessions of up to 90 minutes' duration and used drawing, writing, group presentations, and class-wide theatrical activities, as well as sandplay (using sand, water, and miniature objects) to clarify components of past experiences (Kronick et al., 2018).

The largest study they conducted involved 477 participants from five multiethnic high schools in Canada where they studied the impact of a theatre intervention group among both refugee and immigrant children (Rousseau et al., 2014). The theatre expression program was adapted to be used for a group of students with learning and behavioral problems to facilitate the expression and sharing of group stories by young immigrants and refugees. The authors wanted to achieve a number of goals, including to (a) give support to the construction of meaning in an individual's personal history, (b) foster the grieving processes associated with immigration (separation, transition, loss of expectations) and experiences of academic failure, (c) help consolidate multiple identities, and (d) enhance appreciation of differences and the development of adaptation strategies without increasing marginalization and exclusion. These processes were expected to help alleviate the difficulties and tensions of belonging to a minority group in a postmigration context and foster adolescents' social adjustment and academic performance.

It was a manualized intervention, running for 12 weeks, with one 90-minute workshop per week, incorporated into the regular class timetable and run by two members of the intervention team with the support of a teacher. The workshop leaders acted as guides to encourage the participants to improvise verbally, musically, and through gestures and to explore alternative scenarios (Rousseau et al., 2014). The workshops were structured on the basis of two types of activities: warm-up and improvisation. The improvisation activities often used personal stories from the participants, with a variety of topics explored over the course of the program, including belonging and exclusion, learning (especially experiential learning), family and friends (evoking issues of solidarity and social network), and the topic of transitions (migration, adolescence, or other turning points in the youth's experience).

Although their previous studies had positive findings with improved levels of impairment (Rousseau et al., 2007), lower mean levels of internalizing and externalizing symptoms, and higher mean levels of feeling popular (Rousseau et al., 2005), this study did not, although the intervention group was different from those previously studied, as was the intervention. The study was not associated with greater reductions in self-reported impairment and symptoms compared with active and nonactive control groups. Nonetheless, they did describe some interesting results, with first-generation adolescent migrants having better outcomes than second-generation migrants (Rousseau et al., 2014). It is hoped that this will provide further impetus to gain a better understanding of these treatment differences.

Kalantari et al. (2012) examined the efficacy of Writing for Recovery for bereaved Afghan refugee children in Iran. This is a group intervention for adolescents who have experienced a trauma that can be administered either individually or in a group of up to 50 participants. In this study, the intervention was administered in school groups over 3 consecutive days, with each day consisting of two 15-minute sessions. The writing sessions progress from unstructured writing about innermost feelings and thoughts about one's traumatic event or loss to more structured writing where participants reflect on what advice they would give to another person in the same situation. In this study of 29 participants in the active arm of the trial, their pre–post average scores decreased significantly on a traumatic grief inventory compared with a nonactive control group. Another pilot study of class-wide music therapy on 43 students at an Australian school, which included instrumental improvisation, dancing, song learning, and singing, showed some improvement in externalizing behaviors but with inconsistent results in other domains (Baker & Jones, 2006).

## NARRATIVE EXPOSURE THERAPY

NET was developed as a therapy to address PTSD symptoms as a result of exposure to multiple traumatic events (Fazel, 2018a; Robjant & Fazel, 2010). It has been adapted for child refugee populations as a treatment called KIDNET (Catani et al., 2009; Neuner et al., 2008; Ruf et al., 2010). NET is a manualized intervention and has even been demonstrated to be effective if delivered by lay therapists. It is often delivered in five to 12 sessions. As part of its therapy, which focuses on a verbal processing of the previous traumatic events in intricate detail and in chronological order, a lifeline is created with the child to map the main events in their life. This is a visual and tactile process, where the child describes their life placing stones and flowers to represent either negative "traumatic" or positive events, and is described as the "lifeline." This lifeline becomes a guide for the following therapeutic sessions as the stones that are placed to represent the traumatic events in the child's life are then usually each explored in one of the subsequent therapeutic sessions. So if there are five big stones, then there might need to be five to seven sessions planned, as each session explores one stone. The therapist will need to be aware that some more traumatic events might not be mentioned in early sessions. This is important: As noted, there is a strong urge to "avoid" past traumatic memories, and so the ability to engage with a therapist and test out discussing these past events might be needed before some of the more traumatic memories are described (Fazel, 2019, Fazel et al., 2020). During the subsequent therapeutic sessions, the child will go through each specific traumatic event in intricate detail, and when describing these events, a range of expressive modalities can be used—whatever might assist the child in recalling and describing the negative traumatic event. These can include using play models and physical acting. The therapist then writes down these descriptions and repeats them to the child in the next session to again expose the child to the traumatic memory and facilitate the encoding of the memory in chronological order and with clarity, disrupting the PTSD memories.

The evidence for the use of NET includes a study of 26 refugee children in Germany who were treated individually (Ruf et al., 2010). At both the posttest and follow-up assessments, significant reductions were detected in PTSD symptoms, which persisted at the 12-month follow-up; nonverbal cognitive functioning was also found to have significantly improved. Another study of NET in Sri Lanka, with victims of a tsunami in the context of a previous civil war, compared 31 children who were randomly assigned to six sessions of either NET or meditation and relaxation (Catani et al., 2009). They found no significant differences between the groups; however, both demonstrated significant improvements in PTSD symptoms and functioning.

## SCHOOL-BASED COGNITIVE-BEHAVIORAL APPROACHES

Numerous cognitive-behavioral approaches have been tested in school settings, but only four have been identified for refugee children in schools, of which two were intended to address trauma (Schottelkorb et al., 2012).

Schottelkorb compared trauma-focused CBT with child-centred play therapy in 31 refugee children and reported that both treatments were effective in reducing trauma symptoms (Ehntholt et al., 2005; Schottelkorb et al., 2012; Sullivan & Simonson, 2016). A study looking at six 1-hour manualized CBT group sessions delivered to 15 children in schools in the United Kingdom showed that significant improvements were made in behavioral difficulties and emotional symptoms compared with control refugee children (Ehntholt et al., 2005). This approach is similar in some ways and different in others to NET. The differences lie primarily in the focus of CBT being on one particular traumatic memory rather than all the traumatic memories that child might have been exposed to, hence making it well suited to treat single-episode traumatic events.

Larger investigations have been conducted on traumatized nonrefugee populations using CBT in schools, which merits some discussion—in particular, the use of an intervention called cognitive behavioral intervention for trauma in schools (CBITS) and a primary school adaptation called Bounce Back (Jaycox et al., 2006, 2018; Langley et al., 2015; Morsette et al., 2009; Santiago et al., 2016). This school-based, group and individual intervention is designed to reduce symptoms of PTSD and depression as well as behavioural problems. It uses psychoeducation about trauma and its consequences, relaxation training, learning to monitor anxiety levels, recognizing maladaptive thinking, challenging unhelpful thoughts, social problem-solving, creating a trauma narrative and processing the traumatic event, and facing trauma-related anxieties rather than avoiding them. CBITS focuses primarily on three goals: decreasing current symptoms related to trauma exposure, building skills for handling stress and anxiety, and building peer and caregiver support. It has a multimodal component and so also addresses overall school functioning, academic attainment, peer and parent support, as well as coping skills. The results from trials hold promise that an intervention in a multi-tiered approach can be effective and that symptoms of PTSD and depression decrease postintervention (Morsette et al., 2009).

For example, a study for migrant children aged 10 to 14 years in the United States used CBITS for children with symptoms of trauma and depression (Allison & Ferreira, 2017). After a 10-week program, the children who participated in CBITS had fewer symptoms of trauma and depression, with large effect sizes. The intervention was conducted in Spanish, the language the children spoke at home, and support was also given to the children's teachers and parents/carers. The intervention was facilitated by a school social worker who underwent specialized training, and all the 23 children completed the trial. Following the implementation of CBITS, participants reported experiencing significantly fewer symptoms of trauma and depression with a reduction of 29.3% and 46.9%, respectively. The results reinforce the benefit of providing mental health support within a school setting, especially for minority groups who encounter greater difficulties in accessing services.

## CONCLUSION

Given the multiple and varied needs of refugee children, especially those who have been exposed to multiple potentially traumatic events, schools can play an important role in improving access to treatments and potentially involving wider members of the peer community and school staff into the program. When addressing the impact of exposure to potentially traumatic events in a school setting, it is important to consider both trauma-specific interventions and trauma-informed approaches at the whole-school level, involving families where possible (Chafouleas et al., 2019). Both these approaches play important and complementary roles in treating children and guiding school systems in how best to ensure that they can support the development of refugee children during their crucial first few years in a host country. A broad range of expressive therapies have been introduced to help address the consequences of exposure to potentially traumatic events. At this time, the evidence base to support their widespread rollout remains limited, but given the interest in using these techniques with refugee children, better research and evaluation of these interventions is urgently needed.

The evidence base better supports the use of verbal expressive techniques and verbal processing of previous traumatic events with refugee children; however, the absolute number of children who have been involved in trials remains small, and better enrollment and commitment to building the evidence base is needed. Comparative studies remain even more limited in studying expressive therapies and comparing them to the cognitive-based therapies. There remain a number of considerations for refugee children and any school-based therapy. It is important to try to engage families in some manner—if not in the therapy, then in some way to help address any difficulties they might be experiencing as well as in the parenting role in a new sociocultural context. All members of refugee families are likely to have undergone considerable change and disruption—not only in location but also in their respective roles. Children often master the host language faster and might better understand nuances of culture; at times, they may have to adopt a premature adult role. Parents and other family members might experience isolation and frustration because it can be difficult to find employment opportunities, and often jobs are in an area different from and less aligned with their home country skills and expertise. Therefore, refugee children's parents need to be engaged to ensure the mental health of the whole family is addressed (Fazel & Betancourt, 2018; Fazel et al., 2016). School-based services are well-placed to engage families and provide services for both the adults and the children.

A final consideration is the issue of longer term scalability, sustainability, and implementation of therapies that have been developed for refugee children. Several studies have explored the question of implementation and sustainability in developing interventions in schools to address traumatized populations. This is especially important because so many studies are not implemented on a larger scale (Fazel, 2018a, 2018b; Rolfsnes & Idsoe, 2011). For example a mixed-methods study examined the implementation process of an evidence-based school trauma intervention conducted in 26 schools (Nadeem et al., 2018). Results showed that almost all of the clinics engaged in activities to prepare to implement a new intervention (also termed preimplementation—engagement, feasibility, and readiness), but only 31% of the sites formally started to deliver the program to the children in the schools. Qualitative analysis comparing those that implemented the program to those that did not revealed critical differences in decision-making processes, leadership strategies, and the presence of local champions for the program. Findings indicate that preimplementation and readiness-related consultation should be employed as part of broad-scale implementation and training efforts. Other experiences attest to the importance of leveraging implementation drivers that promote adoption of evidence-based practices in schools (Hoover et al., 2018). Implementation strategies included organizational and state leadership engagement, expert clinical consultation, data systems to measure feedback, and cross-site sharing and accountability. These broader issues must be considered to ensure that the interventions can target the populations they are most likely to benefit and the interventions continue and expand as needed.

Expressive therapies and other school-based mental health interventions for helping refugee children remain a key component of care for both newly arrived and settled refugee populations. Although the dearth of properly evaluated studies is unfortunate given the considerable number of refugee children in the world today, there is reason for optimism as interventions continue to be refined, the measures to capture meaningful change are better defined, and the implementation agenda becomes embedded in the research process. Providing better in-school care for refugee children and their families is likely to be of considerable benefit not only for these children but for the entire school community, particularly if such programs can be a catalyst for better provision and trauma-informed support for all children.

## REFERENCES

Allison, A. C., & Ferreira, R. J. (2017). Implementing cognitive behavioral intervention for trauma in schools (CBITS) with Latino youth. *Child & Adolescent Social Work Journal, 34*(2), 181–189. https://doi.org/10.1007/s10560-016-0486-9

Baker, F., & Jones, C. (2006). The effect of music therapy services on classroom behaviours of newly arrived refugee students in Australia—A pilot study. *Emotional & Behavioural Difficulties, 11*(4), 249–260. https://doi.org/10.1080/13632750601022170

Blackmore, R., Gray, K. M., Boyle, J. A., Fazel, M., Ranasinha, S., Fitzgerald, G., Misso, M., & Gibson-Helm, M. (2020). Systematic review and meta-analysis: The prevalence of mental illness in child and adolescent refugees and asylum seekers. *Journal of the American Academy of Child & Adolescent Psychiatry, 59*(6), 704–714. https://doi.org/10.1016/j.jaac.2019.11.011

Catani, C., Kohiladevy, M., Ruf, M., Schauer, E., Elbert, T., & Neuner, F. (2009). Treating children traumatized by war and tsunami: A comparison between exposure therapy and meditation-relaxation in north-east Sri Lanka. *BMC Psychiatry, 9*(1), 22. https://doi.org/10.1186/1471-244X-9-22

Chafouleas, S. M., Koriakin, T. A., Roundfield, K. D., & Overstreet, S. (2019). Addressing childhood trauma in school settings: A framework for evidence-based practice. *School Mental Health, 11*(1), 40–53. https://doi.org/10.1007/s12310-018-9256-5

Connor, D. F., Ford, J. D., Arnsten, A. F., & Greene, C. A. (2015). An update on post-traumatic stress disorder in children and adolescents. *Clinical Pediatrics, 54*(6), 517–528. https://doi.org/10.1177/0009922814540793

Cook, A., Spinazzola, J., Ford, J., Lanktree, C., Blaustein, M., Cloitre, M., DeRosa, R., Hubbard, R., Kagan, R., Liautaud, J., Mallah, K., Oafson, E., & van der Kolk, B. A. (2017). Complex trauma in children and adolescents. *Psychiatric Annals, 35*(5), 390–398. https://doi.org/10.3928/00485713-20050501-05

Ehntholt, K. A., Smith, P., & Yule, W. (2005). School-based cognitive-behavioural therapy group intervention for refugee children who have experienced war-related trauma. *Clinical Child Psychology and Psychiatry, 10*(2), 235–250. https://doi.org/10.1177/1359104505051214

Fazel, M. (2015). A moment of change: Facilitating refugee children's mental health in UK schools. *International Journal of Educational Development, 41*, 255–261. https://doi.org/10.1016/j.ijedudev.2014.12.006

Fazel, M. (2018a). Psychological and psychosocial interventions for refugee children resettled in high-income countries. *Epidemiology and Psychiatric Sciences, 27*(2), 117–123. https://doi.org/10.1017/S2045796017000695

Fazel, M. (2018b). Refugees and the post-migration environment. *BMC Medicine, 16*(1), 164. https://doi.org/10.1186/s12916-018-1155-y

Fazel, M. (2019). Focusing a lens on refugee families to address layers of avoidance. *The Lancet. Public Health, 4*(7), e318–e319. https://doi.org/10.1016/S2468-2667(19)30107-0

Fazel, M., & Betancourt, T. (2018). Preventive mental health interventions for refugee children in high-income settings: A narrative review. *The Lancet. Child & Adolescent Health, 2*(2), 121–132. https://doi.org/10.1016/S2352-4642(17)30147-5

Fazel, M., Doll, H., & Stein, A. (2009). A school-based mental health intervention for refugee children: An exploratory study. *Clinical Child Psychology and Psychiatry, 14*(2), 297–309. https://doi.org/10.1177/1359104508100128

Fazel, M., Garcia, J., & Stein, A. (2016). The right location? Experiences of refugee adolescents seen by school-based mental health services. *Clinical Child Psychology and Psychiatry, 21*(3), 368–380. https://doi.org/10.1177/1359104516631606

Fazel, M., Hoagwood, K., Stephan, S., & Ford, T. (2014). Mental health interventions in schools 1: Mental health interventions in schools in high-income countries. *The Lancet. Psychiatry, 1*(5), 377–387. https://doi.org/10.1016/S2215-0366(14)70312-8

Fazel, M., Patel, V., Thomas, S., & Tol, W. (2014). Mental health interventions in schools in low-income and middle-income countries. *The Lancet. Psychiatry, 1*(5), 388–398. https://doi.org/10.1016/S2215-0366(14)70357-8

Fazel, M., Reed, R. V., Panter-Brick, C., & Stein, A. (2012). Mental health of displaced and refugee children resettled in high-income countries: Risk and protective factors. *The Lancet, 379*(9812), 266–282. https://doi.org/S0140-6736(11)60051-2

Fazel, M., & Stein, A. (2003). Mental health of refugee children: Comparative study. *BMJ, 327*(7407), 134. https://doi.org/10.1136/bmj.327.7407.134

Fazel, M., Stratford, H. J., Rowsell, E., Chan, C., Griffiths, H., & Robjant, K. (2020). Five applications of narrative exposure therapy for children and adolescents presenting with post-traumatic stress disorders. *Frontiers in Psychiatry, 11*, 19. https://doi.org/10.3389/fpsyt.2020.00019

Hoover, S. A., Sapere, H., Lang, J. M., Nadeem, E., Dean, K. L., & Vona, P. (2018). Statewide implementation of an evidence-based trauma intervention in schools. *School Psychology Quarterly, 33*(1), 44–53. https://doi.org/10.1037/spq0000248

Jaycox, L. H., Langley, A. K., & Hoover, S. A. (2018). *Cognitive behavioral intervention for trauma in schools (CBITS)*. RAND Corporation. https://doi.org/10.7249/TR413

Jaycox, L. H., Morse, L. K., Tanelian, T., & Stein, B. D. (2006). *How schools can help students recover from traumatic experiences: A toolkit for supporting long-term recovery*. RAND Corporation. https://www.rand.org/content/dam/rand/pubs/technical_reports/2006/RAND_TR413.pdf

Kalantari, M., Yule, W., Dyregrov, A., Neshatdoost, H., & Ahmadi, S. J. (2012). Efficacy of writing for recovery on traumatic grief symptoms of Afghani refugee bereaved adolescents: A randomized control trial. *Omega: Journal of Death and Dying, 65*(2), 139–150. https://doi.org/10.2190/OM.65.2.d

Kataoka, S. H., Vona, P., Acuna, A., Jaycox, L., Escudero, P., Rojas, C., Ramirez, E., Langley, A., & Stein, B. D. (2018). Applying a trauma informed school systems approach: Examples from school community–academic partnerships. *Ethnicity & Disease, 28*(Suppl. 2), 417–426. https://doi.org/10.18865/ed.28.S2.417

Keeshin, B. R., & Strawn, J. R. (2014). Psychological and pharmacologic treatment of youth with posttraumatic stress disorder: An evidence-based review. *Child and Adolescent Psychiatric Clinics, 23*(2), 399–411. https://doi.org/10.1016/j.chc.2013.12.002

Kieling, C., Baker-Henningham, H., Belfer, M., Conti, G., Ertem, I., Omigbodun, O., Rohde, L. A., Srinath, S., Ulkuer, N., & Rahman, A. (2011). Child and adolescent mental health worldwide: Evidence for action. *The Lancet, 378*(9801), 1515–1525. https://doi.org/10.1016/S0140-6736(11)60827-1

Kronick, R., Rousseau, C., & Cleveland, J. (2018). Refugee children's sandplay narratives in immigration detention in Canada. *European Child & Adolescent Psychiatry, 27*(4), 423–437. https://doi.org/10.1007/s00787-017-1012-0

La Greca, A. M., Danzi, B. A., & Chan, S. F. (2017). *DSM-5* and *ICD-11* as competing models of PTSD in preadolescent children exposed to a natural disaster: Assessing validity and co-occurring symptomatology. *European Journal of Psychotraumatology, 8*(1), 1310591. https://doi.org/10.1080/20008198.2017.1310591

Langley, A. K., Gonzalez, A., Sugar, C. A., Solis, D., & Jaycox, L. (2015). Bounce Back: Effectiveness of an elementary school-based intervention for multicultural children exposed to traumatic events. *Journal of Consulting and Clinical Psychology, 83*(5), 853–865. https://doi.org/10.1037/ccp0000051

Morsette, A., Swaney, G., Stolle, D., Schuldberg, D., van den Pol, R., & Young, M. (2009). Cognitive Behavioral Intervention for Trauma in Schools (CBITS): School-based treatment on a rural American Indian reservation. *Journal of Behavior Therapy and Experimental Psychiatry, 40*(1), 169–178. https://doi.org/10.1016/j.jbtep.2008.07.006

Murphy, J. M., Abel, M. R., Hoover, S., Jellinek, M., & Fazel, M. (2017). Scope, scale, and dose of the world's largest school-based mental health programs. *Harvard Review of Psychiatry, 25*(5), 218–228. https://doi.org/10.1097/HRP.0000000000000149

Nadeem, E., Saldana, L., Chapman, J., & Schaper, H. (2018). A mixed methods study of the stages of implementation for an evidence-based trauma intervention in schools. *Behavior Therapy, 49*(4), 509–524. https://doi.org/10.1016/j.beth.2017.12.004

Neuner, F., Catani, C., Ruf, M., Schauer, E., Schauer, M., & Elbert, T. (2008). Narrative exposure therapy for the treatment of traumatized children and adolescents (KidNET): From neurocognitive theory to field intervention. *Child and Adolescent Psychiatric Clinics of North America, 17*(3), 641–664, x. https://doi.org/10.1016/j.chc.2008.03.001

Pfefferbaum, B., Nitiéma, P., Tucker, P., & Newman, E. (2017). Early child disaster mental health interventions: A review of the empirical evidence. *Child and Youth Care Forum, 46*(5), 621–642. https://doi.org/10.1007/s10566-017-9397-y

Pfefferbaum, B., Sweeton, J. L., Newman, E., Varma, V., Noffsinger, M. A., Shaw, J. A., Chrisman, A. K., & Nitiéma, P. (2014). Child disaster mental health interventions, part II: Timing of implementation, delivery settings and providers, and therapeutic approaches. *Disaster Health, 2*(1), 58–67. https://doi.org/10.4161/dish.27535

Robjant, K., & Fazel, M. (2010). The emerging evidence for narrative exposure therapy: A review. *Clinical Psychology Review, 30*(8), 1030–1039. https://doi.org/10.1016/j.cpr.2010.07.004

Rolfsnes, E. S., & Idsoe, T. (2011). School-based intervention programs for PTSD symptoms: A review and meta-analysis. *Journal of Traumatic Stress, 24*(2), 155–165. https://doi.org/10.1002/jts.20622

Rousseau, C., Beauregard, C., Daignault, K., Petrakos, H., Thombs, B. D., Steele, R., Vasiliadis, H. M., & Hechtman, L. (2014). A cluster randomized-controlled trial of a classroom-based drama workshop program to improve mental health outcomes among immigrant and refugee youth in special classes. *PLOS ONE, 9*(8), e104704. https://doi.org/10.1371/journal.pone.0104704

Rousseau, C., Benoit, M., Gauthier, M. F., Lacroix, L., Alain, N., Rojas, M. V., Moran, A., & Bourassa, D. (2007). Classroom drama therapy program for immigrant and refugee adolescents: A pilot study. *Clinical Child Psychology and Psychiatry, 12*(3), 451–465. https://doi.org/10.1177/1359104507078477

Rousseau, C., Drapeau, A., Lacroix, L., Bagilishya, D., & Heusch, N. (2005). Evaluation of a classroom program of creative expression workshops for refugee and immigrant children. *Journal of Child Psychology and Psychiatry, and Allied Disciplines*, *46*(2), 180–185. https://doi.org/10.1111/j.1469-7610.2004.00344.x

Rousseau, C., & Heusch, N. (2000). The Trip: A creative expression project for refugee and immigrant children. *Journal of the American Art Therapy Association*, *17*(1), 31–40. https://doi.org/10.1080/07421656.2000.10129434

Ruf, M., Schauer, M., Neuner, F., Catani, C., Schauer, E., & Elbert, T. (2010). Narrative exposure therapy for 7- to 16-year-olds: A randomized controlled trial with traumatized refugee children. *Journal of Traumatic Stress*, *23*(4), 437–445. https://doi.org/10.1002/jts.20548

Santiago, C. D., Fuller, A. K., Lennon, J. M., & Kataoka, S. H. (2016). Parent perspectives from participating in a family component for CBITS: Acceptability of a culturally informed school-based program. *Psychological Trauma: Theory, Research, Practice, and Policy*, *8*(3), 325–333. https://doi.org/10.1037/tra0000076

Schottelkorb, A. A., Doumas, D. M., & Garcia, R. (2012). Treatment for childhood refugee trauma: A randomized, controlled trial. *International Journal of Play Therapy*, *21*(2), 57–73. https://doi.org/10.1037/a0027430

Substance Abuse and Mental Health Services Administration. (2014). *SAMHSA's concept of trauma and guidance for a trauma-informed approach*. https://ncsacw.samhsa.gov/userfiles/files/SAMHSA_Trauma.pdf

Sullivan, A. L., & Simonson, G. R. (2016). A systematic review of school-based social-emotional interventions for refugee and war-traumatized youth. *Review of Educational Research*, *86*(2), 503–530.

Tyrer, R. A., & Fazel, M. (2014). School and community-based interventions for refugee and asylum seeking children: A systematic review. *PLOS ONE*, *9*(2), e89359. https://doi.org/10.1371/journal.pone.0089359

van Westrhenen, N., & Fritz, E. (2014). Creative arts therapy as treatment for child trauma: An overview. *The Arts in Psychotherapy*, *41*(5), 527–534. https://doi.org/10.1016/j.aip.2014.10.004

# 9 TREATMENT FOR REFUGEE CHILDREN AND THEIR FAMILIES

AIMEE HILADO, ANN CHU, AND ALLEGRA MAGRISSO

The United Nations High Commissioner for Refugees (UNHCR; 2019) estimated that there were 70.8 million forcibly displaced persons worldwide at
the end of 2018. More than 25.9 million registered refugees are represented
in this number, with nearly 13 million being children (UNHCR, 2019). Examining the child and youth numbers closely, refugee children and youth were
5 times more likely to be out of school compared with their nonrefugee peers
(UNHCR USA, 2018a). The 7.4 million of school age had limited access to
education—only 61% of refugee children attended a primary school, compared with 91% globally, and 76% of refugee adolescents were not enrolled
in any secondary school (UNHCR USA, 2018a). The crisis in Syria alone has
accounted for 13 million displaced people, with 4.7 million being children
(UNHCR, 2019; UNHCR USA, 2018b). Moreover, there were an estimated
2.4 million very young children (aged birth to 5 years) displaced in refugee
camps and urban areas worldwide (UNHCR, 2018b) who were experiencing
limited access to adequate health care, early childhood programming, and
general resources that ensure very young children are able to meet their
developmental agendas.

https://doi.org/10.1037/0000226-009
*Refugee Mental Health*, J. D. Aten and J. Hwang (Editors)

Thus, there is an entire generation of displaced children and youth growing up in unpredictable and often dangerous circumstances that directly influence their physical and psychological development. Additionally, their developmental outcomes directly influence their families.

This chapter examines the unique needs of displaced families with children, with specific attention to refugee families with very young children aged birth to 5 years. This chapter also highlights relevant interventions that are child focused and target developmental and mental health outcomes. The interventions—child–parent psychotherapy (CPP), sandplay and play therapy, and home visiting—have been studied primarily among young children struggling with trauma-related social–emotional, behavioral, and sensory deficits. Though there is some empirical evidence of effectiveness among immigrant populations broadly, there is limited empirical research on outcomes specific to refugee children (Hilado et al., 2019). Despite this limitation, the interventions have a trauma-informed component that applies to refugee children. The sections on interventions also highlight an ancillary role in which entire family systems can be strengthened as a by-product of the child-focused intervention with the intent of examining how clinical work can strengthen trauma-experienced families. To provide an adequate framework for considering clinical interventions for children and families, we begin with a discussion of the scope of need within refugee families and the needs specific to young children.

## UNDERSTANDING THE IMPACT OF IMMIGRATION ON REFUGEE FAMILIES

### Refugee Status

By definition, a *refugee* is someone who flees their home country and crosses an international border because of a well-founded fear of persecution for reasons of race, religion, nationality, political opinion, or membership in a particular social group (UNHCR, 2018a). Refugees often flee their home country as a result of regional conflicts; climate change; lack of access to basic resources such as health care, education, and employment; or the hope of greater opportunities elsewhere. Thus, the very nature of refugee status reflects an experience of forced migration and protracted periods of uncertainty as individuals, families, and communities move from region to region seeking resettlement options that allow the rebuilding of lives in safety and dignity.

## Stages of Migration

Refugees able to travel as a family unit feel a particular stress in their migration story. As mentioned, this chapter focuses on interventions with young children in the context of their families. To best understand the needs of young children, who typically migrate with their families, or those who grow up in households impacted by immigration trauma, we begin with a discussion of the three stages of a refugee family's migration journey—premigration experiences, experiences in transit, and postmigration resettlement experiences. These stages are understood to have a cumulative impact on a family's dynamics, its structure, and ultimately how that family functions (Hilado & Lundy, 2017). This information on family functioning and the impact of trauma on family systems allows for a clearer discussion of the subsequent impact on child outcomes, the topic at the heart of this chapter.

### Premigration Experiences

To begin, *premigration* refers to the period when a family leaves their country of origin and travels to a refugee processing center. During this time, many refugee families are exposed to violent and traumatic events in their home countries that greatly impact their mental and physical health (Hart, 2009; McMullen et al., 2013). Similar traumatic events may then be experienced once a refugee family arrives at a UNHCR-designated center, is processed, and is assigned refugee status, all experiences that compound vulnerabilities from previous trauma.

The refugee application process for resettlement in the United States is particularly challenging as applicants undergo a rigorous multistep process that begins abroad (U.S. Citizenship and Immigrant Services [USCIS], 2020). It begins with a series of interviews, first with UNHCR field agents; if approved for U.S. resettlement, an agent representing the U.S. Department of State conducts an additional interview, accompanied by medical exams and a series of background and biometric checks across all domestic and international intelligence databases. Refugees applying as a family unit go through an additional protocol based on the nature of the application—intact family or family reunification.

The intact family unit applies together in one interview if all members are in the same location. The adults are interviewed and provide information on behalf of minors (under age 18 years) in the family. Unmarried adults aged 18+ may also be included in the family's application, and in some cases, a married child and spouse can be included in one family's application. Each application is reviewed on a case-by-case basis, and the use of DNA tests to confirm relations between family members is common protocol. In the event a baby is born while a family awaits a resettlement decision, the infant must be added to the application as soon as possible to ensure the file is current and all family members are documented.

For family reunification applications, in which a member in the United States petitions for their family members abroad, the same application process is completed, including interviews, medical exams, and background checks (USCIS, 2020). Additionally, DNA tests are required for both the petitioner in the United States and the applicant family abroad. The family must absorb the cost of these tests initially, but if the application is approved, the cost is reimbursed. This measure is to deter fraudulent family claims through the U.S. Refugee Admissions Program. Moreover, there are priority categories that designate family members who may be approved for resettlement more quickly (American Immigration Council, 2020). Priority is given to parents, spouses, and unmarried children who are minors. Consideration can be given for adult children, their spouses, and potentially grandchildren based on country of origin and available resettlement slots (American Immigration Council, 2020).

Family applications from countries designated as high risk because of terrorism concerns follow an even more rigorous interview protocol (American Immigration Council, 2020). Depending on the country of origin, there are protocols in which each adult member of the family is interviewed separately, in addition to the ongoing medical exams and background checks (American Immigration Council, 2020). The applicants' recollections of the events that are the basis for refugee status need to be identical; otherwise, entire cases can be denied. Many refugees have cited the process for U.S. resettlement as its own traumatic experience because applicants must repeatedly disclose their reasons for fleeing to different agents, recounting each traumatic memory and loss with great detail and having to be sure each story matches over time and across family members. This repetition has the power to intensify the trauma response.[1]

Refugee families tend to be resettled at higher rates than single applicants, but there is no clear equation for which families get priority over others, with the resettlement trends fluctuating each year (RefugeeOne, 2019). Single parents with minor children generally are prioritized over large families with six or more members, but there is great variability by country and world region. Although there is a priority in keeping family cases

---

[1] Authors Hilado and Magrisso are mental health professionals in a refugee mental health program. The remarks in this paragraph reflect statements shared by refugee participants receiving treatment.

together, we have encountered families being separated in the application process.[2] The following client cases are examples of how family separation can occur during the resettlement procedure:

- Four siblings from a Rohingya family living in Malaysia were interviewed separately, and one sibling was not approved for resettlement because her story did not match that of her siblings.

- A Congolese family, while in a refugee camp in Uganda, decided to leave the husband off the application because they believed it would expedite the process. The wife and three children were resettled in the United States and then tried to petition the husband. Because the original application stated that the wife was unmarried, the husband could not join the family despite having marriage paperwork.

Taken together, the premigration experiences of refugee families while fleeing their country of origin and navigating the refugee resettlement application process are fraught with uncertainty, fear, and additional trauma for some. This is the first step of a refugee family's journey and an important element of their migration story.

**Experiences in Transit**
If approved for travel, the experiences of a family while in transit can also have an adverse impact on the entire unit. Many refugee families report selling all their belongings before traveling to their point of departure because only limited goods can be brought to their resettlement country. This can be bittersweet for many families because the process reflects a loss of their personal memories and, for some, of their entire home culture. Some refugee families resettled in the United States report having no clear idea of their final destination and must adapt to the last-minute information of their receiving state; some learn they will be resettled in Chicago, for example, which involves drastically different expectations from resettlement in Los Angeles. The issuance of the so-called U.S. travel bans in 2016[3] that halted

---

[2]The remarks in this paragraph reflect statements shared by refugee participants receiving treatment.
[3]After the 2016 election, the Trump administration implemented a series of executive orders and proclamations that severely limited immigration to the United States and prevented certain citizens from pursuing immigrant visas ("green cards"). These include Executive Order 13769 (January 27, 2017—original travel ban), Executive Order 13780 (March 6, 2017), Presidential Proclamation 9645 (September 24, 2017), Presidential Proclamation 9723 (April 10, 2018), and Presidential Proclamation 9984 (January 31, 2020). Each order or proclamation sought

the U.S. Refugee Admissions Program and banned specific immigrant groups has exacerbated the uncertainty and fear for all U.S.-bound immigrant and refugee groups, many of whom express fear of being denied access despite having approved immigration paperwork. All of these examples reflect the combination of excitement and fear of uncertainty that comes with moving to a new country and specifically to the United States.

**Postmigration Resettlement Experiences**
Lastly, the postmigration resettlement stage involves experiences after a family arrives in their resettlement country, and this stage often presents its own challenges. U.S.-bound refugees have an abrupt adjustment period; they are given a 3-month housing allocation from the U.S. Department of State ($1,250 total per person in 2020) to help with the transition, with the expectation that they will adjust to life in their new city, secure a job to pay rent, and learn to navigate school, health, and social service agencies within that time (American Immigration Council, 2020; Office of Refugee Resettlement, 2020). Although refugee resettlement agencies play a big role in providing both concrete and social supports, much of the pressure of adjustment and becoming economically self-sufficient remains on the family (RefugeeOne, 2019).

## THEMES IN CLINICAL PRACTICE WHEN WORKING WITH REFUGEE FAMILIES

Professionals must consider the following themes that impact refugee families, both individual members and the family system as a whole, as they resettle in the host country:

- changes in family roles: Upon arrival, working-age refugees move quickly to secure a job (often a low-wage, entry-level survival position) with the help of their resettlement agency. Two incomes are often necessary to pay rent and other expenses, requiring women to seek jobs outside the

---

to severely limit entry, including admission through well-vetted immigration programs such as the U.S. Refugee Admissions Program and the U.S. asylum programs, and they were often referred to as "Muslim bans" and characterized by antiimmigrant, xenophobic rhetoric. Each ban was challenged in court, with some resulting in successful injunctions that barred the orders from full implementation. Beginning in March 2020, in response to the COVID-19 pandemic, additional travel restrictions were implemented by country, the U.S. Refugee Admissions Program was suspended, and the borders were closed to arriving asylum applicants.

home—an uncommon practice for many resettled ethnic groups. In some cases, the women of the household have an easier time securing a job based on the hiring sector and thereby assume the role of breadwinner, a role different from what may have been typical in their home country. Such changes often create tensions within the family.

- changes in power dynamics: Refugee children often learn the English language faster than their parents and serve as interpreters in important transactions, including health and public benefits appointments. This capacity shifts the power balance within families as parents and other adults become more reliant on the children, who assume a role that is demanding and critical and often not age appropriate. Refugee parents also sometimes state that the child protection laws in the United States challenge corporal punishment practices that are culturally appropriate back home, leaving parents feeling unable to discipline their children in ways they believe to be effective. Thus, children may be seen as powerful because of their language skills and their parents' understanding of legal protections.

- fears of loss of culture: Parents are often concerned that their children are becoming too "Americanized," as seen when children are less respectful to their elders, more independent and strong willed, and embarrassed to be heard speaking the home language or seen eating native foods around others. The perception of less power because of lack of discipline options also contributes to this concern. Such feelings can create deep divisions within the family, weakening the overall cohesiveness of the unit.

- intergenerational impact of trauma: We have seen young children unable to self-regulate as a result of parents who cannot model compassion, empathy, or self-regulation because of mental health problems related to previous trauma. Trauma has the ability to freeze the parent–child relationship, impeding communication and weakening the bonds between family members. With weakened relationships, entire family systems struggle.

Each theme is experienced differently by each member of a family based on a number of individual factors, such as age, temperament, previous experiences of immigration, coping skills, socioeconomic status, and even health and mental health. The themes are also influenced by the life stage of the family—for example, newly married family, family with previous experience of displacement, or family with adult children (Schriver, 2015). The reactions may range from mild discomfort to pervasive anxiety and sadness that warrant mental health intervention. The variability in adjustment thus requires interventions tailored for each person and need.

## IMPACT OF IMMIGRATION TRAUMA ON YOUNG CHILDREN

Professionals working with refugee families need to consider the entire migration journey and the experiences in each stage that subsequently impact the
entire family system both physically and psychologically (Hilado & Allweiss,
2017). The unique needs of refugee children require yet another level of
understanding and attention. The risk factors for poor developmental outcomes among young children are substantial because the effects of immigration trauma can have a particularly damaging impact when the trauma is
severe and persistent during the first years of a child's life and when there is
no supportive buffer to ameliorate the trauma risk.

The early years are understood to set the foundation for development
across the life span:

> The scientific evidence on the significant developmental impacts of early experi-
> ences, caregiving relationships, and environmental threats is incontrovertible. . . .
> The question today is not whether early experience matters, but rather how
> early experiences shape individual development and contribute to children's
> continued movement along positive pathways. (Shonkoff & Phillips, 2000, p. 6)

It is these early years that establish the basis for children to meet their developmental agenda and full potential (Gopnik et al., 2000; Siegel, 1999).
Conversely, the negative impact of trauma, exposure to violence, and abuse
or neglect during the early years can have repercussions that may plague a
child's life through adulthood with poor health and mental health outcomes
(Anda et al., 2004; Anda, Felitti, Bremner, et al., 2006; Anda, Felitti, Brown,
et al., 2006; Dube et al., 2006; Edwards et al., 2003). The juxtaposition of this
understanding and the overwhelming rates of young children and families
displaced worldwide only intensifies the concern about what is happening
to an entire generation of refugee children and youth for whom traumatic
experiences are a daily reality.

The groundbreaking adverse childhood experiences (ACE) studies of the
1990s clearly highlighted the connection between early experiences and
negative outcomes throughout the life span, illuminating needs that may
not fully be recognized among young refugee children. That is, traumatic
stressors during early childhood through adolescence—specifically, physical,
emotional, and sexual abuse; physical and emotional neglect; and households
experiencing mental illness, domestic violence, parental divorce or separation, substance abuse, and incarceration—represent a common pathway to
a variety of important long-term behavioral, health, and social problems that
may impact functioning throughout the life span, from heart disease to learning difficulties to drug and alcohol use (Anda, 2006; Anda et al., 2004, 2010).
Immigration trauma, though not listed explicitly as an ACE criterion, has

the potential to impact refugees because the trauma can produce behaviors included in the ACE criteria. Furthermore, current immigration policies can result in young children being separated from one or both primary caregivers, which is listed as an ACE stressor. Refugees who are suffering from a mental illness because of past trauma, those who are abusive or neglectful because they are unable to cope with mental health symptoms, and those who become incarcerated as a result of self-destructive behaviors that mask sadness, anxiety, and posttraumatic stress symptoms all potentially raise ACE scores among refugee children.

Already, we are seeing the impact of immigration trauma on young children. Trauma-exposed children may experience emotional and behavioral difficulties in school and within their families because of the adjustment (Goldfinch, 2009; Marans, 2013; Montgomery, 2011; Niaz, 2014); thus, it is not only the experiences in their home country that impact children and their families but also the changes in adapting to a different environment (Hart, 2009; McMullen et al., 2013; Montgomery, 2011). Parents may deliberately try to hide the struggles of relocation with the intention of protecting their children, yet unintentionally leave the children with limited opportunities to discuss their feelings and questions about what is happening (Hart, 2009). Additionally, parents' own traumatic experiences (and the resultant mental and physical health implications) may also affect their children; in some cases, parents may not be able to be adequately attentive to the needs of their children (Montgomery, 2011; van Ee et al., 2012). Moreover, children's early exposure to trauma and untreated trauma can have long-lasting effects on their physical, social, and emotional development, which can impact brain function and development over the life span (Hart, 2009; Niaz, 2014).

The deleterious impact of trauma applies to all young children but is uniquely relevant for young refugee children, who often experience immigration trauma by virtue of their experiences obtaining refugee status. The risk factors may vary, as does the degree of exposure to the risk, yet there is a common denominator: The stressful and traumatic experiences occur within the family and home environment and often in the context of a relationship in the home.

## UNDERSTANDING INFANT-EARLY CHILDHOOD MENTAL HEALTH

As one thinks about the effects of trauma on the youngest refugee children in the family (i.e., those aged birth to 3 years), one must look at the early relationships that are the basis of survival and the foundation of development.

There is no family relationship more important than the relationship between parent or primary caregiver and child (hereafter referred to as the "parent–child relationship"), particularly during the early childhood years. The importance of this relationship is well documented in the early childhood literature (Thompson, 2000; Zeanah, 2019). Often, the critical nature of the attachment relationship is seen in the connection between nature and nurture (or genes and the environment) and understood as the basis for development (Lewontin, 2000; Ridley, 2003; Siegel, 1999). And it is through a strong, positive relationship between parent and child in the early years that gains are seen across the domains of social–emotional, cognitive, language, and physical development (Richter, 2004; Shonkoff & Phillips, 2000; Thompson, 2000).

Immigration trauma, however, has the power to disrupt the development of a strong, positive relationship between the parent and child, an occurrence that mental health professionals see in refugee families. Trauma freezes the parent–child relationship when the refugee parent's availability is compromised by struggles with trauma-related mental health problems. Parents may experience periods of sadness, anxiety, difficulty concentrating, and poor coping skills, all common mental health problems in refugee communities (Slewa-Younan et al., 2015). As a result, parents may be unable to demonstrate and model compassion, empathy, or attuned communication, qualities understood to strengthen the parent–child relationship. Trauma-experienced refugee parents may also be unable to model good coping skills and self-regulation, resulting in parents who react with negative emotion rather than with patience and understanding. The parent–child relationship is strained and even suspended without the parent's ability to tune in to and meet the needs of their child with warm, appropriate nurturance.

All of this has implications for social–emotional development, which is the critical area of development that aligns with what is understood as the basis for mental health among young children (Hughes et al., 2015). Through the years, the work of supporting mental health or social–emotional development in the early years has fallen under several names that have been used interchangeably. The term "infant mental health" focused on supporting the needs of infants aged birth to 2 years and began with the work of psychoanalyst and social worker Selma Fraiberg and her colleagues in 1975. The period was then broadened to include children aged birth to 5 years using the inclusive term "early childhood mental health" (Osofsky & Thomas, 2012). In more recent years, we have seen two additional iterations of the term to include the same time period: "infant, toddler, and early childhood mental health" (Nelson & Mann, 2011) and "infant–early childhood mental health" (I–ECMH; Cohen et al., 2012); we use the term "I–ECMH" hereafter.

Jointly, all four terms refer to an approach to supporting the social–emotional needs of young children through engagement of both the young child and the parent or primary caregiver, given that "a young child's social–emotional development happens within an interactive and relationship-based context" (Hughes et al., 2015, p. 37). Osofsky and Thomas (2012) further noted, "Because the caregiver plays a crucial role as a partner in the infant and young child's social and emotional development, the caregiver's emotional well-being is central to the infant's emotional well-being" (p. 9). This joint focus on parent and child is particularly crucial for refugee families given the broad adverse impact of trauma on the child, parent, and family as a whole. Trauma (and a compromised parent–child relationship as a result of trauma) directly influences I–ECMH. Refugee parents may experience mental health problems because of the combination of previous trauma and the stressors of adjustment to life in a new country. Family stressors—such as lack of resources, large families with complex health and mental health needs, and limited social supports—are yet another layer of risk that influences the presentation of complex trauma in refugee families. These stressors further impact the entire refugee family unit, have a unique impact on each individual member, and have the greatest adverse impact on the youngest members in the refugee family consistent with our discussion of early development.

Therefore, in the next section we describe clinical approaches to supporting refugee families by exploring interventions that focus on supporting I–ECMH through attending to the young child and parent or caregiver simultaneously. In using these approaches, professionals can support the mental health of refugee parents and promote family well-being through this focus.

## TREATMENT MODELS

The reality is that "most potential mental health problems will not become mental health problems if we respond to them early [in life]" (Center on the Developing Child, Harvard University, n.d.). Specifically, attention to mental health needs presented in the first 3 years of a child's life can help that young child resume a healthy trajectory of development and mental well-being. To address this priority, there has been a call for an increase in cross-disciplinary training and cross-discipline collaboration around

I–ECMH (Division for Early Childhood, 2014) and a call for more informa-tion around evidence-based interventions that can support refugee families with young children. Three interventions in particular—child–parent psycho-therapy, sandplay and play therapy, and home visiting—entail clinical strategies that support very young children and their parents and can be used with trauma-experienced, culturally diverse refugee populations. In the sections that follow, each intervention is introduced with a brief his-tory, key elements, primary participants, and intended outcomes of the intervention, followed by a discussion of its relevance for refugee children and families.

## Child–Parent Psychotherapy

### Brief History
Child–parent psychotherapy is an evidence-based treatment model for chil-dren aged birth to 5 years who have been exposed to traumatic events, envi-ronmental adversities, parental mental illness, or harmful parenting practices and who are experiencing mental health, attachment, or behavioral problems. CPP integrates multiple theoretical approaches including developmental perspectives, psychoanalysis, and attachment and trauma theories. CPP uses intervention strategies derived from cognitive behavior, social learning, somatic, and play therapy. CPP is thus similar to many other child psycho-therapies but differs in the centrality of the parent or caregiver in being an active partner during treatment.

CPP originated from infant–parent psychotherapy, a psychoanalytic treat-ment for mental health disturbances for very young children aged birth through 3 years (Fraiberg, 1980). Infant–parent psychotherapy is based on the concept of "ghosts in the nursery"—the now-classic metaphor used to describe the intergenerational transmission of psychopathology as a result of parents reenacting with their young infants their own unresolved or unremembered early relational experiences of helplessness and fear (Fraiberg et al., 1975). The ghosts symbolize early memories that are outside con-sciousness; these nonintegrated memories in turn impact parents' attitudes and behaviors toward their infants. CPP extends infant–parent psycho-therapy by working with children through age 5 and focuses on the emo-tional quality of the parent–child relationship.

Whereas Fraiberg and colleagues (1975) focused on the "ghosts" in the nursery, CPP brought in the counterpoint of "angels" in the nursery to explore experiences of love, acceptance, and safety in the parent's child-hood (Lieberman, Padrón, et al., 2005). The angels symbolize influences of strength and hope that may also be transmitted intergenerationally to heal unresolved conflicts. Hope represents a key guiding value of CPP and one of the main treatment objectives that counterbalances the despair of trauma.

The efficacy of CPP in treating young children exposed to trauma has been documented in five randomized controlled trials with racially, ethnically, and economically diverse samples including anxiously attached toddlers of Latina mothers with trauma histories (Lieberman et al., 1991), toddlers of depressed mothers (Cicchetti et al., 2000), maltreated infants (Cicchetti et al., 2006) and maltreated preschoolers (Toth et al., 2002), and preschoolers exposed to domestic violence (Lieberman, Van Horn, & Ippen, 2005). Findings indicate positive outcomes in a variety of domains, including child and maternal symptoms (Lieberman, Van Horn, & Ippen, 2005), child attributions (of parents, themselves, and relationships; Toth et al., 2002), mother–child relationship and child attachment security (Cicchetti et al., 1999, 2006; Toth et al., 2006), and child cognitive functioning (Cicchetti et al., 2000).

**Key Elements**
The foundational phase of CPP consists of an assessment and engagement period that lasts four to six sessions. Therapists meet individually with the parent or caregiver during the foundational phase with the goal of gathering information and cultivating parental or caregiver engagement. The foundational phase concludes with a feedback session with the parent or caregiver to cocreate a treatment conceptualization and plan. The conceptualization of CPP helps the parent or caregiver understand the potential connections between past trauma experiences and current functioning in the child and how treatment might help.

Using CPP with refugee families with young children can involve an extended foundational phase. Many families have had minimal experience with therapy, and the clinician needs to align the therapeutic frame with the families' cultural norms and parenting practices. Caregivers are often challenged regarding child care options, requiring them to bring their children to foundational phase sessions. Having children present requires navigation by the clinician to obtain information on child and caregiver symptoms and trauma histories; the impact on young children of hearing these discussions needs to be considered.

The first joint parent–child session during the intervention phase is spent with the therapist and parent or caregiver introducing treatment to the child by playing out the child's traumatic experiences with representational objects (e.g., doll figures, dollhouses, ambulances) or with age-appropriate wording.

The explanation of what happened to them is connected to a description of current symptoms. Simple words are used to assure the child that they can share with their parent or caregiver how they feel about what happened. Starting treatment with this frame models the core guiding value of "speaking the unspeakable" (Lieberman et al., 2015) in exploring the impact of trauma exposure on the young child, the parent, and the caregiving relationship.

For many refugee families, the trauma in their home country or during their immigration journey may have occurred in the not-so-distant past and remains unintegrated in the parents' or caregivers' minds and bodies. Many parents avoid thinking or talking about their experiences but understand that their children are being impacted. Many CPP clinicians find themselves working primarily with parents or caregivers to untangle their own trauma histories to strengthen the caregiving relationship. Many refugee families also experience secondary adversities after resettlement such as heightened tensions in the marital relationship (sometimes including domestic violence), separation from extended family in their country of origin, and fear of deportation. Thus, the trauma history becomes a complex narrative with the immigration experience and refugee status forming but a small chapter.

There is no session-by-session guide for CPP. Instead, CPP clinicians provide interventions flexibly according to the family's needs and the spontaneous "ports of entry"—opportunities for entering into the system to create change—offered by the child and parent or caregiver (Lieberman et al., 2015). Interventions can be addressed to the child, the parent or caregiver, or the relationship, with the understanding that all interventions will impact both the parent or caregiver and child. The range of CPP interventions can be largely categorized into the following modalities:

- promoting developmental progress through play, physical contact, and language;
- offering unstructured reflective developmental guidance;
- modeling appropriate protective behavior;
- interpreting feelings and actions;
- providing emotional support and empathic communication;
- providing crisis intervention, case management, and concrete assistance with problems of living;
- addressing traumatic reminders; and
- retrieving and creating benevolent memories (Lieberman et al., 2015, 2019).

The values of the family are interwoven into all the treatment modalities such that clinicians are encouraged to modify and adapt strategies for engagement and treatment based on the developmental issues, parenting practices, and cultural norms of the family while maintaining fidelity to the core CPP components and overall model.

## Primary Participants

One core premise of CPP is that the attachment system is the organizer of children's development and responses to trauma. Problems in infancy and early childhood are best addressed in the context of the primary attachment relationship. Many young children in refugee families experience separation anxiety because of the heightened sense of fear and uncertainty that affects the entire family unit, in particular when separation anxiety represents a normative fear in early childhood (Lieberman, 2018). CPP clinicians work with the parent or primary caregiver in joint dyadic sessions to facilitate increased emotional and behavioral regulation. When safety has been damaged because of exposure to traumatic events, clinicians help parents or primary caregivers resume the role of protector for the child in a reliable and consistent way. When primary caregivers are having difficulty navigating a new country and assimilating to a new culture as a refugee, uncertain of their legal status and future security and unable to secure basic needs such as housing and employment, the goal of establishing safety becomes both paramount and challenging.

## Intended Outcomes

Treatment goals in CPP are prioritized on the basis of the family's needs, with the establishment of a safe environment—physical and psychological safety both in real life and in the therapeutic setting—as the primary target. For refugee families for whom safety remains uncertain, the goal becomes to help children cope with the lack of certainty and to help caregivers create a protective shield for their children within the reality of lack of safety. Treatment is deemed successful when parents or caregivers become reliable protectors of the child and can guide the child and the family toward any of the following key outcomes:

- return to normal development, adaptive coping, and engagement with present activities and future goals;
- increased capacity to respond realistically to threat;
- maintenance of regular levels of affective arousal;
- reestablished trust in bodily sensations;
- restoration of reciprocity in intimate relationships;
- normalization of the traumatic response;
- increased differentiation between reliving and remembering; and
- placement of the traumatic experience in perspective.

### Relevance for Refugee Children and Families

Refugee infants and young children are exposed to highly traumatic events, including accidents, natural disasters, war and terrorism, child maltreatment and neglect, domestic violence, and community violence (for a review, see Chu & Lieberman, 2010). Secondary adversities because of immigration or refugee status may include unemployment; uncertain legal status; uncertain access to food, housing, and transportation; and separation from support systems or communities; such adversities may further adversely impact young children's development (Layne et al., 2011). Additionally, racism and discrimination may further marginalize and isolate refugee families and create changing family dynamics based on shifting gender roles and the parentification of children because of faster acculturation. CPP includes open exploration and a direct, clear, and age-appropriate acknowledgment of the adversities, stressors, and traumatic experiences of the child and parent or caregiver in both the past and present (Lieberman et al., 2015). This acknowledgment helps children make meaning of their experiences.

In work with refugee families, CPP also includes case management and coordinated care to address issues such as housing, food, and employment instability. One additional challenge is the lack of mental health providers with bilingual and bicultural capacities in some regions. In urban areas with large Latinx populations, refugee families from Spanish-speaking countries are able to gain access to services (though typically after a long wait). However, families from other countries often rely on the assistance of professional interpreters. Introducing interpreters into a CPP session creates additional clinical challenges that are beyond the scope of this chapter.

### Case Vignette

Linda,[4] aged 4 years, was referred for services because of bed-wetting at night, social withdrawal, and clinging behavior with her parents when being dropped off at day care. Linda's father, Miguel, was an undocumented immigrant who came to the United States from Guatemala when he was 13 years old. He was the only one in the family who was undocumented. Miguel had previously worked in his cousin's construction business, but it was sold, and he had been out of work for over a year. Linda's mom, Guadalupe, immigrated from Nicaragua when she was 4 years old and was able to obtain legal status through the Deferred Action for Childhood Arrivals program. She worked part

---

[4] To preserve confidentiality, the names and identities of case vignette clients have been disguised. Some components provide composite information to reflect general trends.

time and was the primary income earner; Miguel was now the primary care-giver. This role reversal presented significant challenges in the relationship.

The family was stressed financially, and Miguel reported feeling like a burden on his family. The current political climate was impacting the family's sense of safety; Miguel was constantly thinking about his safety and had started drinking again after 2 years of sobriety. He did not report being connected to any supports in the community. Both parents disclosed having gotten into arguments with each other recently that included physical violence, which Linda might have witnessed. Linda's mom also asked how to explain to Linda the concept of borders. Linda started asking questions after a neighbor friend's father was taken by immigration officers. Linda also asked whether her dad was going to get in trouble with the police again for hurting Mama.

CPP treatment initially addressed the impact that witnessing domestic violence had on Linda. Through treatment, Linda's parents were able to help her make meaning of what she saw and to assure her that they were working on their relationship and doing everything they could to keep her and their family safe. The clinical goal of establishing a sense of safety or protective shield for Linda included addressing the family's mixed status, engaging in safety planning in case Miguel were to be deported, and connecting the family to social supports and resources in the community.

## Sandplay and Play Therapy

Sandplay and play therapy are therapeutic modalities used with adults, children, and families. Both are premised on the value of nonverbal expression in the treatment of a range of mental health issues, including the psychological effects of trauma. Because sandplay and play therapy are practices that do not rely on language as a primary means of expression, they have direct application as a cross-cultural methodology with refugee populations.

### Brief History of Sandplay

Child psychologist Margaret Lowenfeld developed the "world technique," a psychological practice in her therapeutic work with children. Lowenfeld (1979) recognized that there are "impressions and experiences of children that cannot be put into words" (p. 3). She created what her child clients referred to as the "wonder box," a box containing an array of materials including "colored sticks and shapes, beads, small toys of all sorts, paper shapes and match boxes" (Lowenfeld, 1979, p. 3). Children played with materials on the floor, but when Lowenfeld introduced containers of sand and water into the playroom, the children spontaneously integrated materials from the wonder box with the sand and water to create worlds.

Dora Kalff (1966/1980), a Swiss Jungian analyst, is referred to as the originator of the Jungian sandplay method (Mitchell & Friedman, 1994). In 1954, Kalff heard Lowenfeld speak in London about the world technique. Kalff was intrigued by Lowenfeld's work and saw the possibilities of integrating aspects of Lowenfeld's world technique with miniatures, Jungian theory, and the use of sand. Kalff named her approach "sandplay."

### Key Elements of Sandplay

Sandplay is defined as "a natural therapeutic modality that uses the language of symbols to facilitate the expression of the unconscious, archetypical, and internal worlds" (Friedman & Mitchell, 1997). Many categories of miniature figures of people of all ages and races, nature items, houses, fantasy figures, mythic figures, animals, and many others are available for clients to choose from. A tray that is 19.5 in. × 28.5 in. (49.5 cm × 72.4 cm) with a blue base and sides is filled with soft white sand. The therapist gives the simple instruction, "Would you like to make a sand world?" The sand world can be a metaphorical or realistic depiction of inner states or external experiences or conflicts.

### Case Vignette

Ohnmar was a Burmese refugee in his mid-40s who fled to Malaysia. After many years, he and his family were able to resettle in a city in the United States 6 years previously. He continued to struggle with symptoms of posttraumatic stress disorder (PTSD) and major depressive disorder. He was unable to work because of physical disabilities, which contributed to his depression.

After many months of therapy, Ohnmar approached the sand tray. After brushing his hands over the surface of the sand, he piled the sand into two mounds approximating the shape of human bodies. The mounds lay side by side in the center of the tray. He added a gravestone and some trees near the mounds. He began to sob and spoke of a trauma he had experienced as a small child. Ohnmar had watched from his hiding place under a bed as his parents were shot and killed when soldiers stormed into their home. He had carried this sorrow and terror for most of his life. Dormant emotions that had not been spoken became apparent to client and therapist.

### Brief History of Play Therapy

In 1919, Melanie Klein was the first psychoanalyst to make significant contributions to the field of therapeutic practice with children and incorporated play into the therapeutic process (Petot, 1979/1990). She observed that play therapy provided direct access to the child's unconscious. Anna Freud

(1964), another psychoanalyst, believed that play with children was a conduit for forging a therapeutic alliance. Both Klein and Freud believed that play is "the medium through which children express themselves most freely" (Landreth, 2012, p. 29).

A salient influence in the development of play therapy as it is widely used today was the client-centered approach to therapy created by Carl Rogers (1940), a humanistic psychotherapist. Psychologist Virginia Axline (1947) adapted Rogers's client-centered methodology to therapeutic work with children. In Axline's practice, the therapist does not interpret the child's play but mirrors the child's feelings. Educator Garry Landreth's (2012) book *Play Therapy: The Art of the Relationship* developed the key elements of child-centered play therapy as it is used today.

### Key Elements of Play Therapy

According to the Association for Play Therapy (n.d.), *play therapy* is defined as "the systematic use of a theoretical model to establish an interpersonal process wherein trained play therapists use the therapeutic power of play to help clients prevent or resolve psychosocial difficulties and achieve optimal growth and development" (para. 2). Additionally, "the therapist uses play with children because play is children's symbolic language of self-expression" (Landreth, 2012, pp. 16–17). Play is also a universal experience across cultures. It becomes the task of the therapist to understand the functions of play and to learn how to communicate at the developmentally appropriate level with the child about feelings and themes of play.

### Examining the Utility of Sandplay and Play Therapy

Sandplay and play therapy are expressive and projective modalities that have a number of key elements in common, characteristics that make them applicable with refugee populations. In both practices, the client leads the process and content of the session, whether of creating a sand world or in the client's play themes and choice of toys. Sandplay and play therapy are metaphorical expressions of the unconscious. The client's inner world becomes manifest outwardly. The client's process is held in a free and sheltered space (Kalff, 1966/1980). In play therapy, the *therapeutic alliance* is an emotionally safe and trusting relationship established between client and therapist that frees the client to move at their own pace and grow emotionally (Landreth, 2012).

In both modalities, the therapist's function is not to interpret but to witness and accompany the client's process. The therapist is the holding environment for the client's emotional content. Through the therapist's stance of unconditional positive regard (Axline, 1947; Rogers, 1940), the client is aided in resolving inner conflicts and gaining a sense of power and control. Processing trauma content can prompt the client's feelings of dysregulation (Goodyear-Brown, 2010, p. 17). To facilitate a safe environment for the creation of a coherent trauma narrative, the play therapist becomes the holding environment for trauma content, and in sandplay the sand within the boundaries of the tray contains the trauma narrative.

**Primary Participants**
Upheaval and disequilibrium are consequences of the affronts of war. Displacement further compromises refugees' sense of safety. Wounds to the psyche are buried in the unconscious and personal agency diminished. Adult clients report multiple physical symptoms, the emotional impact of trauma held in the body. Children, still in the process of developing a sense of self, are always psychologically impacted by the traumas of war (Zohar et al., 2011). In schools and in families, refugee children's behavior can be pockmarked with multiple maladaptive behaviors such as withdrawal and social isolation, misreading of others' social cues, resistance to the authority roles of parents, and vulnerability to negative influences such as gang affiliation.

Killian and colleagues (2017) found that child-centered play therapy helped Somali refugee children grow in self-awareness and explore what the authors described as "social location." *Social location* is a learning process that we see through play. It requires participants to intimately explore the mechanics of how something works, where it belongs in context with others, and the fit between play objects. By extension, there is a deeper understanding of social location through the relationships represented by those objects. Thus, social location affects what is perceived as acceptable or unacceptable. The vignette that follows describes an example of social location demonstrated in play therapy.

**Case Vignette**
Lely was an 8-year-old Syrian refugee who fled with her family from the war. The family had been in the United States for 1 year. Lely attended second grade in an urban public school. She was referred to therapy because of her aggressive behavior at home and school. She told the therapist that children did not play with her because she spoke Arabic (she also spoke English).

The therapist invited Lely to show her what was happening using the miniature figures of boys and girls, blocks, and chairs and desks. Lely played out a scene demonstrating how she reported to the teacher when other children talked when they should be listening. Lely said that that was what she thought she was supposed to do, but that after she reported this to the teacher, her classmates did not speak to her and excluded her from play. The therapist talked with Lely about the unspoken norms among schoolchildren in the United States and in Syria, explaining that in the United States, correcting behavior is a job left to the teacher.

## Intended Outcomes

Clients experience an easing of inner tension, anxiety, and depression as they concretely portray feelings that are difficult to name. Through the process of sandplay and play therapy, some of the symptoms of PTSD are decreased. Because these modalities allow clients to express themselves in a voice that requires no words, both adults and children become more in touch with themselves and their self-concept improves (Schottelkorb et al., 2012). What has been stored in the unconscious is communicated through the language of play or the creation of a sand world. Inner struggles are "transposed from the inner world to the outer world and made visible" (Kalff, 1966/1980, p. 32). The client's energy becomes more available to deal with the daily tasks necessary for functioning (Goodyear-Brown, 2010).

Elements of a client's story that may have been inaccessible to awareness become concrete, outward manifestations of what the client could not say. The client builds a coherent narrative that challenges cognitive distortions and restructures ways of thinking into constructive and healthy patterns. The discovery of meaning in their posttrauma lives is made possible (Goodyear-Brown, 2010).

## Relevance for Refugee Children and Families

Sandplay and play therapy are of particular relevance for work with refugee children, adults, and families because of their nonverbal and projective nature. Interpretation by the therapist is not necessary and indeed can interrupt the healing process (Bradway & McCoard, 1997). Acting out in the sand or in play is healing in itself.

Loss of memory, defensiveness, and flashbacks or nightmares are symptoms that refugee adults and children live with in their posttrauma lives. Having no choice but to flee from threats to physical and emotional well-being, refugees can continue to feel powerless. They can feel overwhelmed by the demands of adjusting to a new life in a place where nothing feels familiar. Acting out in play and in the sand tray through the use of concrete images can stabilize moods and feelings. By concretely depicting psychological material that can cause fragmentation of a sense of self, refugees who are displaced from their home and country can begin to recover a sense of control over circumstances. Over the course of treatment, as clients construct a narrative of their past through play or sandplay, a sense of agency and the possibilities for a posttrauma life are discovered.

There are challenges to be considered in using sandplay and play therapy with refugee populations. It is beneficial if clinicians receive training in the use of these modalities. To dismiss such practices as "just play" or a "just a technique" is to misunderstand the essence of these practices. The use of miniature figures for expression of feelings may be foreign and uncomfortable to some refugees. Time must be given to the development of a trusting relationship. Neither practice should be forced upon the client but rather extended as an invitation for use in the healing process.

Sandplay and play therapy are also used with refugee family units or small family groups or dyads. As in other forms of family therapy, much can be learned about how a family is coping with trauma and adjusting to resettlement. Coping patterns, family dynamics, roles, and decision-making styles can be seen in play therapy scenes and in themes of the sand world. The following vignette illustrates the use of this intervention with two Burmese children.

### Case Vignette

Salim, aged 12, and his 6-year-old brother, Jabari, had lived in a large U.S. city for 5 years. They had witnessed repeated acts of domestic violence by their father against their mother in their home. The brothers were seen as a dyad in a therapy session. They chose to do a sand world.

Salim immediately drew a line with his finger through the middle of the tray, despite Jabari's protests. A key figure in Salim's sand world was an ominous figure dressed all in black whom he named Evil. (Jabari interjected, "No, he's not," but Salim insisted, saying it was his story.) The Evil figure attempted to invite a child male figure and domestic and wild animals to become evil by climbing up a tree with no leaves and joining him. Battles with Evil for dominance of the other figures ensued, and the ending of Salim's narrative was ambivalent.

At the same time, Jabari constructed his sand world by setting up dyads of a smaller animal with a larger animal, a snake facing an alligator, and a dinosaur attacking a human figure. (As Jabari set up his world, Salim reached over and took a tiger from his brother's side and put it on his side.) Jabari's narration repeated a pattern: The cow ate the dog, the snake ate the alligator, and the dinosaur ate the boy.

In their shared tray relationship, patterns between the brothers were witnessed, as well as how each boy dealt with themes of dominance and conflict. The process allowed the boys to explore emotions—positive and negative—within a safe context while developing a narrative to practice how to communicate those emotions and experiences.

When negative emotions and challenging behaviors arise in session, the process allows an opportunity for the therapist to step in as a supportive guide to work through those feelings and reactions through the tray or in direct conversation. If troubling psychological material is triggered, the therapist's task is to move slowly with the client as emotional content is expressed. The therapist needs to inhabit a steady, reassuring presence, with comments such as "Take your time" or "We can pause for a minute. I will sit here with you." Together, the therapist can help translate behaviors, observe and wonder about reactions with the child, model effective coping, and even suggest strategies to use when negative reactions are experienced. In doing so, the engagement in the context of sandplay work affords new learnings that the child can then integrate into their daily life.

## Home Visiting

### Brief History
Home visiting programs have a long history of supporting vulnerable communities. Documentation of the first home visiting programs can be found as early as the 1880s, when they were used to support new immigrant families adjusting to life in the United State (Charity Organization Society of the City of New York, 1883). Since then, home visiting programs have flourished across a number of human service fields (e.g., child welfare, early education, community health and mental health, immigrant services), supporting individuals from pregnancy to old age (Howard & Brooks-Gunn, 2009) by connecting them with a range of social, health, financial, and community resources that can promote well-being. Substantial data suggest that home visiting programs are effective in part because they have a prevention element: prevention of poor child outcomes (Peterson et al., 2007), reliance on public assistance (Sweet & Appelbaum, 2004), poor birth outcomes (Issel et al., 2011), and high blood lead levels (Brown et al., 2006). There is also documented promotion of breastfeeding (McInnes & Stone, 2001) and increased immunization rates (Koniak-Griffin et al., 2002) associated with home visiting programs.

In early childhood systems, home visiting has become a cornerstone of services for pregnant women and families with young children from birth through school age (Avellar & Supplee, 2013; Duggan et al., 2013). Early childhood research has also demonstrated prevention elements, with a record of home visiting associated with increases in families' health care utilization (Hilado et al., 2019); child well-being, including reduction in child maltreatment (Avellar & Supplee, 2013); and positive maternal behaviors (Nievar & Van Egeren, 2005) that may positively influence child development. Home visiting research has further noted specific child outcomes including improvements in cognitive (Avellar & Supplee, 2013), social–emotional, and language development (Hilado et al., 2019), which are important foundations that allow young children to start school ready to learn and positively engage with others.

What makes home visiting so impactful for families was best described by Sweet and Appelbaum (2004), who stated, "Home visiting programs are linked by their method of service delivery, their goal of helping children by helping the parents of those children, and their focus on younger children" (p. 1435). It is an intervention that is multilevel and multifocused in its approach to supporting the child and family. Specifically, families receive information that promotes the health and well-being of the child (child-focused component) and support for parents and caregivers to improve well-being, mastery, and confidence so they are equipped to meet both their child's and their family's needs (parent-focused component). Home visiting interventions also focus on helping families become competent to navigate the systems that touch the family's life, including the education, health, and social service systems, to further support the diverse needs of the family (family-focused component).

Home visiting is also an intervention that removes some access barriers because the professional goes into the home, which increases the likelihood of engagement and consistent delivery of the intervention. Additionally, professionals are more likely to understand the realities of the family because the intervention is delivered in the most natural environment for the family. More recently, home visiting programs have gained attention as a positive force in supporting I–ECMH and buffering against the negative impact of trauma. This benefit is in part attributable to its relational approach to engaging families, its ability to allow participants to feel heard and supported, and its delivery of important mental health information readily. Home visitors equipped with knowledge of mental health terminology and basic psychological first aid skills are able to share information about the importance of mental health for all family members, assess needs quickly, and refer accordingly as an integrated component of the visit. All of these aspects are particularly relevant when thinking about supporting trauma-experienced refugee families who are in need of adjustment support but are less likely to seek formal early intervention and health or mental health services (Allweiss & Hilado, 2017).

### Key Elements

Home visiting is often delivered by professionals with an early childhood background and a child development associate's degree (minimum); no advanced clinical training is required (Head Start, 2020). The focus, as mentioned, is on promoting the parent–child relationship and parent competence that in turn support child development. Home visiting is not considered therapy, given that its focus is not on treating mental health problems, yet its effects have been documented to be therapeutic, in part because newer home visiting models use many of the clinical strategies used in therapy that yield gains.

Before addressing the clinical components of home visiting, though, we begin with the basics of the intervention. The most effective home visiting programs often share common characteristics related to theory of change, dosage, service protocols and materials, and the relationship between home visitor and family (Paulsell et al., 2010). There are many home visiting models used nationwide (e.g., Baby TALK, Parents as Teachers, Nurse–Family Partnership, Healthy Families, Early Head Start), and each has a theory of how change is conceptualized with families that shapes the mechanisms by which a program model achieves and tracks program goals for the parent, child, and home visitor (Harden, 2010). There is an emphasis on using a developmental parenting approach to supporting the parent–child dyad, meaning that there is an understanding that in the same way young children acquire new skills as they develop, parents can also develop new skills and confidence. With time, parents may feel and be more competent in scaffolding their child's development while attending to their own personal growth.

According to the National Human Services Assembly (2007), high-quality home visiting programs must maintain a high level of engagement (i.e., once a week for 3–6 months, with a service period of 2 years as optimal) to yield benefits; thus, many home visiting programs build this service dosage as a requirement. As for the service protocols and materials, home visiting models typically provide a structure for information sharing that addresses child health and development and parenting competence, often through parent–child activities and linkages to other services (Avellar & Supplee, 2013). Home visiting protocols build in opportunities to assess needs outside the child's developmental needs to ensure the family remains stable. Finally, the various models have a mechanism for recording visits and storing participant information to track outcomes.

**Primary Participants**

There are three primary participants in home visiting interventions: a child, a parent or caregiver, and a home visitor. The intervention focuses on the child and parent (parent–child dyad) who are at the center of the intervention, and the home visitor plays a supportive role of observer, advocate, and informant. Although the parent–child relationship is the focus of the intervention, home visiting interventions equally emphasize the importance of the parent–professional relationship. According to the available literature, a professional's approach to engaging families and the relationship between parent and home visitor appear to be even more important than the specific home visiting model (Sweet & Appelbaum, 2004), and it appears that families are more engaged when the home visitor is able to develop a positive helping relationship with the family (Korfmacher et al., 2007).

It is the relationship—parent–child, parent–home visitor, and home visitor–family—that serves as the vehicle for change in home visiting, and that relationship is built through the clinical strategies used by the home visitor and their approach to working with families. A positive relationship is often successfully developed when home visitors have personal characteristics such as strong listening, observation, organization, probing, interpretation, and prompting skills (National Commission to Prevent Infant Mortality, 1989) as well as conscientiousness and persistence with families (Brookes et al., 2006), all valuable clinical skills. Home visitors must also be trained, monitored, and supported, particularly when working with psychologically vulnerable families; the visitor must have the knowledge and skills to support the physical and mental health of both parent and child (Harden, 2010). These qualities are why home visiting has been seen as valuable in promoting I–ECMH and adult mental health. Finally, a successful home visitor is one who understands that parenting practices are bound to culture, so there needs to be both respect and understanding for the cultural undertones that come with parenting (Gomby, 2005). Today's home visiting programs have evolved to be more client centered, emphasizing culturally appropriate interventions and bringing attention to a person-in-environment framework (Beder, 1998). When these clinical and nonclinical elements are in place, the needle moves on outcomes for the family.

**Intended Outcomes**

Home visiting is based on the fundamental understanding that the experiences in early years set the foundation for development across the life span; thus, home visiting uses protocols that support child development so that young children develop the physical, cognitive, language, and social–emotional skills necessary for self-regulation, enabling them to develop a sense of self and begin school ready to learn. The gains for parent and family are then layered into the intervention. Despite the limited research on home visiting outcomes among refugee families, what is available has shown that home visiting interventions are effective and greatly support families across the areas mentioned (Knox, 1996; Williamson et al., 2014).

There are indeed some documented gains in parenting skills, family functioning, and children's readiness for preschool (Williamson et al., 2014). There are also documented gains showing that families who receive home visiting services have stronger connections with the community, greater access to resources, an increase in positive parent–child interactions, increased home safety, and reductions in social isolation (Knox, 1996); these outcomes are desired in any family but uniquely valuable for refugee families adjusting to life in a new country. Newer studies have been able to document gains across child, parent, and family outcomes specific to refugee populations in which refugee children showed statistically significant gains in social–emotional and language development, refugee parents showed lower stress levels and a greater ability to cope with trauma symptoms, and refugee families were more connected with community resources than those without the intervention (Hilado et al., 2019).

**Relevance for Refugee Children and Families**
The risk factors facing refugee families that are the most concerning are the resultant effects of immigration trauma on mental health and cultural understandings of child development that neglect the importance of the early years and the role of parents in scaffolding early learning. There are also concerns around the lack of knowledge of resources that can meet a family's basic needs for adequate food, affordable housing, and access to health services. Each risk factor can have an adverse impact on refugee families, but the impact is exponentially more damaging to infants and toddlers given what is known about adverse childhood experiences, early childhood mental health, and the lifelong implications of each. Given this context and the research on its effectiveness, home visiting can serve as a powerful opportunity to ameliorate the risk as it is a culturally responsive, relational approach to engaging refugee families. More research is needed that is refugee specific.

*Benefits.* There are elements of the intervention that make home visiting culturally sensitive and ideal for refugee populations. Home visiting is designed to explicitly acknowledge the parent as the expert on their child and the home visitor as an ally. This positioning helps promote the parent–professional relationship because it neutralizes power dynamics to a certain degree, honors parent knowledge and home culture, and allows home visiting to be a collaborative process rather than a top-down, forced intervention, valuable elements when engaging participants unfamiliar with home-based early childhood services. Even when the home visiting professional is not a clinician, the nature of consistent visits and thoughtful support through active listening, attuned communication, dyadic engagement, and assessment of needs—all clinical elements—results in families engaging in a service that is experienced as therapeutic. That feeling of being supported in a holding environment then translates to stronger parent–child relationships and, potentially, stronger refugee families.

Another benefit is that home visiting interventions recognize the interconnectedness that is inherent within family systems by working within the parent–child dyad, engaging all relevant partners so gains can be realized across all members rather than the refugee child only. Additionally, home visiting's relational approach to engaging refugee families is seen as valuable in helping participants open themselves more to others (Hsieh & Bean, 2014), and it is seen as particularly impactful in engaging ethnically diverse families (King et al., 2015). Again, this speaks to an element of home visiting that supports the strengthening of families. Delivering services in the home removes barriers to accessing services when transportation means are difficult. Finally, the home-based nature of the intervention is important especially for immigrants generally, who may avoid leaving their homes for fear of identification by immigration forces and the threats of deportation that are rampant.

***Challenges.*** Despite such benefits, there are issues when home visiting is applied with refugee families. Home visiting services are usually nonexistent in the home countries of refugees served in the United States, and the science around brain development in utero and during the period from birth to age 3 is not readily understood among many arriving refugee populations. This can pose issues in enrollment and engagement. For some refugee families, health and survival (e.g., access to basic nutrients, water, and vaccinations) are the priority of the early years and learning is believed to begin only in the school-age years, a belief inconsistent with available research on the power of the infant and toddler brain and the importance of early development. Additionally, refugee families may not prioritize the needs of their youngest children when basic needs—food, employment, clothing—must be met. In the area of mental health, many refugee parents have struggled with chronic adverse symptoms and do not recognize the impact of those symptoms on themselves or their ability to parent their children, nor are they familiar with the Western concept of early childhood mental health and its importance.

Despite these obvious challenges, supporting I–ECMH and promoting developmental outcomes for young refugee children is important. The examination of home visiting—its components; its benefits to child, parent, and family; its cultural sensitivity—can reveal a relevant option for supporting trauma-experienced refugee families. The intervention itself and related research findings demonstrate its potential for equipping each member—especially the youngest members—with the skills to develop and thrive without being defined by immigration trauma.

**Case Vignette**
Sifuni, a single mother from the Democratic Republic of Congo, and her 2-year-old son, Siddiqi, resettled in Chicago. Upon arrival, Sifuni shared concerns about her son being extremely clingy and difficult to soothe, which hadn't been an issue in the refugee camp. Sifuni herself expressed feeling homesick as she had left many of her relatives and friends behind when she came to the United States. Her case manager recommended home visiting services in which she would receive biweekly visits to support both her and her child. Sifuni was hesitant at first, as she had never heard about home visiting in her home country and was unsure what a stranger could do for her family.

With each visit, Sifuni's home visitor asked her about her adjustment to the city and her observations of her child. The home visitor worked alongside Sifuni, observing her and Siddiqi together, sharing information about what both believed could be happening, and working together on how to support Siddiqi so he would feel more comfortable and less afraid in their new home. The home visitor also shared important child development content and resources Sifuni needed in the community, even bringing her and Siddiqi to important health and public benefit appointments. As Sifuni began to feel more confident in her new surroundings with the help of her home visitor, she found herself also more confident in helping Siddiqi adjust to his new home and supporting his ongoing development.

## CONCLUSION

Each of the three interventions described in this chapter—child–parent psychotherapy, sandplay and play therapy, and home visiting—provides an approach to supporting infant–early childhood mental health and the development of very young refugee children. The interventions often involve refugee parents and caregivers as key participants, and it is through the refugee parent–child interaction (or reflections with parents or caregivers) and relationship that change occurs in the child as well as the parent. The professional also plays an important but indirect role as observer, narrator, bridge between parent and child, and advocate both in and outside the session. Moreover, the refugee child is at the center of each intervention, and the work is based on the child's and parent's subjective and objective experiences, thereby making it culturally sensitive and accessible to participants because their voice is central to the work.

Additionally, considering the nature of the refugee experience for young children and their families, the most impactful interventions will likely be those that demonstrate thoughtful consideration to the experiences of trauma and the feelings of uncertainty, helplessness, and isolation. These factors are addressed through a relational approach to engaging refugee children and their families that is found in each intervention, a relationship that is developed through longer term (6–12 months) treatment. Each intervention provides a strong basis for supporting the development of young refugee children and their parents through thoughtful, consistent engagement that allows the past to be revisited in a way that reduces terror and makes meaning of trauma. The nature of the treatment also focuses on foreseeing the future with hope and opportunity through learning, reflecting, supporting relationships, and building skills.

Ultimately, refugee children and their families suffering from previous trauma are in need of effective treatments to ensure they can thrive, not merely survive. Thus, interventions for young children such as CPP, sandplay and play therapy, and home visiting are healing opportunities that can and must be thoughtfully considered in practice with refugee children and their families.

## REFERENCES

Allweiss, S., & Hilado, A. (2017). The context of migration: Pre-migration, migration, and resettlement experiences. In A. Hilado & M. Lundy (Eds.), *Models for practice with immigrants and refugees: Collaboration, cultural awareness, and integrative theory* (pp. 33–56). Sage.

American Immigration Council. (2020). *An overview of U.S. refugee law and policy.* https://www.americanimmigrationcouncil.org/research/overview-us-refugee-law-and-policy

Anda, R. (2006). *The health and social impact of growing up with alcohol abuse and related adverse childhood experiences: The human and economic costs of the status quo.* National Association for Children of Alcoholics. http://www.nacoa.net/pdfs/Anda%20NACoA%20Review_web.pdf

Anda, R. F., Butchart, A., Felitti, V. J., & Brown, D. W. (2010). Building a framework for global surveillance of the public health implications of adverse childhood experiences. *American Journal of Preventive Medicine, 39*(1), 93–98. https://doi.org/10.1016/j.amepre.2010.03.015

Anda, R. F., Felitti, V. J., Bremner, J. D., Walker, J. D., Whitfield, C., Perry, B. D., Dube, S. R., & Giles, W. H. (2006). The enduring effects of abuse and related adverse experiences in childhood: A convergence of evidence from neurobiology and epidemiology. *European Archives of Psychiatry and Clinical Neuroscience, 256*(3), 174–186. https://doi.org/10.1007/s00406-005-0624-4

Anda, R. F., Felitti, V. J., Brown, D. W., Chapman, D., Dong, M., Dube, S. R., Edwards, V. J., & Giles, W. H. (2006). Insights into intimate partner violence from the Adverse Childhood Experiences (ACE) Study. In P. R. Salber & E. H. Taliaferro (Eds.), *The physician's guide to intimate partner violence and abuse* (pp. 77–88). Volcano Press.

Anda, R. F., Fleisher, V. I., Felitti, V. J., Edwards, V. J., Whitfield, C. L., Dube, S. R., & Williamson, D. F. (2004). Childhood abuse, household dysfunction, and indicators of impaired adult worker performance. *The Permanente Journal, 8*(1), 30–38. https://doi.org/10.7812/tpp/03-089

Association for Play Therapy. (n.d.). *Clarifying the use of play therapy: Guidelines.* https://www.a4pt.org/page/ClarifyingUseofPT

Avellar, S. A., & Supplee, L. H. (2013). Effectiveness of home visiting in improving child health and reducing child maltreatment. *Pediatrics, 132*(Suppl. 2), S90–S99. https://doi.org/10.1542/peds.2013-1021G

Axline, V. (1947). *Play therapy.* Ballantine Books.

Beder, J. (1998). The home visit, revisited. *Families in Society, 79*(5), 514–522. https://doi.org/10.1606/1044-3894.718

Bradway, K., & McCoard, B. (1997). *Sandplay—Silent workshop of the psyche.* Routledge.

Brookes, S. J., Summers, J. A., Thornburg, K. R., Ispa, J. M., & Lane, V. J. (2006). Building successful home visitor–mother relationships and reaching program goals in two Early Head Start programs: A qualitative look at contributing factors. *Early Childhood Research Quarterly, 21*(1), 25–45. https://doi.org/10.1016/j.ecresq.2006.01.005

Brown, M. J., McLaine, P., Dixon, S., & Simon, P. (2006). A randomized, community-based trial of home visiting to reduce blood lead levels in children. *Pediatrics, 117*(1), 147–153. https://doi.org/10.1542/peds.2004-2880

Center on the Developing Child, Harvard University. (n.d.). *Deep dives: Early childhood mental health.* https://developingchild.harvard.edu/science/deep-dives/mental-health/

Charity Organization Society of the City of New York. (1883). *Handbook for friendly visitors among the poor.* Putnam.

Chu, A. T., & Lieberman, A. F. (2010). Clinical implications of traumatic stress from birth to age five. *Annual Review of Clinical Psychology, 6*(1), 469–494. https://doi.org/10.1146/annurev.clinpsy.121208.131204

Cicchetti, D., Rogosch, F. A., & Toth, S. L. (2000). The efficacy of toddler–parent psychotherapy for fostering cognitive development in offspring of depressed mothers. *Journal of Abnormal Child Psychology, 28*(2), 135–148. https://doi.org/10.1023/A:1005118713814

Cicchetti, D., Rogosch, F. A., & Toth, S. L. (2006). Fostering secure attachment in infants in maltreating families through preventive interventions. *Development and Psychopathology, 18*(3), 623–649. https://doi.org/10.1017/S0954579406060329

Cicchetti, D., Toth, S. L., & Rogosch, F. A. (1999). The efficacy of toddler–parent psychotherapy to increase attachment security in offspring of depressed mothers.

*Attachment & Human Development*, *1*(1), 34–66. https://doi.org/10.1080/14616739900134021

Cohen, J., Oser, C., & Quigley, K. (2012). *Making it happen: Overcoming barriers to providing infant–early childhood mental health*. Zero to Three.

Division for Early Childhood. (2014). *DEC recommended practices*. Council for Exceptional Children. https://www.dec-sped.org/dec-recommended-practices

Dube, S. R., Miller, J. W., Brown, D. W., Giles, W. H., Felitti, V. J., Dong, M., & Anda, R. F. (2006). Adverse childhood experiences and the association with ever using alcohol and initiating alcohol use during adolescence. *Journal of Adolescent Health*, *38*(4), 444.e1–444.e10. https://doi.org/10.1016/j.jadohealth.2005.06.006

Duggan, A., Minkovitz, C. S., Chaffin, M., Korfmacher, J., Brooks-Gunn, J., Crowne, S., Filene, J., Gonsalves, K., Landsverk, J., & Harwood, R. (2013). Creating a national home visiting research network. *Pediatrics*, *132*(Suppl. 2), S82–S89. https://doi.org/10.1542/peds.2013-1021F

Edwards, V. J., Holden, G. W., Felitti, V. J., & Anda, R. F. (2003). Relationship between multiple forms of childhood maltreatment and adult mental health in community respondents: Results from the Adverse Childhood Experiences Study. *The American Journal of Psychiatry*, *160*(8), 1453–1460. https://doi.org/10.1176/appi.ajp.160.8.1453

Fraiberg, S. (1980). *Clinical studies in infant mental health: The first year of life*. Basic Books.

Fraiberg, S., Adelson, E., & Shapiro, V. (1975). Ghosts in the nursery: A psychoanalytic approach to the problems of impaired infant–mother relationships. *Journal of the American Academy of Child Psychiatry*, *14*(3), 387–421. https://doi.org/10.1016/S0002-7138(09)61442-4

Freud, A. (1964). *The psychoanalytic treatment of children*. Schocken Books.

Friedman, H. S., & Mitchell, R. R. (1997). The development of sandplay. In Los Angeles Sandplay Association (Ed.), *Sandplay: Coming of age*. http://www.csun.edu/~hcedp007/SP-development.pdf

Goldfinch, M. (2009). 'Putting Humpty together again': Working with parents to help children who have experienced early trauma. *Australian and New Zealand Journal of Family Therapy*, *30*(4), 284–299. https://doi.org/10.1375/anft.30.4.284

Gomby, D. S. (2005). *Home visitation in 2005: Outcomes for children and parents* (Invest in Kids Working Paper No. 7). Committee for Economic Development.

Goodyear-Brown, P. (2010). *Play therapy with traumatized children*. Wiley.

Gopnik, A., Meltzoff, A. N., & Kuhl, P. K. (2000). *The scientist in the crib: What early learning tells us about the mind*. Harper Collins.

Harden, B. J. (2010). Home visitation with psychologically vulnerable families: Developments in the profession and in the professional. *Zero to Three*, *30*(6), 44–51.

Hart, R. (2009). Child refugees, trauma and education: Interactionist considerations on social and emotional needs and development. *Educational Psychology in Practice*, *25*(4), 351–368. https://doi.org/10.1080/02667360903315172

Head Start. (2020). *Education requirements for home visitors*. https://eclkc.ohs.acf.hhs.gov/publication/education-requirements-home-visitors

Hilado, A., & Allweiss, S. (2017). Physical and mental health stabilization: The importance of well-being to the adjustment of new immigrants. In A. Hilado & M. Lundy (Eds.), *Models for practice with immigrants and refugees: Collaboration, cultural awareness, and integrative theory* (pp. 57–76). Sage.

Hilado, A., Leow, C., & Yang, Y. (2019). Understanding immigration trauma and the potential of home visiting among immigrant and refugee families. *Zero to Three, 39*(6), 44–53.

Hilado, A., & Lundy, M. (Eds.). (2017). *Models for practice with immigrants and refugees: Collaboration, cultural awareness, and integrative theory.* Sage.

Howard, K. S., & Brooks-Gunn, J. (2009). The role of home-visiting programs in preventing child abuse and neglect. *The Future of Children, 19*(2), 119–146. https://doi.org/10.1353/foc.0.0032

Hsieh, A. L., & Bean, R. A. (2014). Understanding familial/cultural factors in adolescent depression: A culturally-competent treatment for working with Chinese American families. *The American Journal of Family Therapy, 42*(5), 398–412. https://doi.org/10.1080/01926187.2014.884414

Hughes, M., Spence, C. M., & Ostrosky, M. M. (2015). Early childhood mental health consultation: Common questions and answers. *Young Exceptional Children, 18*(3), 36–51. https://doi.org/10.1177/1096250614558852

Issel, L. M., Forrestal, S. G., Slaughter, J., Wiencrot, A., & Handler, A. (2011). A review of prenatal home-visiting effectiveness for improving birth outcomes. *Journal of Obstetric, Gynecologic, & Neonatal Nursing, 40*(2), 157–165. https://doi.org/10.1111/j.1552-6909.2011.01219.x

Kalff, D. M. (1980). *Sandplay: A psychotherapeutic approach to the psyche.* Sigo Press. (Original work published 1966)

Killian, T., Cardona, B., & Hudspeth, E. (2017). Culturally responsive play therapy with Somali refugees. *International Journal of Play Therapy, 26*(1), 23–32. https://doi.org/10.1037/pla0000040

King, G., Desmarais, C., Lindsay, S., Piérart, G., & Tétreault, S. (2015). The roles of effective communication and client engagement in delivering culturally sensitive care to immigrant parents of children with disabilities. *Disability and Rehabilitation, 37*(15), 1372–1381. https://doi.org/10.3109/09638288.2014.972580

Knox, J. (1996). Homebased services for Southeast Asia refugee children: A process and formative evaluation. *Children and Youth Services Review, 18*(6), 553–578. https://doi.org/10.1016/0190-7409(96)00022-9

Koniak-Griffin, D., Anderson, N. L., Brecht, M. L., Verzemnieks, I., Lesser, J., & Kim, S. (2002). Public health nursing care for adolescent mothers: Impact on infant health and selected maternal outcomes at 1 year postbirth. *Journal of Adolescent Health, 30*(1), 44–54. https://doi.org/10.1016/S1054-139X(01)00330-5

Korfmacher, J., Green, B., Spellmann, M., & Thornburg, K. R. (2007). The helping relationship and program participation in early childhood home visiting. *Infant Mental Health Journal, 28*(5), 459–480. https://doi.org/10.1002/imhj.20148

Landreth, G. (2012). *Play therapy: The art of the relationship* (3rd ed.). Routledge.

Layne, C. M., Ippen, C. G., Strand, V., Stuber, M., Abramovitz, R., Reyes, G., Jackson, L. A., Ross, L., Curtis, A., Lipscomb, L., & Pynoos, R. (2011). The Core Curriculum on Childhood Trauma: A tool for training a trauma-informed workforce. *Psychological Trauma: Theory, Research, Practice, and Policy, 3*(3), 243–252. https://doi.org/10.1037/a0025039

Lewontin, R. (2000). *The triple helix: Gene, organism, and environment.* Harvard University Press.

Lieberman, A. F. (2018). *The emotional life of the toddler.* Simon & Schuster.

Lieberman, A. F., Dimmler, M. H., & Ghosh Ippen, C. M. (2019). Child–parent psycho-therapy: A trauma-informed treatment for young children and their caregivers. In C. H. Zeanah (Ed)., *Handbook of infant mental health* (4th ed., pp. 485–499). Guilford Press.

Lieberman, A. F., Ghosh Ippen, C., & Van Horn, P. (2015). *Don't hit my mommy: A manual for child–parent psychotherapy with young children exposed to violence and other trauma*. Zero to Three Press.

Lieberman, A. F., Padrón, E., Van Horn, P., & Harris, W. W. (2005). Angels in the nursery: The intergenerational transmission of benevolent parental influences. *Infant Mental Health Journal, 26*(6), 504–520. https://doi.org/10.1002/imhj.20071

Lieberman, A. F., Van Horn, P., & Ippen, C. G. (2005). Toward evidence-based treatment: Child–parent psychotherapy with preschoolers exposed to marital violence. *Journal of the American Academy of Child & Adolescent Psychiatry, 44*(12), 1241–1248. https://doi.org/10.1097/01.chi.0000181047.59702.58

Lieberman, A. F., Weston, D. R., & Pawl, J. H. (1991). Preventive intervention and out-come with anxiously attached dyads. *Child Development, 62*(1), 199–209. https://doi.org/10.2307/1130715

Lowenfeld, M. (1979). *The world technique*. Allen & Unwin.

Marans, S. (2013). Phenomena of childhood trauma and expanding approaches to early intervention. *International Journal of Applied Psychoanalytic Studies, 10*(3), 247–266. https://doi.org/10.1002/aps.1369

McInnes, R. J., & Stone, D. H. (2001). The process of implementing a community-based peer breast-feeding support programme: The Glasgow experience. *Midwifery, 17*(1), 65–73. https://doi.org/10.1054/midw.2000.0236

McMullen, J., O'Callaghan, P., Shannon, C., Black, A., & Eakin, J. (2013). Group trauma-focused cognitive–behavioural therapy with former child soldiers and other war-affected boys in the DR Congo: A randomised controlled trial. *Journal of Child Psychology and Psychiatry, and Allied Disciplines, 54*(11), 1231–1241. https://doi.org/10.1111/jcpp.12094

Mitchell, R. R., & Friedman, H. S. (1994). *Sandplay past, present and future*. Routledge.

Montgomery, E. (2011). Trauma, exile and mental health in young refugees. *Acta Psychiatrica Scandinavica, 124*(s440), 1–46. https://doi.org/10.1111/j.1600-0447.2011.01740.x

National Commission to Prevent Infant Mortality. (1989). *Home visiting: Opening doors for America's pregnant women and children.*

National Human Services Assembly. (2007). *Home visiting: Strengthening families by promoting parenting success* [Policy brief].

Nelson, F., & Mann, T. (2011). Opportunities in public policy to support infant and early childhood mental health: The role of psychologists and policymakers. *American Psychologist, 66*(2), 129–139. https://doi.org/10.1037/a0021314

Niaz, U. (2014). Psycho trauma in children exposed to the war atrocities. *Journal of Pakistan Psychiatric Society, 11*(2), 44.

Nievar, M. A., & Van Egeren, L. (2005, April 7–10). *More is better: A meta-analysis of home visiting programs for at-risk families* [Paper presentation]. Biennial meeting of the Society for Research in Child Development, Atlanta, GA, United States.

Office of Refugee Resettlement. (2020). *Refugees*. U.S. Department of Health & Human Services, Administration for Children & Families. https://www.acf.hhs.gov/orr/refugees

Osofsky, J. D., & Thomas, K. (2012). What is infant mental health? *Zero to Three, 33*(2), 9.

Paulsell, D., Boller, K., Hallgren, K., & Esposito, A. M. (2010). Assessing home visiting quality: Dosage, content, and relationships. *Zero to Three, 30*(6), 16–21.

Peterson, C. A., Luze, G. J., Eshbaugh, E. M., Jeon, H.-J., & Kantz, K. R. (2007). Enhancing parent–child interaction through home visiting: Promising practice or unfulfilled promise? *Journal of Early Intervention, 29*(2), 119–140. https://doi.org/10.1177/105381510702900205

Petot, J.-M. (1990). *Melanie Klein: Vol. 1. First discoveries and first systems 1919–1932* (C. Trollope, Trans.). International Universities Press. (Original work published 1979)

RefugeeOne. (2019). *RefugeeOne annual report fiscal year 2019.* http://www.refugeeone.org/uploads/1/2/8/1/12814267/refugeeone_2019_annual_report.pdf

Richter, L. (2004). *The importance of caregiver–child interactions for the survival and healthy development of young children: A review.* Department of Child and Adolescent Health and Development, World Health Organization.

Ridley, M. (2003). *Nature via nurture: Genes, experience, and what makes us human.* Fourth Estate.

Rogers, C. R. (1940). The processes of therapy. *Journal of Consulting Psychology, 4*(5), 161–164. https://doi.org/10.1037/h0062536

Schottelkorb, A., Doumas, D., & Garcia, R. (2012). Treatment for childhood refugee trauma: A randomized, controlled trial. *International Journal of Play Therapy, 21*(2), 57–73. https://doi.org/10.1037/a0027430

Schriver, J. M. (2015). *Human behavior and the social environment: Shifting paradigms in essential knowledge for social work practice* (6th ed.). Pearson.

Shonkoff, J. P., & Phillips, D. A. (Eds.). (2000). *From neurons to neighborhoods: The science of early childhood development.* National Academies Press. https://doi.org/10.17226/9824

Siegel, D. J. (1999). *The developing mind: Toward a neurology of interpersonal experience.* Guilford Press.

Slewa-Younan, S., Uribe Guajardo, M. G., Heriseanu, A., & Hasan, T. (2015). A systematic review of post-traumatic stress disorder and depression amongst Iraqi refugees located in Western countries. *Journal of Immigrant and Minority Health, 17*(4), 1231–1239. https://doi.org/10.1007/s10903-014-0046-3

Sweet, M. A., & Appelbaum, M. I. (2004). Is home visiting an effective strategy? A meta-analytic review of home visiting programs for families with young children. *Child Development, 75*(5), 1435–1456. https://doi.org/10.1111/j.1467-8624.2004.00750.x

Thompson, R. A. (2000). The legacy of early attachments. *Child Development, 71*(1), 145–152. https://doi.org/10.1111/1467-8624.00128

Toth, S. L., Maughan, A., Manly, J. T., Spagnola, M., & Cicchetti, D. (2002). The relative efficacy of two interventions in altering maltreated preschool children's representational models: Implications for attachment theory. *Development and Psychopathology, 14*(4), 877–908. https://doi.org/10.1017/S095457940200411X

Toth, S. L., Rogosch, F. A., Manly, J. T., & Cicchetti, D. (2006). The efficacy of toddler–parent psychotherapy to reorganize attachment in the young offspring of mothers with major depressive disorder: A randomized preventive trial. *Journal of Consulting and Clinical Psychology, 74*(6), 1006–1016. https://doi.org/10.1037/0022-006X.74.6.1006

United Nations High Commissioner for Refugees. (2018a). *The 1951 Refugee Convention.* http://www.unhcr.org/pages/49da0e466.html

United Nations High Commissioner for Refugees. (2018b). *UNHCR demographics population statistics, female and male children age 0–4 years across U.S. resettlement countries.* https://www.unhcr.org/refugee-statistics/download/?url=p9M8

United Nations High Commissioner for Refugees. (2019). *Global trends: Forced displacement in 2018.* https://www.unhcr.org/5d08d7ee7.pdf

United Nations High Commissioner for Refugees USA. (2018a). *Four million refugee children go without schooling: UNHCR report.* https://www.unhcr.org/en-us/news/latest/2018/8/5b86342b4/four-million-refugee-children-schooling-unhcr-report.html

United Nations High Commissioner for Refugees USA. (2018b). *Refugee statistics.* https://www.unrefugees.org/refugee-facts/statistics/

U.S. Citizenship and Immigrant Services. (2020). *Refugee processing and security screening.* https://www.uscis.gov/humanitarian/refugees-and-asylum/refugees/refugee-processing-and-security-screening

van Ee, E., Kleber, R. J., & Mooren, T. T. M. (2012). War trauma lingers on: Associations between maternal posttraumatic stress disorder, parent–child interaction, and child development. *Infant Mental Health Journal, 33*(5), 459–468. https://doi.org/10.1002/imhj.21324

Williamson, A. A., Knox, L., Guerra, N. G., & Williams, K. R. (2014). A pilot randomized trial of community-based parent training for immigrant Latina mothers. *American Journal of Community Psychology, 53*(1–2), 47–59. https://doi.org/10.1007/s10464-013-9612-4

Zeanah, C. H., Jr. (Ed.). (2019). *Handbook of infant mental health* (4th ed.). Guilford Press.

Zohar, J., Yahalom, H., Kozlovsky, N., Cwikel-Hamzany, S., Matar, M. A., Kaplan, Z., Yehuda, R., & Cohen, H. (2011). High dose hydrocortisone immediately after trauma may alter the trajectory of PTSD: Interplay between clinical and animal studies. *European Neuropsychopharmacology, 21*(11), 796–809. https://doi.org/10.1016/j.euroneuro.2011.06.001

# 10

# PEER GROUP AND COMMUNITY-BASED STRATEGIES FOR SUPPORTING REFUGEE MENTAL HEALTH

SAMANTHA ALLWEISS AND MONICA CONNELLY

Community integration has been repeatedly indicated in empirical studies as a key component in supporting psychological well-being for refugees. On the basis of experiences working at RefugeeOne, a Chicago-based refugee resettlement agency, the authors of this chapter describe the ways mental health professionals have been using culturally appropriate and trauma-informed community-based psychoeducation models and peer support groups as best practice strategies to promote the psychological and social well-being of refugees. We pay particular attention to the use of community spaces and peer supports to build social supports and foster healthy adjustment for refugee populations. Specific examples are provided of successful adult group psychoeducation programs and youth peer group interventions based on mindfulness and social and emotional learning (SEL). Finally, we explore the significance of advocacy for increased awareness of and funding for refugee mental health services and ways to extend beyond providing therapeutic interventions by engaging community support systems and advocating for increased access to health, education, and legal resources.

https://doi.org/10.1037/0000226-010
*Refugee Mental Health*, J. D. Aten and J. Hwang (Editors)

## ROLE OF COMMUNITIES IN ACCESS TO MENTAL HEALTH SERVICES

Previous chapters have provided a rich discussion of the factors that push refugees out of their country of origin and highlighted the potential for trauma throughout the migration journey. The cumulative effects of the stressors inherent in the migration journey may leave individuals feeling physically and emotionally depleted, with few internal resources to face the new challenges they confront in their resettlement country. Indeed, research indicates that the stress of resettlement is correlated with poor health outcomes, both physically and psychologically (Agbényiga et al., 2012; Berry, 1997). Table 1 (from Kirmayer et al., 2011, p. E961; see https://www.ncbi.nlm.nih.gov/pmc/articles/PMC3168672/table/t1-183e959/) summarizes factors that affect mental health for adults and youth at each stage of the migration journey This table speaks to the cumulative psychological (e.g., loss of a loved one) and physical (e.g., exposure to harsh and dangerous conditions) traumas endemic to the refugee migration experience.

As indicated in Kirmayer et al.'s (2011) table, stressors continue for refugees after resettlement to a third country. Stressors include learning how to successfully navigate the dominant culture (linguistically, financially, and culturally) while simultaneously grieving for the loss of important familial and social ties. Clients may also internalize guilt and shame about being able to escape and rebuild their lives while many others continue to suffer. When communities are not given adequate support for healing from these traumas, detrimental coping practices, such as the increased rates of substance abuse found within the Somali community, become more pervasive (Im et al., 2017).

Despite the apparent need for mental health services, there are common misconceptions about mental health within arriving refugee communities that serve as barriers to treatment even when services are available. Indeed, the vast majority of refugees who are assessed as needing mental health services never receive care (Birman et al., 2005; Ellis et al., 2010; Jaycox et al., 2002; Saraceno et al., 2007). There are also structural issues, such as lack of transportation, inadequate access to interpreters, and time limitations because of employment needs, that affect access to services. Without understanding the lens through which clients view mental health services and providers, therapists cannot appropriately tailor services to fit the communities they serve.

## BARRIERS TO SERVICES WITHIN REFUGEE COMMUNITIES

The disparity between the number of refugees who need mental health services and the number who access care is startling given findings that refugees are 10 times more likely to experience trauma symptoms than the general population (Fitzgerald, 2017) and are at increased risk for depression and anxiety in their lifetimes (Fazel et al., 2005). Therapists must understand the potential barriers to accessing care and use strategies that increase accessibility. They should acknowledge that each person's experience of trauma and adjustment is framed by previous experiences and knowledge, cultural traditions, and multigenerational perspectives that shape how events (past, present, future) are understood and ultimately influence behavior and guide how individuals react to information. Logically, conceptualizations of mental health can determine how people understand the symptoms they experience as a result of their trauma and can influence their receptivity to mental health interventions.

Among refugee populations served in the mental health program at RefugeeOne, clients often speak about mental health as a stigmatized service, marking one as "unstable," "weak," or "disturbed" if one enters treatment. Mental health is most commonly understood through the disease model, meaning that individuals believe that people who access services are doing so because they have a serious and ultimately incurable mental illness, such as schizophrenia. This belief creates a binary framework for understanding mental health in which individuals are deemed either "sane" or "crazy" (Hassan et al., 2015; Kirmayer et al., 2011). Individuals are often reluctant to discuss their current mental health functioning for fear they will be labeled "abnormal," which could damage their reputation (Ciftci et al., 2012; Hassan et al., 2015). This concern for reputation can be particularly anxiety provoking during the resettlement process as individuals seek to rebuild their support system and establish a sense of community in an unfamiliar city.

For example, refugees from Muslim cultures may understand mental health symptoms to be the will of God, or Allah, bestowed upon the individual to test their faith, to punish them for wrongdoing, or to offer a unique gift or talent (Abu-Ras & Abu-Bader, 2008; Abu-Ras et al., 2008; Gaw, 1993). Acceptance of suffering is seen as a way to show faith in Allah, and therefore refugees may feel that they have to live with the symptoms they are experiencing. Some African communities understand mental health symptoms to be a result of a curse placed on the individual using black magic by someone they have fought with or wronged in some way (Ali & Agyapong, 2016). These curses are commonly thought to occur when someone is granted resettlement and neighbors or friends become jealous and seek retribution. Shared trauma experiences, such in the case of mass rape or genocide, can also lead to entire communities seeing trauma symptoms as part of the human experience. In all these instances, refugees would likely turn to faith-based or spiritual healers instead of seeking services in a mental health setting.

Additional challenges include cultural norms around sharing personal information with those outside of the family; many non-Western cultures prioritize the family unit over the needs of the individual and see it as a violation to share any information that could be damaging to the collective. Given the stigma associated with accessing mental health services, individuals may be concerned that this action could harm the reputation of their entire family, possibly ruining marriage prospects for eligible siblings or children.

Researchers have posited that Western cultures have developed less rigid norms around the expression of psychological experiences whereas other cultures limit this expression (Hsu & Folstein, 1997; Leff, 1998). These societal norms that limit the expression of emotional suffering mean that non-Western refugees are more likely to focus on their physical well-being, understanding psychological distress through somatic symptoms of physical pain or discomfort (Gaw, 1993) such as chronic stomachaches, headaches, muscle aches, or dizziness. Clients experiencing these physical discomforts are likely to seek healing within the medical profession, which leads to misdiagnoses and improper treatment if doctors are not routinely screening patients for mental health needs.

There are also fears about where information about an individual's mental health status will be shared, with concerns that accessing services could have an impact on employability, immigration status, or ability to access public benefits. Some clients have spoken about fears that their children will be removed from the home if they are treated for mental health issues because authorities see this as an indicator that they are not fit to care for their children or that their presence in the home is a safety concern. The current sociopolitical climate in the United States and other countries has heightened concerns about accessing social safety nets as immigrants are frequently hearing about rapidly changing immigration policies focused on creating an inhospitable environment for nonnative residents. Refugees who fear such repercussions would likely deny symptoms altogether and may instruct their family members to do the same.

Another consideration is the power dynamics of the helping relationship. The refugee experience forces individuals to be at the mercy of those assisting them as their paperwork is processed; they must also repeatedly share their trauma story during the screening process to ensure their case is deemed credible. If the professional is not thoughtful, questions posed during a clinical assessment could be seen as mirroring these experiences as refugees are once again asked to share intimate aspects of their history with someone outside of their family (and often community). Refugees may feel powerless to push back against the perceived power inequities, sharing information before they feel emotionally safe. Often, these individuals avoid mental health services after the initial assessment because they see mental health services as disempowering and, at worst, retraumatizing.

Most importantly, refugees are often deprived of knowledge about existing treatment possibilities (Maier & Straub, 2011), which may be the result of a lack of culturally appropriate information about the available services (Fassaert et al., 2009; Sijbrandij et al., 2017). For example, they may believe the only available treatment is psychotropic medications, not knowing that therapy is another effective intervention. Or they may not know where to go to access culturally appropriate services, believing that such resources are not offered or made affordable within their community. If information about services is not adequately disseminated, those with mental health needs may self-medicate through drugs (legal or nonlegal) or alcohol in an effort to mitigate symptoms.

Some or all of the aforementioned challenges may be present in the space if therapists try engaging clients in traditional talk therapy. Additionally, therapeutic models often incorporate Western-centric norms such as individuality, which is not a central value for more communal cultures. Unfortunately, traditional interventions have been focused on individual services, not accounting for family connections or the strengths of the community (Weine, 2011). Therapists must be thoughtful about how they introduce and discuss the topic of mental health; inadequate consideration for cultural contexts could cause individuals to feel defensive, afraid, ashamed, or ignored. Therefore, alternative strategies that target the collective can be more appropriate when initially engaging refugee populations.

## PSYCHOEDUCATION INTERVENTIONS FOR REFUGEE ADULTS AND YOUTH

One effective intervention method is group psychoeducation classes. Researchers have established the connection between adequate social supports for refugees and healthy integration into their new country (Boswell, 2001; Sleijpen et al., 2016; Wilkinson & Marmot, 1998). Ager and Strang (2004) defined *social bonds* as emotional and practical connections to people who share aspects of one's identity (e.g., culture, religion, sexual orientation). These bonds become even more critical in environments that are less welcoming to immigrant or refugee populations and often exist naturally through resettlement agencies or religious institutions (Griffiths et al., 2005; Zetter et al., 2005). Psychoeducation can be seen as both a practical and a social support: It is the process of gathering clients and delivering important information for the purpose of destigmatizing, normalizing, and ultimately supporting mental health needs for those in the community.

## Benefits of Group Psychoeducation

Group psychoeducation is a key component of culturally appropriate mental health services as it is less intensive than one-on-one sessions and self-disclosure is not a requirement for accessing the session. It also serves as a preventive service as facilitators educate members to recognize mental health needs in themselves and others before crises arise. This intervention strengthens communities by increasing productivity and reducing the negative consequences of untreated mental illness, such as legal or financial ramifications (Weine, 2011). It also fosters social connections as discussions of the refugee experience naturally arise, and group members often have shared experiences to draw from during the conversations. Researchers have found that ethnicity-specific groups are most beneficial for refugees, and research within the broader population indicates that homogenous groups are important when initially working with groups to support members' collective identities (Fischman & Ross, 1990; Yalom, 2005).

Psychoeducation is critical for all clinical interventions with refugee populations as it normalizes clients' experiences and provides a framework for discussing client needs. For those unable to access further services because of stigma, personal discomfort, or limitations placed on them during the adjustment process (e.g., poor health, need to attend to children, non-traditional work schedules), individuals leave psychoeducation sessions armed with an understanding of their symptoms. This understanding has been found to reduce anxieties around symptoms, and discussions of healthy coping skills increase available coping resources when clients are dealing with stressful or triggering situations.

Psychoeducation can also be beneficial for refugee youth. A study conducted by Im et al. (2018) on Somali refugee youth in Kenya who received trauma-informed psychoeducation group sessions found that those with moderate to severe trauma symptoms demonstrated a significant decline in mood symptoms (posttraumatic stress disorder [PTSD] and depression) and somatic complaints after engaging in the program. Those who had no symptoms or mild PTSD reported other significant benefits from psychoeducation, such as increased knowledge of available resources, a greater sense of community, and improved coping abilities. This research demonstrates the variety of benefits derived from psychoeducation as it connects to the specific needs of refugee populations. Research also shows that peer-led health education groups can improve overall health outcomes, which indicates that clients benefit from a holistic approach to psychoeducation topics (Webel et al., 2010).

Webel and colleagues (2010) highlighted another benefit of psycho-education: Community members and nonclinicians can facilitate educational sessions. Thus, psychoeducation can be a cost-effective strategy for organizations that do not have therapists on staff. Psychoeducation sessions can also be a critical point at which community leaders who have previously arrived and are currently supporting incoming refugees can be involved. Research indicates that training peers to lead groups has significant beneficial outcomes. For example, a study of an 8-week group psychoeducation program led by peers found that participants experienced decreased social isolation and increased independence at the end of the group (Block et al., 2018). In addition, as shown in a study evaluating peer-led community health workshops with a Bhutanese refugee community, peer-based groups allow for cultural competency that is unparalleled as previously resettled individuals can speak from their own experiences during adjustment (Im & Rosenberg, 2015).

Psychoeducation sessions are commonly formatted as an educational presentation on a relevant topic delivered to a group of refugees from a specific country of origin, ideally with an in-person interpreter to maximize responsiveness to questions or concerns that arise. The goal of psychoeducation is not to pathologize symptoms or focus on mental diagnoses (which are Western concepts); instead, facilitators use culturally sensitive language to discuss symptoms that can keep refugees from living their lives fully and provide strategies to improve functioning.

There are a couple of issues to consider before using psychoeducation in any setting. First, it is important to have a referral process for group members who identify as needing mental health services following a session. Second, facilitators must ensure they conduct adequate research and go through proper training if needed so that accurate information is disseminated. If these steps are taken, then psychoeducation can be implemented at little cost to the agency, and the content can be used repeatedly with new arrivals. An additional benefit of psychoeducation sessions is that they can be used in conjunction with other services. For example, Project SHIFA (Supporting the Health of Immigrant Families and Adolescents), a Boston-based program serving the Somali refugee community, uses psychoeducation to supplement school-based programs by educating parents regarding youth mental health needs. Psychoeducation can also supplement existing case management services by providing additional information on the U.S. health care system and access to benefits.

Although formal group sessions are important, mental health providers must also engage in ongoing psychoeducation with all clients served in individual or group settings as trauma-exposed clients may have impaired short-term memory and may need to hear material repeatedly to help them process the information. Therapists must also engage in reciprocal learning, positioning clients as the expert on their own experiences. For example, therapists must take time to understand that the Western terminology surrounding trauma is culturally bound and may not align with clients' understanding of their symptoms. As discussed later in this chapter, interpreters can serve as valuable tools for therapists' learning. Finally, it is critical to repeatedly instill hope by informing clients that there are paths to healing and that recovery is possible so clients are motivated to seek and continue accessing support.

## Psychoeducation in Practice

Therapists in the mental health program at RefugeeOne conduct group psychoeducation to introduce mental health concepts. Psychoeducation sessions are offered on a monthly basis, both at the agency and in other community spaces, in recognition of the importance and effectiveness of this intervention. The psychoeducation sessions are designed to help clients understand the symptoms they may be experiencing without forcing them to self-identify. These presentations also combat misinformation regarding mental health services, normalize physiological responses, and identify available community-based mental health resources. When appropriate, they also offer strategies for coping (such as basic mindfulness techniques for stress or insomnia) so that individuals have more internal resources to handle the stress of adjustment. The sessions do not require the prolonged time commitment of therapy, which RefugeeOne therapists have found to be a prohibitive factor for those working multiple jobs to support other members of their family.

Staff at RefugeeOne provide a group psychoeducation course on trauma over three sessions in language-specific groups with an in-person interpreter. The purpose of the course is to introduce key trauma concepts using accessible language. Therapists then offer methods for coping with the body's trauma response, introducing cognitive behavior and mindfulness techniques. These sessions are designed to be interactive, and each presentation lasts approximately 1 hour. Staff use image-focused slides with terminology tailored to audience culture and general education levels. Populations that have had limited access to education in their country of origin receive content with simplified terminology, whereas those that have had access to higher education receive information using more technical language. Additionally, the images used in the presentations are adjusted based on the population served as therapists have found that individuals are more responsive to content they feel is relevant to and reflective of their lived experiences.

It is essential that presenters tailor all images used for presentations to the population being served, as this supports non-English speakers with understanding and relating to the content being delivered verbally. Therapists often use color-coded True/False laminated cards as an interactive review activity to ensure understanding of important concepts. Questions are encouraged throughout all presentations, and members often ask questions that stimulate important discussions with other participants.

Content for psychoeducation sessions has been developed with input from colleagues who are members of the communities served. The presentations are tailored on an ongoing basis based on feedback from clients, and pretests and posttests are administered to each group member to ensure their input. The pre- and posttests use an image of a glass of water (Figure 10.1) with a 5-point scale from *empty* to *full*. The questions gauge understanding,

**FIGURE 10.1. Pretest-Posttest Scale for Non-English Speaking Refugee Populations**

**refugee♀NE**

**The Wellness Program — Psychoeducation Series**

Client Name: _____ Age: ____ Sex: M / F  Country of Origin: _____

Topic: _____ Session Number: ____/____ Date: _____

| Please select the number that best represents the statements below. | Pretest | Posttest |
|---|---|---|
| 1. How well do you understand this topic? | 1  2  3  4  5 | 1  2  3  4  5 |
| 2. How much does this topic apply in your life? | 1  2  3  4  5 | 1  2  3  4  5 |
| 3. How helpful would it be to have more information about this topic? | 1  2  3  4  5 | 1  2  3  4  5 |
| Total Score: | | |

*Note.* From *RefugeeOne Wellness Program Service Manual* (p. 4), by RefugeeOne, 2011. Copyright 2011 by RefugeeOne Wellness Program, Aimee Hilado (Clinical Director). Reprinted with permission.

applicability, and desire for more information. This tool has been used successfully with clients with limited reading and writing proficiency; presenters use verbal prompts to contextualize the images, and the interpreter is available for assistance when needed. Feedback is encouraged, and time is provided after every session for clients to speak with presenters regarding any questions, suggestions, or requests for additional information.

Data were gathered on trauma psychoeducation sessions offered to approximately 150 adults in 31 sessions from July 2015 to June 2017. Participants represented Congolese, Rohingya, Burmese, Afghan, Iranian, Iraqi, and Syrian populations, and the assessment tool was successfully administered with each population. Results showed that 85% of Rohingya, 67% of Congolese, 47% of Syrians, and 25% of Iraqis self-reported an increase in knowledge from the program. This research helped staff at RefugeeOne hone content to the specific populations; for example, we received feedback that some information was too oversimplified for the more educated participants, reflected in the smaller percentages of change among the Syrian and Iraqi groups.

Psychoeducation topics were generated based on needs identified within the communities served. In addition to the three-part series focused on trauma, topics include healthy relationships, diabetes management, stress management, tips for navigating the U.S. health care system, and positive parenting strategies. The blending of physical health with mental health topics reinforces the mind–body connection and the importance of attending to both types of need to promote overall well-being. It also helps normalize the concept of mental health by positioning it within a health-focused context. Therapists are purposeful about the way they introduce mental health concepts, deliberately reframing the conversation to destigmatize these important topics. The vignette that follows highlights the critical tenets of psychoeducation: It serves to impart accurate information, normalize challenges individuals and families may be facing, and allow space for clients to benefit from peer support.

### Case Vignette: Facilitating Psychoeducation Workshops With Refugee Adults[1]

As a clinical social work intern at RefugeeOne, I led a set of adult psychoeducation workshops for parents on how trauma impacts child development and how support surrounding social and emotional learning can help children navigate their emotions and relationships with others. We began with a discussion of how exposure to trauma impacts children of any age

---

[1] This case vignette was written by Sara Lytle. Reprinted with permission.

and described some of the signs that a child is struggling with healing from trauma. Immediately, parents began sharing various challenges they were experiencing at home with their children. Many parents talked about struggling with increasingly aggressive behavior and how to set limits and boundaries; others expressed worry about children who were becoming increasingly withdrawn and isolated.

We discussed how children often express their emotions through behavior and how what might look like acting out or being defiant is the result of a child's inner emotional conflict and attempt to self-regulate. Additionally, we emphasized the importance of the home environment, particularly regarding modeling of nonviolent conflict resolution and emotional expression. We addressed the impact of domestic violence, media exposure through television and the Internet, and phone calls with friends and family members discussing traumatic events.

In addition to the psychoeducation information provided by the workshop, it became a space for parents to support one another and share strategies and suggestions. They reported walking away with more information for supporting their children, and this made them feel more confident and less stressed in their home environments.

## PEER GROUP INTERVENTIONS FOR REFUGEE YOUTH

Services for youth often address behavioral issues that can put stress on the entire family and overwhelm parents at a time when they are drained of internal and external resources. When discussing interventions with youth, it is first imperative to acknowledge the diverse ways refugee youth experience the world. This diversity can be masked in the literature by the tendency to overgeneralize by grouping all youth together (Brough et al., 2003). In truth, the intersections of a child's cultural, religious, and gender identities combined with their trauma histories and immigration experiences highlight the complexities within refugee youth identities. Therapists must first listen to each youth's narrative instead of making assumptions about their experiences. However, in order to better understand the overall needs of refugee youth, therapists must examine trends and explore the potential impact of trauma in a refugee child's past and ways it can manifest in their present and future.

Both individual and structural factors highlight the complexity of the resettlement process for youth. High levels of trauma exposure and significant mental health needs often accompany refugee children entering countries of resettlement (Ellis et al., 2008). This is not shocking, considering the fact that most youth grew up in contexts of instability, which increases their likelihood of exposure to violence and repetitive losses. Because refugee youth are more likely to experience trauma in their life than children in the general population through the circumstances surrounding their migration (Berthold, 2000), therapists should use age-appropriate, trauma-informed, and healing-focused interventions.

The perceived stressors that accompany immigration and acculturation may function as reminders of past experiences (Ellis et al., 2008) or may trigger a trauma response and directly or indirectly contribute to the development of mental illness. Therapists should recognize the trauma continuum, meaning that stressors and triggers do not necessarily stop after resettlement, and instead refugees continue to be exposed to trauma through family or friends who remain in the country of origin. Ongoing stressors for refugee youth may also include increased familial responsibility, strained interpersonal relationships, the grief and isolation of family separation or divorce, and the stress of learning to live with a bicultural identity (Ellis et al., 2008). In addition, there is the stress of interacting with their new environment, which may or may not be welcoming to new immigrant populations. The sociopolitical context of the receiving country has been found to be critical for mental health outcomes for all refugees and warrants attention in all interventions, particularly as youth interface with the dominant culture continuously in a school setting (Porter & Haslam, 2005). Sadly, refugee youth in the United States regularly experience bullying and discrimination, which lead to social exclusion from the dominant culture. Efforts to construct meaningful social environments are also impacted by structural factors. For example, a lack of available cultural and linguistic resources, unwelcoming neighborhoods, and an unsupportive school environment can negatively impact the immigration experience.

Of particular concern for youth is identity formation, which begins in childhood and comes to the forefront during adolescence. Refugee youth can struggle to form a cohesive identity as they navigate between the two cultures. Youth can fall anywhere on the spectrum from overidentifying with their culture of origin to overidentifying with their host culture (Brough et al., 2003). Development-focused tasks, such as becoming autonomous and fostering a sense of identity, can be hindered by acculturation stress (Ellis et al., 2008). Aside from the overall stress of postmigration experiences, there are also individual factors that can either facilitate or hinder adjustment. Individual factors include the speed of language acquisition, the presence of social supports, and a sense of belonging within the community (Correa-Velez et al., 2010).

Given that many of these experiences are shared among the refugee youth population, peers can act as a primary source of support and a buffer against the negative effects of the dominant culture. Peer support is a process of mutually receiving support and is based on the foundations of respect and joint responsibility (Mead, 2003). Refugee youth benefit from peer support groups for numerous reasons. First and foremost, these youth are able to identify with one another through shared experiences. Refugee youth disproportionately face trauma exposure, so their lived experiences can be drastically different from those of others in their host country. Furthermore, they face the stress of adjustment and acculturation, which is not experienced by native-born youth. Inclusivity in peer support groups helps alleviate the social isolation and acculturative stress reported by youth (Stewart et al., 2012). Peer support groups operate from a strengths-based and culturally supportive framework, acknowledging that peers have resources that are critical for mutual healing. This framework empowers the individuals in the group and acknowledges the inherent limitations of professionals, particularly those who are not from the cultures of the clients they are serving.

A group dynamic is an important intervention that may help individuals in ways that one-on-one work cannot. Mental Health America (n.d.) reported that peer support services have been proved to

- reduce symptoms,
- reduce hospitalizations,
- decrease lengths of hospital stays,
- increase participation in the community,
- increase social support,
- improve well-being,
- improve self-esteem,
- improve social functioning, and
- encourage more thorough and longer lasting recoveries.

For example, during a therapy group session for 10 adolescent girls from Tanzania attending RefugeeOne's after-school program, a group member shared that she felt scared and anxious after a fire drill at her school that day. She shared that she had no idea what was going on, and it was extremely stressful given her past traumatic experiences. Another group member responded that she felt the same way and could not understand why her teacher and other classmates were not bothered. The whole group identified with the stress felt by this student. They became so passionate that they began speaking Swahili, their native tongue, as this allowed them to converse more fluidly. It was apparent to the group facilitators that it was important for these group members to validate each other's experiences using their own lens. After the group members conversed among themselves for a few minutes, the facilitators noted the girls' relief after processing their experience with others who could identify with their point of view and without having to describe it in their second language. The girls later took the time to summarize the discussion for the facilitators, who validated their need to feel heard and acknowledged the value of peer support.

## Mindfulness Practices With Refugee Youth

Mindfulness interventions can be a strategy to help refugee youth increase affect regulation, improve coping skills, and cultivate healthy relationships with family members, peers, and authority figures. Rumination, anxiety, and trauma recall can all be treated with a toolbox of mindfulness techniques (Hinton et al., 2013). *Mindfulness* is a non-Western technique that focuses on "paying attention in a particular way: on purpose, in the present moment and non-judgmentally" (Kabat-Zinn, as quoted in Saunders, 2015, p. 437). Essentially, mindfulness involves cultivating a nonjudgmental stance toward the self. There are specific cultural adaptations that can be made to this practice (Hinton et al., 2013). Many cultures use different words to describe mindfulness. Cambodians uses the term *saldi*, Latino-Caribbean people use the term *sentidos*, and Buddhist cultures use the term *uppeka*. For people of other cultures that may not have a specific word, mindfulness can be described as "living in the moment with the senses."

*Sensorial mindfulness* is attention to different sensory modalities such as vision, scent, hearing, taste, and touch. Recognition of tension, breathing awareness, and attending to leaf movements are forms of sensorial mindfulness used in practice with refugees. Attending to leaf movements involves instructing youth to make the statement, "May I adjust to each situation just as the leaf is able to adjust to each new breeze," to remind themselves to remain open to new ways of responding to stressful or triggering stimuli (Hinton et al., 2013). This particular intervention is easy to perform and primes emotional and interpersonal flexibility. Sensorial awareness is also practiced through a tea meditation in which youth are asked to pay attention to the appearance of the tea, the way the tea moves in the cup, and the smell, taste, temperature, and weight of the tea. The overall goal of these practices is to shift from a mode of threat avoidance to a mode of pleasurable experiencing.

One of the benefits of mindfulness is that with appropriate training, this tool can be used for anyone in any setting. Mindfulness-based interventions can be very simple and do not need to include complex terminology or abstract concepts. They simply revolve around the experience of processing in a conscious and deliberate way (Brown et al., 2011).

Mindfulness has been taught through various structured and semistructured programs to populations of children, adolescents, and families. Among the numerous available programs, the most widely studied interventions adopt a similar 8-week structure that includes formal meditation practices, mindful movement (synchronizing breath or awareness to movement), and breathing, as well as informal practices that can be integrated in daily life activities. Structured or semistructured programs that focus on breathing techniques, guided meditation, and mindful movement have been found especially beneficial when working with youth (Baxter, n.d.). It is essential to keep youth engaged by providing curriculum that is relevant, easily accessible, and enjoyable. One of the benefits of mindfulness-based interventions is that they are interactive with minimal risk of engagement (Weare, 2012). Youth who have used mindfulness see improvement in their emotional, mental, and physical well-being evidenced by reductions in stress, anxiety, reactivity, and bad behavior. Sleep, self-esteem, self-awareness, self-control, and empathy have also been shown to improve with regular practice.

Mindfulness has a long-term impact on adolescents of increasing focus, enhancing problem solving, and strengthening executive functioning skills. Refugees who have experienced trauma benefit from mindfulness-based interventions because they promote cognitive flexibility (Hinton et al., 2013). Mindfulness promotes brain plasticity by changing the neural networks that were previously wired to a trauma response. This foundation is important for refugee youth as they adjust to new social, linguistic, and cultural contexts. Therapists at RefugeeOne have found that mindfulness in combination with SEL increases the efficacy of both evidenced-based practices in improving emotional and behavior outcomes.

## Social and Emotional Learning Groups With Refugee Youth

Social and emotional learning is a framework for helping youth identify their feelings and express themselves in a healthy and prosocial manner. The Collaborative for Academic, Social, and Emotional Learning (n.d.) outlined five core principles of SEL (Figure 10.2):

1. self-awareness: ability to recognize one's own emotions, attend to needs, and feel capable of completing tasks
2. self-management: ability to cope with stressful situations, maintain control over one's behavior, and set self-directed goals
3. social awareness: respect for difference and ability to care for others

**FIGURE 10.2. Core Principles of Social and Emotional Learning Competencies**

*Note.* SEL = social and emotional learning. From *Social and Emotional Learning (SEL) Competencies*, by Collaborative for Academic, Social, and Emotional Learning, 2017 (https://casel.org/wp-content/uploads/2019/12/CASEL-Competencies.pdf). Copyright 2017 by Collaborative for Academic, Social, and Emotional Learning (CASEL). Reprinted with permission.

4. relationship skills: ability to negotiate wants in relationships, work collaboratively with peers, and ask for support when needed

5. responsible decision making: ability to problem solve in a safe and effective manner and engage in reflective practice in order to learn from the results of one's actions.

Traditional SEL curriculum has been used in school settings and recognizes the importance of family and community engagement.

Trauma can interfere with youths' ability to connect with their emotions, attend to their needs, and cope with ongoing stressors, and the SEL curriculum can be used to increase their internal resilience to combat the negative responses to trauma. Some of the challenges and barriers in traditional youth therapy groups have been a distrust of authority and systems, the stigmatization of mental health services, various cultural and linguistic barriers, and prioritization of other, more seemingly pressing stressors (Ellis et al., 2008). Therapists can overcome some of these barriers by implementing groups in community settings that youth are already familiar with. Barriers can also be effectively addressed by involving the family, using trusted service systems, involving cultural experts, and integrating multiple services.

RefugeeOne involves family by placing siblings together in groups when appropriate and providing family therapy when needed. Parents are a critical part of the therapy, and monthly parent sessions are provided to keep parents updated on their child's progress, reinforce skills learned, and get feedback from parents regarding their child's behavior outside of group. The services are integrated into RefugeeOne's after-school program, which offers school readiness activities and homework support to refugee youth. The program is located in a familiar church, and transportation is provided to take the participants directly from school to the after-school program and then home so that parents do not have the added stressor of providing transportation. Five hundred and five youth received supportive services such as tutoring, advocacy, and support in finding extracurricular activities through the youth program in 2017–18. More than 100 of these children received mental health services in the form of SEL groups.

In addition to the after-school groups, other groups are conducted in spaces offered by partner organizations, such as mutual aid associations and religious study schools that youth attend. Still more youth are served through partnerships with refugee-serving schools in the recognition that therapists in the wellness program have skill sets for working with refugee youth that school staff do not.

Youth can be identified for services by direct service staff, teachers at their respective schools, and family and community members. Because youth tend to manifest mental health issues through changes in behavior, such as withdrawing or acting out, most referrals come from issues children are having with peers, authority figures, or family members. The primary area of concern is often school performance, which is explained within the immigrant experience as preoccupation with the success of future generations as immigrant parents must focus on rebuilding their lives in the new country. Parents often explain that their intent upon resettling is to set their children up for a better life with the understanding that success in school is critical to success in the United States.

Given that peer relationships and identity changes are a universal aspect of youth adjustment, therapists have found peer groups to be an effective framework for therapy. Youth at RefugeeOne are placed in groups based on age, with youth ages 5–7, 8–11, 12–14, and 15–17 placed together to account for emotional development and ensure safety for all participants. For those with high levels of English after being in the United States for at least 2 years, intercultural groups are formed to increase understanding and dialogue across populations. For those with lower English-language skills, groups are formed based on language, and an in-person interpreter is offered to ensure understanding of the topic discussed. Youth below age 11 are placed in coed groups (with the consent of parents and comfort of the youth), whereas older youth are separated by gender identity out of respect for cultural differences and so that topics around psychosexual development can be discussed.

SEL is a framework for assisting youth in the development of emotional self-awareness, affect regulation, and healthy decision-making skills for the purpose of fostering healthy interpersonal relationships and academic success. The groups have been implemented at RefugeeOne in recognition that academic performance hinges on a child's ability to adapt to the norms of U.S. schools and that trauma symptoms can affect the adjustment process through behavioral and psychological manifestations. These groups run weekly for 12 weeks; the content for each week is focused on a specific area of social and emotional learning. The activities are interactive and meant to foster discussion while allowing space for youth to reflect.

A universal theme discussed in these groups is difficulties navigating peer relationships because of cultural differences or poor affect regulation from stress or trauma, which can result in social exclusion or bullying. Younger clients talk about trouble fitting in because of differences in how they look or act. Teens often speak about concerns regarding their identity as they are introduced to norms of U.S. culture that may directly conflict with the expectations for behavior established by their culture of origin. For example, teens from more traditional cultures may have had limited interactions with opposite-sex peers and may struggle with the more fluid interactions that occur in U.S. schools. As these differences come to light, another challenge frequently reported is increased conflict with parents, who may perceive changes in youths' behavior to be a direct affront to their culture of origin.

Another complex issue that surfaces during treatment is the youths' struggle to help their parents understand that they still experience mental health issues even in the physically safer and more stable environment. Parents may feel that their children do not have reasons for concern in comparison with the trauma the parents themselves have endured, assessing their children's symptoms as a sign of weakness that must be addressed through harsher or more involved parenting. Although parents may have the best intentions, this misunderstanding often invalidates the youths' experience and can cause the youth to silently suffer until a mental health crisis occurs. A key tenet of the SEL curriculum is parental education and involvement; therapists speak with parents to update them on the progress of the groups and provide strategies to support their child's social–emotional growth in the home. Parents have reported decreased stress and increased understanding of their child's behavior as a result of youth involvement in the program. The case vignette that follows highlights benefits observed by the facilitator of an SEL group that incorporated mindfulness strategies.

### Case Vignette: Facilitating a Social and Emotional Learning Group With Refugee Youth

I (MC) cofacilitated a therapy group with about 12 participants when I was a social work intern at RefugeeOne. The group took place at RefugeeOne's after-school program. The group members were boys and girls from the Democratic Republic of Congo who ranged in age from 8 to 13 years. During the initial coed session, it became apparent that the boys and girls would feel more comfortable in gender-segregated groups, so we adjusted the structure of the group to attend to cultural norms and ran two smaller groups consecutively on the same day.

The first session was both frustrating and overwhelming because participants had a difficult time remaining calm in order for us to complete introductions and establish the norms of the group. When it was time for the next session, we decided it would be best to use their energy instead of trying to overcome it. We felt that mindfulness-based activities could be helpful for increasing affect regulation and fostering impulse control. When the participants came in, we had everyone take a seat. I led a quick guided meditation involving mindful movements. At the end, I asked everyone to shake their whole body and encouraged participants to dance around. After a couple of minutes, I instructed everyone to freeze, and to notice how their bodies felt. We all took a seat and processed the meditation.

This experience illustrates the importance of flexibility and the effectiveness of applying a strengths-based perspective. Instead of forcing the participants to adapt to the environment, it is much more effective to adapt the environment to suit the needs of the participants.

## SUPPORT SYSTEMS AND ADVOCACY EFFORTS IN THE COMMUNITY

Refugees who immigrate to a new country must search for new communities where they can feel safe and supported. Appropriate systems of support vary by individual but frequently involve schools, community-based refugee support agencies, and institutions of faith. This section discusses important aspects of these community-based supports and highlights the importance of advocacy efforts to ensure these environments are welcoming and supportive.

Public schools serve as a primary space where youth come into contact with the dominant culture. Students' ability to thrive in this new setting is defined by how welcoming they perceive their school to be as their emotional well-being is directly connected to their sense of belonging and engagement in school settings. Youth who feel welcomed into their school also are more likely to be motivated in their academics and to have fewer behavioral issues in the academic setting (Chiu et al., 2012; Hernandez et al., 2009; Suárez-Orozco et al., 2009). School administrations should foster an attitude of inclusivity and make accessible supports for students when needed. For example, sufficient support for English language learning, such as interpretation for parents when issues arise at school and dedicated staff for immigrant students, is necessary so students aren't excluded from the curriculum in the classroom. Schools should ensure that refugee youth are free from verbal or physical bullying and provide spaces for youth to get extra support when needed. Through teaching, research, and practice, schools must provide more opportunities to learn about the new immigrant groups arriving and encourage students to engage with these groups. Refugee parents should be included in important school events and meetings by ensuring that interpretation is provided so they can remain active participants in their child's education.

Appropriate faith institutions are also critical spaces for healing and support. For example, imams (traditional spiritual leaders in the Muslim faith) are often seen as indirect agents of Allah's will and facilitators of the healing process (Abu-Ras & Abu-Bader, 2008; Padela et al., 2011, 2012). Imams may also play central roles in shaping family and community attitudes and responses to illness, and Muslim Americans are more likely to seek support from religious leaders than from mental health professionals (Padela et al., 2012). Ali and colleagues (2005) found that a significant majority (95%) of the 62 imams studied reported spending a large portion of their time emotionally supporting those in their congregation.

One example from practice is a Syrian couple with young children who began experiencing marital stress following the husband's emotional infidelity. The couple sought counseling, where they talked about how their faith was a source of support during difficult times and served as a motivating factor for resolving their issues and avoiding divorce. It was evident that neither client wanted to seek separation, but they were struggling to move forward.

The therapist explored the couple's ties to a mosque in Chicago. They identified an imam who had supported them when they first arrived and agreed to speak with him regarding their strained relationship. During this meeting, their imam counseled the husband regarding the importance of trust and honesty in a relationship and agreed to meet with the family weekly for guidance on fostering a healthy relationship built on the tenets of Islam from the Koran. The wife stopped talking about fears regarding divorce, and the husband spent time at the mosque to decrease his social isolation, which had contributed to their marital strain.

In another example of faith-focused healing, a Christian youth presented with severe depression following a breakup with her first boyfriend, whom she had hoped to marry. The youth was not able to speak with her family about her sadness as they had not approved of the relationship. Similarly, her friends who had not yet been in a relationship were not understanding, so she was able to speak only with her therapist. During one session, this youth talked about her faith as a source of happiness, revealing that she had not gone to church since resettling because she did not know of a church in her neighborhood that held services in her native language. The counselor worked with the youth to find a church and accompanied her once to ensure she knew how to travel there; there she began attending youth Bible study classes. She expressed relief at having a new support system and frequently spoke of the meaning she derived from the verses they discussed. The client eventually phased out of therapy as her depression decreased, and she had a support system as she moved forward.

It is critical for professionals working with new immigrant populations to recognize the role that faith may play in clients' lives and encourage engagement when appropriate. Religion and culture are intertwined, so building an immigrant community should make space for religious elements (Nawyn, 2006). Communities must have spaces for worship and ensure that new immigrants are able to safely get to these spaces. Recent attacks on mosques and synagogues have sent a threatening message to refugee populations, and policies must be enacted to protect all places of worship.

Resettlement agencies are often a primary source of support when refugees initially arrive, offering adjustment services such as English classes, employment counseling, housing support, and case management services. These services are key to stabilizing basic needs for food and shelter as staff ensure clients' access to social safety nets. They can also serve as critical spaces for emotional support as clients meet other newly arrived refugees during English classes or vocational training courses (Nawyn, 2006). Clients are also supported in accessing necessary medical resources to complete immunizations and connect with appropriate physicians. Resettlement agencies are supported in their work by grassroots community-driven organizations, commonly known as "mutual aid associations" (Nawyn, 2006). These organizations are often founded by previously resettled immigrants and refugees of a specific ethnicity to provide support to those still arriving. As refugees phase out of services offered by the resettlement agency (in a time line dictated by the U.S. government), they are offered continued case management services and programming through the mutual aid association. Policies should recognize the continued need to support refugees beyond their initial adjustment period, and funding should be increased to serve these community-driven agencies.

Refugees may also seek support from others who have emigrated from their country of origin in the past, and these individuals can often provide support and guidance through the complexities of adjustment. These community leaders are often identified through their work in community agencies such as resettlement offices, mutual aid associations, or local churches, mosques, or synagogues. Native-born staff working with refugee populations should see these community leaders as cultural brokers who can help clients and staff members navigate cultural differences and provide a bridge that fosters mutual respect and cultural humility (Brar-Josan & Yohani, 2014). For example, when cultural brokers serve as interpreters during individual or group therapy sessions, they can support the therapist in understanding the nuances of nonverbal communication and offer their own assessment of a client's presentation. When possible, it is important to include the interpreter in case consultation as they are a critical piece of the therapeutic alliance. Cultural brokers also demonstrate to the client that someone from their community is advocating for mental health services, which can make them feel more comfortable with accessing services whenever needed. Most importantly, cultural brokers are often at the crux of all interventions mentioned in this chapter as they play a key role in interpreting for youth and adult populations.

## Case Vignette: Angelique

Angelique[2] was a 12-year-old girl from the Democratic Republic of Congo. She was referred to the RefugeeOne wellness program by her school's vice principal after teachers observed changes in her behavior approximately

---

[2] This case vignette is a fictionalized composite.

6 months after her arrival in the United States. Angelique was often observed sitting alone at lunch and rarely spoke in her classes. Her grades had started to slip, and teachers noted that she would zone out during class when not engaged in an activity. A therapist completed the Strengths and Difficulties Questionnaire (Goodman, 2005) with Angelique, who shared that she was feeling nervous all the time when in school because of an incident of bullying that had happened at the end of the previous school year. A girl in her grade had called her names, and other children, including some whom she had seen as her friends, had joined in.

Angelique, who had once enjoyed school, spent the summer dreading the time when she would have to return, and reports to the therapist from her parents indicated that she spent much of her time in her room. Angelique shared that her peers' treatment also triggered memories of violence she witnessed in the refugee camps, where her family was targeted for their religious identity. Angelique had not been able to go to school in the camps, and she often stayed in the tent with her entire family, leaving only if her parents deemed it to be safe. Angelique noted that she felt comfortable when sharing this with the social worker as her parents avoided all talk of the past and scolded her when she brought up these memories. She agreed to attend the after-school program at RefugeeOne, and the social worker explained that she would be meeting other youth who had had similar experiences to her own.

When the group began, Angelique spoke little, often scanning the room. However, during an exercise focused on identifying emotions, Angelique began to speak about her loneliness and need for belonging. She spoke quietly at first, but as other youth nodded along, Angelique became more comfortable and expressive, sharing what it felt like when she was being targeted. Although other group members had not experienced this exact issue, many spoke of feeling like an outsider in their school. Angelique left the session smiling and walked out arm in arm with another group member, an 11-year-old girl from Syria. The group facilitators came together to discuss ideas for continuing to support Angelique by considering three questions:

1. How is the peer group intervention beneficial for Angelique? Are there additional supports we want to put in place for Angelique?

2. How might psychoeducation be useful for other members of Angelique's family? How can we tailor the content, considering the cultural context of this family?

3. What are some Western orientations we should steer away from while tailoring our interventions?

## LESSONS LEARNED: COMMON DENOMINATORS OF IMPACTFUL PEER GROUP AND COMMUNITY-BASED PRACTICE

Therapists working with refugee populations must be cognizant of their personal orientations to practice, which are often Western oriented, and tailor interventions to be inclusive of non-Western cultures. Their practices must reflect the differing community responses to traumatic events and offer content adjusted to the culture of the population being served. Because symptoms are likely to manifest through somatic complaints, there must be a focus on the mind–body connection and on overall well-being.

Trauma-informed care is an orientation to practice that recognizes the prevalence of trauma and the potential for environmental triggers. Trauma-informed practice should be embedded within the organization and take shape in all areas of practice. A trauma-informed lens involves fostering the sense of physical and emotional safety, remaining trustworthy, allowing for autonomy and collaboration during the intervention process, and empowering clients to see their own capacity for healing and growth (Substance Abuse and Mental Health Services Administration, 2014). Practitioners must also resist stereotypes and seek to amend biases so that clients feel respected and treated as individuals with unique histories. As recognized by researcher and author Judith Herman (1992), trauma has the profound impact of removing one's power over one's own life; therefore, practitioners must ensure they do not perpetuate this damage, which can lead to a sense of learned helplessness.

By providing psychoeducation-focused adult sessions in a group setting, therapists give control back to trauma survivors, who walk away equipped with an understanding of symptoms and resources available for support as needed. Clients are provided with the option to self-identify when they are ready to access services, and increased knowledge of common symptoms and available services allows them to self-advocate when needed. Therapists also reduce survivors' sense of isolation by normalizing responses and providing information regarding the prevalence of symptoms.

Youth mindfulness-based and social and emotional learning groups serve a similar purpose of fostering a sense of belonging and inclusion during a critical period of identity formation. Youth are guided through a tailored curriculum that focuses on self-awareness and affect regulation to address trauma symptoms that disrupt their normal mechanisms for coping and can lead to poor school performance and strained interpersonal relationships. Therapists must also attend to structural inequities when they arise as research has highlighted that environmental factors are just as critical to overall well-being as internal coping mechanisms. By nurturing the mind–body connection and attending to micro, mezzo, and macro structures, therapists can promote the overall well-being of refugee adults and youth.

## REFERENCES

Abu-Ras, W., & Abu-Bader, S. H. (2008). The impact of the September 11, 2001, attacks on the well-being of Arab Americans in New York City. *Journal of Muslim Mental Health, 3*(2), 217–239. https://doi.org/10.1080/15564900802487634

Abu-Ras, W., Gheith, A., & Cournos, F. (2008). The imam's role in mental health promotion: A study at 22 mosques in New York City's Muslim community. *Journal of Muslim Mental Health, 3*(2), 155–176. https://doi.org/10.1080/15564900802487576

Agbényiga, D. F., Barrie, S., Djelaj, V., & Nawyn, S. (2012). Expanding our community: Independent and interdependent factors impacting refugees' successful community resettlement. *Advances in Social Work, 13*(2), 306–324. https://doi.org/10.18060/1956

Ager, A., & Strang, A. (2004). *Indicators of integration: Final report* (Development and Practice Report 28). Research, Development and Statistics Directorate, Home Office. https://webarchive.nationalarchives.gov.uk/20110218141321/http:/rds.homeoffice.gov.uk/rds/pdfs04/dpr28.pdf

Ali, O. M., Milstein, G., & Marzuk, P. M. (2005). The imam's role in meeting the counseling needs of Muslim communities in the United States. *Psychiatric Services, 56*(2), 202–205. https://doi.org/10.1176/appi.ps.56.2.202

Ali, S. H., & Agyapong, V. I. O. (2016). Barriers to mental health service utilisation in Sudan—Perspectives of carers and psychiatrists. *BMC Health Services Research, 16*, 31. https://doi.org/10.1186/s12913-016-1280-2

Baxter, E. (n.d.). *Mindfulness in schools: Benefits for students, teachers, and parents.* http://www.suryachandrahealingyoga.com/images/mindfulnessInSchools_ericaBaxter.pdf

Berry, J. W. (1997). Immigration, acculturation, and adaptation. *Applied Psychology, 46*(1), 5–34. https://doi.org/10.1111/j.1464-0597.1997.tb01087.x

Berthold, S. M. (2000). War traumas and community violence: Psychological, behavioral, and academic outcomes among Khmer refugee adolescents. *Journal of Multicultural Social Work, 8*(1–2), 15–46. https://doi.org/10.1300/J285v08n01_02

Birman, D., Ho, J., Pulley, E., Batia, K., Everson, M. L., & Ellis, H. (2005). *Mental health interventions for refugee children in resettlement* [White Paper II]. Refugee Trauma Task Force, National Child Traumatic Stress Network. https://doi.org/10.1037/e315362005-001

Block, A. M., Aizenman, L., Saad, A., Harrison, S., Sloan, A., Vecchio, S., & Wilson, V. (2018). Peer support groups: Evaluating a culturally grounded, strengths-based approach for work with refugees. *Advances in Social Work, 18*(3), 930–948. https://doi.org/10.18060/21634

Boswell, C. (2001). *Spreading the costs of asylum seekers: A critical assessment of dispersal policies in Germany and the UK.* Anglo-German Foundation for the Study of Industrial Society.

Brar-Josan, N., & Yohani, S. C. (2014). A framework for counsellor–cultural broker collaboration. *Canadian Journal of Counselling and Psychotherapy Research, 48*(2), 81–99. https://cjc-rcc.ucalgary.ca/article/view/60942

Brough, M. K., Gorman, D., Ramirez, E., & Westoby, P. (2003). Young refugees talk about well-being: A qualitative analysis of refugee youth mental health from three states. *Australian Journal of Social Issues, 38*(2), 193–208. https://doi.org/10.1002/j.1839-4655.2003.tb01142.x

Brown, K. W., West, A. M., Loverich, T. M., & Biegel, G. M. (2011). Assessing adolescent mindfulness: Validation of an adapted Mindful Attention Awareness Scale in adolescent normative and psychiatric populations. *Psychological Assessment, 23*(4), 1023–1033. https://doi.org/10.1037/a0021338

Chiu, M. M., Pong, S. L., Mori, I., & Chow, B. W. (2012). Immigrant students' emotional and cognitive engagement at school: A multilevel analysis of students in 41 countries. *Journal of Youth and Adolescence, 41*(11), 1409–1425. https://doi.org/10.1007/s10964-012-9763-x

Ciftci, A., Jones, N., & Corrigan, P. W. (2012). Mental health stigma in the Muslim community. *Journal of Muslim Mental Health, 7*(1), 17–32. https://doi.org/10.3998/jmmh.10381607.0007.102

Collaborative for Academic, Social, and Emotional Learning. (n.d.). *What is SEL?* https://casel.org/what-is-sel/#

Collaborative for Academic, Social, and Emotional Learning. (2017). *Social and emotional learning (SEL) competencies.* https://casel.org/wp-content/uploads/2019/12/CASEL-Competencies.pdf

Correa-Velez, I., Gifford, S. M., & Barnett, A. G. (2010). Longing to belong: Social inclusion and wellbeing among youth with refugee backgrounds in the first three years in Melbourne, Australia. *Social Science & Medicine, 71*(8), 1399–1408. https://doi.org/10.1016/j.socscimed.2010.07.018

Ellis, B. H., Lincoln, A. K., Charney, M. E., Ford-Paz, R., Benson, M., & Strunin, L. (2010). Mental health service utilization of Somali adolescents: Religion, community, and school as gateways to healing. *Transcultural Psychiatry, 47*(5), 789–811. https://doi.org/10.1177/1363461510379933

Ellis, B. H., MacDonald, H. Z., Lincoln, A. K., & Cabral, H. J. (2008). Mental health of Somali adolescent refugees: The role of trauma, stress, and perceived discrimination. *Journal of Consulting and Clinical Psychology, 76*(2), 184–193. https://doi.org/10.1037/0022-006X.76.2.184

Fassaert, T., Hesselink, A. E., & Verhoeff, A. P. (2009). Acculturation and use of health care services by Turkish and Moroccan migrants: A cross-sectional population-based study. *BMC Public Health, 9*(1), 332. https://doi.org/10.1186/1471-2458-9-332

Fazel, M., Wheeler, J., & Danesh, J. (2005). Prevalence of serious mental disorder in 7000 refugees resettled in Western countries: A systematic review. *The Lancet, 365*(9467), 1309–1314. https://doi.org/10.1016/s0140-6736(05)61027-6

Fischman, Y., & Ross, J. (1990). Group treatment of exiled survivors of torture. *American Journal of Orthopsychiatry, 60*(1), 135–142. https://doi.org/10.1037/h0079191

Fitzgerald, H. (2017). *Barriers to mental health treatment for refugees in Maine: An exploratory study* [Master's thesis, Smith College]. Smith ScholarWorks. https://scholarworks.smith.edu/theses/1892

Gaw, A. C. (1993). Psychiatric care of Chinese Americans. In A. C. Gaw (Ed.), *Culture, ethnicity, and mental illness* (pp. 245–280). American Psychiatric Association.

Goodman, R. (2005). *Strengths and Difficulties Questionnaire: One-sided self-rated SDQ for 11–17 year olds.* https://www.sdqinfo.org/py/sdqinfo/b3.py?language= Englishqz(USA)

Griffiths, D., Sigona, N., & Zetter, R. (2005). *Refugee community organisations and dispersal: Networks, resources and social capital.* Policy Press. https://doi.org/10.2307/j.ctt9qgknk

Hassan, G., Kirmayer, L. J., MekkiBerrada, A., Quosh, C., el Chammay, R., Deville-Stoetzel, J. B., Youssef, A., Jefee-Bahloul, H., Barkeel-Oteo, A., Coutts, A., Song, S., & Ventevogel, P. (2015). *Culture, context and the mental health and psychosocial wellbeing of Syrians: A review for mental health and psychosocial support staff working with Syrians affected by armed conflict.* United Nations High Commissioner for Refugees.

Herman, J. (1992). *Trauma and recovery: The aftermath of violence.* Basic Books.

Hernandez, D. J., Denton, N. A., & Macartney, S. (2009). School-age children in immigrant families: Challenges and opportunities for America's schools. *Teachers College Record, 111*(3), 616–658.

Hinton, D. E., Pich, V., Hofmann, S. G., & Otto, M. W. (2013). Acceptance and mindfulness techniques as applied to refugee and ethnic minority populations with PTSD: Examples from "culturally adapted CBT." *Cognitive and Behavioral Practice, 20*(1), 33–46. https://doi.org/10.1016/j.cbpra.2011.09.001

Hsu, L. K. G., & Folstein, M. F. (1997). Somatoform disorders in Caucasian and Chinese Americans. *Journal of Nervous and Mental Disease, 185*(6), 382–387. https://doi.org/10.1097/00005053-199706000-00004

Im, H., Ferguson, A. B., Warsame, A. H., & Isse, M. M. (2017). Mental health risks and stressors faced by urban refugees: Perceived impacts of war and community adversities among Somali refugees in Nairobi. *International Journal of Social Psychiatry, 63*(8), 686–693. https://doi.org/10.1177/0020764017728966

Im, H., Jettner, J. F., Warsame, A. H., Isse, M. M., Khoury, D., & Ross, A. I. (2018). Trauma-informed psychoeducation for Somali refugee youth in urban Kenya: Effects on PTSD and psychosocial outcomes. *Journal of Child & Adolescent Trauma, 11*(4), 431–441. https://doi.org/10.1007/s40653-017-0200-x

Im, H., & Rosenberg, R. (2015). Building social capital through a peer-led community health workshop: A pilot with the Bhutanese refugee community. *Journal of Community Health, 41*, 509–517. https://doi.org/10.1007/s10900-015-0124-z

Jaycox, L. H., Stein, B. D., Kataoka, S. H., Wong, M., Fink, A., Escudero, P., & Zaragoza, C. (2002). Violence exposure, posttraumatic stress disorder, and depressive symptoms among recent immigrant schoolchildren. *Journal of the American Academy of Child & Adolescent Psychiatry, 41*(9), 1104–1110. https://doi.org/10.1097/00004583-200209000-00011

Kirmayer, L. J., Narasiah, L., Munoz, M., Rashid, M., Ryder, A. G., Guzder, J., Hassan, G., Rousseau, C., Pottie, K., & Canadian Collaboration for Immigrant and Refugee Health. (2011). Common mental health problems in immigrants and refugees: General approach in primary care. *Canadian Medical Association Journal, 183*(12), E959–E967. https://doi.org/10.1503/cmaj.090292

Leff, J. (1998). *Psychiatry around the globe: A transcultural view* [Gaskell Psychiatry Series]. Gaskell/Royal College of Psychiatrists.

Maier, T., & Straub, M. (2011). "My head is like a bag full of rubbish": Concepts of illness and treatment expectations in traumatized migrants. *Qualitative Health Research, 21*(2), 233–248. https://doi.org/10.1177/1049732310383867

Mead, S. (2003). *Defining peer support.* https://docs.google.com/document/d/1WG3ulnF6vthAwFZpJxE9rkx6lJzYSX7VX4HprV5EkfY/edit

Mental Health America. (n.d.). *Peer services.* https://www.mhanational.org/peer-services

Nawyn, S. J. (2006). Faith, ethnicity, and culture in refugee resettlement. *American Behavioral Scientist, 49*(11), 1509–1527. https://doi.org/10.1177/0002764206288462

Padela, A. I., Killawi, A., Forman, J., DeMonner, S., & Heisler, M. (2012). American Muslim perceptions of healing: Key agents in healing, and their roles. *Qualitative Health Research, 22*(6), 846–858. https://doi.org/10.1177/1049732312438969

Padela, A. I., Killawi, A., Heisler, M., Demonner, S., & Fetters, M. D. (2011). The role of imams in American Muslim health: Perspectives of Muslim community leaders in Southeast Michigan. *Journal of Religion and Health, 50*(2), 359–373. https://doi.org/10.1007/s10943-010-9428-6

Porter, M., & Haslam, N. (2005). Predisplacement and postdisplacement factors associated with mental health of refugees and internally displaced persons: A meta-analysis. *JAMA, 294*(5), 602–612. https://doi.org/10.1001/jama.294.5.602

Saraceno, B., van Ommeren, M., Batniji, R., Cohen, A., Gureje, O., Mahoney, J., Sridhar, D., & Underhill, C. (2007). Barriers to improvement of mental health services in low-income and middle-income countries. *The Lancet, 370*(9593), 1164–1174. https://doi.org/10.1016/S0140-6736(07)61263-X

Saunders, D. C. (2015). Being mindful of mindfulness: Past, present, and future of mindfulness in child and adolescent psychiatry. *Journal of the American Academy of Child & Adolescent Psychiatry, 54*(6), 437–439. https://doi.org/10.1016/j.jaac.2015.03.006

Sijbrandij, M., Acarturk, C., Bird, M., Bryant, R. A., Burchert, S., Carswell, K., & Cuijpers, P. (2017). Strengthening mental health care systems for Syrian refugees in Europe and the Middle East: Integrating scalable psychological interventions in eight countries. *European Journal of Psychotraumatology, 8*(Suppl. 2), 1388102. https://doi.org/10.1080/20008198.2017.1388102

Sleijpen, M., Boeije, H. R., Kleber, R. J., & Mooren, T. (2016). Between power and powerlessness: A meta-ethnography of sources of resilience in young refugees. *Ethnicity & Health, 21*(2), 158–180. https://doi.org/10.1080/13557858.2015.1044946

Stewart, M., Simich, L., Shizha, E., Makumbe, K., & Makwarimba, E. (2012). Supporting African refugees in Canada: Insights from a support intervention. *Health and Social Care in the Community, 20*(5), 516–527. https://doi.org/10.1111/j.1365-2524.2012.01069.x

Suárez-Orozco, C., Pimentel, A., & Martin, M. (2009). The significance of relationships: Academic engagement and achievement among newcomer immigrant youth. *Teachers College Record, 111*(3), 712–749.

Substance Abuse and Mental Health Services Administration. (2014). *SAMHSA's concept of trauma and guidance for a trauma-informed approach.* https://store.samhsa.gov/system/files/sma14-4884.pdf

Weare, K. (2012). *Evidence for the impact of mindfulness on children and young people.* Mindfulness in Schools Project, University of Exeter Mood Disorders Centre.

https://mindfulnessinschools.org/wp-content/uploads/2013/02/MiSP-Research-Summary-2012.pdf

Webel, A. R., Okonsky, J., Trompeta, J., & Holzemer, W. L. (2010). A systematic review of the effectiveness of peer-based interventions on health-related behaviors in adults. *American Journal of Public Health, 100*(2), 247–253. https://doi.org/10.2105/AJPH.2008.149419

Weine, S. M. (2011). Developing preventive mental health interventions for refugee families in resettlement. *Family Process, 50*(3), 410–430. https://doi.org/10.1111/j.1545-5300.2011.01366.x

Wilkinson, R., & Marmot, M. (1998). *Social determinants of health: The solid facts.* World Health Organization.

Yalom, I. (2005). *The theory and practice of group psychotherapy.* Basic Books.

Zetter, R., Griffiths, D., & Sigona, N. (2005). Social capital or social exclusion? The impact of asylum seeker dispersal on UK refugee community organisations. *Community Development Journal, 40*(2), 169–181. https://doi.org/10.1093/cdj/bsi025

# 11

# INTEGRATING INDIGENOUS AND TRADITIONAL PRACTICES IN REFUGEE MENTAL HEALTH THERAPY

E. ANNE MARSHALL

Availability is not the only difficulty for refugees seeking access to mental health services. Western healing methodologies often present as foreign concepts to some refugee populations. Ecological studies (Duran, 2006; Purgato et al., 2017) indicate that integrating Indigenous methods of healing, such as cultural and religious rituals and cultural practices and beliefs, into existing services enhances receptivity and provides more effective outcomes. This chapter describes a "hybrid" therapy approach, in which Indigenous or traditional cultural practices can be integrated with Western therapeutic interventions. The significance of cultural competency in integrating Indigenous practices with refugees is addressed, including relevant ethical issues. Three case studies are included with suggestions for therapy considerations.

Mental health care needs are particularly urgent for refugees and those who have experienced the disruption, and often trauma, of forced migration. Traumatic experiences in their home countries, the stress of forced migration, and the challenges of often multiple relocations have been associated with higher rates of mental health problems among this population (Colucci et al., 2015; Guruge & Butt, 2015). To meet the needs of their ever-growing

https://doi.org/10.1037/0000226-011
*Refugee Mental Health*, J. D. Aten and J. Hwang (Editors)
Copyright © 2021 by the American Psychological Association. All rights reserved.

numbers, therapists and mental health professionals have been advocating for an increased focus on culturally relevant mental health promotion, treatment approaches, and interventions specifically tailored for refugees and forced migrants (Whitley et al., 2013).

Many of these individuals come from countries in which Indigenous or traditional approaches to health, including mental health, are widespread and universally accepted. An Indigenous view of health encompasses the inter-relatedness of spiritual, mental, social, physical, and community aspects (Duran, 2006; Trimble, 2018). These non-Western cultural understandings of mental health and healing are different from most therapy approaches practiced in North America and Europe. Moreover, many refugees come from more collectivist, or community-focused, cultures; the emphasis in Western therapy on individual identity and autonomy may be unfamiliar and uncomfortable for them (Thira, 2014). Thus, therapists need to acquire the appropriate knowledge and skills to support refugees seeking help for mental and emotional difficulties (Andermann, 2014). It is also important to note that, though the potential negative impacts of forced migration are clear, refugees also have significant strengths, resilience, courage, and relational connections. These positive factors can mitigate harmful effects and provide a base for growth and adaptation (Tedeschi & Calhoun, 2004).

In this chapter, I suggest that a "hybrid" approach, blending Indigenous or traditional ways and knowledge with Western mental health therapy, is a culturally appropriate and effective approach for use with refugee populations. Several key considerations for understanding the context of refugee mental health are presented first, including the importance of acknowledging traditional or Indigenous perspectives. Historical trauma, gender role considerations, and barriers to help seeking are also discussed. The hybrid approach to therapy is described, as is the role of cultural brokers. Several principles and strategies to enhance the cultural competency of therapists are outlined. Last, three composite case studies are presented illustrating traditional cultural, family, and community contexts that necessitate a holistic and collaborative approach on the part of the therapist. Suggestions and policy implications are explored throughout the chapter.

## UNDERSTANDING THE CONTEXT OF REFUGEE MENTAL HEALTH NEEDS

The World Health Organization's (WHO's) definition of *mental health* is "a state of wellbeing in which an individual realizes his or her own abilities, can cope with the normal stresses of life, can work productively and is able to make a contribution to his or her community" (Purgato et al., 2017, p. 140).

Refugees forced to leave their home countries after experiencing war or other trauma, family losses, resettlement challenges, and multiple stressors will be affected by diverse circumstances that impact their mental health and well-being. These include premigration family economic and living situations, personal characteristics and abilities, and migration experiences, all set within particular cultural contexts (Andermann, 2014; Kirmayer et al., 2011). To improve outcomes for refugees, culturally and contextually appropriate strategies and resources are required to address their diverse mental health needs.

Kirmayer et al. (2011) described migration as involving three major sets of transitions: changing personal connections and reconstructing social networks, moving from one socioeconomic system to another, and shifting from one cultural system to another. Moreover, the migration trajectory can be divided into three phases: premigration, migration, and postmigration resettlement. Each phase has associated risks and mental health problems. Challenges include communication difficulties related to language and cultural differences; effects of cultural factors on assessment and treatment; differences in family structure that affect adaptation, acculturation, and intergenerational conflict; and elements of acceptance by the host society that affect work and social adjustment. Resettlement typically brings hope and optimism, which can have a positive effect on well-being. However, disillusionment, demoralization, and depression can set in, either because of losses or difficulties associated with migration, or when initial hopes and expectations are not realized. Migrants and their families may face obstacles to advancement in their new home due to structural barriers and inequalities that can be aggravated by exclusionary policies, racism, and discrimination. The impact on mental health is both understandable and significant.

## INDIGENOUS AND NON-WESTERN VIEWS OF MENTAL HEALTH

Research demonstrates that culture provides a resource for positive mental health and fulfills a person's need for identity. However, Indigenous and non-Western cultural understandings of mental health and healing are distinctly different from those found in most North American and European practice settings (Stewart & Marshall, 2016). For the most part, Western mental health treatment is based on an individual and medicalized paradigm of health; in contrast, non-Western and Indigenous world views emphasize holistic views of health and wellness (Stewart & Marshall, 2016). Throughout the world, though, there are many traditional healers known by different names among diverse groups. They often use similar understandings, tools, and techniques such as spiritual ceremonies and rituals, communication with departed family members, touch therapy, herbalism, and music (Fernando, 2018; Vontress, 2018). Traditional healing methods may be the only health care that many refugees have ever known and experienced. Such differing health care experiences can impede effective help seeking for refugees referred to or seeking mental health services from formally trained therapists, including those who may have been trained in cross-cultural or multicultural approaches.

Moreover, the typical Western orientation situates mental health problems within the individual. Thira (2014) and Duran (2006) maintained that mental health should be viewed through a *community lens* that acknowledges social, political, and economic contributing factors. A community cultural orientation recognizes the importance of diverse world views and values, family and kinship connections, the role of community, a holistic understanding of wellness that includes religion or spirituality, and the intergenerational effects of forced or asylum-seeking migration (Marshall et al., 2016).

Understanding and addressing the mental health needs of refugee populations, therefore, requires a sociocultural approach that recognizes the ethnic, familial, community, and national elements that influence how these needs and help seeking are viewed (Andermann, 2014). Spirituality and religion, for example, have assisted many to cope with the oppression they have faced and are integral aspects of healing among Indigenous cultures. Fernando (2018) observed that a type of "spiritual therapy" has been carried out in communities for centuries; ceremonies conducted by elders and traditional healers are common. Beliefs and expectations are particularly important to address. As Vontress (2018) stated, "The belief that a client holds about treatment methodology may be the most important ingredient of therapeutic intervention" (p. 60).

Of further importance to working with refugees is the concept of *historical trauma*. Many refugees are members of ethnic, religious, and other groups that have been either colonized and oppressed, involved in civil war, and/or historically persecuted for generations—and they often exhibit signs of historical trauma. Duran et al. (1998) wrote that the "historical trauma response has been identified and is delineated as a constellation of features in reaction to the multigenerational, collective, historical, and cumulative psychic wounding over time, both over the life span and across generations" (p. 342). The pressures associated with migration and subsequent acculturation can exacerbate existing or latent historical trauma among refugees, which can complicate the mental health symptoms they present to therapists. Experiencing these multiple stressors results in feelings of being overwhelmed emotionally (Tedeschi & Calhoun, 2004). To cope, refugees may turn to substance abuse, violence toward others or themselves, and other forms of self-destructive behavior. Historical trauma is more complex than surface exploration and presenting symptoms reveal, and requires systems-oriented and trauma-informed approaches to therapy (Duran et al., 1998).

Family and kinship relationships and connections are paramount in traditional cultures. Fernando (2018) cautioned that a Western-type technical approach to therapy involving diagnosis and treatment packages, typically including medication, can "take precedence over caring and human relationships as the bedrock of what people with mental turmoil and extreme cases of social suffering need" (p. 69). The importance of family and kinship ties means that systemic approaches and family therapy are often the preferred treatment mode.

## BARRIERS TO SEEKING MENTAL HEALTH SERVICES

Researchers have identified a number of help-seeking barriers among refugees, including limited access to services, misunderstandings due to cultural and language differences, and the perception of stigma associated with mental illnesses (Colucci et al., 2015; Guruge & Butt, 2015; United Nations High Commission on Refugees [UNHCR], 2018). Refugees may not seek out formal help for mental health problems. This can be related to limited familiarity with Western concepts of mental health, and also to the belief that associated problems are a sign of weakness and a source of shame. Vocabulary and language difficulties can further complicate communication between mental health therapists and refugees. Colucci et al. (2015) investigated facilitators of and barriers to mental health service delivery in Australia for young people with refugee backgrounds. Focus groups and key informant interviews with 115 service providers identified eight key themes relevant to increasing the use of mental health services among this population. These were cultural concepts of mental health, illness, and treatment; service accessibility; trust; working with interpreters; engaging family and community; style and approach of mental health providers; advocacy; and continuity of care. Colucci et al. consulted with refugee groups, all of which emphasized the importance of exploring the views and experiences of refugees themselves. This was particularly true when designing and delivering mental health programs.

## GENDER CONSIDERATIONS

Refugee girls and women have particular needs that can go unrecognized within the context of a long history of male-centered refugee settlement policies (UNHCR, 2018). A shift in perspective is critical to identify these needs in the context of existing strengths. The identities of refugee women are complex; understanding them means thinking about barriers and challenges they face through the *intersecting* lenses of gender, class, race, language, trauma, educational background, and migration experience (Beck et al., 2001; Hatoss & Huijser, 2010). Gender inequalities experienced before arriving in settlement countries, for example, often result in girls and women having fewer educational and social opportunities than boys and men. The unequal opportunities in resettlement countries may also be perpetuated in new ones. It is important that therapists explore the impact of these intersecting factors when working with this population (Ellis et al., 2010).

Refugee girls' and women's roles and responsibilities within the family and community may be different from Western values of emancipation and choice (Stewart & Marshall, 2016). With parents sometimes working long hours in multiple jobs—and possibly without a network of extended relatives in the resettlement country—girls and young women can be expected to care for younger siblings, thus limiting extracurricular, social, and postsecondary educational activities. Young women living with parents may be expected to work low-paying jobs and allow young men in the family to pursue higher education. When husbands have been incarcerated, left behind, or even killed in home countries, refugee women may arrive as the head of the household and need to support their children. In these situations, Western therapists may find themselves critical of what may seem to be unreasonable or oppressive expectations placed on girls and women by their families and communities (Ellis et al., 2010). Ethical dilemmas can arise regarding traditional role expectations and refugee women's shifting identities. Therapists need to reflect carefully about how they support these women, whose traditional ethnic, family, and religious values and practices may conflict with their own. Professional development, clinical supervision, and consultation with cultural brokers or legal experts are good resources for information and ethical guidance.

Culturally sanctioned norms and practices regarding gender roles and structural gender inequality within traditionally patriarchal societies remain a challenge in mental health therapy, particularly when addressing sexual- and gender-based violence issues against women that are illegal in Western countries. Barriers to help seeking for intimate partner abuse include shame, social isolation, stigma, concerns about confidentiality, worries about legal documentation, and language obstacles (UNHCR, 2018). To increase access for refugee women, therapist and client gender should be matched when possible, and therapy can be adapted to accommodate home and family responsibilities (Beck et al., 2001). Therapists are in a position to advocate for increased mental health support for these women and girls by challenging structural barriers that segregate and devalue them. At the same time, honoring women's traditional and Indigenous values is also an ethical imperative.

## AN INTEGRATIVE CULTURAL APPROACH TO WORKING WITH REFUGEES

The traditional or Indigenous cultural worldviews and holistic approaches to healing that have been the experience of many refugees are similar to those of Native American and other Aboriginal or Indigenous peoples. For treatment of mental health problems, Native American psychologist Eduardo Duran (2006) suggested a "hybrid" approach—one that integrates complementary Indigenous/traditional and Western paradigms. Together with Western theories and techniques, Duran recommended that therapy incorporate traditional or Indigenous ways of knowing, philosophy, practices, and healing methods. This type of blended approach has been shown to be effective in contexts in which Indigenous spiritual, ancestral, and cultural dimensions—stories, ceremony, language, communal healing—play a vital part in how people live (Duran, 2006). For example, including elders and/or family members in therapy sessions is consistent with Indigenous communal healing principles, and cleansing rituals such as sage smudging or cedar brushing could be incorporated into therapy sessions.

It can be argued that a similar hybrid or blended approach would be appropriate in treating mental health problems among refugees. The cultural backgrounds and lived experience of this population reflect long-standing and cherished cultural, spiritual, and community-oriented values. This means that Western therapists would integrate refugee clients' traditional views and values with Western ways and customs in assessment and treatment planning. Holistic healing practices such as meditation, dietary consultation, and/or social rituals—or Islamic teachings about family traditions and spiritual practices—are examples of elements that can be included in therapeutic treatment planning. Books and journal articles, professional development workshops, training courses, and clients themselves are possible sources of information to help therapists gain relevant knowledge and skills. Given the huge diversity of cultures and practices, however, assistance from settlement services, translators, and individuals such as *cultural brokers* (Yohani, 2013) would most likely be necessary.

Cultural brokers take on a bridging or advocacy role on behalf of individuals or groups (Jezewski & Sotnik, 2001; Yohani, 2013). In mental health settings, they can translate in sessions for therapists and clients when language is a barrier (with appropriate training regarding ethical and confidentiality considerations). Cultural brokers can provide knowledge about Indigenous and traditional practices and beliefs that can promote more appropriate professional communication, practice, or relationships in therapy. They often connect with different spiritual leaders and Indigenous healers in the local community who may be involved in treatment plans. Brokers can also help clients and family members to navigate and interpret legal, health, social welfare, and educational systems in the host country. Cultural brokers are well-informed about and connected to refugee and settlement services; they can advise therapists about programs and options available to meet specific client needs. If there is conflict among family members or between a refugee client and a therapist, a cultural broker may assist as a mediator, particularly if the conflict involves traditional beliefs or practices.

In a study of cultural brokers' experiences with children and families, Yohani (2013) identified several roles that cultural brokers play. Among these are facilitating adaptation, bridging families to community services, interpreting culture/raising awareness, providing support, advocating, and mediating/resolving conflicts. In addition to providing direct assistance to individuals and families, Yohani maintained that cultural brokers can also have an impact at the systemic level. Over time, they can help transform systems and institutions to be more open and flexible about cultural diversity. Cultural brokers can also provide professional development workshops and individual consultation to therapists about Indigenous and traditional spiritual practices, beliefs, and healing approaches.

Ethical considerations can be complex in cross-cultural therapy, given multiple value perspectives, the use of translators, and competing priorities. Vontress (2018) asserted that the issue of professional ethics "has not been adequately addressed in cross-cultural counseling or traditional healing" (p. 61). If refugee clients have indicated that traditional ethnic and/or spiritual practices are important to them and to their family members, therapists should support this as part of ethical practice.

Vontress (2018) also called attention to the lack of adequate training for many who work with migrant and refugee clients, expressing concern about "cultural authenticity when therapists work with clients from cultures other than their own" (p. 60). Consultation and collaboration with cultural brokers, faith leaders, and community members is necessary for ethical practice. For example, many traditional and Indigenous cultures have cherished stories, legends, and parables that have been preserved in their culture for hundreds or even thousands of years; these have been used to educate and socialize children, to promote harmony and social order, and to explain problems such as mental illness (Gone, 2016). Understanding the significance of these stories and teachings can give therapists insight into how refugee clients make sense of certain situations and may aid in making suggestions for intervention strategies consistent with client beliefs. Vontress (2018) described research on traditional healing in Africa, which for him emphasizes the importance of clients' relationships with the universe, ancestors, and the spirit world. Indigenous or native peoples in North America and southern Asia also hold holistic world views that are grounded in spirituality (Duran, 2006; Gone, 2016). According to these views, everything in the universe (people, ancestors, animals, plants, water, mountains, objects, etc.) has a spirit that exists in harmony with other spirits and must be honored. Health and well-being require the holistic integration of physical, mental, emotional, and spiritual aspects—beliefs that contrast with many Western concepts of mental health that exclude religion or spirituality and emphasize cognitive experiences.

Traditional cultures have particular rituals that mark milestone-type events such as coming of age, marriage, and parenthood. These rituals often include prayer, songs or chants, movement or dance, special foods, distinctive costumes, and specific actions performed by members of the family and/or community, which can take place over a number of days or even weeks. Refugees who have been separated from their homeland and extended family may lack opportunities to fully engage in these important rituals. This situation can be a source of distress and/or shame. Communicating respect for rituals and practices can help to build therapeutic alliances and trust (Vontress, 2018). Attending refugee community gatherings or celebrations and observing rituals allows therapists to learn about diverse cultures and to demonstrate their respect for traditional views and beliefs.

## INCORPORATING TRADITIONAL AND INDIGENOUS APPROACHES TO HEALING

Several principles and practices have been found to be helpful for mental health therapists to effectively integrate traditional and Indigenous elements into their work with refugees. These include fostering an open and accepting climate, establishing cultural safety, addressing stigma, and promoting mental health literacy (MHL). Strengths-oriented approaches have also been shown to enhance therapists' intervention effectiveness.

## Fostering a Positive and Accepting Climate

Developing a positive and accepting climate for growth is important when considering sensitive and emotion-focused topics such as refugee mental health (Westerman, 2010). Using open communication styles and avoiding assumptions sends the message that client experiences, thoughts, and feelings are valued and important in therapy. It is vital that therapists pay close attention to the traditional or Indigenous contexts of their clients and avoid generalizing from Western experiences. In recent research with mental health practitioners who worked with refugees, acceptance, relationship building, and trust were universally endorsed as essential for success (Chalmers et al., 2014). Therapists should consider the distinct challenges that some refugees may be facing, such as problems due to ethnic or religious discrimination, gender role expectations, multiple deaths/losses of family and friends, and anger related to past injustices. At the same time, it is important that a therapist not assume that a client is encountering any or all of these problems simply because the client is a refugee. Just as important is identifying strengths and signs of resilience; this emphasizes the positive elements of mental health, in contrast to a problem or deficit focus.

Though therapists may have limited knowledge of traditional and Indigenous groups, Chalmers et al. (2014) suggested that all helping professionals endorse many of the same communication practices with refugees as they do with nonrefugees. These practices include asking whether and where they feel comfortable and safe to talk, taking time to build rapport and trust, being reliable and consistent, listening without interrupting, being genuine, talking calmly, having an awareness of body language, and offering possible courses of action. Many therapists will possess knowledge and skills that are appropriate and adaptable for refugees, particularly if these clients are living in urban environments. As Chalmers et al. contended, those who help migrant populations should not be so focused on cultural differences that they lose sight of emotions that are often universal. Trauma issues, loss, and grief involve emotional needs across diverse populations. Optimal treatment for traditional and Indigenous clients, however, will require knowledge that is relevant to their contexts. This typically involves professional development education, consultation with local refugee resource people and/or cultural brokers, and adaptation of therapy practices to be consistent with traditional family beliefs and values.

## Cultural Safety

Cultural safety is essential to any discussion of mental health therapy with refugees. Practices based on this concept recognize and respect the cultural identities of others and their needs, expectations, and rights (Brascoupé & Waters, 2009; Josewski, 2012). Though all people understand mental health in culturally bound ways, clients' non-Western views are not always acknowledged in mainstream mental health education and service delivery (Pinto-Foltz et al., 2011). A lack of cultural safety is one explanation for traditional or Indigenous refugees' reluctance to seek help or to not continue in treatment.

Cultural safety includes both process and outcome aspects (Josewski, 2012). As a *process*, it provides a critical lens to address the unequal power relations in education and health services delivered to refugee and other minority populations. Therapists need to be aware of how power and privilege operate in their relationships with clients and attend to how their assumptions and knowledge impact the therapeutic alliance. Furthermore, they need to discuss signs and symptoms of mental illness within a cultural context that acknowledges client values and beliefs. Achieving the *outcome* of cultural safety involves adopting culturally sensitive and respectful attitudes and practices as well as making cultural adaptations to standard psychotherapy assessment and treatment (Brascoupé & Waters, 2009). For example, therapists should be sure to ask clients about their spiritual and religious beliefs and practices as part of assessment—fasting, time for prayer, and preparation for celebrations are examples of religious observances that can impact mental health and mental health therapy. Also, family decision-making protocols are important in many Indigenous and traditional societies. Refugees may prefer family therapy sessions that are more consistent with their values and traditions.

### Addressing Stigma

Myths lead to stigmatizing beliefs and attitudes that result in discrimination against those with mental illnesses as well as avoidance of treatment. Stigma continues to be a major hurdle in the help-seeking process, particularly among some traditional cultures (Ellis et al., 2010); marginalization and isolation can even extend to family members. Challenging the underlying myths of stigma is a significant component of promoting positive mental health. Therapists and other health professionals need to understand the multiple elements of stigma and to develop strategies to combat cultural and other stereotypes that undermine positive mental health attitudes and help seeking. It can be a challenge for therapists, on the one hand, to acknowledge and respect different cultural beliefs, yet, on the other hand, to confront discrimination against those who are stigmatized due to mental health problems. Traumatized refugee children can be particularly vulnerable in these instances. Cultural brokers can be helpful allies when addressing stigmatizing beliefs and resistance behaviors among refugee clients and their families (Yohani, 2013). Using idioms of distress (socially and culturally relevant means of experiencing and expressing distress or mental turmoil) can assist therapists to explore client contexts with language that is understandable, socially acceptable, and nonstigmatizing. Cambodians, for example, may use the term "too much thinking" to describe ruminating on difficulties (Kidron & Kirmayer, 2018). Changes in personal hygiene and requests for medicine can also be idioms of distress. Kidron and Kirmayer (2018) suggested that therapists explore client and family local idioms and cultural concepts of distress, and then use this knowledge to adjust mental health interventions to fit clients' lived experience.

## Mental Health Literacy

Promoting MHL among refugee and migrant populations is one element that can contribute to improved mental health. MHL is a relatively recent concept, a more specific aspect of the broader notion of health literacy. The first widely accepted definition was proposed by Jorm et al. (1997): "Mental health literacy comprises the knowledge, beliefs and abilities that enable the recognition, management or prevention of mental health problems" (p. 183). More recently, Bourget and Chenier (2007) proposed a broader definition: "Mental health literacy is the knowledge and skills that enable people to access, understand and apply information for mental health" (p. 4). Their definition puts more emphasis on empowerment, an important concept in health promotion and wellness. Those having MHL are better able to identify mental health "strengths and needs in themselves and others, are better equipped and more empowered to seek appropriate supports, and report lower levels of mental health stigma" (Potvin-Boucher & Malone, 2014, p. 346).

For refugees coming from traditional or Indigenous cultures, any discussion of mental health generally and MHL specifically may be unfamiliar or even a "taboo" topic (as discussed earlier regarding stigma). The UNHCR (2018) has identified the stigma associated with mental illness as a significant barrier to help seeking among immigrant and refugee populations. Mental health therapists are well advised to include an assessment of MHL when working with these individuals and groups. Lack of information can be addressed through education and support; information is readily available in multiple languages through print and online sources. With the assistance of interpreters, if needed, therapists can use culturally familiar terminology and descriptions as part of assessment and treatment. More challenging situations involving denial of symptoms or resistance to treatment, particularly with more vulnerable women and children, may require assistance from cultural brokers or refugee services.

With regard to policy implications, supports for promoting MHL can be part of broader culturally oriented health and education services in the community. Language classes, for example, can include vocabulary and curricula related to mental health concepts. Newcomer education programs for adults and families can incorporate basic MHL concepts. MHL involves more than providing information; it includes support for skill development and advocacy so people can make informed decisions and take effective action to promote positive mental health for themselves and others. A lack of MHL negatively affects understanding, recognition, and treatment seeking for mental illnesses.

### Strengths Orientation

Finally, acknowledging strengths and coping abilities is critically important. By the time they arrive in settlement countries, refugees have already lived through violation of their sense of security, renegotiation of their identities, and loss of their homes and countries. These are obstacles that many in the developed world cannot even fathom overcoming; healing and adjustment take time. However, mental health therapists and scholars are questioning the tendency in developed countries to overemphasize refugee vulnerability and pathology (Hatoss & Huijser, 2010). Focusing only on problems and difficulties neglects the healing potential of resilience. Strengths-based and family systems approaches recognize the protective factors that exist in traditional and Indigenous collectively oriented family and community contexts (UNHCR, 2018). Religious beliefs, elders' wisdom, social rituals, and intergenerational support are viewed as contributing to family and community survival. In time, and with support, refugees may even experience *posttraumatic growth*, defined by Tedeschi and Calhoun (2004) as "the positive change that many people experience as the result of their struggle with highly stressful circumstances" (p. 228). Posttraumatic growth denotes change "that goes *beyond* an ability to resist and not be damaged by highly stressful circumstances; it involves a movement *beyond* pretrauma levels of adaptation" (p. 4).

In therapy, arts-based, narrative, multimedia, and expressive approaches (such as drawing, storytelling, drama, music, and movement) offer excellent opportunities for blending Western and traditional modes and accessing refugees' strengths. Art and music therapeutic techniques can circumvent language and stigma barriers among youth and adult refugees, particularly in group formats (Quinlan et al., 2016). These activities can also increase connections to community, promote self-esteem, prevent social isolation, and build social networks (Correa-Velez et al., 2010; Stewart, 2014).

## COMPOSITE CASE ILLUSTRATIONS

### Case 1: Gender Role Expectations

**Issue**

A year and a half after her arrival, Zara was a young mother struggling with being at home all the time and caring for her young children. She began to experience somatic complaints and depression. One evening, she had to be taken to the hospital for emergency care, with numbness and paralysis in her arms and legs. After extensive tests revealed no physical or neurological problems, Zara was referred for therapy. She reported to the female therapist that she had to stay in the apartment with the children all day and was not allowed to do anything without her husband's approval. She wanted to go to language classes to improve her English and perhaps someday take college courses, but her husband told her that her place was in the home with their baby daughter and 2-year-old son. He also did not want her to go out with the children to a nearby park or do any shopping; he said there was no one to go with her and make sure she was safe. Zara said she had not previously been so restricted, but she loved and respected her husband.

**Intervention**

After seeing Zara alone for a few sessions, the female therapist asked to see the family together. She worked with the couple to first make sure that each understood the other's wishes and worries, taking care to acknowledge the husband's role and observing accepted cultural protocols. While familiar with and acknowledging the family's culture and religion, the therapist also discussed the similarities and differences in gender roles and traditions between their country of origin and their new country, exploring possible scenarios that could be consistent with both. Zara explained that she wanted to attend language classes so she could learn more about parenting, help her children when they entered school, and perhaps study for a child care certificate someday. Although initially reluctant, the husband began to consider options that fit with his traditional cultural values. After consulting with local newcomer services, the therapist found a women's-only language class during the day where Zara could take her children and meet other young neighborhood mothers. The husband agreed that she could go with another young mother who lived close by and was already attending. The classes were held at a local community center where there was also cultural programming. The family was able to attend an Open House event there where the husband was reassured by seeing firsthand that the language classes and early childhood activities were offered in ways that were inclusive and respectful of his values and beliefs. The husband also wanted Zara to be seen by a traditional medicine healer. They located a practitioner in the community who used herbal remedies and visualization; Zara found the sessions to be "soothing and helpful." Thus, the therapist was able to support maintaining family culture and background and to find solutions that were acceptable to both Zara and her husband. She continued to work with the young mother to help her process gender role and other migration issues, and to explore a range of options for meaningful activities to pursue over time. Zara's symptoms receded as the therapy progressed.

**Key Points**
Zara's situation illustrates the frequent occurrence of differing gender roles and expectations. In many cultures, husbands and male relatives determine what women can and cannot do, how they can do it, and when. It is critically important that the therapist respect these differing values and not suggest or imply that Zara should disobey her husband. Searching for mutually acceptable solutions while expanding possible options over time is an effective way to "bridge" different cultures.

## Case 2: Extended Family Disharmony

**Issue**
Kamal, a 13-year-old boy, was referred for mental health therapy after he began bullying younger children and picking fights with peers on the playground at his middle school. He had also stopped doing his homework and his achievement dropped sharply. Kamal's parents insisted that he was happy at home, there were no family troubles, and they could not understand why these things were happening; they did agree that Kamal could attend "a few" therapy sessions when told by the school that he was in danger of failing the school year.

**Intervention**
Initially, Kamal was defensive in therapy. He claimed that younger children were swearing at him and that his peers were stealing his lunch and other

personal items, though these claims could never be substantiated. Kamal was very interested in sports, so the therapist began with game playing and other sports-related metaphors to discuss how young people experience and resolve conflicts. Near the end of his second therapy session, Kamal said he wanted to become a really good soccer player so he could leave home to play on a high-level rep team. He then described a chaotic and conflict-filled home situation where his family of five, which had fled Syria more than two years ago, had recently been joined by his mother's elderly parents and his father's widowed sister and her four children. The 12 people were now living together in a three-bedroom apartment, one family to a bedroom, and there were constant arguments, crying, and not enough to eat. Kamal said he could not do his homework with all the noise and confusion. His father was afraid to go to refugee services for help because he thought he would be reported to the police who would put him in jail for working two jobs. Kamal's grandparents had been relatively well off but lost everything before leaving Syria. They constantly criticized their daughter about the state of the home, the terrible food they had to eat, the sister's badly behaved children, and her husband's inability to better provide for the family. Kamal disclosed that he was upset and angry most of the time. As the eldest son, he felt responsible but didn't know what to do. The male therapist normalized the boy's distress, acknowledging his feelings of responsibility toward his family. The therapist explained that the father would not be jailed, that there were people who could help the family with housing and other problems, and that he would discuss possibilities with Kamal's parents first and then with the family. With the assistance of a cultural broker who spoke Arabic and was known to the local community, the therapist arranged to meet with the parents and, later, the extended family. The broker attended a therapy session with Kamal to explain traditional roles and expectations in such extended families, and then collaborated with the therapist to identify priorities, assess strengths and limitations, and initiate requests for help for the family. The therapist arranged for Kamal to be able to do his homework in the school library at the end of the day and encouraged him to join a community soccer league. The cultural broker continued working with the grandparents, the parents, and the sister's family to advocate for additional housing and temporary financial assistance, and to locate suitable cultural and language activities for the grandparents and the sister's family. The school problems were resolved, and the therapist made sure a referral was made to family services for ongoing assistance.

**Key Points**
This situation underscores the complex extended family and community context that has typically been the experience of many refugees. Traditional

values demanded that Kamal's father take care of the grandparents and his widowed sister's family, although housing and support had originally been granted only for the family of five. Acculturation stress was at the maximum for this family, yet fear, shame, and lack of knowledge were keeping them from seeking help. Critically important, the therapist showed understanding of and respect for traditional family values and roles, while also seeking ways to support the needs of his client, Kamal, within that family system. The assistance of the cultural broker was initially requested by the therapist to address the school situation. However, it quickly became evident that there were many other traditional culture-related family issues needing attention; these were addressed with the help of community resources.

## Case 3: Cultural and Generational Conflict

### Issue

Aisha, a 19-year-old girl, had fled with her family from a rural village in Afghanistan four and a half years earlier. The oldest child, she learned English quickly and did very well in school, particularly in math and science. She had graduated from high school a few months earlier and was working as a clerk in a pharmacy, but dreamed of going to university to study medicine. Aisha's mother was adamant that she get married, which "is what all women should and must do." Her mother wanted an arranged marriage with the son of a well-regarded refugee family, who were from the same region in which they used to live. She expected Aisha to live with her husband's parents but also to take care of her own mother and father as they got older. Aisha's father had been working since their arrival and was able to support the family's basic needs, though Aisha's financial contribution was most welcome. He knew that she had abilities and was proud of her accomplishments. His wife insisted that it was shaming the family to have a daughter not married at the advanced age of 19, let alone her "wanting to take work away from a more deserving man." Every day the mother prayed aloud that Aisha would be married soon and pressured her husband to arrange the marriage. Aisha was not eating or sleeping well, and hardly had the energy to do her work. Her mother said she was being punished for being a disobedient daughter, and wanted her to quit working altogether. Referred by her family doctor, Aisha had come to see a mental health therapist.

### Intervention

The therapist explored Aisha's history and current experiences, taking care to acknowledge the importance of traditions and the expectations of her family. War experiences in their home country and migration difficulties emphasized the importance of safety. They had no male relatives to help support the family and Aisha's siblings were much younger. Aisha's mother wanted her to be safe and cared for—arranged marriage was the only role she knew for women. Her father knew more about the ways of the host country. He wanted his daughter to realize her potential, though he had himself struggled at times with the ignorance and discrimination demonstrated by his coworkers and others. With the help of an interpreter, the therapist held some family sessions. She began with a traditional greeting, demonstrated respect for Aisha's mother's values and beliefs, and acknowledged her wish to see her daughter settled and taken care of. The family agreed to wait until Aisha was physically and mentally well. Her employer arranged a temporary reduced work schedule to help her recover her strength. A community elder who had lived for several years in the host country was invited to one of the family sessions. He shared several stories of young women and men who had found work, married, and remained connected to their cultural and faith communities. He invited Aisha and her mother to help at a weekly well-baby clinic held in the basement of their mosque by an Afghani nurse who had trained in the host country. As Aisha regained her health, the therapist continued to help her explore her educational and personal dreams, encouraging her to connect with respected community mentors who could inspire and support her health care goals. Through their Muslim faith community and the younger siblings' school, Aisha's mother found acceptable volunteer activities that enabled her to make new friends and be exposed to some new ideas. Aisha was able to resume work and to explore correspondence course options.

**Key Points**

Having been acculturated to her new home country through attending school, Aisha found herself torn by conflicting world views. Her mother's traditional values and expectations for women did not fit with how Aisha wished to live her life. Yet she respected her mother and acknowledged that disapproval from the small and close-knit local Afghani community could make things very difficult for her family. Aisha's therapist understood her cross-cultural dilemma but was also ethically bound to prioritize her physical and mental health needs. In the family sessions, the therapist used a culturally appropriate greeting, discussed family values, and included a respected community elder. In this way, she demonstrated respect for the family's traditional views while providing possibilities for new understandings and new stories. With the elder's blessing, Aisha's traditional mother was willing to participate in the baby clinic sponsored by the local mosque, and in other community opportunities that fit with her values yet offered new perspectives regarding women's roles.

## IMPLICATIONS FOR THERAPY PRACTICE WITH REFUGEES

These three cases demonstrate the importance of including traditional and Indigenous cultural context in therapy assessment and treatment. This allows the therapist to effectively address the multiple and intersecting systems that affect their refugee clients. Consultation with refugee and/or community services, faith leaders, and cultural brokers is respectful and informative. Support from those who are familiar with traditional refugee contexts can help in addressing barriers and the stigma associated with seeking mental health treatment, and can provide direct assistance with high-priority needs for well-being, such as housing and employment. Using traditional greetings; acknowledging client and family faith, values, and beliefs; and demonstrating respect for role distinctions and protocols are key behaviors that can be integrated into therapy. Sessions with both immediate and extended family allow therapists to assess family members' knowledge, feelings, and positions regarding the client's situation and to devise culturally appropriate treatment plans. Community social services, schools, and faith institutions offer possibilities for tangible assistance as well as relational connections. Depending on the situation, prayers, rituals, Indigenous healing ceremonies, and traditional medicines can also be part of treatment. Blending helpful elements and minimizing the impact of less positive ones for clients requires skill, diplomacy, and creativity on the part of the therapist. Ongoing consultation, education, and supervision can help therapists understand the conflicts and potential strengths of refugee clients and their families in the context of acculturation processes and challenges. As with all clients, it is realistic to acknowledge, however, that limits exist regarding the change that is possible to achieve in therapy.

## CONCLUDING COMMENTS

Many refugees will continue to forgo beneficial and potentially life-saving mental health treatment unless culturally appropriate assessment and treatment are available. For refugees from traditional and Indigenous contexts, a recommended strategy is to focus on adopting culturally relevant and culturally safe therapy programs and practices, integrating Western and Indigenous and traditional healing approaches and processes. In postmigration contexts, this type of hybrid approach offers a connecting bridge for effective and ethical therapy practice with refugee individuals and families.

This chapter highlights the importance of understanding the key sociocultural aspects of mental health and well-being in providing effective, culturally informed therapy to refugee clients whose traditional values and beliefs pose challenges to Western individualized concepts of mental health and therapy. Consultation, supervision, and professional development can help therapists integrate traditional and Indigenous knowledge and skills for ethical and respectful cross-cultural assessment and intervention. Several promising strategies and resources were noted; most are readily adaptable to diverse environments. Stories of strength and resistance can be found in even the most dire situations. A culturally relevant and culturally safe blended approach to mental health therapy will benefit refugees and support them along their path to mental wellness.

## REFERENCES

Andermann, L. (2014). Reflections on using a cultural psychiatry approach to assessing and fortifying refugee resilience in Canada. In L. Simich & L. Andermann (Eds.), *Refuge and resilience: Promoting resilience and mental health among refugees and forced migrants* (pp. 61–71). Springer. https://doi.org/10.1007/978-94-007-7923-5_5

Beck, E., Williams, I., Hope, L., & Park, W. (2001). An intersectional model: Exploring gender with ethnic and cultural diversity. *Journal of Ethnic & Cultural Diversity in Social Work, 10*(4), 63–80. https://doi.org/10.1300/J051v10n04_04

Bourget, B., & Chenier, R. (2007). *Mental health literacy in Canada: Phase one report of the mental health literacy project.* Canadian Alliance on Mental Illness and Mental Health.

Brascoupé, S., & Waters, C. (2009). Exploring the applicability of the concept of cultural safety to Aboriginal health and community wellness. *International Journal of Indigenous Health, 5*(2), 6–41.

Chalmers, K. J., Bond, K. S., Jorm, A. F., Kelly, C. M., Kitchener, B. A., & Williams-Tchen, A. (2014). Providing culturally appropriate mental health first aid to an Aboriginal or Torres Strait Islander adolescent: Development of expert consensus guidelines. *International Journal of Mental Health Systems, 8*(1), 6–16. https://doi.org/10.1186/1752-4458-8-6

Colucci, E., Minas, H., Szwarc, J., Guerra, C., & Paxton, G. (2015). In or out? Barriers and facilitators to refugee-background young people accessing mental health services. *Transcultural Psychiatry, 52*(6), 766–790. https://doi.org/10.1177/1363461515571624

Correa-Velez, I., Gifford, S. M., & Barnett, A. G. (2010). Longing to belong: Social inclusion and wellbeing among youth with refugee backgrounds in the first three years in Melbourne, Australia. *Social Science & Medicine, 71*(8), 1399–1408. https://doi.org/10.1016/j.socscimed.2010.07.018

Duran, E. (2006). *Healing the soul wound. Counseling with American Indians and other native peoples*. Teachers College Press.

Duran, E., Duran, B., Yellow Horse Brave Heart, M., & Yellow Horse-Davis, S. (1998). Healing the American Indian soul wound. In Y. Daniele (Ed.), *International handbook of multigenerational legacies of trauma* (pp. 341–354). Plenum Press. https://doi.org/10.1007/978-1-4757-5567-1_22

Ellis, B. H., MacDonald, H. Z., Klunk-Gillis, J., Lincoln, A., Strunin, L., & Cabral, H. J. (2010). Discrimination and mental health among Somali refugee adolescents: The role of acculturation and gender. *American Journal of Orthopsychiatry, 80*(4), 564–575. https://doi.org/10.1111/j.1939-0025.2010.01061.x

Fernando, S. (2018). Some thoughts and reflections on therapy and healing across cultures. *Traditional Healing and Critical Mental Health, 1*(1), 69–75.

Gone, J. P. (2016). Alternative knowledges and the future of community psychology. Provocations from an American Indian healing tradition. *American Journal of Community Psychology, 58*(3–4), 314–321. https://doi.org/10.1002/ajcp.12046

Guruge, S., & Butt, H. (2015). A scoping review of mental health issues and concerns among immigrant and refugee youth in Canada: Looking back, moving forward. *Canadian Journal of Public Health, 106*(2), e72–e78. https://doi.org/10.17269/CJPH.106.4588

Hatoss, A., & Huijser, H. (2010). Gendered barriers to educational opportunities: Resettlement of Sudanese refugees in Australia. *Gender and Education, 22*(2), 147–160. https://doi.org/10.1080/09540250903560497

Jezewski, M. A., & Sotnik, P. (2001). *Cultural brokering: Providing culturally competent rehabilitation services to foreign-born persons*. University at Buffalo, Department of Rehabilitation Science, Center for International Rehabilitation Research Information & Exchange. http://cirrie.buffalo.edu/monographs/cb.html

Jorm, A. F., Korten, A. E., Jacomb, P. A., Christensen, H., Rodgers, B., & Pollit, P. (1997). "Mental health literacy": A survey of the public's ability to recognise mental disorders and their beliefs about the effectiveness of treatment. *Medical Journal of Australia, 166*(4), 182–186.

Josewski, V. (2012). Analysing "cultural safety" in mental health policy reform: Lessons from British Columbia, Canada. *Critical Public Health, 22*(2), 223–234. https://doi.org/10.1080/09581596.2011.616878

Kidron, C. A., & Kirmayer, L. J. (2018). Global mental health and idioms of distress: The paradox of culture-sensitive pathologization of distress in Cambodia. *Culture, Medicine and Psychiatry, 43*(2), 211–235. https://doi.org/10.1007/s11013-018-9612-9

Kirmayer, L. J., Narasiah, L., Munoz, M., Rashid, M., Ryder, A. G., Guzder, J., Hassan, G., Rousseau, C., Pottie, K., & the Canadian Collaboration for Immigrant and Refugee Health (CCIRH). (2011). Common mental health problems in immigrants and refugees: General approach in primary care. *Canadian Medical Association Journal, 183*(12), E959–E967. https://doi.org/10.1503/cmaj.090292

Marshall, E. A., Butler, K., Roche, T., Cumming, J., & Taknint, J. T. (2016). Refugee youth: A review of mental health counselling issues and practices. *Canadian Journal of Psychology, 37*(3), 309–319.

Pinto-Foltz, M. D., Logsdon, M. C., & Myers, J. A. (2011). Feasibility, acceptability, and initial efficacy of a knowledge-contact program to reduce mental illness stigma and improve mental health literacy in adolescents. *Social Science & Medicine*, 72(12), 2011–2019. https://doi.org/10.1016/j.socscimed.2011.04.006

Potvin-Boucher, J. T., & Malone, J. L. (2014). Facilitating mental health literacy: Targeting Canadian First Nations youth. *Canadian Journal of Counselling and Psychotherapy*, 48(3), 343–355.

Purgato, M., Tol, W. A., & Bass, J. K. (2017). An ecological model for refugee mental health: Implications for research. *Epidemiology and Psychiatric Sciences*, 26(2), 139–141. https://doi.org/10.1017/S204579601600069X

Quinlan, R., Schweitzer, R., Khawaja, N., & Griffin, J. (2016). Evaluation of school-based creative arts therapy program for adolescents from refugee backgrounds. *The Arts in Psychotherapy*, 47(5), 72–78. https://doi.org/10.1016/j.aip.2015.09.006

Stewart, M. J. (2014). Social support in refugee resettlement. In L. Simich & L. Andermann (Eds.), *Refuge and resilience: Promoting resilience and mental health among refugees and forced migrants* (pp. 91–107). Springer. https://doi.org/10.1007/978-94-007-7923-5_7

Stewart, S. L., & Marshall, E. A. (2016). Counselling indigenous peoples in Canada. In S. Stewart, R. Moodley, & A. Hyatt (Eds.), *Indigenous cultures and mental health counselling. Four directions for integration with counselling psychology* (pp. 73–89). Routledge. https://doi.org/10.4324/9781315681467

Tedeschi, R. G., & Calhoun, L. G. (2004). Posttraumatic growth: Conceptual foundations and empirical evidence. *Psychological Inquiry*, 15(1), 1–18. https://doi.org/10.1207/s15327965pli1501_01

Thira, D. (2014). Aboriginal youth suicide prevention: A post-colonial community-based approach. *International Journal of Child, Youth & Family Studies: IJCYFS*, 5(1), 158–179. https://doi.org/10.18357/ijcyfs.thirad.512014

Trimble, J. E. (2018). Connecting to the spiritual and the sacred through the straight path: Advancing the helping professions through connections with Indigenous nations. *International Journal of Traditional Healing and Critical Mental Health*, 1(1), 52–57.

United Nations High Commission on Refugees (UNHCR). (2018). *Culture, context, and mental health of Rohingya refugees: A review for staff in mental health and psychosocial support programmes for Rohingya refugees.* https://www.unhcr.org/5bbc6f014.pdf

Vontress, C. E. (2018). Traditional healing research in West Africa: Respect, appreciation, and lessons applied to counselling. *International Journal of Traditional Healing and Critical Mental Health*, 1(1), 58–62.

Westerman, T. (2010). Engaging Australian Aboriginal youth in mental health services. *Australian Psychologist*, 45(3), 212–222. https://doi.org/10.1080/00050060903451790

Whitley, J., Smith, J. D., & Vaillancourt, T. (2013). Promoting mental health literacy among educators: Critical in school-based prevention and intervention. *Canadian Journal of School Psychology*, 28(1), 56–70. https://doi.org/10.1177/0829573512468852

Yohani, S. (2013). Educational cultural brokers facilitating the school adaptation of refugee children and families: Challenges and opportunities. *Journal of International Migration and Integration*, 14(1), 61–79.

# 12

## RESEARCH AND RESOURCES IN REFUGEE MENTAL HEALTH

### Reflections and Future Directions

JAMIE D. ATEN, JENNY HWANG, AND KENT ANNAN

As mental health practitioners and researchers, we have the unique and challenging role of cultivating an environment in which people who have lost their homes or been forced out of their country can find stability and partake in a flourishing community. Our ethical duty is to understand that interventions can work only within systems that recognize and reduce oppressive experiences that adversely affect well-being. In developing this book, we placed the parameters of our target population on resettled refugees in countries with a robust mental health infrastructure. The rationale was that by narrowing the scope of the context in which mental health professionals work, we could provide more applicable frameworks and relatable case studies. But we want to reiterate that in working with resettled refugee communities, there is no "one size fits all." A group intervention that works for a Rohingya community may not work for a Sudanese community. A cognitive behavioral therapy approach may work for a Congolese woman but not for a Congolese man or even another Congolese woman. Some interventions may conflict with cultural or religious values, while others may seamlessly integrate into an existing infrastructure. We have heard from an array of practitioners and researchers with varying backgrounds and expertise, and while they present

https://doi.org/10.1037/0000226-012
*Refugee Mental Health*, J. D. Aten and J. Hwang (Editors)

different approaches for interventions and best practices, a unifying theme emerges: effective support requires creative solutions.

In this concluding chapter, we reflect on the recommendations and creative solutions explored by our contributors. Specially, we explore three merging themes: (a) placing the person in context, (b) the need for mental health professionals to expand their thinking about and to provide support to refugees—the dynamic role of mental health professionals, and (c) obstacles and challenges in refugee mental health. We close this chapter with training and resource recommendations for the future direction of refugee mental health.

## PLACING THE PERSON IN CONTEXT

When we hear about the refugee crisis on the news or read studies in our journals, we are often presented with a barrage of numbers and statistics. Even in this book, almost every chapter presented does the same. We have encouraged this emphasis because the numbers are incredibly useful for understanding the challenges facing refugees. These statistics are important in that they help us start to grasp the vast scope of the current crisis. This type of information is vital for raising awareness among psychologists and the public, as well as for mobilizing resources and services. As our authors have pointed out, we need to know refugee statistics. Even more importantly, however, we need to know their stories.

Placing the person in context is one of the most significant components of working with refugees. Before treatment and solutions are suggested, understanding premigration, migration, and postmigration experiences is one of the many ways we place refugee clients in context. Every refugee client that steps into a clinic, hospital, or center carries a story of a long and tumultuous journey (Chapter 2). When a therapist neglects to see a client as a whole in the context of their experience, they are in danger of seeing and treating only the presenting symptoms. A refugee woman may be charged with negligence of her children when in fact she is suffering from depression onset brought on by her premigration traumatic experiences and postmigration financial woes. Placing refugee clients in context also means addressing their discrimination experiences and historical background; it means being aware of the sociopolitical atmosphere and environmental challenges surrounding them. We take one extra step to encourage practitioners to be mindful of how all these elements can interact and encumber these clients (Chapter 5).

In Chapters 5 and 6, the authors discuss some of the ways in which mental health care, as a whole, can be adapted to better serve refugee clients. This includes adapting interventions to be culturally appropriate, noting the limitations of Westernized[1] mental health assessments, and taking an inter-disciplinary approach. The authors of both Chapters 5 and 6 note that adapting Western therapeutic interventions to non-Western groups involves the initial acknowledgment that the interventions are rooted in Western etymology and philosophy and, undoubtedly, have limitations when applied to cultures with different belief and value systems. Practitioners trained in Western pedagogy must challenge their foundational concept of well-being and healing (Kleinman, 1988). Adapting an intervention to be culturally appropriate relies on the active practice of cultural humility—recognizing our own presumptions, prejudices, and tendencies (Chapter 3).

Additionally, mental health professionals must recognize the limitations of Western-centric mental health assessments (Chapter 7). Different cultures yield different expressions of emotions, distress, and mental illness, and without trepidation and awareness for cultural norms, mental health professionals can easily fall into a pattern of overdiagnosing, misdiagnosing, or prescribing incorrect treatment modalities (Desai & Chaturvedi, 2017; Office of the Surgeon General, 2001; Westermeyer, 1987). Therapeutic progress only begins when we can meet our clients where they are, listen for the spoken and unspoken words, place their stories in the context of their experience and the environment, and provide methods of healing that align with their world perspective (Chapter 6).

With emerging research noting postresettlement conditions as a vital factor to the well-being of refugees (Ellis et al., 2016; Ramzy et al., 2017; Vonnahme et al., 2015), it is imperative that mental health professionals treat their clients in the context of their postmigration environment. This ranges from addressing stigmas, prejudices, and racism to understanding accessibility to quality employment, housing, education, religious institutions, and social support as critical determinants of mental health (Chapter 2). Many of our contributing authors recommend taking an interdisciplinary approach to address the mental health needs of refugees holistically. Mental health professionals are encouraged to collaborate across disciplines and professional sectors.

Providing quality mental health care necessitates not only a comprehensive understanding but also a willingness to learn the complexity of the refugee experience. This means taking nontraditional approaches to increase accessibility such as peer group interventions, at-home visits, and indigenous healing methods (Chapters 9, 10, and 11). Placing the person in context

---

[1]*Westernized* refers to the process of adopting or being influenced by Europe and North America.

means avoiding overgeneralizations of refugee communities and individuals, acknowledging their idiosyncrasy, and tailoring therapeutic interventions to their unique needs.

## DYNAMIC ROLE OF MENTAL HEALTH PROFESSIONALS

In supporting both clinical efficacy and a comprehensive ecological framework in refugee mental health, the role of the therapist (or any other mental health professional) may deviate to a less-defined structure. As previous chapters indicate, traditional talk therapy often is not the most efficacious mode of psychotherapeutic intervention. The therapist may take on more elements of a facilitator, social worker, or even an advocate. This adaptability, however, defines a key element in working with refugee populations. Therapists must be flexible and aware of their own limitations. It is vital that they understand their capacity and unexamined bias, as well as acknowledge what they do not know. We repeatedly encourage all mental health professionals to engage from a posture of cultural humility because, in its essence, it enables them to place the person in context, disrupt power dynamics, and prevent a helper–victim dynamic (Chapter 3). With this humility, mental health professionals can refer the client to a more appropriate service provider if needed.

Our authors have also pointed to the fact that psychologists need to expand how we view our professional role. Most practicing psychologists are well versed in providing one-on-one psychotherapy. But as noted by our authors in the previous chapters, if we truly want to help refugees, then we also need to think about how to leverage other skills in our therapy toolbox to provide assistance. Among these are psychoeducational outreach, consultation, group facilitation, case management, and community-based participatory methods. That is, if we are to effectively navigate the complex mental health issues and challenges facing refugees, then we need to start thinking as much—if not more—about how to provide assistance outside the confines of our consulting room walls.

We need to grow in our understanding of and abilities to provide one-on-one care, as well as to address systematic problems through advocacy efforts. Political rhetoric often dictates a nation's investment in immigration and migration resources, and also influences the narrative and attitude toward foreign-born individuals. Thus, advocating for refugee mental health care can involve demands for policy changes that impact funding, resource allocation, and priorities. As Chapter 2 indicates, refugees who experience hostility in their resettled country are more likely to note a negative psychological impact. Treating the person as a whole requires an invested interest in the macro-level systems that influence an individual (Levine et al., 2005). Refugee mental health advocacy can take the form of changing alienating rhetoric, raising awareness of unique needs, promoting accessibility to care, or even restructuring our existing infrastructures to be more inclusive.

Recently, our professional "home"—the American Psychological Association (APA)—announced a plan for strategically realigning resources and structures to be better positioned to not just provide services but to also advocate for our community. As practitioners and researchers, we also need to think in similar ways when it comes to our refugee clients and the refugee communities that we serve.

## CHALLENGES IN REFUGEE MENTAL HEALTH

An infrastructure to support quality mental health care for refugees has always met with challenges, whether they be funding issues, vacillating migration policies, or simply a lack of resources (e.g., limited translators; Chapter 2). But in regard to service delivery challenges, the complexity of the refugee experience is what often posits nearly imponderable situations, as noted throughout the book. Here we note two specific challenges—conflicting ethical values and cultural differences in mental health.

### Conflicting Ethical Values

Ethical guidelines written for the context of more traditional psychotherapeutic settings may conflict when working with a more complex population like refugees. What is considered ethical in one culture may be deemed unethical in another, and navigating these gray areas induces service providers to seek consultation, supervision, and collaboration (Chapter 4). For example, different refugee populations may have varying child-raising practices in which corporal punishment is appropriate. This, though, could conflict with child abuse policies in the residing country, and thus escalate into a complex dilemma of cultural sensitivity, acculturation, and ethical duties for the therapist.

### Perspectives on Mental Health

Most of the development of mental health as a discipline and practice stems from a Western perspective. Thus, the concept of mental illness and counseling may feel foreign to certain refugee populations (Chapters 2 and 6). Furthermore, cultural values and beliefs circumscribe how symptoms can manifest. Studies have identified idioms of distress (see Chapters 6 and 11 for more details) in non-Western cultures that resemble *Diagnostic and Statistical Manual of Mental Disorders*–categorized mental illnesses. However, symptom manifestations and causality for the idioms of distress are rationalized through the context of a culture's existing belief system, and this, unfortunately, can lead to misdiagnosis or negligence by a Western-trained therapist. In cultural practices where indigenous healing methods are prevalent, therapists may collaborate with local healers in the community (Chapter 11). Caution is warranted, however, if the healing methods are deleterious in any capacity.

## RESOURCE AND RESEARCH RECOMMENDATIONS

This book is part of a bigger narrative in refugee mental health awareness. For decades, many organizations and individuals have relentlessly advocated, researched, and provided services for refugee communities. We strongly encourage our readers to educate themselves about the available services and the strides made in the realm of refugee mental health. Below we list a few major networks in North America and a few key international bodies that share best practices, research developments, trainings, and other resources for serving refugees. We also encourage you to do your own homework and get to know and learn from others in your own "backyard" such as local advocates, community leaders, volunteers, and resource centers. Likewise, we argue that as mental health professionals, we need to do more to get connected and collaborate with U.S. resettlement agencies; these are listed by state in Appendix 12.1. By no means is the following meant to be an exhaustive list, but rather is a sample of organizations that offer a wide range of refugee mental health resources and services and can be a good place for exploring what sorts of resources are already available.

### North America Resources

### Refugee Mental Health Resource Network
Originally an initiative from APA's Division 56 (Trauma Psychology) to address the need for mental health expertise in working with refugees and immigrants, the Refugee Mental Health Resource Network (https://refugeementalhealthnet.org/about/) is now a web-based listing of a professional community of volunteer psychologists and mental health professionals

who are working with or interested in working with refugee communities. They provide webinars, trainings, and other resources on various issues that rise in treatment with refugees.

### Refugee Health Technical Assistance Center

Funded by the Office of Refugee Resettlement in collaboration with various leading refugee-serving organizations, the Refugee Health Technical Assistance Center (https://refugeehealthta.org/) is an online platform that distributes resources and provides trainings and workshops. In addition, it hosts webinars for all service providers working with or interested in learning more about working with refugee communities.

### National Child Traumatic Stress Network

The National Child Traumatic Stress Network (NCTSN) was developed in 2000 as part of the Children's Health Act to raise the standard of care and increase access to services for children and families who experience or witness traumatic events. It is now an extensive network of hundreds of centers, hospitals, universities, and community-based programs that work to provide evidence-based interventions to treat childhood trauma. As a comprehensive initiative, NCTSN provides resources and trainings specifically for services providers working with refugee and immigrant children (NCTSN, n.d.).

### Office of Refugee Resettlement

A State Department program that is part of the Administration for Children and Families office, the Office of Refugee Resettlement (ORR; https://www.acf.hhs.gov/orr) helps administer the resettlement of refugees in the United States. Established with the passing of the Refugee Act of 1980, the ORR has since been the focus for all refugee resettlement procedures and regulations in the United States. The ORR functions as a central platform for resources and resettlement data. Its main responsibility is to support federal agencies, voluntary agencies, and state partners in the resettlement of refugees. On the ORR website, readers can find information on resettlement agencies in each state, ongoing training opportunities for service providers, and other resource availability.

### Center for Victims of Torture

The Center for Victims of Torture (CVT; https://www.cvt.org/) is an independent NGO dedicated to healing survivors of torture and violent conflicts. Employing a diverse group of mental health professionals, CVT provides a wide variety of direct care for survivors. With the overlap of the refugee experience and torture survivors, CVT is a prominent psychosocial service provider for refugee communities. It provides manuals and reports on research and program evaluations of psychosocial interventions.

### U.S. Committee for Refugees and Immigrants

The origins of the U.S. Committee for Refugees and Immigrants (USCRI; https://refugees.org/) dates back to 1911, when Edith Terry Bremer started an international institute in New York City to provide specialized services for foreign-born individuals. USCRI quickly grew into a vast nationwide network and exists today as a centralized platform for service providers to share resources, trainings, and services for immigrants and refugees.

## International Resources

### World Health Organization

Established in 1948 as the international public health arm of the United Nations, the World Health Organization (WHO; https://www.who.int/) employs more than 7,000 people from more than 150 countries. A vast network of doctors, public health specialists, scientists, epidemiologists, emergency relief personnel, economists, and others, WHO globally responds directly and indirectly to emergencies related to health concerns, including mental health. It frequently provides resources, reports, and trainings that may pertain to the well-being of refugees (WHO, 2019).

### United Nations High Commissioner for Refugees

The United Nations High Commissioner for Refugees (UNHCR; https://www.unhcr.org/en-us/about-us.html) is the official U.N. program established to protect the rights of refugees. The UNHCR is an international presence that responds globally to all refugee crises. It regularly partners with organizations, academic institutions, and governments to provide services and research best practices. As the official resettlement entity, the UNHCR has the latest statistics on resettlement trends and provides numerous resources and the latest research on refugees.

## Cultural and Language-Specific Resources

### Community Interpreter Services

Established in 1986, Community Interpreter Services (CIS; https://community interpreterservices.org/who-we-are/) assists people with limited English proficiency (LEP) in accessing legal, medical, educational, and corporate services through the provision of interpretation and written translation. CIS partners with more than 150 trained interpreters and translators, who collectively are fluent in over 90 languages. CIS is a social enterprise of Catholic Charities of Boston (Community Interpreter Services, 2020).

### Cross-Cultural Interpreting Services (Heartland Alliance)

Cross Cultural Interpreting Services (CCIS) is a full-service language provider specializing in interpretation and translation services. Established in 1996 as a Heartland Alliance program, the purpose of CCIS is to improve access to services for individuals with LEP. CCIS was the first program of its kind in Illinois to recruit, assess language skills, and train in the medical interpreting field. CCIS provides ongoing interpreter trainings (Heartland Alliance, 2020).

### Asian Pacific Development Center

Asian Pacific Development Center (APDC; https://www.apdc.org/), a Colorado-based organization, is a mental health clinic that provides comprehensive services to refugees and immigrant communities. APDC aims to offer culturally and linguistically appropriate mental health care. In addition to mental health care services, APDC collaborates with the Colorado Language Connection to provide interpreters, medical interpreter translation trainings, language proficiency testing, and other workshops (APDC, 2020).

## Research

As our contributing authors have repeatedly noted, conducting robust mental health research on refugee communities is a challenge. Cultural nuances, participation engagement, and varying psychosocial complexities are just a few factors that make studies of refugees particularly difficult to facilitate. Additionally, the stigmatization of mental illness in many refugee communities can impede individuals from seeking treatment, despite its availability (Chapter 2), further limiting the scope of refugee mental health research. The Western-centric framework that dominants overall mental health research also poses limitations in capturing diverse experiences of suffering and healing. In this regard, we note the need for more and continuing research on

- prevalence and scope of mental illnesses and stressors among different refugee communities,
- efficacy of therapeutic interventions and advocacy programs among different refugee groups,
- culture-bound syndromes and idioms of distress,
- efficacy of culturally adapted interventions,

- longitudinal impact of pre- and postmigration experience,
- refugee-led community-based initiatives,
- trauma narratives of the refugee experience, and
- resiliency factors in different refugee communities.

David Turton, an anthropologist and former director of the Refugee Studies Centre, once stated that "research into other's suffering can only be justified if alleviating that suffering is an explicit objective" (Turton, 1996, p. 96). This beckons researchers to a sense of moral responsibility when engaging in research involving vulnerable populations. From this perspective, we encourage researchers of refugee mental health to reflect on their motives and contemplate how their research can have both scientific value and empowering results for refugee communities. We pose a few basic questions researchers can ask themselves before and throughout their research journey:

- What are my priorities for this research study?
- Who will directly benefit from this research? How?
- Am I linguistically and culturally competent to carry out this research? If not, do I have a plan to work with people who are?
- Is my research design based on former studies, is it community participatory, or both? Is this the best research design for the question I am asking?
- What is my framework of understanding mental health?
- What is my knowledge and awareness of the community I plan to research?
- What is my role in data collection?
- Do I have external pressure or biases for yielding certain outcomes?
- What is my plan for disseminating my findings and how will it help the participants?
- Am I in a position of power that could possibly exploit the community?

## Recommendations

Despite the efforts made to integrate multiculturalism into service provider trainings, there is still a gap in comprehensive trainings and standardization for navigating cultural appropriateness and the "gray" areas of ethical duties. We note a particular need for

- holistic trainings on implicit biases for graduate students in the field of mental health,
- curriculums that operate from a posture of cultural humility than cultural competence,
- supervisor trainings on navigating complex cultural-related ethical dilemmas,

- training requirement for working with interpreters,
- training requirement for working with cultural brokers, and
- more accessible and culturally appropriate evidence-based interventions.

Finally, and most notably, we advocate for stronger collaborative and interdisciplinary efforts to support refugee well-being. This translates as an integrative team of doctors, lawyers, social workers, case managers, advocates, community leaders, cultural brokers, therapists, and refugee clients themselves all working together to enhance the quality of life for refugee communities.

## MOVING FORWARD

Whether you are a practitioner, graduate student, or researcher, we are grateful for your time and interest. We believe that a concern for quality mental health care for refugee communities is a step toward a better, more caring society. War, violence, and uncertainty have shaped the stories of many resettled refugees, but with the help of humble, effective interventions there is an opportunity for them to create new and empowering stories. And it is our unique role and a privilege to walk alongside them in the journey toward healing. We, as the volume's editors, along with the contributors, have witnessed the transformative change that can unfold in therapy sessions, in homes, and in communities. Unquestionably, the task can be daunting and is never lightly undertaken; there are times of feeling discouraged and overworked with little support. In these moments, we remember that the greatest movements that brought equality, dignity, and justice to society always began with a few individuals who relentlessly cared for the well-being of others.

---

## APPENDIX 12.1

## RESETTLEMENT AGENCIES IN THE UNITED STATES

In the United States, each state chooses how it will fund and execute refugee resettlement programs. States can choose to have (a) a state-administered refugee program; (b) a Wilson Fish Program, in which state government is bypassed and allows the federal Office of Refugee Resettlement to fund and organize directly with local voluntary agencies; or (c) a public–private partnership.

| State | Category | Agency |
|-------|----------|--------|
| Alabama | Wilson Fish | Catholic Social Services Refugee Program |
| Alaska | Wilson Fish | Catholic Social Services |
| Arizona | State | Arizona Immigrant and Refugee Services |
| | | Catholic Charities Community Services |
| | | IRC Phoenix & Tucson |
| | | Refugee Focus |
| | | Lutheran Social Services of Southwest |
| Arkansas | | Catholic Charities Immigration Services |
| California | State | East African Community of Orange County |
| | | World Relief Garden Grove |
| | | Immigration and Refugee Services |
| | | International Institute of Los Angeles |
| | | International Rescue Committee–Los Angeles, Oakland, Sacramento, San Diego, San Jose, Turlock |
| | | African Community Resource Center |
| | | Immigration and Resettlement Program |
| | | Interfaith Refugee and Immigration Ministry of the Episcopal Diocese of Los Angeles |
| | | Jewish Family Service–Silicon Valley, San Diego |
| | | World Relief Modesto |
| | | Catholic Charities–Oakland, San Bernardino, San Diego |
| | | Opening Doors, Inc. |
| | | Sacramento Food Bank & Family Services |
| | | Alliance for African Assistance |
| | | Jewish Family & Children's Services– San Francisco, East Bay |
| | | PARS Equality Center |
| Colorado | Wilson Fish | Lutheran Family Services Rocky Mountain– Denver, Colorado Springs, Greeley |
| | | ECDC African Community Center |
| | | International Rescue Committee |
| Connecticut | State | International Institute of Connecticut |
| | | Catholic Charities Migration & Refugee Services |
| | | Integrated Refugee and Immigrant Services |
| Delaware | State | Catholic Charities |

| State | Category | Agency |
|-------|----------|--------|
| Florida | State | Coptic Orthodox Charities–Clearwater, Tampa |
| | | Gulf Coast Jewish Family & Community Services |
| | | Church World Services–West Palm Beach, Miami |
| | | Catholic Charities Bureau, Inc.–Jacksonville, NW Florida, Palm Beach, Diocese of St. Petersburg, Diocese of Venice |
| | | Lutheran Social Services–Northeast Florida |
| | | World Relief–Jacksonville, Miami, Tallahassee |
| | | International Rescue Committee–Miami, Tallahassee |
| | | Youth Co-Op, Inc.–Miami, Palm Springs |
| | | Lutheran Services Florida–Miami, Orlando, Tampa |
| | | Episcopal Migration Ministries |
| Georgia | State | International Rescue Committee–Atlanta |
| | | Lutheran Services of Georgia |
| | | Migration and Refugee Services, Catholic Social Services, Inc. |
| | | Refugee Resettlement & Immigration Services of Atlanta |
| | | World Relief Atlanta |
| Hawaii | State | Pacific Gateway Center |
| Idaho | Wilson Fish | Agency for New Americans |
| | | International Rescue Committee Boise |
| | | Jannus, Inc. |
| | | College of Southern Idaho Refugee Program |
| Illinois | State | World Relief–Aurora, Chicago, Moline, DuPage |
| | | Catholic Charities–Chicago, Rockford |
| | | Ethiopian Community Association of Chicago |
| | | Heartland Alliance of Human Needs and Human Rights |
| | | Jewish Child and Family Services of Chicago |
| | | RefugeeOne |
| Indiana | State | Catholic Charities of Fort Wayne-South Bend, Inc |
| | | Catholic Social Services |
| | | Exodus Refugee Immigration, Inc. |
| Iowa | State | Catherine McAuley Center |
| | | Catholic Charities |
| | | USCRI Des Moines |

| State | Category | Agency |
|-------|----------|--------|
| Kansas | State | International Rescue Committee–Garden City, Wichita |
| | | Catholic Charities of Northeast Kansas |
| | | Episcopal Wichita Area Refugee Ministries |
| Kentucky | Wilson Fish | Western Kentucky Refugee Mutual Assistance–Bowling Green |
| | | Kentucky Refugee Ministries, Inc.–Lexington, Louisville |
| | | Catholic Charities |
| | | Western Kentucky Refugee Mutual Assistance–Owensboro |
| Louisiana | Wilson Fish | Migration and Refugee Services, Catholic Charities |
| | | Migration & Refugee Services |
| | | Immigration and Refugee Services, Catholic Charities Archdiocese of New Orleans |
| Maine | State | Catholic Charities Maine |
| Maryland | Public-Private | Jewish Community Services |
| | | International Rescue Committee–Baltimore, Silver Spring |
| | | World Relief Anne Arundel |
| | | JSSA Newcomer Resettlement |
| | | ECDC African Community Center |
| | | Lutheran Social Services of National Capital Area |
| Massachusetts | Wilson Fish | Jewish Family Service of MetroWest |
| | | Refugee & Immigrant Assistance Center |
| | | International Institute of New England–Lowell |
| | | Catholic Charities |
| | | Jewish Family Services of Western Massachusetts |
| | | Ascentria–West Springfield, Worcester |
| | | Refugee and Immigrant Assistance Center |
| Michigan | State | Jewish Family Service of Washtenaw County |
| | | Lutheran Social Services of Michigan–Battle Creek, Grand Rapids, Troy |
| | | Catholic Charities of South East Michigan |
| | | USCRI Detroit |
| | | Bethany Christian Services-PARA |
| | | Refugee Services/St. Vincent Catholic Charities |

| State | Category | Agency |
|---|---|---|
| Minnesota | Public-Private | Lutheran Social Services of Minnesota–Minneapolis, St. Cloud<br>Minnesota Council of Churches<br>Arrive Ministries<br>Diocese of Winona Catholic Charities<br>International Institute of Minnesota<br>Migration & Refugee Services |
| Mississippi | State | Migration and Refugee Center<br>Catholic Charities |
| Missouri | State | Diocese of Jefferson City<br>Della Lamb Community Services<br>Jewish Vocational Services<br>International Institute of St. Louis<br>International Institute of Southwest Missouri |
| Montana | State | N/A |
| Nebraska | State | Catholic Social Services<br>Lutheran Family Services–Lincoln, Omaha<br>Southern Sudan Community Association |
| Nevada | Wilson Fish | ECDC African Community Center<br>Refugee Assistance Program |
| New Hampshire | State | Ascentria Care Alliance<br>International Institute of New Hampshire |
| New Jersey | State | Refugee Microenterprise Development, Diocese of Camden<br>Jewish Vocational Services of MetroWest<br>International Rescue Committee Elizabeth<br>Church World Services Jersey City |
| New Mexico | State | Catholic Charities of Central New Mexico<br>Lutheran Family Services Rocky Mountains |
| New York | State | USCRI Albany<br>Catholic Charities–Amityville, Brooklyn, Buffalo<br>American Civic Association Inc.<br>IRSA Camba, Brooklyn, Buffalo<br>International Institute of Buffalo<br>Jewish Family Service of Buffalo & Erie County<br>Journey's End Refugee Services, Inc. |

| State | Category | Agency |
|---|---|---|
| | | Refugee Resettlement Program/Catholic Charities, Diocese of Brooklyn |
| | | Catholic Charities Community Services |
| | | FEGS Health & Human Services |
| | | International Rescue Committee New York |
| | | Catholic Family Center |
| | | Interfaith Works of Central New York |
| | | Northside CYO/Catholic Charities |
| North Carolina | State | Carolina Refugee Resettlement Agency |
| | | Catholic Charities Diocese of Charlotte |
| | | Church World Services–Durham, Greensboro |
| | | World Relief–Durham, High Point |
| | | North Carolina African Services Coalition |
| | | Diocese of East Carolina Interfaith Refugee Ministry–New Bern, Wilmington |
| | | Lutheran Family Services in the Carolinas |
| | | USCRI North Carolina |
| North Dakota | Wilson Fish | Lutheran Social Services of North Dakota New Americans–Bismarck, Fargo, Grand Forks |
| Ohio | State | International Institute of Akron |
| | | World Relief Akron |
| | | Catholic Social Services of SW Ohio |
| | | Migration and Refugee Services |
| | | International Services Center |
| | | Catholic Charities/Migration and Refugee Services |
| | | US Together, Inc.–Cleveland, Columbus, Toledo |
| | | Community Refugee and Immigration Services |
| | | World Relief Columbus |
| | | Catholic Social Services of the Miami Valley |
| Oklahoma | Public-Private | Catholic Charities–Oklahoma City, Tulsa |
| Oregon | Public-Private | Catholic Charities |
| | | Lutheran Community Services Northwest |
| | | SOAR Ecumenical Ministries of Oregon |
| Pennsylvania | State | LCFS of Eastern Pennsylvania–Allentown, Lancaster |
| | | Catholic Charities International Institute of Erie |
| | | Catholic Charities–Harrisburg, Pittsburgh |
| | | Church World Services–Lancaster |
| | | HIAS Pennsylvania |

| State | Category | Agency |
|---|---|---|
| | | Nationalities Service Center |
| | | Acculturation for Justice Access and Peace Outreach |
| | | Jewish Family & Children's Services of Pittsburgh |
| | | Northern Area Companies |
| | | Catholic Social Services of the Diocese of Scranton |
| Rhode Island | State | Dorcas International Institute of Rhode Island |
| | | Immigration and Refugee Services |
| South Carolina | State | Lutheran Family Services in the Carolinas |
| | | World Relief Spartanburg |
| South Dakota | Wilson Fish | Lutheran Social Services of South Dakota–Huron, Sioux Falls |
| Tennessee | Wilson Fish | Bridge Refugee Services, Inc. |
| | | World Relief Memphis |
| | | Catholic Charities |
| | | Nashville International Center for Empowerment |
| Texas | Public-Private | International Rescue Committee–Abilene, Dallas |
| | | Catholic Charities of the Texas Panhandle |
| | | Refugee Services of Texas, Inc.–Amarillo, Austin, Dallas, Fort Worth, Houston |
| | | Caritas of Austin |
| | | Refugee & Empowerment Services |
| | | Catholic Charities/Diocese of Fort Worth, Inc. |
| | | World Relief Fort Worth |
| | | Alliance for Multicultural Community Services |
| | | Catholic Charities of the Archdiocese of Galveston-Houston |
| | | Interfaith Ministries for Greater Houston |
| | | YMCA International Services |
| | | Catholic Charities–San Antonio |
| Utah | State | Catholic Community Services, Diocese of Salt Lake City |
| | | International Rescue Committee Salt Lake City |
| Vermont | Wilson Fish | Vermont Refugee Resettlement Program |

| State | Category | Agency |
|---|---|---|
| Virginia | State | Catholic Charities-Diocese of Arlington–Arlington, Fredericksburg |
| | | International Rescue Committee Charlottesville |
| | | Lutheran Social Services of National Capitol Area |
| | | Church World Services–Harrisonburg, Richmond |
| | | Commonwealth Catholic Charities–Newport News, Richmond, Roanoke |
| Washington | State | Jewish Family Services of Greater Seattle |
| | | World Relief–Seattle, Tri-Cities, Spokane |
| | | Diocese of Olympia |
| | | International Rescue Committee–Seattle |
| | | Spokane Neighborhood Action Partners |
| | | Lutheran Community Services Northwest–Tacoma, Vancouver |
| Washington, DC | State | Catholic Charities of Diocese of Washington |
| West Virginia | State | Migration & Refugee Services |
| Wisconsin | State | Resettlement & Immigration Services Catholic Charities |
| | | Lutheran Social Services of Wisconsin and Upper Michigan–Milwaukee, Madison |
| | | International Institute of Wisconsin |
| | | Migrant and Refugee Services, Catholic Charities–Milwaukee, Sheboygan |

*Note.* From *Find Resources and Contacts in Your State*, by the Office of Refugee Resettlement, 2019 (https://www.acf.hhs.gov/orr/state-programs-annual-overview). In the public domain.

## REFERENCES

Asian Pacific Development Center. (2020). https://www.apdc.org/

Birman, D. (2005). Ethical issues in research with immigrants and refugees. In J. E. Trimble & C. B. Fisher (Eds.), *The handbook of ethical research with ethnocultural populations & communities*. SAGE.

Community Interpreter Services. (2020). About us. https://communityinterpreter services.org/who-we-are/

Desai, G., & Chaturvedi, S. K. (2017). Idioms of distress. *Journal of Neurosciences in Rural Practice, 8*(Suppl. 1), S94–S97. 10.4103/jnrp.jnrp_235_17

Ellis, B. H., Hulland, E. N., Miller, A. B., Bixby, C. B., Cardozo, B. L., & Betancourt, T. S. (2016). *Mental health risks and resilience among Somali and Butanese refugee parents*. Migration Policy Institute.

Heartland Alliance. (2020). *Cross cultural interpreting services*. https://www. crossculturalinterpretingservices.org/

Kleinman, A. (1988). *Rethinking psychiatry: From cultural category to personal experience.* Free Press.

Levine, M., Perkins, D., & Perkins, D. (2005). *Principles of community psychology: Perspectives and applications* (3rd ed.). Oxford University Press.

National Child Traumatic Stress Network. (n.d.). *Special populations.* NCTSN Learning Center. https://learn.nctsn.org/course/index.php?categoryid=60

Office of Refugee Resettlement. (2019, April 30). *Find resources and contacts in your state.* https://www.acf.hhs.gov/orr/state-programs-annual-overview

Office of the Surgeon General, Center for Mental Health Services, National Institute of Mental Health. (2001). Culture counts: The influence of culture and society on mental health. In *Mental health: Culture, race, and ethnicity. A supplement to mental health: A report of the Surgeon General.* https://www.ncbi.nlm.nih.gov/books/NBK44249/

Ramzy, L. M., Jackman, D. M., Soberay, A. D., & Pledger, J. (2017). Refugee resettlement in the U.S.: The impact of contextual factors on psychological distress. *Universal Journal of Public Health, 5*(7), 354–361. https://doi.org/10.13189/ujph.2017.050703

Turton, D. (1996). Migrants and refugees. In T. Allen (Ed.), *In search of cool ground: War, flight, and homecoming in Northeast Africa* (pp. 96–110). Africa World Press.

Vonnahme, L. A., Lankau, E. W., Ao, T., Shetty, S., & Cardozo, B. L. (2015). Factors associated with symptoms of depression among Bhutanese refugees in the United States. *Journal of Immigrant and Minority Health, 17*(6), 1705–1714. https://doi.org/10.1007/s10903-014-0120-x

Westermeyer, J. (1987). Cultural factors in clinical assessment. *Journal of Consulting and Clinical Psychology, 55*(4), 471–478. https://doi.org/10.1037/0022-006X.55.4.471

World Health Organization. (2019). *About us.* https://www.who.int/

# Index

Traffickers, 21
Transcendental meditation (TM), 145
Transition period, trauma experienced
    during, 50–51, 109–110
Transportation costs, 111–112
Trauma
    assessing exposure to, 168–169
    continuum of, 262
    cumulative impact of, 36–38
    definition of, 36
    exposure to, as barrier to accessing
        therapy, 196–199
    historical, 284–285
    impact of immigration, on children,
        222–223
    intergenerational, 221
    premigration, 109–110
    during transition period, 50–51,
        109–110
    and trauma story, 142, 157–158
Trauma healing programs, 69
Trauma-informed care movement (TICM),
    138
Traumatic life narratives (in HEART
    model), 157–158
Traumatic withdrawal syndrome (TWS),
    110
Tribe, R. H., 146
Trump, Donald, and administration,
    28–29, 34, 77, 107–108
Turkey, 23, 28, 140
Turton, David, 312
Two-person relational model, 54
TWS (traumatic withdrawal syndrome),
    110

**U**

Uganda, 23, 26, 146
UNHCR. *See* United Nations High
    Commissioner for Refugees
United Arab Emirates, 108
United Kingdom, 104–105, 198
United Nations, 5–7, 45
United Nations High Commissioner for
    Refugees (UNHCR), 6–7, 19–23, 29,
    107, 111, 140, 149, 215, 292, 310
United Nations Refugee Convention
    (1951, amended 1967), 6–8, 19,
    104–105
United Nations Relief and Rehabilitation
    Administration (UNRRA), 5–6

United States
    effects of current policies/climate in,
        34–35, 77–78, 107–108
    Muslim Ban in, 107–108
    refugee processing in, 29–34
    refugee resettlement in, 30–31, 103
    Syrian refugees in, 28–29
Universal Declaration of Human Rights, 6
Universal health coverage, 90
UNRRA (United Nations Relief and
    Rehabilitation Administration), 5–6
U.S. Committee for Refugees and
    Immigrants (USCRI), 310
U.S. Department of Defense, 31, 117
U.S. Department of Homeland Security
    (DHS), 31
U.S. Department of State, 30–33, 220
U.S. Department of Veteran Affairs, 117
U.S. Federal Emergency Management
    Agency, 149
U.S. Refugee Admissions Program, 218,
    220
U.S. Refugee Resettlement Program, 29,
    30, 34
U.S. travel bans, 219–220
USCRI (U.S. Committee for Refugees and
    Immigrants), 310

**V**

Viber, 106, 111
Vietnam, refugees from, 7n1, 8–9, 143
Vietnam War, 7n1
Violence
    exposure to, 9
    sexual, 110, 155
    towards others or selves, 284–285
Voluntary migration, 20
Vontress, C. E., 284, 288–289

**W**

Walker, D. K., 36, 37
Walsh, F., 68
Webel, A. R., 257
Western cultures, 254
West Papuan refugees, 171, 177
WGR (Working Group on Resettlement), 7
WhatsApp, 106, 111
WHO. *See* World Health Organization
WHO guidelines, 89–93

# About the Editors

**Jamie D. Aten, PhD,** is the founder and executive director of the Humanitarian Disaster Institute and associate professor and Blanchard Chair of the Humanitarian Disaster Leadership program at Wheaton College. He is a disaster psychologist and disaster ministry expert. He has received more than $6 million in grant funding to study disasters, trauma, and faith issues around the globe and has been recognized with the American Psychological Association's (APA's) Division 36 (Society for the Psychology of Religion and Spirituality) Margaret Gorman Early Career Award and the Mutual of America Merit Finalist Award. Dr. Aten also received the 2016 Federal Emergency Management Agency Community Preparedness Champion Award at the White House. He is the coeditor or coauthor of seven books, including three other APA titles. See https://www.jamieaten.com and @drjamieaten

**Jenny Hwang, MA,** is a doctoral student in clinical-community psychology at the University of Maryland, Baltimore County. She previously worked as the managing director for the Humanitarian Disaster Institute at Wheaton College. She earned a bachelor's degree in clinical psychology from Boston College and a master's in international disaster psychology from the University of Denver. As a mental health professional, Ms. Hwang has worked with refugees from Burma, Iraq, Syria, Nepal, North Korea, Somalia, Ethiopia, Rwanda, and Burundi. Her research interests include global mental health in the contexts of disaster settings, community resiliency, human trafficking, cross-cultural communication; and mental health in Black, Indigenous, and People of Color.